The World's Population

THE WORLD'S POPULATION

An Encyclopedia of Critical Issues, Crises, and Ever-Growing Countries

Fred M. Shelley

 ABC-CLIO

Santa Barbara, California • Denver, Colorado • Oxford, England

Library of Congress Cataloging-in-Publication Data

Shelley, Fred M., 1952-
  The world's population : an encyclopedia of critical issues, crises, and ever-growing countries / Fred M. Shelley.
     pages cm
  ISBN 978-1-61069-506-0 (hardback : alk. paper) — ISBN 978-1-61069-507-7 (ebook)
1. Population—Encyclopedias.   2. Population—Environmental aspects—Encyclopedias.
3. Population—Economic aspects—Encyclopedias.   4. Birth control—Encyclopedias.
I. Title.
  HB871.S534 2015
  304.6—dc23   2014017421

ISBN: 978-1-61069-506-0
EISBN: 978-1-61069-507-7

19 18 17 16 15   1 2 3 4 5

This book is also available on the World Wide Web as an eBook.
Visit www.abc-clio.com for details.

ABC-CLIO, LLC
130 Cremona Drive, P.O. Box 1911
Santa Barbara, California 93116-1911

This book is printed on acid-free paper ⊗

Manufactured in the United States of America

CONTENTS

PREFACE

How many people live on the earth today? How has this number of people changed in the past? Will the number of people currently living on the earth continue to rise, as it has in recent decades? How many more people can the earth support? Why do people move from place to place? Where do these people come from, and where do they go? All of these questions involve human populations. Many of the most fundamental questions facing societies as they plan for the future involve population-related questions such as these. The entries in this encyclopedia have been prepared in an effort to shed light on such questions.

Questions associated with population can be divided into two broad categories. Some of these questions involve numbers of people themselves, and how these numbers vary from place to place. Ultimately, population changes over time reflect births and deaths: populations increase when people are born and they decrease when people die. The second broad category of population-related questions involves movement from place to place. Large numbers of people are moving to certain regions, countries, and cities throughout the world, while people are leaving other places to move elsewhere. Thus questions associated with births and deaths are complemented by questions associated with migration, or where people live and where they move to, and move away from, over the course of their lifetimes.

Experts on population are known as demographers. Demographers study questions associated with births, deaths, and migration. Some of their analyses are global, involving the population of the entire world as it changes over time. Other demographic analyses are done for individual regions of the world, such as Europe, Asia, the Middle East, and sub-Saharan Africa. Many others are undertaken for individual countries. Most countries throughout the world conduct censuses, or formal counts of their populations, at regular intervals. Information gathered from these censuses is used to determine population changes over time, and it is often compared between countries. Censuses not only count total numbers of people within a country's population, but they also break this information down regionally and locally. For example, the United States census counts people by state and by counties, cities, and towns within each state. Thus, census data enable demographers to analyze population issues at the local scale.

The entries presented in this encyclopedia are based on the types of questions studied by demographers. Many of these entries reflect the basic questions associated with demography, including measurements of births, deaths, and changes in numbers of births and deaths historically as well as in the present day. Where these people are is also fundamental to demography. More than 7 billion people live on the earth today, but their distribution across the earth's surface varies greatly. Some places are teeming with millions of people in very small areas, while other large areas, such as northern Africa's Sahara Desert, are virtually uninhabited. These conceptual questions are associated with migration also, including how many people move from place to place and the reasons underlying this movement. These questions involving births, deaths, and movement represent the fundamental building blocks of demographic analysis and how such analysis is related to larger questions associated with the world economy, culture, and the global environment. They also include how natural disasters, famines, and means of economic production affect populations.

The encyclopedia includes entries about well-known individuals who have made important contributions to the study of demography. These include historical figures such as Thomas Malthus, Adam Smith, and Karl Marx. Others have contributed their insights into population-related questions more recently. The encyclopedia also includes entries about organizations that deal with population-related questions. Some, such as the United States Bureau of the Census, are charged with the collection and analysis of population data. Others are advocacy organizations whose goals are to promote changes in population-related policies, locally and globally. Such organizations include international organizations, such as agencies of the United Nations; agencies of individual governments, including the Bureau of the Census; and nongovernmental organizations.

Other entries in this encyclopedia consider individual places. The earth today is divided politically among approximately 200 independent countries, whose population varies greatly. More than half of the world's people live in Asia, and more than a third of the world's people live in the world's two largest countries by population, China and India. This encyclopedia includes entries about all of the more than 30 countries around the world with populations of more than 40 million, ranked in order of population. These countries are found throughout the world and include countries in Europe, such as the United Kingdom, France, and Germany; countries in the Middle East, including Egypt and Iran; countries in Latin America, including Brazil and Mexico; and countries in Africa, including Nigeria, Ethiopia, and Kenya.

An increasing number of the world's people live in cities. Demographers estimate that about half of the world's people today live in cities, with this percentage expected to increase to 60 percent or more within the foreseeable future. More and more people live in metropolitan areas with populations of more than 10 million. This encyclopedia includes entries for each of these large metropolitan areas, which are often called megacities, ranked in order of population. Reflecting the overall distribution of the world's population, more than half of the world's megacities are located in Asia. However, other megacities, such as New York, Mexico City, Rio de Janeiro, London, Lagos, and Cairo, are found elsewhere. Finally, the encyclopedia includes the texts of statements made by leaders of organizations and excerpts taken from the work of scholars whose research is important to the history of demographic thought. It also includes links to numerous demography-related Web sites as well as to books and articles that provide further insights into the topics with which each is associated.

INTRODUCTION

Approximately 7.2 billion people inhabit the earth today, and their numbers are growing daily. Demographers estimate that the world's population is increasing by between 130 and 150 million people every year. Can the earth sustain this increasing population without compromising the quality of human life and without major impacts on the world's biosphere? Can we provide adequate amounts of food? Are there sufficient resources to sustain the world's population? How can more and more people coexist without potentially catastrophic economic and cultural conflicts? How are populations affected by globalization, and how does globalization affect populations? Ultimately, the major conflicts facing the world today are related closely to questions involving population. The purpose of the encyclopedia is to address population-related questions in hopes of shedding light on relationships between population issues and other major problems of contemporary and future global concern.

Experts on population undertake analysis of several fundamental questions. How many people are there in the world today? How does this number of people compare with the number of people historically, and why? Where do these people live? Why are some areas of the world, such as southern and eastern Asia, densely populated, whereas others are uninhabited or sparsely populated? Why do people move from place to place? Where do they go, and why? By addressing these questions, demographers can contribute to our understanding of how the international community, and individual countries, can deal with the major issues of concern throughout the world today.

Those studying population address many different types of questions, as indicated throughout this encyclopedia. However, these questions can be divided into three broad although not entirely unrelated categories. First, how many people are there? Second, where do these people live? Third, what are the relationships between the numbers, location, and movement of people and questions such as globalization, environmental change, war, food availability, and cultural differences and conflicts? All of these categories are addressed in historical perspective as well as in the present.

In each case, students of population also look to the future and endeavor to make predictions about how population numbers and distributions will evolve over time. In this way, demographic analysis can inform policymakers who seek potential ways to address urgent economic, environmental, and cultural problems affecting the global community.

Perhaps the most fundamental question involving population is simply the question of how many people there are on the earth's surface. Although estimates of populations in the distant past are necessarily unreliable, demographers believe that the earth's population between 10,000 and 12,000 years ago, at the end of the last Ice Age, was between 1 and 10 million. At this time, people survived by hunting and gathering. Most were nomads who could not store food. They were dependent on the vagaries of nature. When game and/or edible plants were scarce or absent, many people starved.

While nobody knows precisely how many people were living on the earth between 8000 and 10,000 BCE, it is certain that the world's population began to increase quickly after agriculture was invented and came into common use in Asia, Africa, the Middle East, and Europe. Agricultural societies had several advantages over hunting and gathering societies. Farmers could obtain far more food per acre than could hunters and gatherers. They were much better able to count on reliable food supplies. They could give up their nomadic lifestyles and settle permanently near their fields. Permanent settlement enabled people to store food for future use, reducing the risk of short-run food shortages. Surplus food could also be exchanged with people in other communities for other types of food as well as for tools, weapons, and other artifacts. For these reasons, agricultural societies sustained much larger populations than did hunting and gathering societies. It is no coincidence that the few remaining hunting and gathering societies in the world today live in sparsely populated areas.

The earth's population increased steadily over the next several millennia. It has been estimated at between 200 and 300 million around CE 1, 2,000 years ago. Over the next 1,700 years, the population of the world grew slowly but steadily. However, worldwide population declines occurred at various times during the Middle Ages. For example, it has been estimated that the world's population declined by as much as 15 percent during the 14th century. This decline in the world's population was especially noticeable in Europe, which suffered through two major calamities: the Great Famine of 1315–1317, and the Black Death epidemic of the 1340s and 1350s. Each of these catastrophic events is believed to have resulted in the deaths of as much as a quarter of Europe's population at the time. The population of China, which then as now was the largest country in the world by population, also fluctuated widely in response to famines, epidemics, natural disasters, and political turmoil. Over the long run, however, the world's population increased until it reached an estimated 1 billion people in the early 19th century.

Over the past 200 years, the earth's population has grown to more than seven times what it was in 1800. Thus the world's population grew by about 750 million in the 1,800 years since CE 1, and by about 6 billion since 1800—in other words, from about 400,000 people per year between CE 1 and 1800, and about 30 million since. The number of people added to the world's population continues to increase annually, although the rate of population growth has begun to slow down.

The rapid increase in the world's population since the late 18th century is associated with the Industrial Revolution. In 1800, well over 95 percent of the world's people were farmers, but the percentage of people who earn their livings via agriculture has decreased steadily ever since. The Industrial Revolution was associated with various technological advances that allowed the death rate to decline quickly. Modern medical science developed, and with modern medical science came knowledge of what caused various infectious and epidemic diseases and how these diseases could be prevented and cured. As it became recognized that many diseases spread under conditions of poor sanitation and contaminated food and water, public health measures were implemented and enforced. As a result of these advances in medical science and technology, diseases caused much lower rates of mortality and more people lived longer, enabling them to become parents as adults. Declining death rates resulted in rapid population increases, especially given the fact that birth rates remained high.

Over the past few decades, birth rates in most countries around the world have declined. Families have become smaller, and many women bear fewer children than did their mothers or grandmothers. As birth rates decline, population growth rates also drop. In many developed countries, birth rates are now considerably lower than death rates. If this trend continues, populations of these countries are expected to decline. Such has been the case in recent years in Russia, Japan, and other developed countries. However, birth rates remain high in many less developed countries, especially in Africa. In these countries, populations are continuing to grow at rapid rates. The model of demographic transition, described in this encyclopedia, is central to the understanding of population change over time as it relates to the industrialization process in countries throughout the world.

Demographers focus not only on absolute numbers of people, of course, but also on where these people live. In order to do so, they examine population density, or the number of people per unit of land area. Throughout the world, several population clusters, or large areas with high population densities can be identified. There are five major population clusters in the contemporary world. These include East Asia (eastern China, Japan, South Korea, and Taiwan); South Asia (India, Pakistan, and Bangladesh); Southeast Asia (especially western Indonesia, Singapore, Malaysia, Vietnam, and southern Thailand); Western Europe; and northeastern North America. More than 60 percent of the world's people live in one of these population clusters, and more than half of the world's people live in Asia.

Other large metropolitan areas and nearby areas, such as the areas including Mexico City, Lagos, Rio de Janeiro, Cairo, and Buenos Aires, also have high population densities, albeit over smaller areas. By contrast, many areas have few or no people. Most of these sparsely populated regions including Siberia, the Sahara Desert, the Himalaya Mountains, the rainforests of the Amazon River basin, and the deserts of central Asia and central Australia have climates that are too cold, too dry, or are otherwise unsuitable for agriculture. In general, with the exception of northeastern North America, the areas of the world in which these large population clusters arose are places in which agriculture was developed and practiced intensively beginning thousands of years ago.

Populations change as a result not only of births and deaths, but also because of migration. Throughout history, people have moved from place to place. Until the development of agriculture, most humans were nomads, and even today more than 30 million people, primarily in Eurasia and the Middle East, continue to practice nomadism. While agriculture allowed people to settle in more permanent communities, over the long run many societies moved over longer distances in order to settle new areas. The history of many countries is associated with large-scale migrations. For example, the ancestors of many people of Southeast Asia today are believed to have moved from southwestern China more than a thousand years ago. The ancestors of millions of persons living in present-day northern India, Pakistan, and Bangladesh are believed to have moved originally from southwestern Asia, perhaps from present-day Iran or Turkey. And of course the large majority of Americans are descended from immigrants from other parts of the world.

Migration has, of course, had dramatic impacts on societies worldwide. While migration is usually conceptualized as a voluntary process, in fact millions upon millions of people have been forced to move against their will. Over the course of history, stronger societies have driven weaker ones away from the most productive and fertile lands. For example, the Indo-Aryans who now dominate the populations of northern India, Pakistan, and Bangladesh are believed to have encountered Dravidian peoples who were already living in these areas. The Indo-Aryans, with their superior numbers and more advanced technology, drove the Dravidians into peninsular southern India, where many of their descendants live today.

In general, migration of more technologically advanced societies has driven indigenous peoples from their ancestral lands. The large-scale movement of Europeans to North and South America, for example, resulted in dramatic declines in Native Americans and other indigenous peoples of the western hemisphere. Many Native Americans died from European diseases from which they had no immunity. Others were killed in warfare, or were enslaved and died from neglect and overwork. Many of those who remained were driven onto reservations or other territories, and as in the case of the United States and Canada these reservations tend to be located on unproductive lands. The population of North and South

America was augmented, of course, by the arrival of millions of Africans who were kidnapped, transported by ship across the Atlantic Ocean, and enslaved.

Today, migration remains a very important component of demographic analysis. Migration has considerable impacts on the populations of many countries, although the number of international migrants is small relative to the number of people who move within their countries of birth. The number of international migrants, or people who live as adults in countries other than those in which they were born, is estimated at about 230 million, or about 3 percent of the world's population. Even in most countries with long histories of political oppression and/or poverty, more than 90 percent of people born in these countries live in the same country as adults. Nevertheless, significant numbers of residents of many countries are immigrants. For example, an estimated 13 percent of U.S. residents were born in other countries. Worldwide, it has been estimated that about 9 percent of residents of developed countries are international migrants, as compared to less than 1.5 percent in less developed countries. The concentration of international migrants in the United States and other developed countries reflects a combination of economic opportunity and political and religious freedom that are often absent in other parts of the world. Many of these immigrants are unskilled or semiskilled laborers. Others are highly educated professionals, and still others are refugees who have been displaced from their native countries in response to political and/or religious persecution.

Finally, demographers focus on relationships between population and other critical economic, environmental, and cultural problems. These relationships are often complex and are often reciprocal. In other words, population change affects the global economy, the world's physical environment, and relationships between cultures. These in turn affect populations.

For example, it is well established that human activity is having a significant and increasing impact on the earth's biosphere. Increasing surface temperatures, habitat fragmentation, species extinction, and sometimes toxic levels of air and water pollution are well documented. These changes are occurring in large part because of efforts to support larger and larger populations.

In this context, industrialization has triggered the process of demographic transition, which allowed explosive population growth worldwide over the past two centuries. But more and more people mean that there are more and more mouths to feed. Hence once-pristine habitats are being cleared for agriculture, reducing habitat available for wild plants and animals that are critical to the long-run sustainability of the ecosystems in which they live. More intensive manufacturing, mining, and industrial production are responsible for increasing levels of air and water pollution. However, the intensification of agricultural and industrial production needed to sustain a larger population worldwide has also imperiled the earth's physical environment. Surface temperatures are rising, causing sea levels to rise and threatening the millions of people around the world who live in coastal cities and low-lying rural environments. Mortality in areas polluted as a result of industrial activity has increased to levels far beyond other areas. For example, life expectancy in the Siberian city of Norilsk, which is the world's leading center for nickel mining and refining, is nearly 10 years less than that of Russia as a whole because nickel mining and refining is very highly polluting and results in the discharge of large quantities of toxic chemicals into the atmosphere and into the region's surface water supplies.

Similarly, globalization has affected populations in that it provides more incentives for people to move in search of employment, especially from less developed countries where wages are much lower than in developed countries. Much of this movement is from rural to urban areas, which have become overcrowded and also face major problems with the creation of slum areas along with polluted air and water.

The relationships between population and the major challenges facing the world of the 20th century underscore the importance of understanding the fundamentals and dynamics of population. Understanding population change, movement, and impacts on economy, environment, and culture is essential to developing effective methods by which these problems can be addressed, both locally and globally.

Part I: Entries

Age-Specific Death Rate

The age-specific death rate, which is sometimes called the age-specific mortality rate, is the ratio between the number of people in a population who are of a particular age and who die in a given year to the overall number of people of that age in that population. In other words, the age-specific death rate is the percentage of people of a given age who die within a given period of time. Thus, the age-specific death rate breaks down the crude death rate by age of the population. Age-specific death rates, like crude death rates and crude birth rates, can be calculated for subsets of populations broken down by gender, race, ethnicity, religion, and other population characteristics.

Age-specific death rates among adults increase as people age. Because of infant mortality, the age-specific death rate is higher for children who are less than one year old than it is throughout the rest of childhood and young adulthood. In 2007, the death rate for infants less than one year old in the United States was 6.7 per 1,000. In other words, about 0.67 percent of newborn infants did not survive until their first birthdays. The age-specific death rate for children less than a year old is also known as the infant mortality rate. The death rate for children between one and two years of age was 0.46 per 1,000. The rate continued to drop until reaching a low of 0.09 per 1,000 at age 10. After age 10, the age-specific death rate began to increase. It climbed to 0.62 per 1,000 at age 17, primarily because the number of deaths from accidents and homicides increases among people in their late teens and their twenties.

The age-specific death rate in the United States increases slowly during young adulthood and middle age, and then increases more rapidly as people move into old age. At age 62, the death rate reached 10 per 1,000 in 2007. In other words, about 1 percent of Americans aged 62 died during their 63rd year. It increased to 20 per 1,000, or 2 percent of people in their 70th year, at age 70, to 34 per 1,000 at age 75, 56 per 1,000 at age 80, 90 per 1,000 at age 85, and 144 per 1,000 at age 90. In other words, more than 14 percent of people aged 90 in a given year die within the next year. Because women tend to live longer than do men, age-specific death rates are generally lower for females than for males throughout the life span.

The general trend of declining age-specific life expectancy during childhood followed by increases in age-specific life expectancy as people become older can be found from data in other highly developed countries. For example, in Denmark the infant mortality rate is about 6.1 per 1,000. It drops below 2 per 1,000 between ages 5 and 15, then begins to increase slowly. At age 50, the age-specific mortality rate is about 5.5 per 1,000. In other words, Denmark's age-specific death rate in the early fifties is approximately equal to its infant mortality rate. As in the United States, the age-specific death rate begins to increase more rapidly over the remainder of the life span.

In less developed countries with lower life expectancies and higher crude death rates, the general pattern of increasing death rates with increasing age is similar, but actual age-specific death rates are higher. For example, the infant mortality rate in the African country of Burkina Faso in 1999 was 113 per 1,000 for boys and 104 per 1,000 for girls. In other words, more than 10 percent of infants born in Burkina Faso fail to survive until their first birthdays. As in the United States, the lowest death rates in Burkina Faso occur among children between 10 and 14. The death rate in Burkina Faso increased to about 20 per 1,000 for people between ages 40 and 45. For those from ages 60 to 65, the death rate in Burkina Faso was 40 per 1,000 for men and 35 per 1,000 for women, as opposed to about 10 per 1,000 in the United States. Hence persons in their sixties are three to four times more likely to die in Burkina Faso relative to those in Denmark or the United States.

Life tables and other information about age-specific death rates are used by actuaries in determining insurance rates. They are also valuable in calculating remaining life expectancies for people at different ages. In other words, a life table can be used to estimate the average number of additional years that a person of a given age can expect to live. In effect, this estimate becomes an age-specific life expectancy. For example, according to age-specific death rate information the average American aged 62 in 2007 had a remaining life expectancy of about 20.9 years, or an overall life expectancy of about 83 years. Additional life expectancy also declines with advancing age. In the United States in 2007, the remaining life expectancy was about 30 years at age 51, about 20 years at age 63, about 10 years at age 77, and about 3 years at age 95.

See Also: Crude Birth Rate; Crude Death Rate; Infant Mortality Rate; Life Expectancy; Population Pyramid; United States of America

Further Reading

Elizabeth Arias. "United States Life Tables, 2007." United States Center for Disease Control, National Vital Statistics Reports, September 28, 2011. http://www.cdc.gov/nchs/data/nvsr/nvsr59/nvsr59_09.pdf.

Alan D. Lopez, Joshua Salomon, Omar Ahmad, Christopher J. L. Murray, and Doris Mafat. "Life Tables for 191 Countries: Data, Methods, and Results." World Health Organization, 2010. http://www.who.int/healthinfo/paper09.pdf.

United States Social Security Administration. "Actuarial Life Tables 2007." April 20, 2012. http://www.ssa.gov/oact/STATS/table4c6.html.

H. Wang, L. Dwyer-Lindgren, K. T. Lofgren, J. K. Rajaratnam, J. R. Marcus, A. Levin-Rector, C. Levitz, A. D. Lopez, and C. J. L. Murray. "Age-specific and Sex-specific Mortality in 187 Countries, 1970–2010: A Systematic Analysis from the Global Burden of Disease Study 2010." *The Lancet* 380 (2012): 2071–94.

Agriculture and Population

Agriculture, or the systematic cultivation of domestic plants and animals, revolutionized human history several thousand years ago. Agriculture allowed human populations to increase rapidly.

Agriculture was developed about 10,000 to 12,000 years ago in various parts of the world, including present-day China, India, Mesopotamia, and the Nile Valley, although anthropologists do not know the extent to which agriculture in different areas was invented independently. Agriculture began after humans domesticated plants to be cultivated. Animals were also domesticated both as sources of food and in order to provide muscle power needed to plow and otherwise produce food.

Agriculture also depended on availablity of reliable water supplies. The places in which agriculture was first developed are located near rivers, including the Nile River in present-day Egypt, the Tigris and Euphrates Rivers in Mesopotamia, the Hwang Ho River in present-day China, and the Indus and Ganges River valleys in present-day India. In these areas and elsewhere, irrigation techniques were developed in order to use these waters for farming. These irrigation methods were

The Egyptian artist Sennedjem lived and worked about 1300 B.C. Sennedjem's artwork depicted contemporary life in Egypt. His tomb, discovered in 1886, contains examples of his art such as this mural of a man sowing seeds. (DEA/G. DAGLI ORTI/Getty Images)

essential particularly in the Nile Valley and in Mesopotamia, where the climate is too dry for farming and agriculture would be impossible without irrigation.

As agriculture was developed and perfected, it began to replace hunting and gathering because agriculture offered several advantages. Whereas hunters and gatherers depended on highly unreliable food supplies, agriculture allowed the production of steady and reliable food supplies. Hunters and gatherers were nomads who were forced to move from place to place in search of food. Thus hunters and gatherers could not accumulate possessions. Moreover, hunters and gatherers were at the mercy of food availability. When game became scarce or when the berries, nuts, and roots upon which they subsisted failed to ripen, many hunters and gatherers starved. On the other hand, farmers could settle in one place, relying on their lands to produce food year after year. Thus farmers could accumulate wealth and property. They began to build dwellings and other structures, and eventually they began to build cities.

Agriculture also made possible the division of labor. Not everyone had to be active in food production, as individuals produced enough surplus food to feed the rest of the population including rulers and government officials, religious leaders, traders, and merchants. Eventually, however, the division of labor made possible by agriculture contributed to the development of social classes, with the status of farmers varying from one society to another. The ancient and traditional caste system of India was an extreme example of this division, with individuals confined to the caste in which they were born. Each caste was governed by an elaborate set of rules that governed institution of marriage, raising children, and food production and consumption.

Settlement was made easier by the fact that farmers could store food for future use. Not only could excess food be stored for later consumption, but surplus food could also be exchanged among societies for other types of food, clothing, tools, weapons, or other items of value. Indeed, many buildings in very early societies were granaries used to stockpile food for use in the event of later crop failures or famines. All of these factors contributed to the fact that populations in ancient agricultural societies grew to be much larger than those in hunting and gathering societies. The work of Ester Boserup focuses upon some of the demographic impacts of transition from hunting and gathering to agriculture.

The number of people who could be supported by agriculture, however, varied in accordance with the agricultural environment in which people lived. Some forms of agriculture were more conducive to higher population densities than were others. Agricultural production includes subsistence agriculture and commercial agriculture. Subsistence farmers produce food for their own consumption, whereas commercial farmers produce food for sale. A commercial farmer produces far more food than does a subsistence farmer.

Some types of subsistence farming are associated with higher population densities than are others. Shifting cultivation, often known as slash-and-burn agriculture, has long been practiced in tropical rainforest environments in which soil fertility is low. This type of agriculture is associated with communal land ownership. A group of people who may live in a village own the surrounding lands in common. The farmers select a plot of land. They cut down trees and other vegetation with machetes, axes, and knives, and then burn the cut vegetation. The ashes fertilize the soil and crops are planted on the burned plot. However, after a few years, the cleared land loses fertility, especially in rainforest environments with their poor soils, and crop production on this land ceases. Another plot of land is chosen and the process repeats itself.

At any given time, only a small percentage of the land available to a society is under cultivation. Most of the land lies fallow, regenerating its fertility until it is cleared eventually. Thus slash-and-burn agriculture supports relatively few people and population densities are low. Today, slash-and-burn agriculture is disappearing for several reasons. Population pressure, often associated with reduced crude death rates locally and elsewhere, forces more land to go into production at any given time. Given the fact that relatively infertile tropical soils require sometimes considerable time to regenerate their original levels of fertility, an increase in the amount of land under cultivation means that the land that is under cultivation is less productive. In modern societies, farmers also face increasing pressure to grow crops commercially, rather than for their own subsistence. Descendants of farmers who once practiced slash-and-burn farming now produce crops and livestock commercially, and these products are exported rather than consumed locally. In some cases, farmers who once practiced slash-and-burn agriculture have strong economic incentives to produce crops sold illegally on the black market. For example, opium poppies that are used in the production of heroin and other illegal drugs are grown in large quantities in parts of South America and Southeast Asia that prior to recent decades were used for slash-and-burn cultivation. Also, slash-and-burn agriculture is associated with communal land ownership. However, in many contemporary societies, land is viewed as a commodity that is owned individually and can be bought and sold.

In many areas of the world where there is not sufficient rainfall to grow crops, traditional food production involved pastoral nomadism. Under this system, nomads raised cattle, goats, sheep, camels, and other domesticated animals, in contrast to hunters and gatherers, who moved from place to place following wild animals. Pastoral nomads traveled with their flocks from place to place over the course of the year. They subsisted on meat and milk from the animals, and traded animals and animal products for fruits, vegetables, clothing, tools, and other goods. Pastoral nomadism, like slash-and-burn farming, also supported only small populations.

Today, an estimated 30 to 40 million people still practice pastoral nomadism. Most live in Eurasia or Africa, especially in central Asia and the Middle East. However, pastoral nomadism is on the decline, as is slash-and-burn agriculture. The decline of pastoral nomadism has been caused in part by the modern system of international boundaries. Many of these boundaries cross territory occupied traditionally by various nomadic societies. Governments now pressure nomads to remain within their boundaries rather than continue to follow their herds across international borders. Many pastoral nomads have given up their nomadic lifestyles, often moving to settled dwellings in cities and towns where they work in manufacturing and at other jobs for wages.

In areas with more fertile soils and with reliable sources of water, intensive subsistence agriculture developed. Large plots of land were cultivated year after year, with the result that much higher amounts of food were produced. The food not consumed immediately was stored for future use or traded for other commodities. Intensive subsistence agriculture supports much higher population densities than did slash-and-burn farming or pastoral nomadism. Efforts are made to organize production in such a way as to use as much of the available land as possible. For example, terracing or cutting away slopes is undertaken in order to create flat fields in hilly areas, allowing agricultural production in places that are otherwise too steep for cultivation.

Intensive subsistence farming has been practiced in many parts of the world for thousands of years and it remains an important source of food today. Many areas in which intensive subsistence farming was practiced in ancient times remain among the most densely populated areas of the world, notably in eastern China, northern India, Java, and the Nile River valley of contemporary Egypt. However, in ancient and medieval times, many persons who practiced intensive subsistence agriculture lived on the edge of survival. Crop failures, droughts, floods, and natural disasters could wipe out crops entirely or cause dramatic declines in crop yields, leaving these areas in danger of famine. Moreover, malnourished people were more susceptible to epidemic disease, further increasing short-run crude death rates in these societies. In the United States and other developed countries, most farmers are commercial farmers, as opposed to subsistence farmers. Commercial farmers produce large quantities of food for sale and export, often with the help of many forms of modern technology. As an economy shifts from subsistence agriculture to commercial agriculture, far fewer people are needed to produce enough food to support large populations. As a result, rural population densities in the United States and other developed countries in which intensive subsistence farming is no longer practiced tend to be considerably lower than in less developed countries.

Agricultural work forces in places whose agricultural economies are dominated by commercial agriculture are also much smaller than in places in which intensive subsistence agriculture is still practiced. According to recent estimates by the World Bank, for example, only about 1 percent of the United States' labor force is involved in agriculture, as opposed to more than 40 percent in countries such as China, India, and Indonesia. Thus the development of large-scale commercial farming has been associated with ongoing rural to urban migration and urbanization. Thus throughout recorded history, the development and practice of agriculture have been associated closely with demographics and changes in populations.

Although intensive subsistence farming continues to be practiced in many areas within less developed countries, commercial farming is by no means limited to developed countries. Commercial farming is commonplace in many less developed countries as well. In many places, fruits and vegetables that can only grow in hot, humid climates are produced commercially in less developed countries and exported to the United States, Europe, and other developed countries. For example, nearly 60 percent of all of the world's cocoa beans, which are used to make chocolate, are grown in the West African countries of Côte d'Ivoire and Ghana. India leads the world in the commercial production of bananas, followed by Uganda, China, the Philippines, and Ecuador. Many of these tropical crops are grown commercially on plantations that are often owned by absentee landlords or large corporations, with the actual labor done by often poorly paid employees. However, in many cases, international observers have claimed that some of the labor undertaken on these plantations is done by children and/or by slaves. Human rights organizations such as the International Organization for Migration have been active in calling attention to human trafficking, slavery, and dangerous working conditions faced by workers on these plantations.

See Also: Boserup, Ester; China; Crude Death Rate; Egypt; Famine; Hunting and Gathering; India; Indonesia; International Organization for Migration; Philippines; Population Density; Rural to Urban Migration; Slavery

Further Reading

Jared Diamond. *Guns, Germs, and Steel: The Fates of Human Societies*. New York: W. W. Norton, 1997.

Charles B. Heiser. *Seed to Civilization: The Story of Food*. New York: W. H. Freeman, 1990.

T. Douglas Price and Anne Birgitte Gebauer, eds. *Last Hunters, First Farmers: New Perspectives on the Prehistoric Transition to Agriculture*. Santa Fe, NM: School of American Research, 1995.

World Bank. "Employment in Agriculture (% of Total Employment)." Geneva: World Bank, 2014. http://data.worldbank.org/indicator/SL.AGR.EMPL.ZS.

American Eugenics Society

The American Eugenics Society was an organization founded in 1922 to support the eugenics movement in the United States. Its early founders and patrons included many influential and wealthy individuals, such as John D. Rockefeller, Henry Ford, J. P. Morgan, Jr., and Margaret Sanger. The society was active in promoting eugenics through both scholarly and public activity, drawing analogies to the selective breeding of plants and livestock as often undertaken by farmers. It began publishing the journal *Eugenics Quarterly* in 1954.

After World War II, the eugenics movement became discredited worldwide, although the society remained active in promoting aspects of eugenics, including knowledge of genetics and population control programs. As the eugenics movement continued to be discredited, however, interest in the society and its activities declined. The society was renamed the Society for Biodemography and Social Biology in 1972. It continues to publish a scholarly journal, *Biodemography and Social Biology*.

See Also: Eugenics; Rockefeller, John D.; Sanger, Margaret

Further Reading

Rich Remsberg. "Found in the Archives: America's Unsettling Early Eugenics Movement." *NPR*, June 1, 2011. http://www.npr.org/blogs/pictureshow/2011/06/01/136849387/found-in-the-archives-americas-unsettling-early-eugenics-movement.

Society for Biodemography and Social Biology Web Site. http://www.biodemog.org/.

Asiatic Barred Zone

The Asiatic Barred Zone was a provision of the Immigration Act of 1917, which was a law restricting immigration into the United States. Its overall purpose was to prevent

> idiots, imbeciles, epileptics, alcoholics, poor, criminals, beggars, any person suffering attacks of insanity, those with tuberculosis, and those who have any form of dangerous contagious disease, aliens who have a physical disability that will restrict them from earning a living in the United States . . ., polygamists and anarchists, those who were against the organized government or those who advocated the unlawful destruction of property and those who advocated the unlawful assault or killing of any officer

from entering the United States. The act was one of several laws, including the Johnson-Reed Act of 1924, the purpose of which was to control and curtail the flow of immigrants into the United States. The act was passed originally by Congress in 1916 and vetoed by President Woodrow Wilson. In February 1917, Congress overrode Wilson's veto and the act became law.

One of the provisions of the act was to create the Asiatic Barred Zone, which prohibited further migration from most parts of Asia into the United States, regardless of whether prospective Asian immigrants met one or more of the criteria specified in the act itself. Numerous migrants from China had migrated to the United States during the middle and later years of the 19th century. Chinese American workers provided much of the labor used to complete construction of the United States' first transcontinental railroad in 1869. However, many native-born Americans began to resent Chinese workers, who were seen as threatening their own jobs. In 1882, Congress passed the Chinese Exclusion Act, which banned further immigration into the United States from China. This law was followed by an agreement between the governments of the United States and Japan. This "gentleman's agreement" stated that Japan would not issue passports for its citizens to work in the continental United States, while the United States would honor the rights of those Japanese immigrants already in the country, along with their immediate families. Japanese nationals could continue, however, to emigrate to what was then the Territory of Hawaii.

In effect, the Asiatic Barred Zone extended the American ban on immigration from China and Japan to other parts of East and South Asia. The zone included present-day Indonesia; Southeast Asia; the Indian subcontinent, including present-day India, Pakistan, and Bangladesh; Central Asia; present-day Iran; present-day Turkey; and Asian portions of the Middle East. Islands of the Pacific Ocean, with the exception of the Philippines, which was then a U.S. possession, were also part of the zone. Specifically, the law stated that

> the following classes of aliens shall be excluded from admission to the U.S. . . . . [P]ersons who are natives of islands not possessed by the United States adjacent to the Continent of Asia, situated south of the 20th parallel latitude north, west of the 160th meridian of longitude east from Greenwich, and north of the 10th parallel of latitude south, or who are natives of any country, province, or dependency situated on the Continent of Asia west of the 110th meridian of longitude east from Greenwich and south of the 50th parallel of latitude north. . . .

This provision of the Immigration Act of 1917, which established the zone, was repealed in 1952.

See Also: Bangladesh; China; Indonesia; Iran; Japan; Johnson-Reed Act; Migration; Pakistan; Philippines; Turkey; United States of America

Further Reading

Erika Lee. *At America's Gates: Chinese Immigration during the Exclusion Era, 1882–1943.* Chapel Hill: University of North Carolina Press, 2007.

Frank Van Nuys. *Americanizing the West: Race, Immigration, and Citizenship.* Lawrence: University Press of Kansas, 2002.

Baby Boom

A baby boom is a population increase resulting from a rapid increase in a country's crude birth rate. Baby booms have occurred throughout history and around the world. However, the term "baby boom" usually refers to the rapid increase in the birth rate of the United States after World War II. Americans born between 1946 and the early 1960s are often called "baby boomers."

The United States went through the Great Depression in the 1930s, and entered World War II in 1941. During this period, crude birth rates in the United States fell quickly. The crude birth rate of the United States was about 26 per 1,000 in 1924, but dropped to below 20 per 1,000 from 1933 through 1940. Although this decline could be attributed in part to demographic transition in which crude birth rates drop, some historians believe that fertility dropped in part because of very poor economic conditions and despair over the future of younger generations. Persons who were unemployed or impoverished would refuse to start families out of concern that they would not be able to provide for their children if the Depression were to continue. During World War II itself, of course, millions of American military personnel were stationed overseas. Thus the birth rate remained low until the end of the war.

After the war ended, the United States entered a prolonged period of prosperity. Returning military personnel were anxious to settle down and start families. The U.S. government facilitated their return to civilian life through the enactment of the Servicemen's Readjustment Act of 1944, which was commonly known as the G.I. Bill of Rights. The G.I. Bill also provided low-cost loans for returning military personnel, whether or not they had served in combat, to purchase homes. It thus stimulated a boom in housing construction, especially in suburban areas outside New York and other large cities. It also authorized payment of tuition for veterans to attend colleges or trade schools.

These provisions of the G.I. Bill made it much easier for veterans to raise families. As they began to do so, the United States' crude birth rate rose quickly. It increased to about 24 per 1,000 in 1947, and peaked at above 26 per 1,000 in 1948. The crude rate remained above 25 per 1,000 through most of the 1950s. Not until the late 1960s did it once again drop below its prewar average of about 19 per 1,000.

The baby boom also affected total fertility rates, which increased from about 3.1 in the early 1950s to more than 3.7 by 1957. The demographer Richard Easterlin analyzed this phenomenon in research undertaken between the 1960s and the 1980s. Easterlin argued that total fertility rates rose in accordance with economic prosperity and greater levels of confidence about the future. According to this argument, prospective parents who believed that they had the means to provide their children with a higher standard of living than they had had themselves would choose to have larger families. Easterlin's argument is consistent with birth-rate data from the baby-boom period, but it appears to be less accurate today because baby boomers and their descendants have chosen to have fewer children than the model would have predicted.

The impact of the baby boom has been felt ever since the United States' crude birth rate spiked during the years after World War II. School and college enrollments rose rapidly in order to accommodate the large numbers of children being born. As students and young adults, baby boomers spearheaded the counterculture and initiated profound societal changes that continue to the present day. However, changes in the global economy meant that many baby boomers were unable to achieve the levels of prosperity that their parents envisioned for them.

World War II ended in August 1945. Thus, baby-boom children will start to turn 70 in late 2015, and by 2014 all baby boomers reached the age of 50. Thus baby boomers have reached and are beginning to pass late middle age. The aging of the baby-boom generation brings with it a host of new demographic issues. For example, the aging of baby boomers coupled with consistently lower crude birth rates has resulted in a steady increase in the median age of the United States. Hence the percentage of the population that is elderly is increasing. Already, this implies that more resources must be devoted to providing health care for this burgeoning elderly population.

A higher median age also means that the dependency ratio, or the ratio of people working to the number of children added to the number of elderly people, is declining. In other words, fewer and fewer working-age adults are becoming responsible for the support of more and more persons who are elderly. This has also generated concern that government-sponsored programs for care of the elderly, including Social Security, will no longer be able to provide the resources needed for supporting the growing number of aging baby boomers. The future of social security programs, and particularly of Medicare and other programs associated directly with the health of the elderly population, has become an issue of increasing concern in U.S. politics today.

See Also: Demographic Transition Model; Dependency Ratio; Easterlin, Richard; New York; Total Fertility Rate; United States of America

Further Reading

Richard Easterlin. "The American Baby Boom in Historical Perspective." *American Economic Review* 51 (1961): 869–911.

Rusty Monhollon, ed. *Baby Boom: People and Perspectives*. Santa Barbara, CA: ABC-CLIO, 2010.

Doug Owram. *Born at the Right Time: A History of the Baby Boom Generation*. Toronto: University of Toronto Press, 1997.

Berlin Wall

The Berlin Wall was a border fence or separation barrier built in the divided city of Berlin, Germany, during the Cold War. Its purpose was to keep residents of East Berlin, which was the capital city of Communist-ruled East Germany between 1945 and 1989, from crossing the border into West Berlin. The Berlin Wall became one of the best-known symbols of the Cold War.

After World War II, the Nazi government of Germany was dismantled. Germany was divided into four occupation zones. Each zone was controlled by one of the four major Allied powers: the United Kingdom, France, the United States, and the Soviet Union. Under Soviet influence, the area of Soviet occupation in eastern Germany became a Communist-controlled state called the German Democratic Republic, but known informally as East Germany. The United Kingdom, France, and the United States agreed to combine their occupation zones into what would become the Federal Republic of Germany or West Germany.

Germany's capital city of Berlin is located within what was the Soviet occupation zone. It was also divided among the four powers. The Western powers refused to

Residents of East Germany and West Germany standing on the Berlin Wall in front of the Brandenburg Gate on November 10, 1989, one day after the Wall was torn down. Germany reunified, with Berlin as its capital, in 1990. (AP Photo)

allow the portions of Berlin that they occupied to become part of East Germany. Instead, the three Western sectors of West Berlin were combined as a part of West Germany, although West Berlin was surrounded by East German territory and was separated from the rest of West Germany by approximately 100 miles of road. In 1948, the Soviets attempted to force West Berlin into East Germany by blockading roads and railroads to keep food and other supplies from reaching West Berlin. In response, the United States and other Western countries initiated the Berlin Airlift, by which supplies were brought into West Berlin by airplane. Eventually the Soviets relented and discontinued the blockade.

During the 1950s, West Germany prospered and its economy grew steadily, far outpacing the stagnant East German economy. Recognizing the prosperity and freedom of West Germany, many East Germans crossed the border into West Germany. A barbed-wire border fence along the boundary was constructed, but the boundary between East Berlin and West Berlin remained open and thousands of East Germans made their way to East Berlin, crossed the border between East Berlin and West Berlin, and then left for other parts of West Germany in order to escape to the West. Migration to West Germany became part of the brain drain, in that a disproportionate percentage of those leaving East Germany were young and highly skilled professionals.

On August 13, 1961, the East German government officially closed the border between East Berlin and West Berlin and construction of the Berlin Wall began. Its purpose was to stop migrants and refugees from leaving East Germany. The concrete wall was reinforced with barbed wire and land mines. East German soldiers were stationed along the Wall and were ordered to shoot to kill those attempting to cross it. Over the 25 years, the Wall was reinforced and strengthened by the East German government, aided by the Soviet Union. The Wall's purpose remained to stop cross-boundary migration, although as tensions between the West and the East relaxed during the 1970s and 1980s, the two governments allowed limited interaction between people in the two parts of the city.

The Berlin Wall soon became a symbol of the Cold War and conflict between the democratic, capitalist West and the communist East. During the three decades after the Wall was built, U.S. Presidents John F. Kennedy and Ronald Reagan issued what would become iconic statements in support of West Berlin and in opposition to the Wall. During a visit to West Berlin in 1963, Kennedy stated, "[A]s a free man, I take pride in the words "*Ich bin ein Berliner*" [I am a Berliner]." In 1987, Reagan also visited West Berlin. Referring to the Soviet Union's leader, Reagan said, "Mr. Gorbachev, tear down this wall!" By this time, the economies of East German and other Soviet satellites were disintegrating and popular support for overthrowing East Germany and other Communist dictatorships increased. The East German government opened the gates on November 9, 1989, and allowed people to cross into West Berlin. A year later, Germany officially reunified and destruction of the

Wall began. Today, the Berlin Wall is symbolic of the Cold War and efforts on the part of autocratic governments to prevent people from leaving their countries.

See Also: Border Fences; Brain Drain; France; Germany; Russia; United Kingdom; United States of America

Further Reading

David Childs. *The Fall of the GDR: Germany's Road to Unity*. London: Longman, 2001.

Frederick W. Taylor. *The Berlin Wall: A World Divided, 1961–1989*. New York: HarperCollins, 2007.

Black Death

The Black Death was an epidemic of bubonic plague that decimated the population of Europe during the 14th century. Historians estimate that between a third and half of Europe's people died during this epidemic between 1348 and 1352. Overall, the world's population is believed to have declined by 10 to 20 percent during the 14th century, largely because of the plague and its impacts on the population. The outbreak of this disease triggered one of the most devastating epidemics in history.

The term "Black Death" may refer to the fact that the skin of many victims darkened as death approached. It may also refer to the gloomy outlook faced by victims and their relatives and friends, given that most people who contracted the disease died quickly and that medical knowledge of how to prevent and treat the plague was very rudimentary. Today, it is well known that bubonic plague is caused by a bacterium that is transmitted to people by biting fleas, which in turn are transported by rats. Thus control of rat populations has been undertaken in such a way as to reduce the incidence of bubonic plague greatly.

Outbreaks of bubonic plague have occurred from time to time throughout premodern history, including a serious epidemic known as the Justinian Plague that affected eastern and southern Europe in the sixth and seventh centuries CE. The specific outbreak that resulted in the Black Death is believed to have originated in China. From East Asia, it spread to Europe via trading, both over land and by sea. At that time, European mariners had not yet circumnavigated Africa, so many trade goods were transported to the Middle East by ship, and hence to Europe by land. Rats aboard trade ships are believed to have escaped from these ships while they were in port. Thus the Black Death first became evident in port cities, eventually spreading to the countryside.

The Black Death epidemic was first observed in Turkey and southern Europe along the coast of the Mediterranean Sea in 1347. From there it spread northward

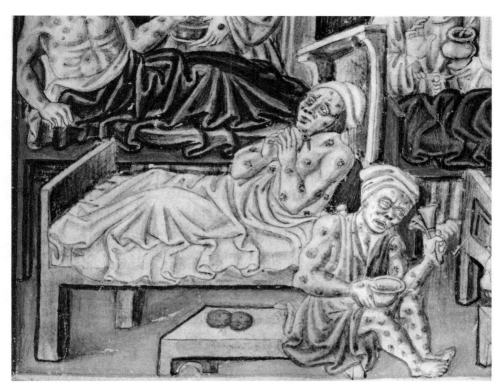

The Black Death was one of the most severe epidemics in recorded history. This epidemic of bubonic plague is believe to have killed off a third or more of Europe's population in the middle of the fourteenth century. This image depicts plague victims in Perugia, Italy. (DEA/A. DAGLI ORTI/Getty Images)

and westward, reaching Paris in 1348, London in 1349, and Scandinavia in 1350. Mortality rates were very high, with an estimated 50 to 75 percent of those who were infected eventually perishing from the disease. The majority died within a few days after becoming infected.

The impacts of the Black Death were greatest in southern Europe, closest to where it is believed to have arrived from East Asia, and where the epidemic lasted longest. The highest death rates were in Italy, France, and Spain, where as many as 75 to 80 percent of the people were killed by the disease. The death rate is believed to have been much lower in England and present-day Germany, where less than a quarter of the population succumbed to the plague. Death rates were higher in cities than in rural areas, in part because medieval cities were very crowded, dirty, and unsanitary, and therefore provided many breeding grounds for rats.

Lacking knowledge of modern medical science, contemporary Europeans turned to other possible explanations for the arrival and spread of the disease. Many saw the disease as a form of divine punishment for sinful activities. Others blamed transient, wandering, or outcast populations including Jews and Roma (gypsy) people. Many European Jews were persecuted or executed and some Jewish communities were destroyed and burned. In the long run, the Black Death, as well as the Great Famine of 1315–1317, ushered in fundamental changes in Europe's culture, including the rise of scientific thinking, greater distrust of authority, and eventually the Protestant Reformation.

The Black Death subsided in the early 1350s. However, outbreaks of bubonic plague occurred periodically in Europe, the Middle East, and Asia for the next several centuries. For example, an outbreak of plague in 1576 and 1577 killed a third of the people of Venice, and others caused substantial mortality in London in 1623 and 1665. The last major outbreak of plague to strike Europe affected the French city of Marseille in 1720. A later major epidemic struck Asia in the late 19th century, causing as many as 10 million fatalities in China and India. By the 20th century, medical researchers had isolated the cause of bubonic plague and how the disease is spread, enabling them to promote public health measures to reduce the spread of the disease and to identify cures for those who were infected with it. Today, bubonic plague cases are reported occasionally at various locations around the world, although large-scale epidemics of the disease no longer take place.

See Also: China; Epidemics; France; Germany; Great Famine of 1315–1317; Italy; Justinian Plague; London; Paris; Spain; Turkey

Further Reading

J. P. Byrne. *The Black Death*. London: Greenwood, 2004.

Norman F. Cantor. *In the Wake of the Plague: The Black Death and the World It Made*. New York: Free Press, 2001.

David Herlihy and Samuel K. Cohn. *The Black Death and the Transformation of the West*. Cambridge, MA: Harvard University Press, 1997.

Blackbirding

Blackbirding is the practice of tricking or kidnapping persons and transporting them to distant countries as laborers. Although the term refers primarily to Australia and the Pacific Islands, blackbirding has been practiced all over the world and continues in some areas today.

Blackbirding was first practiced in Australia. Many of Australia's original settlers of European ancestry arrived via convict transportation to an area already inhabited by Australia's indigenous population of Aborigines. However, by the middle of the 19th century, Australia faced a significant shortage of agricultural labor, especially after large numbers of Aborigines died of exposure to European diseases. The shortage of labor was especially acute in Queensland in northeastern Australia, where sugar plantation owners demanded large labor forces. The planters turned to the nearby islands of Melanesia and Polynesia in the southwestern Pacific Ocean as sources of labor.

Some laborers from the Pacific islands moved to Australia voluntarily as indentured servants. However, the majority arrived involuntarily. Blackbirding ships visited these islands and tricked local people into boarding the ships, often on the pretense of trade opportunities or providing them with gifts. Other locals were kidnapped directly. Once the locals boarded or were forced aboard, the ships would set sail for Australia before their passengers could disembark. Once the ships landed in Australia, the victims of blackbirding were unloaded and put to work on farms. Many became slaves.

Historians estimate that more than 50,000 persons from the Pacific Islands were blackbirded to Australia during the 19th century. Most worked under harsh conditions, and some died from European diseases to which they had no immunity. The high death toll associated with blackbirding is evident from the first census of Australia taken in 1901, in which only about 10,000 people of Pacific Islands origin were recorded despite the fact that more than 50,000 had been transported to Australia during previous decades. Blackbirding was also used to provide labor on plantations in Fiji and other areas of the South Pacific.

Although the term blackbirding is no longer used, the practice of using deceit and kidnapping persons into labor or servitude continues today. For example, many plantation workers in West Africa are teenagers who come from very poor countries and are lured into agricultural labor on cocoa plantations, coffee plantations, and other farm enterprises by the pretense of high wages. However, these promised high wages are not paid. Impoverished teenagers, many of whom are illiterate or have only rudimentary formal educations, have no way of returning home and have little choice but to remain as poorly paid and poorly treated agricultural laborers. Similar types of trickery are also used to entice young women who are promised good jobs, educations, and opportunities to support their families across international borders into the sex trade.

See Also: Census; Convict Transportation; Indentured Servitude; Indigenous Populations; Slavery

Further Reading

Blong Yu Mi. "History of the Trade." N.d. http://www.blackbird.vu/index.php/about-blackbird/history-of-the-trade.

Emma Christopher, Cassandra Pybus, and Marcus Buford Rediker. *Many Middle Passages: Forced Migration and the Making of the Modern World*. Berkeley: University of California Press, 2007.

Border Fences

Border fences, which are also known as separation barriers, are structures that have been erected by governments in order to restrict immigration between neighboring countries. Generally, border fences are built by governments of wealthier countries in order to separate these wealthier countries from their poorer neighbors and to reduce illegal immigration across these boundaries. Proposals to build and maintain these border fences are often controversial and have led occasionally to armed conflict.

A controversial border fence has been built along the southern boundary of the United States adjacent to its border with Mexico. The purpose of this border fence was not only to restrict the flow of illegal immigrants from Mexico into the United States, but also to curb the large flow of illegal drugs into the United States.

In 2005, U.S. Representative Duncan Hunter proposed legislation to construct a fence along the entire boundary between United States and Mexico. Hunter's proposal to fence the entire boundary was not enacted. However, Congress passed the Secure Fence Act, which was signed into law by President George W. Bush in

Family members are reuniting at a section of the U.S.-Mexico border fence near San Diego, California. Although the border fence along the border is highly controversial, residents living on the American side of the border can visit family members and friends in Mexico under the supervision of U.S. Border Patrol agents. (John Moore/Getty Images)

2006. The act authorized construction of 700 miles of physical barriers along the boundary. Congress appropriated $1.2 billion for the project, which would extend along about half of the boundary. As of 2013, most of the fence as authorized has been completed. The barriers are 21 feet high and are dug six feet underground to prevent immigrants and drug smugglers from tunneling underneath the fences to enter the United States illegally. More than 20,000 U.S. Border Patrol agents are stationed along the boundary.

Critics of the fence project have questioned its effectiveness. They have also argued that the fence will restrict the movement of legal immigrants and U.S. citizens as well as illegal immigrants. Others have argued that the fence has had environmental effects, especially by disrupting the natural migration routes of wild animals that live along the boundary and by altering natural drainage patterns. The constructed sections of the fence have also divided tribal lands owned by three Native American nations. However, proponents of the project have argued for authorization to construct the remaining sections of the boundary. In 2013, this question was discussed in Congress as part of a larger debate over U.S. immigration policy. Proposals to expand the fence have been accompanied by proposals to use drones and staff the fence with as many as 40,000 additional border patrol agents.

CEUTA'S AND MELILLA'S BORDER FENCES

In Spain, border fences have been built around the exclaves of Ceuta and Melilla in order to keep African and Middle Eastern migrants out of Europe.

Ceuta and Melilla are located along the Mediterranean coast of Africa. Both are small cities under Spanish sovereignty, although they are surrounded by Moroccan territory and claimed by Morocco. The two exclaves have a combined population of about 160,000. Because these cities are politically part of Spain, over many years, large numbers of persons have crossed their boundaries with Morocco and from Ceuta and Melilla have crossed the Mediterranean Sea into Europe.

In 1993, the Spanish government built a border fence about 10 feet high around the border between Ceuta and Morocco. After several people died while trying to climb the fence, its height was raised to about 20 feet in 2005. In 2014, Spain announced its intention to expand border security in Ceuta and Melilla. These efforts were condemned by Morocco, which does not recognize Spanish sovereignty over the cities and has demanded that Spain tear down the border fences and hand the cities over to Morocco.

Further Reading

Ashifa Kassam. "Spain to Raise Security around Morocco Territories over Immigration Fears." *The Guardian*, March 6, 2014. http://www.theguardian.com/world/2014/mar/06/spain-security-morocco-territories-immigration.

Another controversial border fence has been built in India along its border with Bangladesh. The boundary between the two countries is nearly 2,500 miles in length. India has long tried to restrict movement from poor and densely populated Bangladesh into wealthier India, although as in North America restriction of the illegal drug trade has also been cited as a reason to fence the border between the two countries. Currently, a fence along 2,116 miles, or more than 80 percent, of the boundary, is authorized. The fence is more than 10 feet high and is reinforced with concrete and barbed wire. By 2013, more than two-thirds of the project had been completed and construction is being undertaken along other sections of the fence. On several occasions, Indian border patrol agents, some of whom have shoot-to-kill orders, have shot and killed Bangladeshi citizens attempting to cross the fence. The fact that many of the victims were unarmed civilians sparked outrage on the Bangladeshi side of the boundary.

Border fences have been built in several other countries in recent years, including Saudi Arabia, Egypt, Cyprus, and Israel. Other separation boundaries have been built and maintained in the past, but are no longer used or enforced. Examples include the Great Wall of China and the Berlin Wall.

See Also: Bangladesh; Berlin Wall; Egypt; Great Wall of China; India; Mexico; Saudi Arabia; States, Nations, and Population; United States of America

Further Reading

Brad Adams. "India's Shoot-to-Kill Policy on the Bangladesh Border." *The Guardian*, January 23, 2011. http://www.theguardian.com/commentisfree/libertycentral/2011/jan/23/india-bangladesh-border-shoot-to-kill-policy.

Pushpita Das. "India-Bangladesh Border Management: A Review of Government's Response." *Strategic Analysis* 32 (2008): 667–88.

Michael Dear. "Mr. President, Tear Down This Wall." *New York Times*, March 11, 2013. http://www.nytimes.com/2013/03/11/opinion/mr-president-tear-down-this-wall.html?ref=borderfenceusmexico&_r=0.

The Economist. "Secure Enough: Spending Millions More on Fences and Drones Will Do More Harm Than Good," June 22, 2013. http://www.economist.com/news/united-states/21579828-spending-billions-more-fences-and-drones-will-do-more-harm-good-secure-enough.

Borlaug, Norman

Norman Borlaug (1914–2009) was an American biologist and agronomist whose pioneering work in agricultural production technologies led to the Green Revolution. He was honored for his work with the Nobel Peace Prize in 1970.

Borlaug was born in Cresco, Iowa. He earned a bachelor's degree in biology from the University of Minnesota, and a PhD in genetics and plant pathology from the same institution in 1942. In 1944, Borlaug moved to Mexico as a member of a research team assembled by the Cooperative Wheat Research Production Program, which was sponsored by the Rockefeller Foundation and the Mexican ministry of agriculture. The purpose of the program was to promote increasing food production in order to alleviate hunger. While in Mexico, Borlaug conducted research on improving wheat production by developing drought-resistant, disease-resistant, high-yielding wheat varieties in order to increase per-acre wheat production. Many of these high-yielding wheat varieties were dwarf varieties whose shorter, thicker stems gave them more wind resistance and reduced the risk of toppling or lodging. These new varieties of wheat became widely available throughout the country. By the mid-1960s, Mexico had become self-sufficient in food production and had become a net exporter of wheat despite its rapidly increasing population.

During the 1960s, Borlaug extended his efforts to South Asia, where wheat yields in India and present-day Pakistan doubled during that decade. By this time, the term "Green Revolution" had been coined to describe the research about and introduction of high-yielding crop varieties and other agricultural technologies to increase food production. The impacts of the Green Revolution on agriculture in these and many other countries remain evident today. For example, per-hectare wheat yields in Mexico rose from about 1,000 kilograms per hectare in the 1950s to over 4,000 kilograms per hectare today. The efforts of Borlaug and many other researchers and practitioners have been credited with saving as many as several hundred million lives, which might otherwise have been lost due to famine and starvation.

Recognizing deforestation as a significant environmental problem especially in developing countries, Borlaug believed that higher per-acre crop yields would reduce levels of deforestation. He advocated increasing agricultural productivity on the highest-quality farmland in order to promote environmental preservation. He also analyzed relationships between crop yields and population growth. Borlaug argued that unless crop yields increased at a rate faster than that of population growth, famine and starvation would intensify and populations would decrease. Thus Borlaug's views on relationships between population, agricultural production, and the economy paralleled those articulated by Thomas Malthus nearly two centuries earlier.

Borlaug's critics argued that per-acre food production in less developed countries could not continue indefinitely, and that reliance on pesticides, fertilizers, and other new technologies would contribute to long-run environmental degradation. In response, Borlaug argued that only through these new technologies could many people in less developed countries hope to avoid large-scale food shortages. In the 1980s, Borlaug and his associates attempted to expand the Green

Revolution into Africa, but his efforts were resisted by some environmentalist groups. Resistance was intensified in opposition to Borlaug's support for the use of genetically modified organisms (GMOs) in efforts to expand food production.

Throughout his career, Borlaug called attention to the value of population control. He saw the need to curb population growth in order to stay within the limits to which food production on a per capita basis could be increased. At one point, he stated that the world could feed as many as 10 billion people if high-yielding technologies were used effectively and wisely. At the same time, he predicted that the world would need to double its food production by 2050 in order to keep up with expected population growth, especially in developed countries.

Borlaug is remembered today as the father of the Green Revolution. Although his ideas remain controversial, his contributions to food supply have certainly alleviated starvation and famine and have allowed the world to buy more time to deal with the effects of continuing population growth on food supply.

See Also: Bangladesh; Food Production and Security; Green Revolution; India; Malthus, Thomas; Mexico; Pakistan

Further Reading

Leon Hesser. *The Man Who Fed the World: Nobel Peace Prize Winner Norman Borlaug and His Battle to End World Hunger*. Dallas, TX: Durban, 2006.

Noel Veitmeier. *Our Daily Bread: The Essential Norman Borlaug*. Lorton, VA: Bracing Books, 2011.

Boserup, Ester

Ester Borgesen Boserup (1910–1999) was a Danish economist who is best known for her conceptualization of the relationship between population pressure and agricultural production in pre-industrial societies. Boserup's theory challenged Thomas Malthus's argument that population growth in pre-industrial societies is limited by agricultural production.

Boserup was born in Copenhagen and earned a bachelor's degree in theoretical economics from the University of Copenhagen in 1935. She worked as an economist for the Danish government from 1935 until 1947, when she began to work for the United Nations Economic Commission of Europe. Beginning in the late 1950s, she worked as an independent consultant and writer. Her best-known work, *The Conditions of Agricultural Growth*, was published in 1965. In her later years, Boserup investigated the relationships between gender and agricultural productivity in less developed societies. In this work, she demonstrated that in many such societies, intensification of cultivation generated much higher work demands on women.

In *The Conditions of Agricultural Growth*, Boserup examined the relationship between population growth and agricultural production in pre-industrial agricultural societies. Malthusian theory postulated that food supply limited population growth. Boserup theorized that population pressure created an incentive for societies to develop new technologies to support their increased populations. For example, many pre-industrial societies in tropical rainforest areas have long practiced slash-and-burn agriculture. Under this system of agriculture, a community clears a relatively small area of nearby land to cultivate at any given time, with the rest of the land left fallow. Vegetation on the plot chosen is cut down and burned (hence the term "slash and burn"). Ash from the fire fertilizes the soil, and crops are grown on the cleared land. Once the land's fertility begins to decline, the cultivated land is abandoned and the process is repeated on another plot. Thus at any given time, most of the land occupied by the community remains fallow.

Slash-and-burn agriculture becomes less and less feasible as population increases. With more people, a higher percentage of the local land base must be cultivated in order to support the larger population. If population continues to grow, most or all of the land must be cultivated in order to feed the entire community. Hence slash-and-burn agriculture is replaced by more land-intensive and labor-intensive forms of agricultural production. In recent years, the ecological impacts of more intensive cultivation in such areas have been noticed, particularly in some areas of the Amazon Basin region of Brazil and in Indonesia, where as much as half of the land base has been deforested. Larger agricultural populations also mean that the overall labor requirements needed to support these increased populations also rise. In pre-industrial areas with dense populations such as China and India, farmers must work much longer hours in order to produce sufficient quantities of food to support themselves.

Although Boserup's theory was seen originally as challenging Malthus's views, in the larger context the two theories can be regarded as complementary. Both theories conceptualize relationships between productivity, technology, and population. Malthus's theory is based on an assumption that per capita food productivity is static; Boserup's theory suggests that population increases provide incentives to increase per capita food production in order to support larger populations without decreasing the availability of food to support each person. More generally, both approaches develop the concept that food supply limits population growth in the long run, even if technology allows for increased food supply. The larger issue becomes the maximum numbers of people that technology can support, both locally and globally.

See Also: Agriculture and Population; Brazil; China; India; Indonesia; Malthus, Thomas

Further Reading

Ester Boserup. *The Conditions of Agricultural Growth: The Economics of Agrarian Change under Population Pressure.* London: Allen and Unwin, 1965.

Ester Boserup. *Population and Technological Change: A Study of Long Term Trends.* Chicago: University of Chicago Press, 1981.

Brain Drain

The brain drain refers to the movement of highly educated persons from less developed to developed countries. Participants in the brain drain include physicians, scientists, engineers, academics, and other professionals who were born in less developed countries but practice their professions in developed countries.

Persons who participate in the brain drain are motivated by both push factors and pull factors. Push factors include the lack of opportunity to practice one's profession. For example, scientists working in less developed countries are unlikely to have access to funding, laboratory equipment, or other supplies needed to undertake their research activities. In many cases, highly educated professionals are motivated to leave their native countries because of a fear of political or religious persecution. Educated persons are often seen by officials of autocratic governments as threats to their regimes and are unwilling to remain in countries in which they may be subject to arrest or persecution. Pull factors include much higher levels of economic opportunity associated with the practice of a profession, along with political and religious freedom.

The brain drain has significant impacts on both less developed and developed countries. In effect, the brain drain represents the flight of human capital from less developed to developed countries. Many educated natives of less developed countries obtain their education and training in their native countries. When these persons take their talents and skills abroad, their countries of birth lose the investments that they have made in educating them and preparing them for professional success. Moreover, the expertise of persons with technical and scientific skills that would be valuable to a less developed country's development is no longer available.

Many countries actively encourage in-migration by highly educated professionals and people with important technical skills. For example, the law in Singapore distinguishes "foreign workers" from "foreign talents." Highly skilled workers and professionals are regarded as "foreign talents" and are given priority in housing and education along with a fast track to Singaporean citizenship. On the other hand, "foreign workers" are international labor migrants who are often paid poorly and have few rights under Singaporean law.

The movement of highly educated people between countries has had profound impacts on world history. For example, thousands of Jewish scientists, writers, and other intellectuals left Nazi Germany in the 1930s to escape persecution. These escapees included world-renowned intellectual figures including Albert Einstein, Thomas Mann, and John von Neumann. Thousands of highly trained professionals left the Soviet Union and Eastern Europe when these countries were under Communist Party rule. Most of these scholars, scientists, engineers, and physicians moved to Western Europe, the United States, or Israel. After communism collapsed in these countries, their citizens became free to leave and many did. An estimated 500,000 scientists and engineers have left Russia for Western Europe or the United States since 1991.

The brain drain has affected less developed countries. In 2005, it was estimated that nearly 80 percent of natives of Jamaica who hold college degrees live outside Jamaica, with the majority living in the United States. More than three-quarters of educated Haitians have also left the country. After Haiti was decimated by a major earthquake, the government of Haiti pleaded with these expatriates to return to their native country in order to help Haiti rebuild itself.

See Also: Illegal Immigration; International Labor Migration; Push Factors and Pull Factors; Singapore; United States of America

Further Reading

BBC News. "Russian Brain Drain Tops Half a Million," June 20, 2002. http://news.bbc .co.uk/2/hi/europe/2055571.stm.

Lucie Cheng and Philip Q. Yang. "Global Interaction, Global Inequality, and Migration of the Highly Trained to the United States." *International Migration Review* 32 (1998): 626–54.

Caglar Ozden and Maurice Schiff. *International Migration, Remittances, and Brain Drain.* New York: World Bank, 2007.

Bureau of Population, Refugees, and Migration

The Bureau of Population, Refugees, and Migration (PRM) is an agency under the jurisdiction of the United States Department of State. Its purpose is to "[provide] aid and sustainable solutions for refugees, victims of conflict and stateless people around the world, through repatriation, local integration, and resettlement in the United States." Thus the major purpose of PRM is to address questions associated with refugees, although it also addresses other issues associated with migration and population policies. In this context, PRM's mission statement reads,

> The mission of the Bureau of Population, Refugees, and Migration (PRM) is to provide protection, ease suffering, and resolve the plight of persecuted and uprooted people around the world on behalf of the American people by providing life-sustaining assistance, working through multilateral systems to build global partnerships, promoting best practices in humanitarian response, and ensuring that humanitarian principles are thoroughly integrated into U.S. foreign and national security policy.

What is now PRM was established in 1980 as the Bureau of Refugee Programs. Its present name was adopted in 1994, and its mission was adjusted to reflect its larger jurisdiction over population-related issues as they relate to the foreign policy of the United States. PRM is headed by a director who holds the rank of Assistant Secretary of State for Population, Refugees, and Migration Affairs. The bureau represents the United States formally on international organizations such as the United Nations Population Fund.

PRM's primary focus remains the plight of refugees, especially those who seek to move to and/or seek political asylum in the United States. In doing so, PRM manages the process by which refugees can apply for admission to the United States. Refugees whose applications are approved are given assistance in resettling in the United States. In this capacity, PRM works in conjunction with the Office of the United Nations High Commissioner for Refugees, the United States Department of Homeland Security, and the United States Department of Health and Human Services. Periodically, PRM issues policy statements concerning United States policies with respect to refugees, international migration, and world population. For example, in 2013 the director of PRM, Anne Richard, issued a statement about PRM's policy regarding international migration. The text of this statement can be found elsewhere in this encyclopedia and can be accessed at http://www.state.gov/j/prm/releases/remarks/2013/219010.htm.

See Also: International Labor Migration; Refugees; United Nations High Commissioner for Refugees; United Nations Population Fund; United States of America

Further Reading

David North. "The Immigration Managers—The Department of State." Center for Immigration Studies, October 5, 2009. http://cis.org/north/state.

U.S. Department of State Web Site. http://www.state.gov/j/prm/about/index.htm.

Carrying Capacity

Carrying capacity is the maximum size of a population of a species that can be sustained given the long-run availability of resources necessary to sustain that population. The concept of a carrying capacity is critical to the ongoing debate among demographers about Thomas Malthus's view that population is constrained by resource availability.

The concept of carrying capacity was developed originally by biologists studying animal populations over time. In examining data on species abundance, these biologists noted that populations of various species would continue to increase until reaching a point at which they would begin to decline. The carrying capacity was defined as the number of animals of that species above and beyond which the population could no longer sustain itself. This number was associated with one or more limiting or regulating factors such as the availability of food or water. If too little food was available, some of the animals would starve to death and the population would once again drop to below carrying capacity, with the process repeating itself eventually. Biologists and ecologists have undertaken numerous studies of carrying capacity in various species of animals.

Carrying capacity has been adapted to the study of human populations. One of the first demographers to apply the concept, although the term was not in use at that time, was Thomas Malthus. Malthus believed that the earth's population was constrained by available food and other resources. Eventually, it would reach a point at which sufficient food was no longer available, and the population would crash. In that way, Malthus conceptualized the world's carrying capacity as fixed. However, today it is recognized generally that carrying capacity can be increased via technology, innovation, and the development of new resources. Today, the earth supports far more people than was the case in Malthus's day, and the average standard of living has increased greatly. Those recognizing food as a limiting factor on the human population point to the fact that the rate of food production increase has been greater than the rate of global population increase over the past several decades. The rate of food production increase has been accelerated by the Green Revolution. However, some have predicted that populations will increase at rates faster than the rate of increase in food production. In that case, a carrying capacity will be reached eventually, although in numerical terms, this increased carrying capacity would far exceed what would have been predicted in Malthus's day.

The concept of carrying capacity underlies the tragedy of the commons. The tragedy of the commons model postulates that individual self-interest is associated with outcomes that are detrimental to the group as a whole. For example, the original formulation of the model suggests that as farmers add more and more cattle to a commonly held pasture, the pasture becomes overgrazed and the cattle starve. In effect, the pasture has exceeded its carrying capacity. However, one could argue that carrying capacity could be increased, for example by developing grass seed that would produce more grass per acre. Thus each cow would need less land upon which to survive, thereby allowing a larger number of cattle to survive on the pasture.

Although it is recognized that human activities have increased the earth's carrying capacity for its human populations, it is also recognized that the resources of the earth are finite. Demographers have attempted to estimate the long-run carrying capacity of the earth. In effect, they are attempting to determine the number of people who can be sustained given the earth's finite resources. Some have argued that the world's population has already exceeded its carrying capacity and therefore that the world's population is likely to collapse in the foreseeable future. For example, Paul Ehrlich has argued that the world has already exceeded its carrying capacity and that the earth's maximum sustainable population may be less than 2 billion. Others have argued that the earth can sustain a much larger population, 10 billion or more.

See Also: Demography; Ehrlich, Paul; Green Revolution; Malthus, Thomas; Tragedy of the Commons

Further Reading

Lester Brown. *World on the Edge*. New York: Norton, 2011.

Nathan F. Sayre. "The Genesis, History, and Limits of Carrying Capacity." *Annals*, Association of American Geographers, 98 (2008): 120–34.

Cause-Specific Death Rates

Within a population, the cause-specific death rate is a measure of the percentage of people who have died from a specific cause at any given point in time. Whereas crude death rates are based on the overall number of deaths in a population regardless of cause, cause-specific death rates provide more information to demographers because various causes of death are more likely to affect people of different ages over the course of the life span. Thus cause-specific death rates are often analyzed in conjunction with age-specific death rates.

Some causes of death tend to impact young adults at higher rates than is the case with older people. For example, young adults are more likely to be victims of homicide than are older adults. In the United States in 2012, for example, the homicide rate for Americans aged between 18 and 24 was about 14 per 100,000 people. This rate dropped to 9 per 100,000 between ages 25 and 44 and to less than 2 per 100,000 people aged 65 or older. HIV/AIDS is another disease whose effects are greatest among young adults in the United States and other countries. Similarly, young adults are more likely to be killed in motor vehicle or other accidents than are older persons.

Other causes of death are more likely to affect the elderly. In the United States, the two leading causes of death are heart disease and cancer. In both cases, the likelihood that a person will suffer from one or both of these diseases increases with age. The relationship between age and death rates associated with cancer is illustrated by data from the United Kingdom between 2009 and 2011. For persons aged 55 and 59, the death rate from cancer was about 500 per 100,000. However, it increased to almost 4,000 per 100,000 for people aged 70 to 74 and over 12,000 per 100,000 aged 85 or more.

Cause-specific death rates also vary between countries. For example, death rates from HIV/AIDS are considerably higher in sub-Saharan Africa than in any other part of the world. However, death rates from diseases that affect the elderly primarily, including cancer and heart disease, are higher in developed countries than in less developed countries. For example, recent estimates indicated death rates from cancer of over 150 per 100,000 people in the developed countries of Canada, Denmark, Lithuania, and Poland. On the other hand, cancer death rates were less than 80 per 100,000 in less developed Niger, Sudan, and the Central African Republic.

These much lower death rates from cancer occur because overall life expectancy in these countries is less than that in the developed world, and also because their very high crude birth rates reduce the median ages in these countries. In countries whose populations contain relatively few elderly people, a lower percentage of people contract or die from cancer over the course of their lifetimes. Fewer contract cancer in these countries because more die from other causes earlier in life. Cancer death rates are also very low in countries such as Kuwait and the United Arab Emirates, whose populations include large numbers of international labor migrants who tend primarily to be young adults.

Deaths by violence also vary considerably among countries. In some countries, many people who have died from violence have been killed during civil wars and international conflicts. Today, the highest rates of death by violence are found in parts of Latin America and Africa. In many of these countries, high rates of death by violence can be linked to wartime conditions. Not only are combatants killed in battle, but many people also die during wartime from malnutrition, epidemics, famine, and other causes. Many of these victims are refugees who may have no access to medical care and succumb to various diseases that could be treated easily if medical resources and services were available to them.

Overall, analysis of cause-specific death rates as they vary over the course of the lifespan and between cultures provides very useful information for demographers and policymakers. Effective efforts to reduce death rates from different causes must begin with careful analysis of how mortality trends from place to place and over time.

See Also: Age-Specific Death Rate; Crude Death Rate; Demography; Epidemics; Famine; Life Expectancy; Median Age; Niger; Refugees; United Kingdom; United States of America

Further Reading

Cancer Research UK. "Cancer Mortality by Age," 2012. http://www.cancerresearchuk.org/cancer-info/cancerstats/mortality/age/.

Ahmedin Jemal, Melissa M. Center, Carol DeSantis, and Elizabeth M. Ward. "Global Patterns of Cancer Incidence and Mortality Rates and Trends." *Cancer Epidemiology, Biomarkers, and Prevention* 19 (2010): 1893–1907.

World Life Expectancy. "Leading Causes of Death in the World," n.d. http://www.worldlifeexpectancy.com. Interactive Web site illustrating death rates from various causes on a country-by-country basis.

Census

A census is an official counting of the population of a given country or place. Through a census, a government obtains information about the number of people living in that place, along with other information such as age, gender, place of residence, occupation, religious identity, language spoken, marital status, and ethnicity.

Censuses have been taken since ancient times. Greek city-states and the empires of Egypt, the Roman Empire, India, and China are known to have conducted censuses more than 2,000 years ago. Information gathered from these censuses was used by governments in a variety of ways, including the assessment of land values, the collection of taxes, and identifying possible military conscripts. Today, most governments conduct censuses on a regular basis, usually every 10 years. Information from these censuses is used extensively by demographers in assessing population and migration trends.

In the United States, the U.S. Constitution mandates that a census be taken every 10 years. Information from the census is used to apportion seats in the House of Representatives among the states on the basis of their populations. The first official census of the United States was taken shortly after the nation became independent in 1790, with the most recent having been taken in 2010. The censuses of the United States population are administered by the United States Bureau of the Census.

Historically, censuses were conducted by census takers who traveled from place to place counting and interviewing people at their residences. Today, censuses are often conducted by mail. Regardless of the method used to identify people, no census can be completely accurate. Census information is related to geography, and an accurate census would require linking each person to his or her place of

New York City is one of the most diverse cities in the world, with large numbers of immigrants from every continent. New York's diversity makes it difficult to conduct censuses accurately because of language barriers and because many immigrants are wary of disclosing where they live. Here ethnic Russians in Brooklyn are informed about the upcoming 2010 census. (Spencer Platt/Getty Images)

residence. Of course, many people throughout the world have multiple residences, often in two or more countries. Other people move at the time of the census and may not be counted either at their prior residences or their new residences.

In the United States and other countries, there are systematic biases associated with determining the population of a given place. Certain segments of the population tend to be undercounted relative to their actual numbers. Immigrants and expatriates are often undercounted. Many illegal immigrants refuse to cooperate with census takers or forms out of fear that their whereabouts will be discovered by government officials and they will be deported. Homeless people, who lack fixed addresses, are also overlooked in many censuses. People who do not speak the country's official or predominant language, such as English in the United States, may not be able to communicate verbally or in writing with census officials and are therefore not counted either. Most experts agree that poor people and members of ethnic minority groups, in addition to immigrants and non-English speakers, are undercounted in the U.S. census.

Systematic undercounting can have significant consequences to undercounted populations and to places in which these undercounted people live. Apportionment in Congress and in state and local legislative bodies is conducted on the basis of census population figures. In addition, the amount of federal funds available for various government programs in particular places is tied to the official census populations of these places. Thus if the census population of a given city is counted as 10 percent less than the actual number of people who live there, that city will get 10 percent less funds that it would have received if the census count had been fully accurate.

See Also: China; Demography; Egypt; Expatriates; Illegal Immigration; India; United States Bureau of the Census; United States of America

Further Reading

Bernard Baffour and Paolo Valente. "Census Quality Evaluation: Considerations from an International Perspective." New York: United Nations Economic and Social Council, 2008. http://unstats.un.org/unsd/censuskb20/Attachments/2008UNECE_ECE-GUIDd4f2 af9398dd 41958dc212c1e649c693.pdf.

John Goering. "Segregation, Race, and Bias: The Role of the U.S. Census." Washington, DC: United States Bureau of the Census, 2005. http://www.census.gov/hhes/www/housing/housing_patterns/pdf/goering.pdf.

David A. Love. "2010 Census Undercount Could Spell Disaster for Blacks, Latinos." *The Grio*, May 24, 2012. http://thegrio.com/2012/05/24/2010-census-undercount-could -spell-disaster-for-blacks-latinos/.

Channelized Migration

Channelized migration, sometimes known as chain migration, involves migration flows from specific origins to specific destinations. This practice impacts the distribution of population at local and regional levels around the world, involving international as well as within-country migration flows.

The gravity model, which links migration levels to the populations of origins and destinations and the distance between them, has been shown to predict levels of migration at a large scale well. However, the gravity model does not account for more specific relationships between places of origin and places of destination. Long-distance migrants who move to new environments often select destinations based on the experience of friends and relatives who have already migrated. Moving to communities in which friends and relatives are already living facilitates the transition to a new environment. These friends and relatives can help the migrants obtain jobs or farmland and can help teach newcomers about the culture, language, and customs of these newcomers' new environments. As well, transition is facilitated by the presence of others who share a common origin. People living in the same communities as previous migrants are more likely to speak, read, and write the same first languages and to attend social events and religious services in common.

There are numerous examples of channelized migration, both contemporary and historical, within the United States and other countries. The history of ethnic settlement in the United States is linked closely to the process of channelized migration. For example, many settlers from the Netherlands moved to southwestern Michigan or to central or northwestern Iowa. Even today, Michigan and Iowa have the largest percentages of people who, according to the census of the United States, report Dutch ancestry. Similarly, channelized migration helps to account for the large populations of Norwegian Americans in Minnesota and North Dakota, Finnish Americans in the Upper Peninsula of Michigan, and Irish Americans in large cities such as New York, Chicago, and Boston.

The impact of channelized migration continued during the 20th century. After the United States curtailed foreign immigration in the early 1920s, large numbers of African Americans in the South moved to Northern cities in search of industrial employment. As with European immigrants, these African American migrants gravitated toward destinations in which people from their home states and communities were living already. Thus many African Americans living in Northeastern cities came originally from the Carolinas whereas migrants to Detroit and Chicago tended to come from Alabama, Mississippi, and Arkansas. Similarly, many people from rural West Virginia and Kentucky moved along the "hillbilly highway" from Appalachia to industrial centers such as Detroit. The process of channelized migration helps also to account for the more recent concentration of refugees from Vietnam in Southern California and from Cuba in South Florida.

Channelized migration also helps to account for patterns of international labor migration in Europe and other parts of the world Since World War II, very large numbers of persons from the Middle East, Africa, and elsewhere have moved to the countries of the European Union. However, the specific distribution of these migrants varies, with countries of origin linked to countries of destination. For example, many migrants into France have come from the former French colonies of Algeria and Morocco, whereas far more international labor migrants moving into Germany have arrived from Turkey. Channelized migration is also prevalent among persons who move to oil-rich, wealthy countries such as Saudi Arabia, the United Arab Emirates, and Kuwait. Throughout the world, the process of channelized migration has reinforced place ties between origins and destinations, for example by encouraging remittances to relatives and friends in areas of origin.

See Also: Census; Germany; Gravity Model; International Labor Migration; Migration; New York; Push Factors and Pull Factors; Remittances; Saudi Arabia; Turkey; United Arab Emirates; United States of America; Vietnam

Further Reading

Martin Cadwallader. *Migration and Residential Mobility*. Madison: University of Wisconsin Press, 1992.

Curtis C. Roseman. *Migration as a Spatial and Temporal Process*. Washington, DC: Association of American Geographers, 1971.

Climate Change and Population

Over the past several decades, it has come to be recognized that the earth's climate is changing. The large majority of scientists who have examined long-term changes in climate attribute many of these changes to human activity, and in particular long-run increases in emission of carbon dioxide and other chemicals into the atmosphere during and since the Industrial Revolution. Climate change has already impacted populations in many parts of the world, especially in less developed countries.

In examining climate change, it is important to distinguish climate from weather. Weather represents atmospheric conditions including temperature, precipitation, and wind speed and direction at any given point in time. Climate, on the other hand, refers to long-term trends in these and other measures of the state of the atmosphere. Thus climate can be conceptualized as "average" weather. At any given point in time, weather in a particular place can deviate substantially from long-term averages. Thus the weather on a given day in a particular community can be much warmer, much colder, much wetter, or much drier than the long-run average in that community.

Global climate change is likely to affect populations worldwide in the future. Higher surface temperatures are especially prevalent near and north of the Arctic Circle, causing glaciers to melt and sea-ice cover to diminish. This image illustrates the retreat of Briksdal Glacier in Norway. (Tony Waltham/Robert Harding World Imagery/Getty Images)

Over the past several decades, observed surface temperature throughout the world has been increasing. The average surface temperature has increased by nearly 1 degree Celsius (1.6 degrees Fahrenheit) since the early 20th century. Much of this increase has taken place since the 1970s. Sometimes, those who are skeptical that humans are responsible for global temperature increases will point to unusually cold weather events to debunk the idea of global warming. However, the fallacy of this reasoning is related to the difference between weather and climate. Although it may be unusually cold in one area of the world, on average the weather has tended to be warmer than normal in other places on the earth's surface. The result is that most of the years with the highest worldwide average temperatures have occurred during the early 21st century.

Most scientists attribute global warming to human activity. Industrial activity and other activities involving the burning of fossil fuels emit substantial amounts of carbon dioxide. As a result, the overall concentration of carbon dioxide in the atmosphere worldwide has increased from an estimated 270 parts per million in the 18th century to over 400 parts per million today—about a 50 percent increase in less than 250 years. Carbon dioxide is a greenhouse gas. Analogous to a greenhouse, carbon dioxide traps heat by preventing it from escaping into space. Thus heat energy is turned back toward the earth's surface, increasing temperatures at the earth's surface.

Climatologists have developed numerous models predicting the effect of continued global warming on surface climates. Although the specifics of the models vary, the models suggest that the general global warming trend will increase as long as the emission of carbon dioxide and other greenhouse gases continues to intensify. Climate change has already had many different impacts on atmospheric conditions, both globally and locally. These impacts are expected to intensify as greenhouse gas emissions continue to increase.

What are the potential impacts of global climate change? One widely observed impact is melting of glaciers and ice caps in the polar latitudes. Observations have confirmed that mountain glaciers as well as the ice cap of Greenland have decreased in size over the past century. Currently, global sea levels are estimated to be rising at between 3 and 3.5 millimeters annually. If this trend continues, sea levels will increase by as much as 30 centimeters, or more than a foot, by the end of the 21st century.

Continued sea-level rise can affect many of the very large populations throughout the world who live in coastal areas. Low-lying coastal cities such as Amsterdam, Lagos, Mumbai, and New Orleans would become subject to flooding and inundation. Devastation could be especially intense in the impoverished and very densely populated country of Bangladesh, which contains substantial amounts of land less than 10 feet above sea level. Government officials in the low-lying island countries of Kiribati in the Pacific Ocean and Maldives in the Indian

Ocean have recognized that much of their land areas could be completely under water in the event of continuing sea-level rise. Persons who are threatened with displacement because of climate change or other long-run changes in the environment caused by human activities are known as environmental refugees.

Climate change is also likely to affect patterns of precipitation. Climate models have identified places that are likely to become wetter or drier in the event of continued global warming. Many have predicted that semi-arid places throughout the world will experience reduced precipitation, resulting in desertification and increasing stresses on populations. For example, experts have predicted that the semi-arid Sahel region of Niger and other countries will experience more frequent and severe droughts, reducing agricultural productivity and making it more difficult for people in these countries to obtain sufficient food. Some have predicted that climate change may increase the frequency of extreme weather events, including major tropical cyclones such as the devastating Typhoon Haiyan that killed as many as 10,000 people in the Philippines in November 2013.

Climate change could affect patterns of agricultural productivity in other parts of the world as well. Long-term climate change could make currently productive areas too warm, too wet, or too dry to produce various crops. Although this loss of agricultural potential could be offset by increased productivity in places currently less suitable for farming, some experts have predicted that on balance the earth's potential to produce sufficient food to support its growing population may be declining.

The impacts of climate change on population are likely to vary geographically. As the examples of Bangladesh and Niger illustrate, these impacts are likely to be greatest in poor and less developed countries. These countries are generally experiencing rapid population growth and given their low incomes, have relatively few resources to plan for or cope with the impacts of climate change. Efforts to reduce the rate of global warming worldwide have been initiated, although the extent that the developed countries are willing to accept responsibility for global warming is a matter of considerable debate. Representatives of less developed countries have argued that while the effects of global warming are greatest in less developed countries, industrial activity and burning of fossil fuels responsible for this global warming have been concentrated in the developed parts of the world. However, representatives of many developed countries have come to recognize climate change as a factor with potentially large impacts on the world's population. For example, U.S. secretary of state John Kerry delivered remarks on this subject in a speech in Jakarta, Indonesia, on this topic in February 2014. Excerpts from the text of Secretary Kerry's remarks can be found elsewhere in this encyclopedia.

See Also: Agriculture and Population; Environmental Refugees; Jakarta; Lagos; Mumbai; Population Density

Further Reading

International Panel on Climate Change. "Climate Change 2013: The Physical Science Basis," 2013. http://www.ipcc.ch/report/ar5/wg1/.

John Kerry. "Remarks on Climate Change," February 16, 2014. http://www.state.gov/secretary/remarks/2014/02/221704.htm.

John Seager. "Population Growth, Climate Change Putting More People at Risk." *Huffington Post*, November 8, 2013. http://www.huffingtonpost.com/john-seager/population-growth-climate_b_4296894.html.

Judith Stephenson, Karen Newman, and Susannah Mayhew. "Population Dynamics and Climate Change: What Are the Risks?" *Journal of Public Health* 32 (2010): 50–56.

Convict Transportation

Convict transportation, which is also known as penal transportation, was the process of exiling convicted criminals by transporting them to distant places. Convict transportation was an important source of population in Australia and other countries.

Exile, or the forced removal of persons from society, has been practiced in Western societies since ancient times. During and after the Middle Ages, people convicted of crimes that were not deemed severe enough for capital punishment were sentenced to exile. Some exiles were also political prisoners or prisoners of war. Exile was sometimes temporary and in some cases was permanent. Persons sentenced to temporary exile had the right to return home after a specified period of time, although many persons remained in the places to which they had been exiled.

In order to facilitate exile, governments organized efforts to transport exiled persons overseas. For example, in 1718, the British government enacted the Transportation Act. The Transportation Act authorized the transport of convicted offenders to British colonies in North America for a period of seven years. From the British point of view, the Transportation Act served two purposes. At a time when Britain's population was beginning to grow rapidly, its prisons were becoming overcrowded and transportation helped to reduce the prison population. At the same time, North American planters and other entrepreneurs faced a serious shortage of labor, which could be supplied by these transported exiles as well as by indentured servants and slaves. Many of these transported convicts remained in what is now the United States and Canada rather than returned to Britain after their seven-year exiles were completed.

After the Transportation Act was implemented, the British government paid ship owners and captains to transport convicts across the Atlantic Ocean to North America. The practice went into effect in 1720 and continued until it was halted in 1776 during the American Revolution. Historians have estimated that between 50,000 and 100,000 convicts were transported from Britain to North America between 1720 and 1776. After the American Revolution, the British government could no longer transport convicted criminals to North America. Beginning in 1787, the British began to transport convicts to Australia. More than 150,000 convicts were transported to Australia between 1787 and 1868, when the practice of transportation was outlawed by the British government. By the middle of the 19th century, transported convicts and their descendants made up a significant proportion of Australia's population of European origin.

See Also: Indentured Servitude; International Labor Migration; Slavery; United Kingdom; United States of America

Further Reading

Charles Bateson. *Convict Ships, 1787–1868*. Sydney: A. H. and A. W. Reed, 1976.

A. Roger Ekirch. *Bound for America: The Transportation of British Convicts to the Colonies, 1718–1775*. New York: Oxford University Press, 1990.

Crude Birth Rate

The crude birth rate in any place is the ratio between the numbers of births in a given year in that place and the total population of that place. Usually, the birth rate is expressed in terms of number of births per 1,000 people in a particular place. For example, suppose that 1,800 babies are born in a given year in a city of 100,000 people. In this case, the ratio of births to population is 1,800:100,000. Thus, the birth rate is 18 per 1,000. Birth rates can also be expressed as percentages. In this example, the birth rate would be 1.8 percent.

In 2012, the world's crude birth rate was estimated at 19.1 births per 1,000 people. However, crude birth rates vary considerably between countries. Generally speaking, crude birth rates are higher in developing countries and lower in developed countries. In 2010, the United Nations estimated crude expected birth rates for 199 countries and territories throughout the world. All eight of the sovereign countries with the highest expected birth rates are located in Africa. These include Niger (47.7 per 1,000), Zambia (46.5), Mali (45.0), Malawi (44.5), Uganda (43.9), Chad (43.4), Somalia (43.0), and Burkina Faso (42.4).

These are followed by Afghanistan (42.3) and the Democratic Republic of the Congo (42.1).

On the other hand, most of the countries with the lowest estimated birth rates are developed countries. The 10 sovereign countries with the lowest birth rates include Bosnia and Herzegovina (8.2 per 1,000), Japan (8.5), Austria (8.6), Germany (8.7), Portugal (8.8), Italy (9.1), Malta (9.1), Singapore (9.5), Cuba (9.6), and Croatia (9.8). Thus 7 of the 10 countries with the lowest estimated birth rates are located in Europe. In all of these countries, total fertility rates are below replacement-level fertility. The birth rate in the United States for the period 2010–2015 has been estimated at 13.7 per 1,000, below Chile at 14.0 and above Australia at 13.5. The demographic transition model provides an explanation for these differences in birth rates observed throughout the world.

Crude birth rates can be calculated for subsets of populations as well as entire populations. For example, crude birth rates can be estimated for people in particular age cohorts. Thus the crude birth rate can be calculated for teenage mothers as a ratio of births to women aged 15 to 19 to the total population of women aged 15 to 19. Similarly, the crude birth rate can be estimated for different ethnic or religious groups.

The United Nations has estimated age-specific birth rates at five-year intervals for countries throughout the world, with some of these estimates taken from information derived from national censuses. In 2006, for example, the age-specific crude birth rate for women aged 15 to 19 was 41 per 1,000. In other words, about 4 percent of women in this age cohort had children in 2006 (a few had twins or multiple births). The crude birth rate for women aged 20 to 24 was 103 per 1,000 and peaked at 118 per 1,000 for women aged 25 to 29. It then declined to 94 per 1,000 for women aged 30 to 34, 46 per 1,000 for women aged 35 to 39, and 10 per 1,000 for women over 40.

Age-specific crude birth rates in less developed countries are higher. For example, the crude birth rate among women aged 15 to 19 in Sierra Leone in 2007 was estimated at 14.6 per 1,000, or about 3.5 times greater than that of the United States. The rate rose to 222 per 1,000 women aged 20 to 24 and fell slightly to 217 per 1,000 for women aged 25 to 29. It dropped to 187 per 1,000 for women aged 30 to 34; to 145 per 1,000 for women aged 35 to 39; and to 107 per 1,000 for women over 40 years of age. The fact that age-specific crude birth rates are much higher in less developed countries such as Sierra Leone relative to those in the United States illustrates that total fertility rates, or the average number of children born to a woman over the course of her lifetime, are much higher in less developed countries than in developed countries such as the United States. The difference in age-specific birth rates between Sierra Leone and the United States is particularly great among teenage women and among women over 40, illustrating that American women who have only one or two children tend to have them while in their twenties or early thirties, whereas women in Sierra Leone, with larger numbers of children, begin bearing them earlier and continue to do so later in life.

See Also: Democratic Republic of the Congo; Demographic Transition Model; Germany; Japan; Niger; Population Pyramid; Replacement-Level Fertility; Singapore; Total Fertility Rate; United States of America

Further Reading

United Nations, Department of Economic and Social Affairs, Population Division, Population Estimates and Projections Section. *World Population Prospects, the 2012 Revision.* http://esa.un.org/unpd/wpp/Excel-Data/fertility.htm.

United States Central Intelligence Agency. *CIA World Factbook 2012.* Washington, DC: U.S. Government Printing Office, 2012. https://www.cia.gov/library/publications/the-world-factbook/fields/2054.html.

Crude Death Rate

The crude death rate in a given place is the ratio between the number of deaths occurring in a given year in that place and the total population of that place. The crude death rate is calculated in the same way as the crude birth rate and is also expressed generally in terms of number of deaths per 1,000 people in an entire population. For example, if 900 deaths occur in a city of 100,000 people in a given year, the crude death rate would be 900:100,000, or 9 per 1,000. Death rates, like birth rates, can also be expressed in percentage terms. In this example, the crude death rate would be 0.9 percent. The crude death rate is also known as the mortality rate.

Crude death rates vary throughout the world, although the differences between places are not as great as in the case of crude birth rates. Worldwide, the crude death rate was estimated by the U.S. Central Intelligence Agency at 8.6 per 1,000 in 2009. In general, crude death rates are higher in developing countries relative to developed countries. Nine of the 10 countries of the world with the highest death rates are located in Africa. These 10 countries include Swaziland (30.8 per 1,000), Angola (24.1), Lesotho (22.1), Sierra Leone (21.9), Zambia (21.3), Liberia (20.7), Mozambique (20.1), Afghanistan (19.2), Djibouti (19.1), and the Central African Republic (17.8). The 10 countries with the lowest crude death rates as of 2009 were the United Arab Emirates (2.1 per 1,000), Kuwait (2.4), Qatar (2.5), Saudi Arabia (2.5), Jordan (2.8), Brunei (3.3), Libya (3.5), Maldives (3.7), Oman (3.7), and Solomon Islands (3.8). The crude death rate for the United States in 2009 was 8.4 per 1,000, or slightly less than the worldwide crude death rate.

These lists illustrate factors that affect death rates in different countries. The countries with the highest death rates are all less-developed countries that lack sufficient medical care to treat diseases when they occur. Transportation to hospitals and other medical care opportunities is often poor or absent, especially in rural areas. Thus people who contract serious illnesses or suffer from accidents cannot reach medical facilities in time to receive life-saving treatment. The very high crude death rates in southern African countries including Swaziland, Angola, and Lesotho have been attributed also to the widespread incidence of the HIV/AIDS virus in this area of the world. In general, high death rates are related to poor and insufficient medical care, poor public health, and the prevalence of untreated epidemic diseases.

On the other hand, many of these countries, including the United Arab Emirates, Kuwait, Qatar, and Saudi Arabia, are wealthy, oil-rich countries. Medical care facilities are much better than in very poor, less-developed countries. As well, these countries have large populations of immigrants, many of whom are international labor migrants, who come from poorer countries to these places in search of employment. Most of these immigrants are young adults, reducing the percentage of older people who are more likely to die in any given year in their new countries' populations.

Crude death rates can be estimated for subsets of populations such as ethnic or religious groups, as is the case with crude birth rates. In addition, the age-specific death rate and the cause-specific death rate can be estimated. Age-specific death rates represent the ratios between the number of deaths in a specific age category and the total population in that age category. Not surprisingly, age-specific death rates increase with age although in some countries, maternal mortality is still some-what prevalent. Nevertheless, many countries have reported progress in reducing the number of mothers who die during pregnancy or in childbirth. In sub-Saharan Africa, for example, rates of maternal mortality dropped by 41 percent in a 20-year period beginning in 1990.

Cause-specific death rates represent the ratios between deaths from specific diseases and other causes relative to the population. These also vary by cause of death. Older people are more likely to die from cancer or heart disease, whereas younger people are more likely to die from violence or in motor vehicle accidents.

See Also: Age-Specific Death Rate; Cause-Specific Death Rates; Crude Birth Rate; HIV/AIDS; International Labor Migration; Saudi Arabia; United Arab Emirates; United States of America

Further Reading

UNFPA. "Sub-Saharan Africa's Maternal Death Rate down 41 Percent." May 17, 2012. http://esaro.unfpa.org/public/public/cache/offonce/news/pid/10767.

United States Central Intelligence Agency. *World Factbook 2012*. Washington, DC: U.S. Government Printing Office, 2012. https://www.cia.gov/library/publications/the-world-factbook/.

Demographic Transition Model

The demographic transition model provides an explanation for population changes over time. It shows changes in crude birth rates, crude death rates, and rates of natural increase over time as societies have transitioned from pre-industrial to industrial to post-industrial economies. This process is known as demographic transition. The model of demographic transition as used today was first articulated by an American expert on demography, Warren Thompson (1887–1973).

In medieval Europe and in other parts of the world, births and deaths were recorded as they took place. These records have been used by modern demographers to estimate birth rates and death rates in pre-industrial societies. The analysis of these records confirms that birth rates, death rates, and total fertility rates were much higher in pre-industrial times than they are today. Death rates fluctuated dramatically over time because of epidemics of infectious diseases and large-scale famines. For example, much of northern Europe experienced the Great Famine of 1315–1317. Several years of unusually chilly, rainy weather resulted in widespread crop failure and resulted in millions of fatalities. Later in the 14th century, Europe's population was devastated by epidemics of bubonic plague, or the "Black Death." As many as a third of Europe's people died from these epidemics in the 14th century alone. As a result, life expectancy was very low relative to today's standards. Over the long run, birth rates and death rates were approximately equal and populations were stable.

Death rates declined rapidly as societies began to industrialize. The development of modern medical science enabled people to understand the causes of and to treat infectious diseases that would previously have caused fatalities. Immunizations and public health programs were developed to prevent diseases from spreading. Infant mortality declined quickly, and a far larger percentage of newborn babies survived to adulthood.

Birth rates remained high, however, even as death rates dropped rapidly. Birth rates remained high for several reasons. In many societies, children were regarded as a form of social security and were expected to care for their parents when the parents became elderly. Many cultures afforded women few alternatives to early marriage and childbearing, and these norms were reinforced by various religious traditions. As death rates declined and birth rates remained high, rates of natural increase rose and populations increased rapidly.

Eventually, birth rates began to decline as families chose to have fewer and fewer children. Today, birth rates in most industrialized countries are as low as, and in many cases lower than, death rates. Hence total fertility rates are less than two and rates of natural increase in these countries are negative.

The process of demographic transition, thus, can be divided into four stages. At the first stage, birth rates are high, death rates are high, and populations over the long run are stable. At the second stage, death rates drop and birth rates remain high and populations increase rapidly. At the third stage, birth rates begin to decline and populations continue to increase at a slower rate. At the fourth stage, both birth rates and death rates are low and populations stabilize. The United States and the countries of Europe are at this fourth stage of demographic transition. Less developed countries are in the second and third stages, with rapid population increases. The demographic transition model explains the fact that more than 90 percent of newborn babies today are born in less developed countries. Some demographers identify a fifth stage of demographic transition associated with declining total fertility rates that remain below replacement-level fertility, and therefore with long-run population declines. This idea has been applied particularly to various countries whose total fertility rates have remained consistently below two including Japan, Germany, and Russia.

See Also: Black Death; Crude Birth Rate; Crude Death Rate; Epidemics; Famine; Germany; Great Famine of 1315–1317; Japan; Life Expectancy; Rate of Natural Increase; Replacement-Level Fertility; Russia; Total Fertility Rate; United States of America

Further Reading

Kingsley Davis. "World Population in Transition." *Annals*, American Academy of Political and Social Science (1945): 1–11.

David Herlihy and Samuel K. Cohn. *The Black Death and the Transformation of the West.* Cambridge, MA: Harvard University Press, 1997.

William C. Jordan. *The Great Famine: Northern Europe in the Early Fourteenth Century.* Princeton, NJ: Princeton University Press, 1996.

Dudley Kirk. "The Demographic Transition." *Population Studies* 50 (1996): 361–87.

Demography

Demography is the systematic study of human populations. Demographers measure population characteristics and calculate, analyze, and interpret statistics about births, deaths, and migration at global, national, regional, and local scales of analysis.

Plato, Aristotle, Cicero, and many other ancient writers investigated questions of population. In the late 18th century, Thomas Malthus developed his theory that population growth would be constrained by resources available by interpreting observations of increasing populations in the United Kingdom during the Industrial Revolution. In other words, Malthus postulated that populations would be limited by the country's carrying capacity. In the middle of the 19th century, life expectancy tables began to be computed in order to set insurance rates and premiums. These tables were based on observation of age-specific death rates. However, demography as a systematic field of study dates back to the late 19th century. By this time, many countries had established regular censuses in order to obtain data about their populations.

Data from these censuses give demographers information that they need in order to calculate crude birth rates, crude death rates, total fertility rates, population densities, and other standard measures of population location and change. Censuses not only count individuals, but they also are used to obtain information such as age, gender, ethnicity, and location of each individual. This information is used to calculate and analyze age-specific birth and death rates and cause-specific death rates. This information is used to calculate population projections, and is used to advise governments about population policies.

See Also: Age-Specific Death Rate; Carrying Capacity; Cause-Specific Death Rates; Life Expectancy; Malthus, Thomas; Population Density; Total Fertility Rate

Further Reading

Jay Weinstein and Vijayan K. Pillaj. *Demography: The Science of Population*. New York: Pearson, 2000.

Douglas Yaukey, David L. Anderton, and Jennifer Hickes Lundquist. *Demography: The Study of Human Population*. 3rd ed. Long Grove, IL: Waveland Press, 2007.

Dependency Ratio

Within a population, the dependency ratio is a measure of the percentage of people in a place of country who are outside the labor force. Knowledge of the dependency ratio is important to understanding both natural increase and migration.

The purpose of a dependency ratio is to estimate the percentage of people within a population who are of working age, or considered economically productive. The dependency ratio is thus calculated as the ration of the sum of the total numbers of young people and old people to the number of working-age people in a population. Usually, the working-age population is defined as people between the ages of 15 and

64. Thus, the dependency ratio is the ratio of the number of people aged 14 or less or aged 65 or more to the number of people between 15 and 64. This ratio is generally multiplied by 100. For example, if a country has twice as many people between 15 and 64 as it does people either under 15 or older than 64, its dependency ratio is 1 to 2 and is expressed as a value of 50 per 100. Low dependency ratios imply that many people are of working age, whereas higher dependency ratios mean that a relatively small percentage of the population is responsible for the support of the young and the elderly. The two components of the dependency ratio—the very young and the elderly—can be separated from each other for purposes of analysis and comparison.

Dependency ratios vary considerably between places and over time. In places where populations are growing rapidly because of high crude birth rates and total fertility rates, dependency ratios are high because there are large numbers of children who must be supported by working-age adults. In such countries, the median age is low. A high dependency ratio is thus typical of industrializing countries that are in the second stage of demographic transition. As of 2012, the countries with the highest dependency ratios were Niger, Uganda, Chad, Somalia, Angola, and Mali. All of these countries have very high birth rates and very high total fertility rates. All have dependency ratios of over 100, meaning that less than half of the population is between the ages of 15 and 64.

However, dependency ratios also increase in countries with high life expectancies, especially when crude birth rates are low. This means that a shrinking percentage of working-age people must support a larger and larger population of elderly people. Such is the case in Japan, which has one of the highest median ages in the world given its high life expectancy and low birth rate. In 2012, Japan had a dependency ratio of 60, which was the highest of any highly developed country. Japanese government officials are currently considering how Japanese society can manage to take care of its growing elderly population. The dependency ratio in the United States was 50. This dependency ratio is comparable to those of other developed countries, such as Australia (50), the Netherlands (50), Norway (52), and Germany (52). The lowest dependency ratios are reported in countries with very large expatriate populations of working age in their labor forces. In 2012, the countries with the lowest dependency ratios were Qatar (17), the United Arab Emirates (17), Bahrain (25), and Singapore (34).

Dependency ratios are also affected by migration. For example, in many less developed countries, people have moved to the United States and other developed countries as international labor migrants. Because most international labor migrants are young adults, the population remaining in the community of origin is composed increasingly of children and the elderly. A smaller percentage of working-age adults remain to support these younger and older people. Moreover, many of these people of working age may be disabled and/or poorly educated, further reducing their potential economic productivity. However, the impacts of a high dependency ratio on the communities from which international labor migrants originate are mitigated often by remittances.

Dependency ratios also vary within countries. For example, in the United States, many rural areas, such as parts of Appalachia and the Great Plains, have high dependency ratios because young working-age adults move away, leaving the elderly behind. States such as West Virginia and Nebraska have among the highest dependency ratios of any of the states. At the same time, places with large retirement communities, such as parts of Florida, also have high dependency ratios because of the influx of elderly persons who have retired there after working and raising their families in other states.

See Also: Crude Birth Rate; Expatriates; Germany; Japan; Life Expectancy; Median Age; Migration; Rate of Natural Increase; Remittances; Singapore; United Arab Emirates; United States of America

Further Reading

United States Bureau of the Census. "Aging Boomers Will Increase Dependency Ratio, Census Bureau Projects," 2010. http://www.census.gov/newsroom/releases/archives/aging_population/cb10-72.html.

World Bank. "Age-Dependency Ratio: Percentage of Working-Age Population, 2012. http://data.worldbank.org/indicator/SP.POP.DPND.

Diaspora

A diaspora is the large-scale, generally forced migration of an ethnic or national group. Typically, a diaspora involves movement from a relatively small area of origin to a large number of destination places. Diasporas have had significant impacts on population distributions throughout history.

The word "diaspora" comes from the Greek word *diaspeiro*, meaning "scattering." Diasporas are generally caused by religious persecution, political persecution, or forced expulsion from one's home country. Although people who move during diasporas can be considered refugees, diasporas can be distinguished from movement of refugees in general in that diasporas involve large-scale movement by large numbers of people over a short period of time. In addition, people involved in diaspora migration generally retain a strong sense of collective cultural identity, as well as ongoing attachment to their ancestral homelands. In many cases, migrants retain a hope that they will one day be able to return to their homelands.

In 1915, the government of the Ottoman Empire forced millions of Armenians to march long distances across present-day Turkey. Many Armenians were massacred during this Armenian genocide. Millions more left the country during and after World War I for the United States and other countries. (AP Photo)

The term diaspora was associated originally with the expulsion of Jews from the Roman province of Judaea, most of which is located in present-day Israel. In 66 CE, Jews in Judaea revolted against Roman control. The Roman Empire's armies defeated the Judaean rebels in battle. After defeating the Jewish armies, the Romans laid siege to the Jewish holy city of Jerusalem and destroyed the sacred Second Jewish Temple in 70 CE. Thousands of Jews were killed during and after the siege, and over the next several decades, the Romans continued to persecute Jews while Romanizing the area. As a result, many of Judaea's Jews left Judaea. Some left voluntarily, and others were captured and sold into slavery elsewhere in the Roman Empire.

Over the next 1,500 years, the Jewish population continued to disperse, with many going to Europe and others staying in the Middle East and nearby areas. These dispersed Jewish populations maintained their cultural identities as Jews, including the practice of Judaism and the use of the Hebrew language. These scattered Jewish communities maintained a belief that the area around Judaea would once again become a homeland for Jews. This hope was fulfilled with the creation of independent Israel in 1948.

One of the major diasporas of the 20th century was the Armenian diaspora during and after World War I. What is now western Armenia was annexed to the Ottoman Empire, which was administered from the present-day city of Istanbul (then known as Constantinople), during the 16th century. The Ottomans allowed the Armenians to live and retain their culture, language, and autonomy without government interference until shortly before the empire was deposed during World War I. Beginning in 1915, however, the Ottoman government began large-scale persecution of its Armenian population. Historians estimate that more than a million Armenians were massacred over the next several years in what came to be known as the Armenian Massacre. More than half a million Armenians left the region, establishing Armenian communities in other parts of the world. Today, most historians recognize the Armenian Massacre as an instance of genocide. More Armenians left in response to persecution by the Soviet Union, which incorporated Armenia in the early 1920s. An estimated 7 million people of Armenian ancestry live outside Armenia today, including about 500,000 living in the United States.

The term "diaspora" has been applied to many other large-scale movements of refugees forced to move in response to wartime conditions and persecutions throughout the world. Examples include the expulsion of approximately 100,000 South Asians by the government of Uganda in the 1970s, and movement of Cubans to the United States after Fidel Castro's government took control of Cuba beginning in 1959. It has been applied also to migration associated with natural disasters, for example to the movement of people displaced from New Orleans to other cities in the United States in 2005. Diasporas have resulted in the complete or nearly complete elimination of ethnic communities in countries of origin. For example, nearly all of the Jews living in Poland at the outset of World War II were massacred as part of the Holocaust or left the country. Diaspora communities have also had significant economic, political, and cultural impacts on their countries of destination, as is evidenced by the influential Jewish and Armenian communities in the United States.

See Also: Environmental Refugees; Genocide; Istanbul; Slavery; Turkey; United States of America

Further Reading

Robin Cohen. *Global Diasporas: An Introduction.* 2nd ed. Abington, UK: Routledge, 2008.

Stephane Dufoix. *Diasporas.* Berkeley: University of California Press, 2008.

Earth Summit

The term "Earth Summit" refers to three international conferences on population, the global environment, economic development, and sustainability sponsored by the United Nations. The three conferences include the United Nations Conference on

Environment and Development, which took place in Rio de Janeiro in 1992. The Rio de Janeiro conference was followed by the World Summit on Sustainable Development, which was held in Johannesburg in 2002, and the United Nations Conference on Sustainable Development, which took place in Rio de Janeiro in 2012.

The 1992 conference included representatives of 172 countries, including more than 100 heads of state. It also included representatives of numerous nongovernmental organizations with active interest in population-related and economic development issues and concerns. More than 10,000 journalists from throughout the world also participated. This conference focused primarily on development and environmental issues, although many of the issues discussed involved population growth and movement indirectly.

One of the major outcomes of the 1992 conference was the development of the Framework Convention on Climate Change. This led to the drafting of the Kyoto Protocol, which is an international treaty intended to reduce emission of greenhouse gases, in 1997. It was recognized that the Kyoto Protocol, if agreed upon by the world's developed countries, would implement policies that would have the effect of reducing global warming and climate change, perhaps reducing the potential for increased numbers of environmental refugees. However, the Kyoto Protocol has yet to be ratified by the United States and has been renounced by Canada.

The 1992 conference also recognized the impacts of environmental change on indigenous peoples. Delegates agreed "not [to] carry out any activities on the lands of indigenous peoples that would cause environmental degradation or that would be culturally inappropriate." After this conference, UN officials stated that "[the] Earth Summit influenced all subsequent UN conferences, which have examined the relationship between human rights, population, social development, women and human settlements—and the need for environmentally sustainable development."

After the 1992 Conference, the UN General Assembly ratified the Rio Declaration on Environment and Development. The Rio Declaration consisted of 27 principles that had been discussed and supported by delegates to the conference. These principles included Principle 5, which reads, "All States and all people shall cooperate in the essential task of eradicating poverty as an indispensable requirement for sustainable development, in order to decrease the disparities in standards of living and better meet the needs of the majority of the people of the world." Principle 6 reads, "The special situation and needs of developing countries, particularly the least developed and those most environmentally vulnerable, shall be given special priority. International actions in the field of environment and development should also address the interests and needs of all countries." (The complete text of the Rio Declaration can be accessed at http://www.un.org/documents/ga/conf151/aconf15126-1annex1.htm.)

Later, a more detailed action plan known as Agenda 21 was developed. Its preamble states in part,

Humanity stands at a defining moment in history. We are confronted with a perpetuation of disparities between and within nations, a worsening of poverty, hunger, ill health and illiteracy, and the continuing deterioration of the ecosystems on which we depend for our well-being. However, integration of environment and development concerns and greater attention to them will lead to the fulfillment of basic needs, improved living standards for all, better protected and managed ecosystems and a safer, more prosperous future. No nation can achieve this on its own; but together we can—in a global partnership for sustainable development.

Agenda 21 mentions populations and demographic change more specifically, in particular by pointing out that continued population growth could imperil the global environment. The complete text of Agenda 21 can be accessed at http://www .unep.org/Documents.Multilingual/Default.asp?documentid=52.

The Johannesburg conference took place on the tenth anniversary of the 1992 Rio Conference. Among its goals was to examine ways to better implement the principles of the Rio Declaration. At the time, conference organizers wrote,

At the 1992 Earth Summit in Rio, the international community adopted Agenda 21, an unprecedented global plan of action for sustainable development. But the best strategies are only as good as their implementation. Ten years later, the Johannesburg Summit presents an exciting opportunity for today's leaders to adopt concrete steps and identify quantifiable targets for better implementing Agenda 21.

The outcome of the Johannesburg Summit was the Johannesburg Declaration on Sustainable Development, whose complete text can be accessed at http://www .un-documents.net/jburgdec.htm.

The Johannesburg Declaration reiterates the UN's commitment to sustainable development. In Articles 21 and 22, the declaration states,

We recognize the reality that global society has the means and is endowed with the resources to address the challenges of poverty eradication and sustainable development confronting all humanity. Together, we will take extra steps to ensure that these available resources are used to the benefit of humanity. In this regard, to contribute to the achievement of our development goals and targets, we urge developed countries that have not done so to make concrete efforts to reach the internationally agreed levels of official development assistance.

However, the U.S. government did not participate in the Johannesburg meeting, likely undercutting the conference's long-run global impact.

The 2012 conference in Rio de Janeiro was held on the 20th anniversary of the original Earth Summit in the same city. Its goals linked those of the two previous Earth Summits by asking for renewed commitment to sustainability on the part of governments throughout the world, and considering ways to promote a sustainable global economy along with effective institutional frameworks to coordinate local, national, and global changes in how to address environmental problems. The 2012 conference was even larger than the first Rio conference. It was attended by delegates from 192 countries and about 130 heads of state. However, the heads of government of the United States, the United Kingdom, and Germany did not attend, leading observers to question the extent to which the leaders of these countries were truly committed to international efforts to promote a sustainable economy.

The major outcome of the 2012 conference was a nonbinding document known as "The Future We Want." This document reiterates the UN's commitment to sovereignty and reducing environmental degradation, although it does not include specific targets and goals. Underlying the report are objectives including,

> We reaffirm our commitment to strengthening international cooperation to address the persistent challenges related to sustainable development for all, in particular in developing countries. In this regard, we reaffirm the need to achieve economic stability and sustained economic growth, promotion of social equity, and protection of the environment, while enhancing gender equality and women's empowerment, and equal opportunities for all, and the protection, survival and development of children to their full potential, including through education. We resolve to take urgent action to achieve sustainable development. We therefore renew our commitment to sustainable development, assessing the progress to date and the remaining gaps in the implementation of the outcomes of the major summits on sustainable development and addressing new and emerging challenges. We express our determination to address the themes of the Conference, namely a green economy in the context of sustainable development and poverty eradication, and the institutional framework for sustainable development.

Above and beyond general questions of sustainability and development, "The Future We Want" examines questions such as agriculture, climate change, poverty, trade, globalization, and food security. The text of "The Future We Want" can be accessed at http://www.uncsd2012.org/content/documents/727The%20Future%20We%20Want%2019%20June%201230pm.pdf.

In general, the three Earth Summits have resulted in the creation of blueprints for global action on improving the quality of the environment and planning for economic growth and development. It is recognized that the burdens of climate change, poverty, and environmental degradation are being borne most heavily by the least developed countries. However, lack of support from some developed countries, including the United States, may be limiting the degree to which the principles developed during the three Earth Summits will be acted upon worldwide in the foreseeable future.

See Also: Climate Change and Population; Environmental Refugees; Germany; Globalization; Rio de Janeiro; United Kingdom; United States of America

Further Reading

United Nations. "UN Conference on Environment and Economic Development 1992," 1992. http://www.un.org/geninfo/bp/enviro.html.

United Nations. "Johannesburg Summit 2002," 2002. http://www.un.org/jsummit/html /basic_info/basicinfo.html.

United Nations Conference on Sustainable Development. "The Future We Want," 2012. http://www.uncsd2012.org/content/documents/727The%20Future%20We%20Want% 2019%20June%201230pm.pdf.

Easterlin, Richard

Richard A. Easterlin (1926–) is an American economist and demographer. He is best known for his research on the American baby boom, including economic explanations of why the crude birth rate in the United States rose sharply shortly after World War II and declined quickly during and after the late 1960s.

Easterlin was born in Ridgefield Park, New Jersey. He earned an ME degree in engineering from the Stevens Institute of Technology in 1945. He then switched his academic interests to economics, earning an MA in economics in 1949 and a PhD in economics in 1953 from the University of Pennsylvania. He joined the economics faculty at the University of Pennsylvania, eventually becoming the William R. Kenan, Jr., Professor of Economics. In 1982, he became professor of economics at the University of Southern California, where he has remained active ever since.

Easterlin's first major publication on demography, "The American Baby Boom in Historical Perspective," was published in 1961. In this paper, Easterlin challenged a then-prevalent assumption that people have fixed preferences as to family size. Rather, he argued that people prefer larger families under conditions of economic prosperity, as was true of the United States during the years after World War II. Thus he argued that the increased total fertility rate in the United States during the 1950s could be explained on the basis that parents after World War II felt that they could afford more children than did those who started families during the Great Depression. This argument came to be known as the "Easterlin hypothesis."

The assumption underlying the Easterlin hypothesis is that people aspire to maintain a standard of living higher than that of their parents. Thus, under favorable economic conditions, people believe that they will be able to provide their high standard of living to their offspring. However, parents who doubt that they can maintain this standard of living will have fewer children. In other words, people who do not believe that they will be able to provide a standard of living consistent with their aspirations about the future will delay or forgo childbearing.

Demographic data from the period before and during the U.S. baby boom are consistent with the Easterlin hypothesis. However, by the 1970s it had become evident that the Easterlin hypothesis could not explain continuing declines in the crude birth rate. Rather, it had become clear that most prospective parents, even if prosperous, preferred smaller families.

See Also: Baby Boom; Crude Birth Rate; United States of America

Further Reading

Richard Easterlin. "The American Baby Boom in Historical Perspective." *American Economic Review* 51 (1961): 869–911.

Richard Easterlin. *Happiness, Growth, and the Life Cycle.* New York: Oxford University Press, 2010.

Richard Easterlin. *The Reluctant Economist: Perspectives on Economics, Economic History, and Demography.* New York: Cambridge University Press, 2004.

Ehrlich, Paul

Paul R. Ehrlich (1932–) is an American biologist, ecologist, and demographer. Throughout his career, Ehrlich has been a strong proponent of Thomas Malthus's views about how human population growth is limited by a lack of resources.

Ehrlich was born in Philadelphia and earned a bachelor's degree from the University of Pennsylvania before earning his PhD in zoology from the University of Kansas in 1957. He joined the faculty of Stanford University in 1959 and remained a member of the Stanford faculty throughout his career.

Ehrlich's best-known early work, *The Population Bomb*, was first published in 1968. In this book, he argued that the world was quickly becoming overpopulated and that strong action would be needed to prevent catastrophic famines, epidemics, and social disruption associated with continued population increases. In effect, Ehrlich was arguing that the world had already reached its population carrying capacity by the 1960s.

At the time, Ehrlich made predictions that have proven to be incorrect. For example, he predicted that hundreds of millions of people worldwide would face starvation by the end of the 20th century. His critics regarded Ehrlich as a "doomsday" prophet. However, Ehrlich's supporters credited him with raising global awareness of population-related issues, thereby promoting the implementation of policies that would alleviate the predicted impacts of continuing population increases. In his later work, Ehrlich acknowledged that his prediction of impending catastrophe had been inaccurate. However, he argued that such catastrophes were bound to happen eventually. In effect, Ehrlich viewed the Green Revolution and other programs to increase global food supplies as ones that would postpone, but not resolve, long-run impacts of population growth. Ehrlich has been an advocate for strong, government-sponsored family planning programs intended to reduce birth rates dramatically.

Ehrlich has also argued that the United States and other developed countries must also reduce per capita natural resource consumption in order to reduce human impacts on the environment and to make the world's population more sustainable. In making this argument, Ehrlich noted that increased numbers of people are likely to rely on more and more marginal lands for sustenance, increasing the likelihood that population growth will result in long-run environmental consequences.

See Also: Carrying Capacity; Crude Birth Rate; Epidemics; Famine; Green Revolution; Natural Resources and Population

Further Reading

Paul R. Ehrlich. *The Population Bomb*. New York: Ballantine, 1968.

Paul R. Ehrlich and Anne H. Ehrlich. *The Population Explosion*. New York: Touchstone Press, 1991.

Environmental Refugees

An environmental refugee is a person who has been displaced from his or her country of residence because of natural disasters or possible long-run changes in the global environment. In light of ongoing global climate change and global warming, it is expected that more and more persons living in various parts of the world will become environmental refugees in the foreseeable future. In effect, the concept of environmental refugee status extends the traditional definition of a refugee as a victim of political or religious persecution to persons forced to move because of changing environmental conditions. The United Nations Environmental Program has defined environmental refugees as "those people who have been forced to leave their traditional habitat, temporarily or permanently, because of a marked environmental disruption (natural and/or triggered by people) that jeopardized their existence and/ or

A major earthquake struck near Port-au-Prince, Haiti, in 2010. The earthquake caused more than 150,000 fatalities and displaced several hundred thousand people. Many of these displaced persons moved to refugee camps, where United Nations personnel have been active in helping them. (AP Photo/Ariana Cubillos)

seriously affected the quality of their life." The problem of actual and potential environmental refugees is greatest in impoverished and less developed countries.

Environmental refugee status can be observed and assessed on several time horizons. In the short run, natural disasters such as floods and earthquakes have triggered large-scale international migration on the part of persons living in the vicinity where these disasters have occurred. For example, thousands of Haitian people left Haiti after the country was devastated by a major earthquake that caused upwards of 150,000 fatalities and great damage to its infrastructure in 2010. An estimated 50,000 moved to the United States, where they were given temporary asylum and permitted to obtain jobs. Employment of these refugees allowed them to send remittances to relatives, friends, and other earthquake victims in Haiti.

Environmental refugees have also moved in response to longer-term environmental changes. A good example of this movement can be found in the Sahel region of northern Africa immediately south of the Sahara Desert. This semi-arid region, which extends across Africa from Sudan westward to Mauritania, has long been subject to periodic droughts. However, drought conditions have been especially severe since the late 1960s. Only in 4 of the 40 years between 1971 and 2010 has the amount of rain falling in the Sahel region been greater than long-term normal, and temperatures throughout the period have averaged well above normal. These drought conditions have intensified ongoing population problems in the Sahel, which is one of the most impoverished places in the world and whose countries have very high crude birth rates, rates of natural increase, and total fertility rates.

The hotter and drier weather in recent years has affected the Sahel to the point that desert conditions have spread southward and many parts of the region are no longer suitable for agriculture. Nomads living in the region found that there was no longer sufficient vegetation to support their herds of domestic grazing animals. In response, large numbers of people from the Sahel have migrated, with many moving southward to countries such as Nigeria and Côte d'Ivoire. As is the case with other refugees, these countries lack the infrastructure to absorb large numbers of Sahelian environmental refugees.

The number of people who can be classified as environmental refugees is expected to increase over the course of the 21st century in response to long-run global climatic and environmental change. Most experts on climate science believe that human activity is largely responsible for ongoing climate change, including significant increases in global surface temperatures. In that sense, the situation currently being faced by residents of the Sahel region can be seen as a harbinger of situations likely to face people worldwide in decades to come.

One major problem is expected rise in sea levels. Warmer weather is already causing glaciers in Greenland, Antarctica, and other places to begin melting. As glaciers melt, water runs off into the oceans, causing overall sea levels to rise. Experts have estimated that sea levels around the world may rise by as much as two to six feet by 2100.

Rising sea levels are likely to have serious consequences for cities, larger areas, and even entire countries located at or near sea level. Several of the world's megacities, including Kolkata, Lagos, Jakarta, Bangkok, and Dhaka, are located at or near sea level. Many other large cities throughout the world, including Amsterdam, Venice, Copenhagen, Miami, and New Orleans, are also built on low-lying, flat land and are also likely to be affected by global sea level increases. Sea level rise may inundate portions of these and other cities, forcing residents to abandon their homes and move inland. Some have also predicted that sea level rise may trigger more intense tropical storms, such as the typhoon that devastated the Philippines in November 2013.

Sea level increases can affect larger areas in addition to coastal cities. Bangladesh may be among the hardest-hit countries because more than a third of its land surface, including its most heavily populated areas, is located less than 25 feet above sea level. Moreover, Bangladesh is susceptible to intense tropical cyclones (hurricanes), including a storm that caused nearly 500,000 fatalities in 1970 and another that resulted in 150,000 fatalities in 1991. Sea level rise may cause such storms to intensify in the future. Sea level rise is already inducing many Bangladeshis to move as environmental refugees to India, which is attempting to control in-migration

---

KIRIBATI DEALS WITH SEA-LEVEL RISE

Kiribati is a small island country located along the equator in the Pacific Ocean. It consists of 33 inhabited islands scattered across more than a million square miles of ocean. The islands have a total land area of about 310 square miles and a population of about 104,000.

All but one of Kiribati's islands are atolls, which are formed from coral reefs, encircle lagoons, and have flat topographies only a few feet above sea level. Thus Kiribati is highly vulnerable to the possibility of sea-level rise associated with global climate change. Such would force many people in Kiribati to become environmental refugees. Already, rising seas are encroaching on Kiribati's coast, and many of its supplies of fresh water have become contaminated. Its president, Anote Tong, has argued that Kiribati needs to prepare for what he calls "migration with dignity." In 2008, Tong stated, "We may be beyond redemption. We may be at the point of no return, where the emissions in the atmosphere will carry on contributing to climate change, to produce a sea-level change so in time our small nation will be submerged."

Further Reading

Bernard Lagan. "Kiribati: A Nation Going Under." *The Global Mail*, April 15, 2013. http://www.theglobalmail.org/feature/kiribati-a-nation-going-under/590/.

---

from Bangladesh in part through the construction of a border fence along the boundary between the two countries.

Entire countries, especially those located on islands, are being affected by potential sea level rise. Two island countries of particular concern are Kiribati in the Pacific Ocean and the Maldives in the Indian Ocean. Both occupy low-lying, flat islands generally less than 15 feet above mean sea level. In these and other cases, governments have begun efforts to prepare for possible large-scale evacuation. However, to date other countries have been generally reluctant to accept people claiming environmental refugee status as migrants.

The actual and potential displacement of environmental refugees has begun to attract international attention. For example, a nongovernmental organization known as Living Space for Environmental Refugees (LiSER) has been founded to coordinate and call attention to environmental refugees. (Read the text of the LiSER mission statement elsewhere in this encyclopedia.)

See Also: Agriculture and Population; Bangladesh; Climate Change and Population; Crude Birth Rate; Dhaka; Globalization; India; Jakarta; Kolkata; Lagos; Mumbai; Rate of Natural Increase; Total Fertility Rate; United States of America

Further Reading

Charles Kenny. "The Haitian Migration." *FP*, January 9, 2012. http://www.foreignpolicy.com/articles/2012/01/09/the_haitian_migration.

Bernard Lagan. "Australia Urged to Prepare for Influx of People Displaced by Climate Change." *The Guardian*, April 16, 2013. http://www.theguardian.com/environment/2013/apr/16/australia-climate-change-refugee-status.

Alice Thomas. "Sahel Villagers Fleeing Climate Change Must Not Be Ignored." *The Guardian*, August 2, 2013. http://www.theguardian.com/global-development/poverty-matters/2013/aug/02/sahel-climate-change-displacement-migration.

Manish Vaid and Tridivesh Singh Maini. "The Changing Climate of Bangladeshi Migration to India." *East Asia Forum*, March 23, 2013. http://www.eastasiaforum.org/2013/03/23/the-changing-climate-of-bangladeshi-migration-to-india/.

World Bank. "Warming Climate to Hit Bangladesh Hard with Sea Level Rise, More Floods and Cyclones, World Bank Report Says," June 19, 2013. http://www.worldbank.org/en/news/press-release/2013/06/19/warming-climate-to-hit-bangladesh-hard-with-sea-level-rise-more-floods-and-cyclones-world-bank-report-says.

Epidemics

An epidemic is an occurrence of an infectious disease that spreads rapidly, often affecting very large numbers of people over a widespread area and resulting in numerous fatalities and considerable social disruption. Epidemics have had major impacts on populations throughout history. Some of the best-known epidemics in history include the bubonic plague epidemic or Black Death that struck Europe in the 14th century, and the Spanish flu epidemic that is believed to have caused as many as 75 million fatalities worldwide after World War I.

Epidemics are usually defined on the basis of comparing death rates during disease outbreaks to long-term death rates. The term *pandemic* is used to describe an epidemic that occurs over a very large area. Thus the Spanish flu epidemic of 1918–1919 has been referred to as a pandemic. The term "epidemic" has also been applied to diseases and social disruptions with long-run or indirect impacts on populations such as criminal activity, diabetes, alcoholism, and obesity.

Epidemics often occur when diseases strike populations that have little or no immunity to the viruses, bacteria, or other agents that cause disease. Many epidemics, such as epidemics of influenza, involve contagious diseases. Others, such as bubonic plague epidemics, involve diseases spread by contact with insects and other pests. Consumption of infected food or water supplies can also result in epidemics. For example, outbreaks of cholera result from people consuming food infected with bacteria that cause that disease. Such epidemics are often associated with a lack of sanitation and public health.

Epidemics can have substantial effects on populations, sometimes over very large areas. The Justinian Plague, which occurred in 541 and 542 CE, had major and long-lasting impacts on the Eastern Roman Empire. For example, it is believed that the Black Death caused the death of a quarter to a third of Europe's people during the 1340s and 1350s. Epidemics occurred throughout the western hemisphere and other areas after European contact as Europeans spread tuberculosis, smallpox, and other diseases to which local indigenous populations had no immunity. In some areas, as many as 90 percent of Native Americans and other indigenous North Americans succumbed to these diseases during the first few decades of European colonization.

THE H1N1 FLU EPIDEMIC OF 2009

In 2009, an epidemic of influenza affected people throughout the world. The epidemic was caused by a strain of the H1N1 virus that was responsible for the Spanish flu epidemic of 1918–1919. The disease was called "swine flu" as it was first reported in domestic pigs before it affected humans. Although the World Health Organization estimated that 18,000 deaths were caused by this epidemic, other estimates put the death toll at between 300,000 and 500,000 people. One reason for the discrepancy in the number of fatalities is that many persons, especially in less developed countries, were infected and died without medical treatment.

Where the strain of the H1N1 virus originated is unknown. However, significant numbers of cases were reported in Mexico in January 2009. From there the disease spread quickly to the United States and to other parts of the world. Between 50 and 90 million people contracted the disease worldwide. The highest cause-specific death rates were reported in Latin America, whose infection rate was 20 times that of Europe.

Further Reading

Liz Szabo. "Flu Pandemic in 2009 Killed 10 Times More Than Thought." *USA Today*, November 26, 2013. http://www.usatoday.com/story/news/nation/2013/11/26/h1n1-pandemic-killed-10-times-more-than-thought/3758711/.

In general, the impacts of epidemics have been reduced over the past two centuries. Once the causes of epidemic diseases were identified, vaccinations and other measures to prevent outbreaks were implemented. Cures were developed in order to treat victims of these diseases who might otherwise have died. Public health measures such as sanitization and quarantine were adopted in order to retard the spread of diseases. Thus the control of epidemics was related closely to demographic transition and to the very rapid decline in death rates that has accompanied industrialization. However, epidemics continue to affect people throughout the world. Many are caused by viruses and other agents to which immunity is limited, in some cases because of mutations. For example, the global epidemic of HIV/AIDS is believed to have claimed more than 20 million victims worldwide over the past three decades. Medical research directed at isolating the causes of HIV/AIDS, preventing its spread, and treating its victims is ongoing.

See Also: Black Death; Demographic Transition Model; HIV/AIDS; Justinian Plague; Spanish Flu

Further Reading

Leon Gordis. *Epidemiology*. 4th ed. Philadelphia: Saunders, 2008.

Ray M. Merrill. *Introduction to Epidemiology*. 6th ed. Sudbury, MA: Jones and Bartlett, 2012.

Eugenics

Eugenics is the view that selective breeding can improve the "quality" of human populations. Drawing inspiration from Charles Darwin's theories of natural selection and from observation of selective breeding of animals and plants, proponents of eugenics believed that people with "desirable" traits such as high intelligence and physical vitality should be encouraged to reproduce whereas those lacking such traits should be discouraged from or forbidden to bear children.

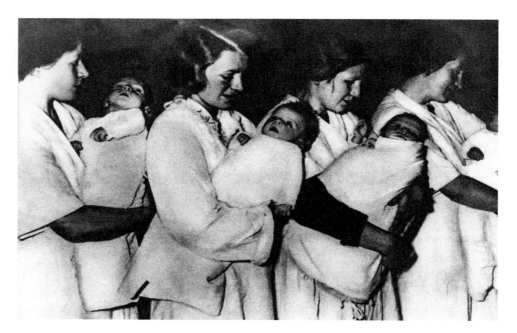

The Eugenics movement, which flourished in the early twentieth century, became discredited during the rule of the Nazis in Germany before and during World War II. Nazi officials exterminated millions of Jews, Roma, and other non-Aryan people in an effort to promote "racial purity," while women of pure German ancestry were encouraged to give birth. (Keystone-France/Gamma-Keystone/Getty Images)

The ideas of eugenics were developed in the late 19th century, after Darwin's theories of evolution had become accepted widely within the scientific community. The British scientist Sir Francis Galton (1822–1911), who was a cousin of Darwin's, believed that various human traits including intelligence were inherited. Galton coined the term "eugenics" in 1883, and he argued that systematic efforts could and should apply Darwin's theory of natural selection to human populations. Proponents of eugenics founded various organizations such as the American Eugenics Society in order to promote their views.

During the early 20th century, many countries adopted and practiced policies inspired by concepts of eugenics. Many of these policies prohibited people who were considered "inferior" from having children. These policies include compulsory sterilization and forced abortions on the part of people who were disabled, "feeble-minded," and mentally ill. In some countries, such as Nazi Germany, such people, along with members of specified ethnic and racial groups such as the Jews in Germany, were identified, isolated from society, and sterilized, euthanized, or murdered.

Sterilization of the mentally ill was practiced in many countries in addition to Germany during the early 20th century. In addition, concepts of eugenics were used to discourage fertility among people of lower social classes on the grounds that upper-class people were perceived to be more intelligent and productive. In the United States, well-known public figures including Margaret Sanger promoted these ideas of eugenics. Thousands of Americans were sterilized during this period, with these actions justified on the basis of eugenics concepts. However, the concepts of eugenics became discredited after they were used by the Nazis to justify their identification of Germans as a "master race" and their relentless extermination and genocide of Jews and other minorities.

After World War II, the principles of eugenics came to be recognized as a severe violation of human rights. However, its advocates have continued to argue in favor of the use of scientific principles in population planning. The American Eugenics Society's president, Harry L. Shapiro, wrote in 1959,

Eugenics has always been a joint enterprise of scientists and laymen interested in applying to population problems the best scientific knowledge of the time. One might have expected that a belief in the possibility of improving the quality of human population and a faith that acceptably sound means could be found for doing so might have attracted from the very beginning greater enthusiasm, particularly among men and women dedicated to science and aware of its varied achievements. But, in fact, eugenics has never been a widely popular movement. . . . [T]he zeal of early eugenists not adequately grounded in science, or of eugenists who were operating in areas where science had nothing positive to say, had in the past led to the advocacy of programmes that subsequently were discredited and shown to be of little value. And this in some circles did eugenics little or no good. This points up the difference between science and a programme. The discredited theories of science have not discredited science.

The use of these scientific concepts in population control at both the individual level and at the larger scale remains highly controversial. For example, proponents of abortion have argued that genetic screening allows the abortion of fetuses believed to be afflicted with Down's syndrome and other genetic disorders. However, the ability to detect the sex of an unborn child has also enabled sex-selective abortion, which has been practiced frequently in China given that country's one-child population policy.

See Also: American Eugenics Society; China; Euthanasia; Galton, Sir Francis; Genocide; Germany; One-Child Policy; Sanger, Margaret

Further Reading

Jerry Bergman. *Hitler and the Nazi Darwinian Worldview: How the Nazi Eugenic Crusade for a Superior Race Caused the Greatest Holocaust in World History.* Kitchener, ON: Joshua Press, 2012.

Edwin Black. *War against the Weak: Eugenics and America's Campaign to Create a Master Race.* New York: Dialog Press, 2012.

Nancy Ordover. *American Eugenics: Race, Queer Anatomy, and the Science of Nationalism.* Minneapolis: University of Minnesota Press, 2003.

Harry L. Shapiro. "Eugenics and Future Society." *The Eugenics Review* 51 (1959): 89–92, http://www.ncbi.nlm.nih.gov/pmc/articles/PMC2973509/.

Euthanasia

Euthanasia is the practice of deliberately ending one's life with the assistance of medical personnel in order to relieve pain and suffering. Euthanasia differs from suicide in that it is undertaken with the assistance of medical professionals, and it is therefore called sometimes "assisted suicide." Some countries have legalized euthanasia, but the practice is controversial in part because of evidence that not all instances of euthanasia are entirely voluntary and because it is considered inconsistent with some religious traditions. Even in countries in which euthanasia is legal, however, death rates from euthanasia are low. In the Netherlands, for example, euthanasia and physician-assisted suicide has been legal since the early 1990s. About 2,300 deaths, or about 2 percent of all deaths in the Netherlands, occur as a result of euthanasia.

Euthanasia is associated with relief from pain and suffering, or with the presence of a terminal and incurable illness. The Oxford English Dictionary defines euthanasia as "the painless killing of a patient suffering from an incurable and painful disease or in an irreversible coma." There are two types of euthanasia: active euthanasia and passive euthanasia. Active euthanasia involves the direct injection of lethal drugs or other substances that cause death. Passive euthanasia involves the prescription of lethal drugs or the withholding of life-extending medical treatments.

Euthanasia is believed to have been practiced in ancient Greece and Rome, but was rejected by Christian theologians who regarded the practice as inconsistent with the Christian philosophy of the sanctity of life. Debate over the legality, morality, and practice of euthanasia in the modern world began in the late 19th century in part because of the invention of chloroform, morphine, and other drugs that could reduce pain or render patients unconscious. These medications allowed people to be euthanized painlessly.

Proponents of euthanasia have emphasized the idea that euthanasia is a voluntary action, and a decision to end one's life must be made rationally by people in full command of their mental faculties. However, in some societies euthanasia has been practiced involuntarily. Before and during World War II, Nazis in Germany euthanized disabled and elderly people, as well as Jews and other religious minorities, involuntarily. Advocates of eugenics in the United States and other countries have argued for euthanizing people with severe physical or mental disabilities.

The role of physicians and other medical professionals in euthanasia cases has also been controversial, even when euthanasia is a completely voluntary act. Family members and other associates of euthanasia patients have doubted the degree to which these patients have made decisions to end their lives completely voluntarily, without pressure and coercion. In countries in which euthanasia is illegal, physicians and others who have assisted in euthanasia have been accused of murder and have been prosecuted for this crime. In the United States, perhaps the best-known medical professional associated with euthanasia was Jack Kevorkian (1928–2011). Kevorkian claimed to have assisted more than 100 people to commit suicide. In 1999, Kevorkian was convicted by a Michigan jury of second-degree murder and served eight years in prison.

Today, the legal status of euthanasia varies between countries and, in the United States, among the states. However, euthanasia is illegal in most countries. As of 2013, active euthanasia was legal only in the Netherlands, Belgium, and Luxembourg. It is illegal throughout the United States, although the U.S. states of Montana, Oregon, Vermont, and Washington permit physician-assisted suicide. In Switzerland, physicians may prescribe lethal drugs with the consent of the patient but may not administer these drugs to the patient. More generally, many countries allow patients to decline medical treatment that would extend their lives. Many people sign legal documents that preserve their rights to decline such medical treatment should they become incapacitated eventually.

See Also: Eugenics; Germany; United States of America

Further Reading

Amanda Gardner. "Dutch Euthanasia Rates Steady after Legalization." *ABC News*, March 23, 2014, http://abcnews.go.com/Health/Healthday/story?id=4506995.

Michael Manning. *Euthanasia and Physician-Assisted Suicide: Killing or Caring?* Mahwah, NJ: Paulist Press, 1998.

Robert Orfali. *Death with Dignity: The Case for Legalizing Physician-Assisted Suicide and Euthanasia*. Minneapolis: Mill City Press, 2011.

Expatriates

Expatriates are persons who live for extended periods of time outside their countries of birth or citizenship. In some areas, expatriates represent a significant proportion of their resident populations.

There is no precise definition of an expatriate. In a large sense, all of the more than 200 million people who live outside their home countries and have immigrated to other countries can be considered expatriates. However, persons who reside temporarily in another country but remain attached to their home countries are generally not considered expatriates. Examples of such nonexpatriates include foreign students, military personnel stationed overseas, and employees of international corporations assigned to work in other countries. However, many countries regard international labor migrants as expatriates, whether or not they intend eventually to return to their home countries.

Not all expatriates are guest workers or international labor migrants. An increasing number of highly educated professionals including scientists, engineers, and academics live and work outside their home countries. Such individuals have been referred to as "global professionals." In many cases, they are part of the brain drain. Other expatriates are outside the labor force. For example, many Americans and Europeans have retired to other countries, generally to places with attractive physical environments and a relatively low cost of living. The most common destinations for Americans retiring abroad are Mexico, Central America, and various Caribbean countries.

Millions of people around the world live as expatriates. Currently, it is estimated that there are about 6 million expatriates from the United States and about 3 million from the United Kingdom. In a few countries such as the United Arab

Emirates, expatriates make up more than half of the resident population. Many expatriates residing in the United Arab Emirates come from much poorer countries of origin, including India, Pakistan, and Bangladesh. Most expatriates retain strong ties to their countries of origin. However, some eventually renounce their citizenship in their home countries and become permanent residents or citizens of the countries to which they have relocated.

See Also: Bangladesh; Brain Drain; India; International Labor Migration; Pakistan; United Arab Emirates; United Kingdom; United States of America

Further Reading

Justlanded.com. "Expatriates Worldwide," 2009. http://www.justlanded.com/english/Common/Footer/Expatriates/How-many-expats-are-there.

Brian Knowlton. "More American Expatriates Give Up Citizenship." *New York Times*, April 25, 2010. http://www.nytimes.com/2010/04/26/us/26expat.html?_r=0.

Harold Perkin. *The Third Revolution: Professional Elites in the Modern World.* London: Routledge, 1996.

Famine

Famine is defined as a chronic shortage of food over a substantial area. Historically, famines have caused millions of death throughout the world. Today, famine has been eradicated largely in the developed world, although famines continue to be significant causes of death in less developed countries.

Famines have several causes. Many result from crop failure that occurs in response to drought, flooding, pest infestations, or natural disasters. Famines also have economic and political causes. Many famines have occurred because governments withhold food, because roads and other transportation supply lines used to provide food are cut off during wartime, and/or because people do not have money to purchase food.

Famines not only cause death by starvation and malnutrition, but they can also cause death rates to increase because people who lack sufficient food are more vulnerable to epidemics or infectious diseases. In pre-industrial societies, it was difficult or impossible to transport food to persons suffering from famine because transportation of these food supplies was unavailable or prohibitively expensive. Thus famines were commonplace in ancient and medieval times. Historians have documented that more than 200 famines were recorded in the British Isles in the past 2,000 years, or about one every decade. In much larger and more populated China, about 2,000 famines have been recorded during the same two millennia.

Civil and international conflicts continue to force large numbers of people to leave their home countries as refugees. Many of these refugees are impoverished and are forced to settle in refugee camps, where they often lack basic services, food, and water. Here, representatives of the United Nations' World Food Program distribute food to refugees in Dolo, Somalia, where refugees face a severe threat of famine. (AP Photo/Jason Straziuso)

Over the past 150 years, famines have disappeared from the developed world, and the disappearance of famine is associated with demographic transition. The Irish Potato Famine, which occurred between 1845 and 1852, was the last major famine in Western Europe. Famine in developed countries has been eradicated for several reasons. Overall food supplies have increased as a result of improved agricultural technology. Human diets are more diverse, with people no longer reliant on only one or two types of food for sustenance. Improved transportation has made it easier to transport food quickly and cheaply, and freezing and refrigeration techniques make it possible to store food for long periods of time for future use. Ease of transportation also allows food to be shipped quickly to feed people who have experienced natural disasters or crop failures.

In the 20th and 21st centuries, most famines have occurred in less developed countries. Contemporary famines are not the direct result of food shortages at a global level, but are normally associated with political and economic problems. Over the past century, many significant famines have taken place in places in wartorn areas. Several major famines occurred during World War I and World War II. A major famine took place in Russia in 1916 and 1917, and it was followed by another in 1921 in the aftermath of the Russian Revolution. During World War II, several famines occurred in war-torn areas of Eastern Europe. An even larger famine, the Great Bengal Famine, took place in present-day Bangladesh. As many as three million people lost their lives as a result of the Great Bengal Famine, which occurred in part because food supply lines between Bangladesh and present-day Myanmar, which was then controlled by Japan, were cut as a result of the war. The Great Bengal Famine was one of the events that eventually triggered the Green Revolution. The most devastating famine of the 20th century was the Great Chinese Famine of 1958–1962. This famine, which resulted in more than 40 million fatalities, was a result of substantial political upheaval and social disruption associated with China's unsuccessful "Great Leap Forward" planning policies.

Sometimes, famines intensify in war-torn areas because food is used also a political weapon by factions competing with one another for power. For example, famine in Somalia in the early 1990s was exacerbated by the fact that Somalia lacked a functioning central government, and local warlords cut off food supplies for political purposes as they struggled for control of the country. Another major famine has occurred in Somalia and throughout the Horn of Africa between 2006 and 2008. The United Nations has estimated that more than 11 million people in Somalia, Kenya, Ethiopia, and Djibouti have been affected by this famine, which occurred as a result of drought coupled with ongoing military conflicts.

Demographers, economists, and geographers are divided as to whether the number and intensity of famines will increase throughout the world in the 21st century. One reason for the decreasing number of famines is that even though world populations have increased rapidly over the past two centuries, our ability to produce and transport food has, for the most part, increased at an even faster rate. The Green Revolution and other coordinated efforts have applied scientific agricultural methods and modern technology to improve crop yields in Mexico, India, Africa, Southeast Asia, and other places. As a result of these efforts, increased food production has offset population increases. However, many experts believe that society is reaching a limit as to how much additional food can be produced. Taking a Malthusian view, these experts predict that famines will increase as long as populations continue to increase relative to food supplies.

On the other hand, observers have also noted that famines have seldom taken place in democratic societies. In one study, the effects of food shortages in democratic India were compared to those in autocratic East African societies. In the impoverished and densely populated Indian state of Odisha (formerly known as Orissa), there were several occasions on which local food production dropped as a result of crop failure or severe weather conditions. Despite food shortages, only several hundred people in Odisha have perished as a result. In contrast, famines in Somalia and other East African countries caused hundreds of thousands of

---

FAMINE IN SOMALIA

In Somalia, a combination of drought, political turmoil, and lack of access to food supplies is causing widespread famine. With a population of about 10.5 million, Somalia is one of the poorest countries in the world. It is embroiled in civil war, and has lacked a fully functional central government for more than two decades. Per capita gross domestic product is less than $600, and only about 30 percent of adult Somalis are literate.

Although much of Somalia is arid and the amount of arable land is limited, agriculture remains an important economic activity. Agricultural production has been curtailed, however, by ongoing civil war as well as by drought, which was especially severe between 2008 and 2011. By 2012, more than half of Somalia's domestic cattle and goats had died from lack of water, and numerous crops had failed. The shortage of agriculture production drove food prices up rapidly, making it very difficult for already impoverished people to afford to buy food. Contemporary estimates suggest not only that thousands of people in Somalia have perished, but also that more than 20 percent of the famine's survivors suffer from malnutrition.

Further Reading

The Economist. "Once More into the Abyss," July 7, 2011, http://www.economist.com/node/18929467.

Oxfam International. "Famine in Somalia: Causes and Solutions," July 2011. http://www.oxfam.org/en/emergencies/east-africa-food-crisis/famine-somalia-what-needs-be-done.

---

fatalities during the same time period. The linkage between democracy and reduced impacts of famine has been attributed to the fact that under democratic governance, governments are accountable to the people who elected them. Governments that are unsuccessful in responding effectively and quickly to famine conditions or in alleviating hunger and suffering are likely to be voted out of office in future elections. Educational activities and programs to provide credit to impoverished farmers, allowing them to expand production, are also seen as valuable to efforts to reduce the threat of famine.

Modern technology, including effective transportation and scientific agriculture, has alleviated the threat of famine caused by natural forces. However, famine continues to occur in places in which crop shortages coincide with war, political turmoil, or economic problems. Whether the world can continue to feed itself, and whether large-scale famines can be prevented in the future, remains an open question.

See Also: Bangladesh; China; Crude Death Rate; Food Production and Security; Great Bengal Famine; Great Chinese Famine; Great Famine of 1315–1317; Green Revolution; India; Irish Potato Famine; Malthus, Thomas; Mexico; Russia

Further Reading

Dan Banik. "Poverty, Inequality, and Democracy: Growth and Hunger in India." *Journal of Democracy* 22 (2011): 90–104.

William A. Dando. *Food and Famine in the 21st Century*. Santa Barbara, CA: ABC-CLIO, 2012.

William A. Dando. *The Geography of Famine*. Silver Spring, MD: V. H. Winston, 1980.

Celia W. Dugger. "Ending Famine, Simply by Ignoring the Experts." *New York Times*, December 2, 2007. http://www.nytimes.com/2003/03/01/arts/does-democracy-avert -famine.html?pagewanted=all&src=pm.

Michael Messing. "Does Democracy Avert Famine?" *New York Times*, March 1, 2003. http:// www.nytimes.com/2003/03/01/arts/does-democracy-avert-famine.html.

Food Prices and Population

As populations grow throughout the world, many demographers have debated the eventual carrying capacity of the earth to support human populations. Hence the question of relationships between food prices and population is a very important one.

The concept of carrying capacity posits that one or more limiting factors will force populations downward once carrying capacities have been reached. Many regard the availability of food as a major limiting factor for human populations. Considering the extent to which food may be a limiting factor for human populations requires examination of food availability, both from the standpoint of production and from the standpoint of prices of food. The question of food prices is also related to examination of Thomas Malthus's theories of the relationships between population and resources in that Malthus postulated that the world would run out of sufficient food as populations continued to increase. Moreover, starvation would increase because food prices would rise in light of short supply, and poorer people would no longer be able to afford enough food to survive.

The price of any commodity is based on supply and demand, with prices decreasing with increased supply and increasing with increased demand. The relationship between supply and demand is especially critical in the case of food, because demand for food is inelastic. Demand for any product can be divided between inelastic and elastic demand. Inelastic demand implies that prices are affected little by economic conditions, whereas elastic demand implies that demand decreases substantially as economic conditions deteriorate. Thus demand for luxury items and expensive vacations is elastic. On the other hand, food is an essential commodity that is necessary to survival, and therefore demand for food is inelastic.

Inelasticity of demand for food helps to explain the fact that the percentage of one's income spent on food decreases with increased per capita incomes. Today, the average person in the United States and in most countries of the European Union spends less than 10 percent of his or her income on food. On the other hand, studies have confirmed that residents of less wealthy and developed countries such as Egypt, Indonesia, and Nigeria spend more than 40 percent of their incomes on food. Given the inelasticity of demand for food, this difference means that people in less developed countries are affected far more by increased food prices than are people in developed countries such as the United States.

Rising food prices put less developed countries at a much greater risk of famine relative to developed countries. In recent years, riots and other conflicts have broken out over increased food costs as governments endeavor to mediate between the interests of farmers and food producers who favor price increases and consumers who want prices to decline.

Although Malthus predicted that food supplies would run out with increasing population, since World War II, increases in food production have exceeded increases in population. Thus food prices have declined in real terms as supply increases faster than demand, although local food shortages and price increases continue to occur. The increasing food supply is due to the impacts of the Green Revolution and other efforts to produce larger quantities of food.

However, whether the general trend of increased food supply relative to demand will continue is problematic. Some have predicted that food supply will continue to increase faster than the rate of population increase, pointing out that the rate of population increase worldwide may be declining as more and more countries experience demographic transition. Others, following Malthus, argue that the world is reaching its limit of food production capacity, in part because increased reliance on technology is causing environmental degradation and ecological destruction and also because of the potential impacts of global climate change on food production. Those taking the latter view have predicted the possibility of food shortages locally and perhaps globally in the foreseeable future. They recognize also the possibility that food prices will increase to the point that the poor, especially in less developed countries, will no longer be able to purchase sufficient quantities of food.

See Also: Carrying Capacity; Egypt; Famine; Food Production and Security; Globalization; Green Revolution; Indonesia; Nigeria

Further Reading

MIT Technology Review. "The Cause of Riots and the Price of Food," August 15, 2011. http://www.technologyreview.com/view/425019/the-cause-of-riots-and-the-price-of-food/.

Charlotte Rye. "Are We Entering a Global Food Crisis?" *Populationmatters.org*, August 2001. https://www.populationmatters.org/documents/food_crisis.pdf.

Sophie Wenzlau. "Global Food Prices Continue to Rise." Worldwatch Institute, April 11, 2013, http://www.worldwatch.org/global-food-prices-continue-rise-0.

Food Production and Food Security

How much food can the world produce? And to what extent can individual countries, cultures, and people in local areas be certain of having sufficient supplies of food to support their populations? Questions such as these are questions of food production and food security.

The world's crude birth rate continues to exceed its crude death rate. Currently, the world's rate of natural increase is estimated at between 1.5 and 2 percent annually. Thus the total number of people living in the world is continuing to increase and more and more food is necessary to produce this increasing number of people. At the same time, levels of food production are also increasing. New technology, such as that associated with the Green Revolution, has resulted in often-dramatic increases in food production. The question becomes whether increases in food production resulting from more efficient and productive agriculture will continue at a faster rate than the rate of population growth.

This question has been debated for more than 200 years. In the late 18th century, Thomas Malthus postulated that food production could not keep up with the needs associated with a growing population. Hence Malthus believed that food production would be a factor in determining the earth's carrying capacity. Once the carrying capacity was exceeded, populations would decline. However, Malthus did not anticipate the extent to which food production would increase in accordance with demands for food. Today, some experts believe that the extent to which the world's food production capacity can be increased has become limited. However, optimists point to evidence that world food production is increasing at a faster rate that the rate of population increase, which may be slowing down as more and more less developed countries complete the process of demographic transition.

Whether or not food production worldwide can exceed global population growth, there is no doubt that the relationships between food availability and population growth vary from place to place around the world. Especially in less developed countries, shortages of food production result in famines, which can be exacerbated under wartime conditions and/or during periods of drought, flooding, or other environmental stresses. The possibility of local food shortages raises the question of food security. Food security refers to the availability of food for present and future use. In ancient times, transition from hunting and gathering to farming made possible very large increases in food security, because food could be stored for future use.

Today, food security is measured in terms of the likelihood that food will be available in a particular place at a particular time. It can also be examined at a global level as well as at a more local scale. In other words, while the world may have enough food to feed itself people in certain areas may lack food security and therefore may not have enough food. Levels of food security vary in accordance with several factors. The most basic consideration is the amount of food that is produced and available for future use. The amount of food that can be produced is affected by environmental conditions such as water availability. Some experts have predicted that global climate change may affect food production in that currently productive food-producing areas may become hotter and drier, reducing their food production capacities.

Food security levels are also affected by food prices. Even when sufficient food is available, people may not be able to afford to purchase food. Thus food shortages will affect the poor more than they will wealthy people, who have more resources to buy food even when shortages occur and prices rise. Food prices as a function of income vary considerably, with people in less developed countries spending as much as half of their incomes on food. High levels of spending on food, relative to overall income, reduces food security in that people become dependent on scarce economic resources to obtain sufficient amounts of food.

Measures of food security also involve the quality of food as well as its quantity. A simple measure of food security is the number of calories consumed per day, with fewer calories implying greater threats to food security. However, many people throughout the world suffer from malnutrition even if they consume sufficient amounts of food because they may not have the opportunity to eat foods that have high nutritional value.

Food security also involves questions of distribution. Not only must there be sufficient food, but the technology to distribute food to consumers must also be available. Lack of food security can cause famine under wartime conditions, when food supply lines may be cut because roads and bridges are destroyed, blown up, or blockaded by enemy forces. Food is used as a political weapon by dictators and warlords who can use food as a weapon to advance their political goals.

The international community has taken many steps to address issues of food security. Efforts to reduce birth rates and to reduce global population increase can result in declining increases in the demand for food. Continued use and implementation of agricultural technology can result in increased production capacity. Economic growth and improved provision of public services, especially in rural areas, have also been viewed as means to increase local food security levels. Health is also related to food security in that better nutrition can allow farmers to produce more food in order to boost supplies.

Although global food production levels continue to increase faster than global population growth rates, it is an open question whether this trend will continue on a global as well as on a local scale. To the extent food security declines, food shortages will become more commonplace. In general, problems of food security will have far more impacts on the poor and/or residents of less developed countries than they will have in other parts of the world.

See Also: Agriculture and Population; Carrying Capacity; Climate Change and Population; Crude Birth Rate; Crude Death Rate; Demographic Transition Model; Famine; Food Prices and Population; Globalization; Hunting and Gathering; Malthus, Thomas

Further Reading

John Ingram, Polly Ericksen, and Diana Liverman, eds. *Food Security and Global Environmental Change*. London: Routledge, 2010.

Bryan L. McDonald. *Food Security*. New York: Polity Press, 2010.

United Nations Food and Agriculture Organization. *The State of Food Insecurity in the World 2003*. ftp://ftp.fao.org/docrep/fao/006/j0083e/j0083e00.pdf.

Galton, Sir Francis

Sir Francis Galton (1822–1911) was a British psychologist, economist, explorer, statistician, and geographer who is regarded today as a founder of the concept of eugenics.

Galton was born near Birmingham, England, and was a half-cousin of Charles Darwin. He was educated at Trinity College, University of Cambridge, where he studied mathematics. He then began to study medicine, but abandoned his studies and became a well-known African explorer, including travel along the Nile River into present-day Sudan and an expedition into South-West Africa (present-day Namibia). His family's wealth enabled him to pursue his intellectual interests on a full-time basis, and throughout the later years of his life he was an active member of the Royal Society, the British Association for the Advancement of Science, and the Royal Geographical Society.

The publication of *The Origin of Species* by his cousin Darwin in 1859 spurred Galton's interest in human heredity. He developed a system to measure specific traits of individuals, including their height and weight as well as what were described as "mental traits" or supposed measures of intelligence. He argued that intelligence is inherited, arriving at this conclusion from observation of his own family and other families that had produced generations of prominent scholars, scientists, artists, business leaders, and government officials.

These observations encouraged Galton to advocate policies encouraging these "intelligent" people to have more children, whereas less intelligent people would be discouraged from or forbidden procreation. In this way, the human race could be "improved." In his book *Hereditary Genius*, published in 1869, he wrote that an ideal society would be one in which "the pride of race was encouraged . . .; where the weak could find a welcome and a refuge in celibate monasteries or sisterhoods, and lastly, where the better sort of emigrants and refugees from other lands were invited and welcomed, and their descendants naturalized."

In 1882, Galton coined the term "eugenics." At that time, many members of the British upper classes married late and had small families while members of the lower classes tended to have much larger families. In keeping with the ideas set forth in *Hereditary Genius*, Galton argued that members of these upper-class families who had proven their ability to produce "successful" persons should be encouraged to marry at an early age and raise large families, with government providing incentives to promote these large families if necessary. Today, of course, the concepts of eugenics as developed originally by Galton have been largely discredited.

See Also: Eugenics

Further Reading

Michael Bulmer. *Francis Galton: Pioneer of Heredity and Biometry*. Baltimore: Johns Hopkins University Press, 2003.

Sir Francis Galton. *Hereditary Genius: An Inquiry into Its Laws and Causes*. London: Macmillan, 1869. Online edition available at http://galton.org/books/hereditary-genius/galton-1869-Hereditary_Genius.pdf.

Sir Francis Galton. *Memories of My Life*. New York: E. P. Dutton, 1909.

Nicholas Wright Gillham. *A Life of Sir Francis Galton: From African Explorer to the Birth of Eugenics*. London: Oxford University Press, 2001.

Gender and Population

Throughout the world, gender plays an important role in demography. The role of gender in population analysis can be observed with respect to many factors, including the human sex ratio; various demographic characteristics such as crude birth rates, crude death rates, and life expectancy; and patterns of migration.

In looking at gender and population, it is important to distinguish the concept of gender from the concept of sex. Sex is a biological construct, based on whether a person is male or female regardless of the cultural implications of one's sex. For example, human sex ratios measure the percentage of people in a given population who are male or female. Gender, on the other hand, is a cultural construct.

Female illiteracy is an important issue in less developed countries. In Afghanistan, the harsh Taliban regime forbade girls to attend school. After education was banned for five years, girls such as these attending the Manu Chera School in Kabul are returning once again to the classroom. (AP Photo/Marco Di Lauro)

Analysis of gender involves understanding of the implications of being male or being female within a society, as these implications affect a society's economy and culture.

Although human sex ratios are based on numbers of males and females without regard to the gender implications of one's biological sex, they are influenced strongly by gender-related issues. For example, human sex ratios defined as the ratio of males to females in a population are higher in countries such as China and India as compared to the United States and Europe. Higher sex ratios in many Asian countries, where a majority of people are men, are related to the fact that in many Asian countries there is a strong preference for sons over daughters. Traditionally, in many Asian cultures, not only do sons carry on the family name but daughters also typically marry into other families. Thus a daughter, who will not contribute to a family's economic well-being as an adult, becomes an economic burden during her childhood before she marries. China's one-child policy has resulted in even stronger preference for boys over girls given that many families are limited to a single child. In China and other Asian societies, sex-selective abortion is practiced frequently in order to increase the likelihood that a family's only child will be a boy.

Countries such as Kuwait and the United Arab Emirates have even higher human sex ratios. In these and other wealthy Middle Eastern countries, a large percentage of the population at any given time consists of international labor migrants who move from poorer countries in order to obtain employment. Because a large majority of these international labor migrants are men, human sex ratios in these countries are very high. For example, Kuwait's human sex ratio was estimated at 1.66 in 2012. In other words, there were about 166 men in Kuwait's population for every 100 women.

Sex differences in literacy rates have also affected populations throughout the world. In the United States, Canada, the countries of Europe, and other developed countries, literacy is universal. Virtually all men and virtually all women are able to read and write, and therefore there is no sex difference in literacy rates. However, in less developed countries, literacy rates are considerably higher among men than among women. For example, 48 percent of males but only 29 percent of females in Ethiopia are literate. In Niger, 42 percent of males and 15 percent of females are literate.

In the contemporary global economy, illiteracy reduces economic opportunity dramatically. Illiterate people are often unable to find productive work other than farming and manufacturing. Female illiteracy also intensifies pressure on young women to marry at an early age and to bear large numbers of children. Thus, illiteracy is linked to high total fertility rates in these and other less developed countries. High total fertility rates are also linked to a lack of contraception, and this lack of contraception may in turn be related to cultural and religious norms and taboos. Also, women in less developed countries may lack access to effective prenatal care and to health care in general. Moreover, children raised in large families are less likely to have the opportunity to attend school, thereby perpetuating this cycle across generations. Scholars have demonstrated a strong linkage between family size, literacy rates, and economic opportunity in less developed countries.

Other implications of gender as related to population include violence against women and the prevalence of sex trafficking. Throughout the world, a large majority of victims of domestic violence are women. In some cultures, violence against women is regarded as an acceptable practice and many women die as a result each year.

Sex trafficking is a major issue throughout the world. A very large majority of persons who are kidnapped, tricked, or sold to the international sex trade are girls and young women. Increasing human sex ratios in Asia, for example, have been associated with an increase in sex trafficking, as young women are sent to these countries, often against their will and illegally, as prostitutes. The human rights organization Equality Now has estimated that of the more than 20 million people who live today as slaves, as many as 80 percent are part of the commercial sex trade. More than 90 percent are women and girls, and a third are less than 18 years of age. These factors illustrate the often profound impacts of gender on population worldwide. Many observers and experts claim that these impacts will decrease only if more attention is paid to women's rights, women's health, literacy, and overall changes in the social and economic status of women worldwide.

See Also: China; Crude Birth Rate; Crude Death Rate; Demographic Transition Model; Ethiopia; Globalization; Human Sex Ratio; India; International Labor Migration; Niger; One-Child Policy; Rate of Natural Increase; Sex Trafficking; Slavery

Further Reading

Csar Chelala. "A Sad Worldwide Gender Gap." philly.com, November 11, 2005. http://articles.philly.com/2005-11-11/news/25431504_1_maternal-deaths-reproductive -health-gender.

F. Nii-Amoo Dodoo and Ashley E. Frost. "Gender in African Population Research: The Fertility/Reproductive Health Example." *Annual Review of Sociology* 34 (2008): 431–52.

Equalitynow.org. "Sex Trafficking Factsheet," 2013. http://www.equalitynow.org/sites /default/files/Global_Sex%20_Trafficking_EN_v3.pdf.

U.S. Department of State. "The Facts about Child Sex Tourism," 2009. http://2001-2009 .state.gov/documents/organization/51459.pdf.

Genocide

Genocide is the organized, systematic killing of members of a particular nation, culture, religious group, or ethnic group. Genocide is regarded as a crime under international law. Throughout history, genocide has resulted in substantial and long-lasting demographic change.

In 1948, the United Nations adopted the Convention on the Prevention and Punishment of the Crime of Genocide. The convention was adopted in part in response to the atrocities of the Holocaust, or the systematic genocide of Jews in Germany and Eastern Europe perpetrated by the Nazis before and during World War II. According to the convention, genocide is defined as:

> any of the following acts committed with intent to destroy, in whole or in part, a national, ethnic, racial or religious group, as such: killing members of the group; causing serious bodily or mental harm to members of the group; deliberately inflicting on the group conditions of life, calculated to bring about its physical destruction in whole or in part; imposing measures intended to prevent births within the group; [and] forcibly transferring children of the group to another group.

Observers of genocide have noted that it involves several processes. For example, the president of the nongovernmental organization Genocide Watch, Gregory H.

Stanton, has identified what he calls the "eight stages" of genocide. These include classification, symbolization, dehumanization, organization, polarization, preparation, extermination, and denial. Historians examining instances of genocide such as the Holocaust can observe each state as the process unfolded. (The text of Mr. Stanton's statement concerning the eight stages of genocide can be found elsewhere in this encyclopedia.)

Although genocide is often associated with mass murder, genocide goes beyond killing. It involves systematic efforts to destroy cultures and their social, political, and economic institutions. Genocide has often occurred in conjunction with ethnic cleansing, or the forcible removal of members of a particular ethnic group from a given country. However, the overriding goal of ethnic cleansing is the removal, not necessarily the mass murder, of its victims.

About 80 countries have adopted laws based on the convention to prevent genocide. In these countries, persons accused of perpetrating genocide can be tried, convicted, and punished. The International Criminal Court, which was established in 2002, is authorized to try cases of genocide involving countries that are signatories to the Convention. Prior to the establishment of the court, accusations of genocide were heard in international tribunals established for the

Genocide remains a major issue throughout the world, especially in less developed countries. As many as 500,000 people in Rwanda are believed to have lost their lives in a mass genocide in the 1990s. In this 2004 photograph, a genocide survivor prays at a mass grave containing the remains of genocide victims. (AP Photo/Sayyid Azim)

purposes of hearing specific cases. For example, the Nuremberg Trials were set up by the Allies after World War II to try Nazi officials accused of genocide. More recently, ad hoc tribunals were established to deal with instances of genocide in the former Yugoslavia and in Rwanda in the 1990s.

Genocide has occurred throughout history, but its scale and scope increased in the 20th century as a result of population increases and technological developments that facilitated mass execution. During and after World War I, millions of Armenians were massacred during the last days of the Ottoman Empire. The Armenian Massacre remains a major point of contention between Turkey and Armenia today. In the 1930s, Soviet leaders authorized genocide by killing or exiling millions of members of ethnic minority groups. Since World War II, instances or accusations of genocide have occurred in Ethiopia, the Democratic Republic of the Congo, Liberia, China, and other parts of the world. International awareness of genocide on the part of organizations such as Genocide Watch along with globalized communication and transportation may help to reduce the occurrence of genocide in the future.

See Also: China; Democratic Republic of the Congo; Ethiopia; Eugenics; Genocide Watch; Germany; Turkey

Further Reading

Doris L. Bergen. *War and Genocide: A Concise History of the Holocaust*. Boulder, CO: Rowman and Littlefield, 2009.

Maria Pritchard. *Genocide: A History from Carthage to Darfur*. London: RW Press, 2013.

Gregory H. Stanton. "The Eight Stages of Genocide." genocidewatch.org, 1998. http://www.genocidewatch.org/aboutgenocide/8stagesofgenocide.html.

Genocide Watch

Genocide Watch is a nongovernmental organization whose goal is to call attention to issues associated with genocide throughout the world. According to its mission statement, "Genocide Watch exists to predict, prevent, stop, and punish genocide and other forms of mass murder. We seek to raise awareness and influence public policy concerning potential and actual genocide. Our purpose is to build an international movement to prevent and stop genocide." In support of this mission, Genocide Watch works with other international organizations to monitor incidents of genocide around the world. It is part of an umbrella organization known as the International Alliance to End Genocide. (Details about the International Alliance can be found at http://genocidewatch.net/partners-and-projects/international-alliance/.)

Genocide Watch was founded in 1999 and is headquartered in Washington, D.C. Among its other projects, it issues periodic alerts calling attention to actual or suspected genocide situations in countries worldwide. The alert system includes three stages: genocide watch, genocide warning, and genocide emergency. A genocide watch occurs when "early warning signs indicate the danger of mass killing or genocide." A genocide warning occurs when "genocide is imminent, often indicated by genocidal massacres." A genocide emergency is declared when "genocide is actually underway." As of early 2014, Genocide Watch had identified Ethiopia, the Democratic Republic of the Congo, Somalia, Syria, Myanmar, and several other countries as facing genocide emergencies. Genocide warnings had been posted for China, Nigeria, and other primarily less developed countries.

See Also: China; Democratic Republic of the Congo; Genocide; Myanmar; Nigeria

Further Reading

Genocide Watch Web Site. http://genocidewatch.net/.

Gregory H. Stanton. "What Is Genocide?" genocidewatch.org, 2002. http://www.genocide watch.org/genocide/whatisit.html.

Globalization

Globalization refers to the increasing integration of production, distribution, and exchange of people, goods, services, capital, and ideas around the world. In the words of journalist Thomas Larsson, globalization "is the process of world shrinkage, of distances getting shorter, things moving closer. It pertains to the increasing ease with which somebody on one side of the world can interact, to mutual benefit, with somebody on the other side of the world." The process of "world shrinkage" has had profound effects on population, which in turn impact the globalization process itself.

Societies have interacted with one another since ancient times, exchanging goods and services in such a way that both societies benefit. Globalization is the result of extending this process of exchange in accordance with steady improvements in technology, communications, and transportation. Ancient and medieval societies were largely isolated from one another. Trade linkages between cultures existed via which people could exchange goods and services. However, most trade was conducted locally. Long-distance trade took place, for example along the Silk Road between Europe and present-day China, but such trade was very expensive and time-consuming. Thus many items traded along the Silk Road were luxury items such as silk, gold, jewels, and spices. Ordinary items such as food and clothing were produced and consumed locally. The expense of long-distance transportation of food meant that many people living in places with shortages of food perished as a result of famines.

Over time, the cost of long-distance transportation decreased. Europeans who sailed west across the Atlantic Ocean hoped to reach East Asia, which they believed contained vast quantities of precious metals and other valuables. As overland caravans were replaced by ships, the cost of long-distance transportation declined. It continued to decrease as sail power was replaced by steam power. On land, transportation via railroads, motor vehicles, and aircraft replaced transportation on food or via the use of animals. All of these technologies reduced transportation costs dramatically, allowing people to travel much further at a much lower cost.

McDonald's restaurants are found in more than 100 countries worldwide. They are regarded widely as symbols of American culture and therefore as symbols of globalization. Some critics see McDonald's and other American-based fast food chains as contributing to the destruction of local cultures. (Xiaofeng123/Dreamstime.com)

The declining cost of transportation was paralleled by the declining costs of communications. Long-distance communication prior to the 20th century was expensive and slow. Today, people can communicate with one another throughout the world instantaneously via the use of the telephone, radio, television, and the Internet. These technologies enable people throughout the world to learn about food shortages, famines, epidemics, and natural disasters very rapidly. The cost of transportation and communications were lowered not only by improvements in technology, but also by governments' refusal to inhibit movement—in other words, through the support of free trade. Under conditions of free trade, governments do not tax movements of goods and services, reducing their overall costs.

All of these developments contributed to globalization. Cheaper, faster, and more efficient transportation and communication allowed people to interact with one another over longer distances at much less cost. People themselves could move further and faster. Goods could also be exchanged over long distances. Ideas, philosophies, and new technologies also flowed around the world at much faster rates of speed. Reduced transportation costs also mean that these costs are no longer prohibitive relative to the overall distribution of goods and services. This fact helps to explain why production of many industrial items has moved to less developed countries. For example, many staple items of clothing worn by Americans, such as T-shirts, jeans, shorts, shoes, and socks are manufactured in less developed countries, where labor is far cheaper than in the United States. It is much cheaper to produce these staple items in less developed countries and ship them to consumers in the United States than it is to produce them in the United States, where labor costs are much greater.

Globalization and population interact in many different ways. Perhaps most fundamentally, globalization influences patterns of migration. The number of international migrants throughout the world continues to increase, including the many international labor migrants who move from less developed countries to developed countries in search of employment opportunities. Cheap and fast communication allows these international labor migrants to remain in contact with relatives and friends in their countries of origin. It also facilitates the sending of remittances from these international labor migrants to those remaining in their home countries.

Cheaper and cheaper shipment of goods also affects population. For example, prior to the 20th century, it was all but impossible to alleviate famine by shipping food to people in affected areas. Today, the technology to ship needed food supplies around the world in a cost-effective manner is firmly in place. However, in some cases this shipment is disrupted by human activities, including wars and political conflicts that create barriers to effective movement of food supplies. Globalized communications can also be cut off as a result of political forces; for example, some autocratic societies restrict citizen access to social media and/or control what can be broadcast or published in local mass media. On the other hand, proponents of globalization argue that it facilitates worldwide efforts to address ongoing societal problems such as environmental degradation, in that it makes it easier for counties and other stakeholders to coordinate their activities and facilitates international agreements. However, critics of excessive globalization argue that in the long run, the process contributes to greater levels of inequality and promotes environmental degradation.

See Also: Agriculture and Population; Carrying Capacity; Climate Change and Population; Food Prices and Population; Food Production and Security; Gender and Population; International Labor Migration; Remittances

Further Reading

Thomas L. Friedman. *The World Is Flat: A Brief History of the Twenty-First Century*. 3rd ed. New York: Picador, 2007.

Peter Hugill. *World Trade since 1431: Geography, Technology, and Capitalism*. Baltimore: Johns Hopkins University Press, 1995.

Thomas Larsson. *The Race to the Top: The Real Story of Globalization*. Washington, DC: Cato Institute Press, 2001.

Jorgen Osterhammel and Niels P. Petersson. *Globalization: A Short Introduction*. Translated by Dona Geyer. Princeton, NJ: Princeton University Press, 2009.

Gravity Model

The gravity model is a mathematical construct applied to the analysis of population. It has long been used to predict the amount of migration between pairs of places.

The model is based on Sir Isaac Newton's law of gravity, which postulates that the gravitational attraction between two celestial objects is determined by their mass and the distance between them. Gravitational attraction increases as two objects become closer together, and it decreases with increasing distance between them. The concept of gravitational attraction has been applied to many different types of spatial interaction between places, not only flows of migrants but also trade flows, traffic volume, and numbers of telephone calls and other types of communication. The gravity model is the foundation of Ernst Ravenstein's Laws of Migration that he articulated in the late 19th century.

As applied to migration, the gravity model predicts that the number of people moving between one place and another is related to their size and the distance between them. As an example, the gravity model suggests that there will be more migration between Germany and Poland than there will be between Germany and Portugal, which is further from Germany and has fewer people than has Poland. Similarly, we can expect more migration between New York and Chicago than between New York and Des Moines, which is further away from New York and smaller in population than Chicago.

Empirical observations, both historical and contemporary, have demonstrated that the gravity model is often useful in predicting migration flows. Many demographers and social scientists who have analyzed migration flows associated with the gravity model have sought and interpreted exceptions to the model, or cases in which actual migration flows are considerably less or considerably more than are predicted by using the model. Situations in which actual migration is less than predicted are often associated with barriers to migration, especially in the case of international migration.

Some countries refuse to allow people to leave or enter. For example, between the 16th and 19th centuries, Japan did not allow anyone to move into or out of the country. Japan isolated itself further by restricting trade with other countries to two ports with strict limits on the number of foreign ships allowed to use the ports. Hence there was very little migration between Japan and nearby China, although both countries were and are large and located relatively near each other. Japan's self-imposed isolation came to an abrupt end in 1854, when a U.S. Navy fleet under the command of Commodore Matthew Perry (1794–1858) opened Japan's ports forcibly to foreign trade.

Today, the boundary between North Korea and South Korea serves as a barrier to migration. North Korea and South Korea are adjacent, and they share a common language, culture, and history. However, there is very little migration between the two countries because of profound differences between the Communist government of North Korea and the democratic capitalist system used in much more prosperous South Korea. This barrier has been in place since the Korean War ended in 1953.

In other cases, migration between pairs of places is greater than might be expected based on the gravity model. Places that are especially attractive to international labor migrants or other immigrants may receive far more migrants than might be expected on the basis of the gravity model. Many migrant flows are affected by cultural, linguistic, and economic ties. Thus, during the 19th century, European immigrants to the United States did not disperse evenly after crossing the Atlantic Ocean. Rather, many tended to settle in places already inhabited by people from the same country who spoke the same language and practiced the same religion as did the more recent immigrants. In some cases, this process of channelized migration involved the movement of large numbers of immigrants from one small region in Europe to one small region in the United States. People often moved to places where their relatives or friends were living already. As an example, migration from Norway to Minnesota was much greater than would be expected as a result of the gravity model because of these cultural and personal ties. Many more migrants moved from Norway to Minnesota than from Norway to New York, Pennsylvania, or Ohio although these states are larger and closer to Norway than is Minnesota. Similarly, cases of channelized migration among African Americans between the rural South and cities of the North between the 1920s and the 1950s are cases in which migration levels are much greater than would be predicted.

Critics of the gravity model claim that the model has little theoretical foundation, and that it is based on observation and induction rather than being based on deduction from postulates. Nevertheless, the gravity model is a useful starting point for analysis of migration flows.

See Also: Channelized Migration; International Labor Migration; Japan; Migration; Ravenstein, Ernst; South Korea

Further Reading
William J. Reilly. *The Law of Retail Gravitation*. New York: Knickerbocker Press, 1931.

John Vanderkamp. "The Gravity Model and Migration Behaviour: An Economic Interpretation." *Journal of Economic Studies* 4 (1977): 89–102.

Great Bengal Famine

The Great Bengal Famine was one of the most severe famines of the 20th century. The famine, which took place in 1943, is believed to have resulted in between 2 and 4 million fatalities in present-day Bangladesh and eastern India, including the city of Kolkata. The Great Bengal Famine occurred during World War II, and its history illustrates how many modern-day famines have taken place in response to a combination of natural and political factors.

During World War II, present-day Bangladesh and India were part of the British Empire, which was one of the Allied powers fighting against Japan. Japan had seized

The Great Bengal Famine, which began in 1943, was one of the most severe famines of the twentieth century. The Famine resulted from crop failure at a time that food supplies to affected persons were cut off during World War II in India and Southeast Asia. Here a British soldier shares his rations with four Indian children who lacked food because of famine conditions. (AP Photo)

control of much of Southeast Asia, and the area along the frontier between British India and Japanese-occupied Southeast Asia was the scene of many battles. Under these wartime conditions, food was scarce. Much of what food was available was used to feed the British and Indian armies, and the government of British India lacked the resources needed to alleviate hunger among civilians.

Rice is a staple food of eastern India. In the fall and winter of 1942, however, the rice crop in eastern India largely failed. Rice yields were reduced substantially because of large-scale flooding caused in part by a devastating tropical cyclone. The unusually wet weather contributed to the spread of a fungus known as brown spot. This blight is believed to have ruined well over half of the rice that was produced in the region, rendering it inedible.

Because of wartime conditions, governments had great difficulty supplying food to alleviate the famine. Food was already in short supply throughout British India, with little surplus to be transferred to the afflicted areas. More importantly, Japan controlled the major trade routes between India and Southeast Asia, from which food was normally imported into India. The British colony of Burma (present-day Myanmar) was the world's leading exporter of rice at the time. However, Burma was captured by Japan, which blockaded trade routes and diverted the surplus rice away from British India. Not only were supplies of rice from Burma into British India cut off, but thousands of refugees from Burma moved across the border and increased the number of people unable to obtain sufficient food supplies. Within British India, scarce food was hoarded and stockpiled rather than supplied to the hardest-hit areas of the colony. Shipping of food supplies from overseas was very difficult because ships would have to cross war-torn waters, many of which were controlled by the Japanese Navy. All of these factors contributed to a sharp rise in food prices, and many of the victims of the famine were urban residents who did not have land to produce their own food and could not afford to purchase it.

The extent to which the Great Bengal Famine was caused by natural forces, wartime conditions, government inaction, or greed and speculation may never be known. However, efforts to prevent famines of similar magnitude helped to generate the Green Revolution and its dramatic increase in food production and supply throughout India and many other parts of the world.

See Also: Bangladesh; Famine; Green Revolution; India; Kolkata; Myanmar; Refugees

Further Reading

P. R. Greenough. *Prosperity and Misery in Modern Bengal: The Famine of 1943–1944*. New York: Oxford University Press, 1982.

Mark B. Tauger. "Entitlement, Shortage, and the 1943 Bengal Famine: Another Look." *Journal of Peasant Studies* 31 (2003): 45–72.

Great Chinese Famine

The Great Chinese Famine, which took place between 1958 and 1962, was one of the most devastating famines of the 20th century. The story of the Great Chinese Famine illustrates how contemporary famines are the result of the convergence between natural conditions and faulty or ineffective human management practices.

Various parts of China have been impacted by famine throughout the course of recorded history. More than 2,000 famines, or an average of one a year, have been recorded in various parts of present-day China during the past two millennia. However, the impact of these famines was dwarfed by the Great Chinese Famine. Historians believe that more than 40 million people perished as a direct or indirect result of the famine during a five-year period.

During the late 1950s, the Communist government of China implemented the "Great Leap Forward" policy. The intent of the Great Leap Forward was to transform China quickly from an agrarian to an industrial society. The government collectivized agriculture and attempted to prohibit private farming. Farmers were encouraged, and later required, to join agricultural collectives. Others were forced to abandon their farms and to move to cities as industrial workers.

The intent of the collectivization policies was to increase grain production to be used to provide food for people living in urban areas. These grains were also earmarked for export, with the idea of providing foreign exchange to be used to expand industrial production. However, the Great Leap Forward proved disastrous. The period between 1958 and 1962 was the only period in recent Chinese history in which China's economy failed to grow.

During the period in which the Great Leap Forward policies were implemented, many parts of China experienced severe droughts. Other agricultural areas experienced major floods. These natural disasters affected per-acre crop production, and resulted in reduced food production. Food production was reduced even more by government policy associated with the Great Leap Forward. The forced movement of Chinese peasants to the cities resulted in a shortage of agricultural labor. In addition, the government implemented what proved later to be unscientific and ineffective cultivation practices. For example, irrigation projects were developed hastily without input from experienced engineers. Local peasants were forced to work on these and other projects, and many forced to work long hours without adequate food starved and perished.

The Great Leap Forward policies also guaranteed food supplies to industrial workers and urban residents, with agricultural workers forced to subsist on what food was left over after guaranteed supplies were taken to cities. Unrealistic production quotas were imposed on many collective farms, and agricultural workers were punished and sometimes killed, tortured, or beaten severely when they failed to meet these quotas. Even in those places in which the quotas were reached, the fact that food was earmarked for the cities resulted in food shortages in the countryside. Thus rural areas bore the brunt of the failed policies, and fatalities associated with the Great Leap Forward were concentrated in rural and agricultural regions. Across China, the crude death rate spiked from about 12 per 1,000 in 1958 to 15 in 1959, 25 at the height of the famine in 1960, and 15 in 1961.

As weather conditions improved and food shortages abated in the early 1960s, crude death rates declined once again to pre-famine levels. In summarizing what had happened, the Chinese government blamed the widespread famine on the poor weather conditions. Only later did government officials begin to admit that the famine was caused at least in part by poor and ineffective planning and management practices. Today, it is recognized by historians that the Great Leap Forward policies, and their implementation, were largely responsible for this greatest famine of the 20th century.

See Also: China; Crude Death Rate; Famine

Further Reading

Frank Dikotter. *Mao's Great Famine: The History of China's Most Devastating Catastrophe, 1958–62.* Orlando, FL: Walker and Company, 2010.

Jisheng Yang. "The Fatal Politics of the PRC's Great Leap Famine." *Journal of Contemporary China* 19 (2010): 755–76. http://dx.doi.org/10.1080/10670564.2010.485408.

Great Famine of 1315–1317

The Great Famine of 1315–1317 was one of the most devastating famines in the history of Europe. The famine resulted in millions of fatalities and proved to be a defining moment in medieval European history.

The famine was concentrated in northern continental Europe, especially present-day Germany and northern France, although its effects extended into England, present-day Italy, and present-day Russia. It was caused by unusually cool, rainy weather that resulted in widespread crop failure. Paleoclimatologists now know that the period between about 950 and 1300, known to historians as the High Middle Ages, was characterized by warmer than normal temperatures throughout Europe. Under these favorable weather conditions, crop yields increased. More plentiful food supplies contributed to significant increases in Europe's population. The population of Europe has been estimated at between 25 and 30 million at the time of Charlemagne in 800 CE, but is believed to have increased to more than

100 million by 1300. Thus, the population density of Europe increased by more than three times during the Medieval Warm Period.

The Medieval Warm Period came to an end in the early 14th century, when a period of several hundred years of unusually cool temperatures known as the Little Ice Age began. Beginning in the spring of 1315, Europe experienced sustained periods of cool and rainy weather, especially relative to the milder weather of the previous three centuries. Bad weather prevented crops from ripening, reducing food supplies for both people and livestock. What supplies of food had been stored were depleted quickly. Food shortages caused rapid increases in food prices. Many who could not afford food starved to death. Others were weakened by lack of food and succumbed to bronchitis, pneumonia, and other infectious diseases.

In order to survive, many peasants were forced to slaughter their draft animals or to eat seed grains that would otherwise have been used to plant crops the following year. Crime rates rose rapidly as people turned to stealing food. Children and the elderly were abandoned. Some historians believe that the folk tale "Hansel and Gretel," in which a poor woodcutter was forced to abandon his children, who were captured by a wicked witch, was inspired by the events of the Great Famine of 1315–1317.

The unusually cool and wet weather continued into 1316 and 1317 when once again heavy and persistent rains prevented many crops from ripening. Starvation levels increased as food shortages mounted and food prices continued to rise. Some rulers of European countries affected by the famine attempted to impose measures intended to alleviate its impacts, but by and large, these monarchs did not have the resources to address these issues effectively. Although the weather began to improve in 1318, food supplies did not return to their pre-famine levels until well into the 1320s.

The overall death tolls from the Great Famine of 1315–1317 are not known with any precision, but it has been estimated that more than 5 percent of England's population died during this period, with even higher death rates in present-day Germany, France, the Netherlands, and Belgium. Additional famines, many associated with poor weather and with outbreaks of the bubonic plague, or Black Death, occurred throughout the rest of the 14th century.

The Great Famine of 1315–1317 had long-lasting consequences for European society and for global history. The famine undermined the authority of the Roman Catholic Church, which at the time dominated Europe. Many Europeans saw the famine as God's punishment for the corruption and excesses of the church. This led to increased questioning of the authority of the church and its hierarchy, leading eventually to the Protestant Reformation. With an increase of violence and lawlessness came outbreaks of war, notably the Hundred Years' War between England and France that broke out in 1337 and lasted until 1453. More generally, the period of population growth and relative prosperity that characterized the High Middle Ages in Europe came to an abrupt end. Populations declined throughout Europe, and in some places, population levels did not recover until well into the 19th century.

See Also: Black Death; Famine; France; Germany; Italy; Russia; United Kingdom

Further Reading

William C. Jordan. *The Great Famine: Northern Europe in the Early Fourteenth Century.* Princeton, NJ: Princeton University Press, 1996.

Ian Kershaw. "The Great Famine and Agrarian Crisis in England." *Past and Present* 59 (1973): 3–50.

Great Wall of China

The Great Wall of China is a long border fence or separation barrier that extends across the northern portion of China. Its purpose was to restrict migration from Central Asia, whose inhabitants were seen as threats to the Chinese government, into China itself.

The Great Wall is not a single fence. Rather, it consists of numerous, discontinuous fortifications constructed near the boundary over a period of 2,000 years. The wall extends roughly along the southern boundary of China's Inner Mongolian Autonomous Region. Its total length has been estimated by archaeologists at as many as 13,000 miles. Various portions of the wall were constructed using bricks, stone, wood,

The Great Wall of China was built to keep Central Asians from invading the population centers of China. Construction began more than 2,500 years ago, and the Wall was reinforced and defended for more than two thousand years. Today the Great Wall is one of China's main tourist attractions. (Silvershot55/Dreamstime.com)

and other building materials. Earth was also tamped and moved in order to increase the height of the wall, in part to make it easier for soldiers to patrol it. In some places, movement was restricted further by digging trenches parallel to the wall itself.

Construction of a wall along China's northern frontier is believed to have begun about 600 BCE and continued intermittently into the 16th century CE. Around 221 BCE, the Qin dynasty (from which China takes its name) unified most of modern-day eastern and central China for the first time. The Emperor Qin Shi Huang (260–210 BCE) undertook a systematic effort to construct the wall, and to add to its existing segments, in order to stop military incursions from Central Asian tribes and to restrict the movement of nomads from Central Asia into China. Given the expense of transporting building materials, where possible, the wall was constructed using rammed earth and locally available resources.

Much of the original Qin dynasty wall has eroded, and little remains today. However, over the next 1,700 years, the wall was rebuilt and expanded by later Chinese dynasties. Rulers of these dynasties reinforced the wall not only to prevent military attacks and movement of nomadic peoples, but also to regulate trade and to impose taxes and duties on cross-border movement of goods. These security functions were reinforced by the construction of numerous watchtowers and by thousands of soldiers stationed along the wall.

Construction of the wall reached its apex during the Ming Dynasty, which governed China between 1368 and 1644. The Ming succeeded the Yuan Dynasty, which was founded originally by Mongol invaders under the leadership of Genghis Khan. After they seized power, the Ming emperors were intent on eliminating the possibility of further Mongol invasions. Historians believe that 25,000 watchtowers were built along the wall during the Ming dynasty's rule, and that as many as several hundred thousand troops were stationed along the border. The Ming also constructed smaller walls parallel to the main line of the Great Wall as further insurance against invasions from the north and west. However, construction and maintenance of the wall was largely discontinued after the Q'ing dynasty, which seized power from the Ming in 1644. Today, the wall is used primarily as a tourist attraction and as a representation of Chinese imperial history.

See Also: Border Fences; China

Further Reading

Jennifer Abbey. "Great Wall of China Longer Than Previously Reported." *ABC News*, July 18, 2012. http://abcnews.go.com/blogs/headlines/2012/07/great-wall-of-china-longer -than-previously-reported/.

Julia Lovell. *The Great Wall: China against the World, 1000 B.C.–A.D. 2000*. New York: Grove Press, 2010.

John Man. *The Great Wall*. London: Bantam Press, 2008.

Green Revolution

The Green Revolution was a global effort to use technology in order to increase agricultural production in less developed countries. The goal of the Green Revolution was to alleviate famine and to provide food for rapidly growing populations. Many of the activities of the Green Revolution took place between the 1940s and the 1970s, but these efforts continue today.

The Green Revolution began during and after World War II, when the international community recognized that rapid population growth was making it difficult for less developed countries to provide enough food. Large-scale famines such as the Great Bengal Famine and the Great Chinese Famine gained worldwide attention. Moreover, international observers recognized rapid population growth in many developing countries, leading to concern about potential food shortages and additional famines. In response, researchers developed varieties of rice, wheat, and other grains whose cultivation could produce higher per-acre yields. The introduction of these new grains was coupled with the use of pesticides, fertilizers, and other technologies. The development of these technologies was facilitated by consortia of organizations, including the United Nations, governments of individual countries, private corporations, and nongovernmental organizations. Many of these technologies were first developed in Mexico, where the American biologist and agronomist Norman Borlaug undertook pioneering research. Borlaug came to be known as the "Father of the Green Revolution," and was recognized for his work with the Nobel Peace Prize of 1970.

The Green Revolution resulted in dramatic increases in grain outputs throughout Mexico, India, Latin America, Africa, and elsewhere, helping to alleviate hunger among rapidly growing populations. Estimates suggest that the increased food supplies associated with the Green Revolution saved as many as hundreds of millions of people from starvation.

While the Green Revolution was highly successful in increasing food supplies and reducing the risk of famine, it has had several other consequences. The Green Revolution encouraged farmers to produce for national and international markets, rather than for local consumption. In other words, many replaced subsistence farming with commercial farming. Farmers shifted from locally consumed crops with no external market value to crops with value on the international market such as wheat, rice, corn, and cotton. Many farmers who had previously grown several crops shifted to growing only a single crop. Growing only a single crop over a large area is known as monoculture. Monoculture has made places more dependent on individual crops, increasing the impact of global market conditions on local economies as well as increasing the risk of food shortages under crop failure conditions, as in the case of the Irish potato famine.

Another consequence of the Green Revolution has been to increase the gap between wealthier and poorer farmers. Wealthier farmers could more easily afford the new technologies associated with the Green Revolution. Poorer farmers, who had more difficulty keeping up, were more likely to give up farming. The result has been consolidation of many farms into larger units. Smaller farmers who were forced off the land often moved to cities, contributing to rural to urban migration. Despite these problems, the Green Revolution has played a very important role in the histories of many less developed countries. Regions that have historically been plagued by famine have become self-sufficient in food production, and in some cases now export considerable amounts of food.

The state of Punjab in India illustrates the success of the Green Revolution. Punjab is located in northern India, adjacent to the boundary between India and Pakistan. Punjab is densely populated, with about 25 million people living in an area of 20,000 square miles, smaller than South Carolina. Historians have recorded numerous instances of famine in Punjab. During the 1960s and 1970s, however, the Punjab government along with the government of India invested heavily in the Green Revolution. Crop yields increased dramatically, and Punjab is sometimes referred to as the "breadbasket of India." Despite its small land area, according to government statistics found on its official government Web site (http://www.punjabgovt.gov.in), Punjab produces 20 percent of India's wheat, 14 percent of its cotton, and 9 percent of its rice. In part because of the Green Revolution, Punjab has the highest per capita income and the lowest poverty rate in India.

In spite of these successes, problems remain. Some experts on agriculture in Punjab believe that the fertility of the soil may be decreasing because of excessive reliance on fertilizers and pesticides. Moreover, Punjab's climate is relatively dry compared with many other parts of India. Irrigation is often necessary to water crops, and groundwater resources are being depleted. The challenge for Punjab is to address these important environmental problems while maintaining its prosperity and production levels.

The Green Revolution continues today, with ongoing efforts to expand food production through improved crop varieties. One major initiative is the New Rice for Africa (NERICA) program. Rice is a dietary staple of many West Africans, although more than half of the rice consumed in West Africa is imported. The NERICA project is intended to promote self-sufficiency in rice production in West Africa, and in that way to promote economic development.

NERICA is sponsored by a consortium including the United Nations Development Programme, the government of Japan, and the African Development Bank. The purpose of the program has been to crossbreed African rice (*Oryza glaberrima*) with varieties of Asian rice (*Oryza sativa*). African rice has been cultivated in West Africa for thousands of years. It is well adapted to the West

African environment and is resistant to local pests and to droughts. However, per-acre rice yields are low compare to those of Asian rice. Many African farmers have begun to cultivate higher-yielding Asian rice, but Asian rice requires more water and is much more susceptible to pests and diseases. The NERICA project has involved creating hybrid varieties that combine the positive features of both rice species.

The NERICA rice varieties have been introduced in several African countries, particularly in Guinea. Guinea is a former French colony with a land area of about 95,000 square miles (slightly larger than Kansas) and a population of 9.4 million. The government of Guinea has encouraged farmers to begin growing NERICA rice. However, many farmers in Guinea have difficulty getting access to new rice varieties because of lack of money and credit, government corruption, poor transportation, and lack of storage facilities.

Although the Green Revolution has undoubtedly prevented millions of people from famine and starvation, questions remain as to whether its success can continue. In Punjab and elsewhere, large-scale reliance on technology to produce food has endangered the land's natural productivity. Whether these technologies can provide food for more and more people in rapidly growing less developed countries remains to be seen.

See Also: Agriculture and Population; Bangladesh; Borlaug, Norman; Famine; Food Production and Security; India; Mexico; Pakistan

Further Reading

Amarjeet Kaur. "The Cost of India's Green Revolution." *World Development Movement*, July 31, 2013. http://www.wdm.org.uk/food-and-hunger/cost-india%E2%80%99s-green-revolution.

H. K. Jain. *Green Revolution: History, Impact, and Future*. Houston: Studium Press, 2010.

Michael Morris, Hans P. Binswanger-Mhkize, and Derek Byerlee. *Awakening Africa's Sleeping Giant: Prospects for Commercial Agriculture in the Guinea Savannah Zone and Beyond*. Washington, DC: World Bank, 2009.

Vandana Shiva. *The Violence of Green Revolution: Third World Agriculture, Ecology, and Politics*. London: Zed Books, 1992.

Hardin, Garrett

Garrett Hardin (1915–2003) was an American biologist who is best known for his development of the tragedy of the commons model, which has been used as a metaphor for the dangers associated with increased population.

Hardin was born in Dallas, Texas, and earned a BS degree in zoology from the University of Chicago in 1936 and a PhD in microbiology from Stanford University in 1941. He joined the faculty of the University of California–Santa Barbara in 1946 and became Regents' Professor of Human Ecology in 1963. He retired formally from this position in 1978, but remained active in research for the rest of his life.

Hardin's influential article "The Tragedy of the Commons" was published in 1968. In this article, Hardin set forth his argument that pursuit of individual self-interest could lead to disaster for an entire group of individuals. Thus this model is in contrast with the theories of Adam Smith, who argued that pursuit of self-interest results in mutual benefit. Hardin's theory differs from Smith's in that he postulated that the degree to which individual self-interest could benefit a community was limited by resource availability. He applied the model to questions of population by pointing out that individual parents benefit from bearing children. However, if fertility rates increase, the population will increase to the point that it can no longer support itself and will therefore begin to decline. In that sense, Hardin's model is consistent with Thomas Malthus's view that population growth is necessarily constrained by resource availability.

Hardin's views on the tragedy of the commons remain influential today, although critics point out that the model ignores the impact of technology and human ingenuity in averting overpopulation and environmental disaster. In support of population control, Hardin was an advocate of eugenics, including the possibility of forced sterilization of those regarded as "unfit" to reproduce. He was also a strong supporter of legalized abortion and euthanasia. Hardin was also criticized for arguing that international efforts to relieve famine in less developed countries was counterproductive in that survival of more people would increase the overall number of people in a society, therefore contributing to higher rates of population growth over the long run.

Despite these criticisms, Hardin's model of the tragedy of the commons remains an important work. His model has guided contemporary thinking about population issues and many other aspects of managing the global environment.

See Also: Malthus, Thomas; Smith, Adam; Tragedy of the Commons

Further Reading

Garrett Hardin. *Living within Limits: Ecology, Economics, and Population Taboos.* Oxford: Oxford University Press, 1993.

Garrett Hardin. "The Tragedy of the Commons." *Science* 162 (1968): 1243–48.

History of World Population

The world's population, estimated at about 7.2 billion as of 2014, has grown steadily throughout the course of recorded history. However, the rate of population growth has increased at a much faster rate over the past two centuries.

Today, most countries throughout the world conduct regular censuses, with which they obtain reasonably reliable estimates of their populations. Although it is impossible to count the world's population with complete accuracy, the world's population can thus be estimated with a reasonable degree of precision. Censuses were conducted in various parts of the world since ancient times, but only in recent decades are there sufficient data to estimate changes in the world's population with accuracy. Some countries did not conduct regular censuses until well into the 20th century. Thus it is impossible to provide more than a rough estimate of how the world's population changed during ancient and medieval times. Nevertheless, demographers are in broad agreement about the pattern of worldwide population growth and change over the past 2,000 years. Population estimates going back several thousand years earlier have also been made, but these estimates are far more speculative.

According to the United States Bureau of the Census, estimates made by various demographers and organizations of the world's population about 10,000 years ago have ranged from 1 million to 10 million. Although these estimates vary widely, it is clear that the earth's population began to increase quickly as people in various parts of the world developed agriculture and abandoned hunting and gathering, which supports much smaller populations. Estimates of the world population as of about 1 CE, or 2,000 years ago, range from 170 million to 400 million. Over the next 1,000 years, populations are believed to have grown very slowly. Estimates of the world's population as of 1000 CE range from 250 million to 400 million. Populations in various areas fluctuated frequently as a result of famine, epidemic diseases, and natural disasters.

Slow growth continued over the next seven centuries. In fact, most demographers estimate that the world's population decreased considerably during the 14th century, when Europe in particular was faced with the Great Famine of 1315–1317 and the Black Death. After 1400, however, world populations rebounded, reaching about 600–650 million by 1700. The world's population is believed to have reached a billion during the early 19th century.

Since 1800, the world's population has been growing at an increasing rate. It nearly doubled during the 19th century, reaching about 1.7 billion by 1900. It passed the 2 billion mark around 1930, and reached 3 billion in the late 1960s. Over the past 50 years, the world's population has more than doubled. It is estimated to have surpassed 7 billion in late 2011, and is currently increasing at a rate of between 130 and 150 million annually. In other words, the world's rate of natural increase is nearly 2 percent per year.

Ongoing rapid increases in the world's population since the early 19th century reflect demographic transition. Historically, both crude birth rates and crude death rates worldwide were very high compared to these rates today. Thus the rate of natural increase, or the difference between the crude birth rate and the crude death rate, remained low. However, as countries industrialized, their crude death rates declined dramatically, in part because of the development of modern medical science and technology. Crude birth rates remained high, and thus the rate of natural increase rose quickly. Today, crude birth rates are declining in many parts of the world, and as a result, the world's rate of natural increase may be slowing down. It remains to be seen if the world's rate of natural increase will drop to or below zero and, if so, the number of people who will make up a stable population.

See Also: Agriculture and Population; Carrying Capacity; Crude Birth Rate; Crude Death Rate; Epidemics; Famine; Rate of Natural Increase

Further Reading

Carl Haub. "How Many People Have Ever Lived on Earth?" *Population Reference Bureau*, 2005. http://www.prb.org/Publications/Articles/2002/HowManyPeopleHaveEverLivedo nEarth.aspx.

United States Bureau of the Census. "Historical Estimates of the World's Population." 2013 (with regular updates). http://www.census.gov/population/international/data/worldpop /table_history.php.

HIV/AIDS

The human immunodeficiency virus (HIV) is a virus that causes progressive deterioration of the human immune system. Persons infected with HIV have difficulty fighting off infections, tumors, or other illnesses. HIV is the cause of Acquired Immune Deficiency Syndrome (AIDS). Since the early 1970s, AIDS has caused millions of fatalities worldwide. Thus AIDS is recognized as one of the most severe epidemics of the late 20th and early 21st centuries. According to statistics presented on the World Health Organization's Web site (http://www.who.int/ mediacentre/factsheets/fs360/en/), as of 2012, nearly 36 million people worldwide, or 0.2 percent of the world's population, were infected with HIV.

Unlike many types of viruses, HIV does not spread through indirect exposure. Rather, the spread of HIV depends on direct contact between an infected person and other persons. HIV is spread via sexual intercourse, sharing of infected hypodermic needles, breastfeeding of infants, blood transfusions, and other direct

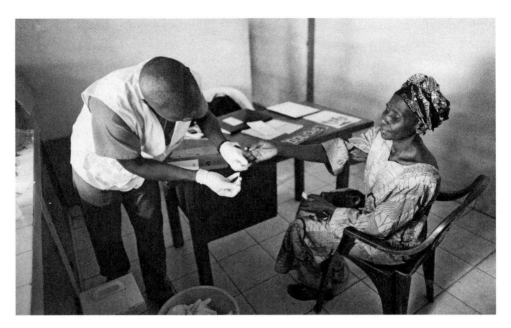

This woman in the Central African Republic is one of millions of Africans who have been infected with HIV. HIV/AIDS has caused millions of fatalities worldwide, with the highest death rates from HIV/AIDS occurring in Africa. In some African countries, high death rates from HIV/AIDS have resulted in substantial declines in life expectancy. (Ton Koene/picture-alliance/dpa/AP Photo)

transmission via transfer of body fluids between people. Pregnant women infected with HIV can also transfer the virus to their unborn children. There is no evidence that HIV is spread via casual or indirect contact with other HIV patients, for example by being in the same room with an HIV-positive individual.

Scientists now recognize that HIV evolved among nonhuman primates in West Africa during the late 19th or early 20th century. After it spread to humans, the virus and the AIDS disease spread to Haiti and then to the United States, Europe, and Asia. In the United States, AIDS was first recognized as a medical condition by the U.S. Center for Disease Control in 1981.

AIDS has now been documented worldwide, although the large majority of AIDS cases and fatalities continue to be found in sub-Saharan Africa. Official figures are believed to be underestimates because AIDS and HIV are associated with homosexual activity, drug abuse, and prostitution. About 2.6 million AIDS-related fatalities have been documented, and experts believe that the actual number of people who have succumbed to AIDS is considerably higher because their deaths were attributed to infections or other immediate causes. The countries with the largest number of AIDS cases included South Africa (3.5 million), Nigeria (2 million), the United States (1.6 million), India (1.5 million), and Thailand (1.2 million). The fatalities attributed worldwide to AIDS include nearly half a million children. Millions of other children have been orphaned after their parents have perished from the disease.

About three-quarters of HIV/AIDS cases and fatalities are in sub-Saharan Africa, where the World Health Organization estimates that 1 in 20 adults, or 5 percent of the region's adult population, are infected with HIV. The highest incidence rates are in the southern part of Africa, including South Africa, Botswana, Lesotho, Zimbabwe, and Zambia. HIV/AIDS is most likely to strike young adults, and it has had profound impacts on countries in which the disease is prevalent. Life expectancies in these and other African countries have declined markedly, while death rates have risen. For example, South Africa's life expectancy declined from about 63 years in the early 1990s to less than 50 years in 2003.

As well, the prevalence of HIV/AIDS has reduced the size of the labor force, increasing the dependency ratio in that there are fewer young adults in the population whose labor can support the young and the elderly. High dependency ratios also mean that there are fewer workers whose incomes can be taxed. Governments have been forced to spend increasing amounts of limited financial resources on treating persons affected with the disease. Fewer resources are therefore available for education, transportation, communications, and other projects, as well as for AIDS prevention policies. However, coordinated efforts on the part of scientists and physicians to understand the causes, spread, and prevention of HIV and AIDS have reduced the number of confirmed cases and fatalities. In 2011, about 32,000 Americans were diagnosed with AIDS, with 15,529 fatalities. The death rate from AIDS has declined steadily since the disease was first recognized in the 1980s. Nevertheless, HIV/AIDS remains a major epidemic, especially in less developed countries that lack the resources to provide effective prevention, education, and treatment of the diseases.

See Also: Crude Death Rate; Epidemics; India; Life Expectancy; South Africa; Thailand; United States of America

Further Reading

Victoria A. Harden. *AIDS at 30: A History*. Dulles, VA: Potomac Books, 2012.

Jacques Pepin. *The Origins of AIDS*. Cambridge: Cambridge University Press, 2011.

Human Sex Ratio

The human sex ratio of a population is the ratio of men to women within that population. Human sex ratios vary widely between different areas of the world.

Human sex ratios also vary by age, with the ratio of men to women declining with advancing age.

Generally, demographers who calculate and analyze human sex ratios examine them as ratios of men to women, or as the percentage of men within populations, although they can also be analyzed as ratios of women to men or as the percentage of women within populations. In this article, human sex ratios are presented as ratios of men to women. For example, a human sex ratio of 1.05 means that there are 105 men for every 100 women.

Current estimates suggest that there are about 1.01 males for every female in the world's population. To the extent that these estimates are accurate, this implies a human sex ratio of 1.01 or 101 per 100. Analysis by medical experts suggests that the ratio of newborn boys to newborn girls at birth is about 1.06 worldwide. In other words, slightly more baby boys are born relative to baby girls. However, this ratio may be inflated in some countries by sex-selective abortion, in which parents choose to abort female fetuses. The human sex ratio at birth in both China and India, where sex-selective abortion is not uncommon, has been estimated at 1.12. China's high human sex ratio, especially among the young, has been attributed to that country's one-child population policy.

Human sex ratios vary not only geographically, but also with age. Human sex ratios decrease with age, in light of the fact that life expectancy is considerably higher among women relative to men. Worldwide, the human sex ratio for people over 65 has been estimated at about 0.78. It tends to be even lower in developed countries with high life expectancies and low birth rates. For example, the human sex ratio for people over 65 is estimated at 0.53 in Lithuania, 0.59 in Hungary, and 0.60 in Slovakia. The lowest human sex ratio among the elderly in the world today is 0.44 in Russia, where the difference between male and female life expectancy is among the largest in the world. On the other hand, in some less developed countries, the human sex ratio among the elderly approaches 1. This is true because life expectancies are lower and because women are more likely to die in childbirth.

For entire populations, human sex ratios vary widely throughout the world. Generally, they are lower with more women than men in developed countries, and are higher with more men than women in less developed countries. Currently, human sex ratios are less than 1, with more women than men, in the United States, Canada, Japan, Australia, and throughout Europe. On the other hand, many less developed countries, including China and India, have human sex ratios greater than one. Southern Africa is an exception to the general trend. Here, human sex ratios are generally less than 1 in light of the global epidemic of HIV/AIDS, the incidence of which is higher in southern Africa than anywhere else. Because men are much more likely to die as a result of HIV/AIDS than are women, the human sex ratio declines accordingly.

In the United States, human sex ratios are consistent with overall global trends. The human sex ratio in the United States has been estimated at 1.05 at birth, 1.04 for people aged under 15, 1 between 15 and 64, and 0.75 for people aged over 65.

See Also: China; Gender and Population; India; Life Expectancy; One-Child Policy; Russia; United States of America

Further Reading

Therese Hesketh and Zhu Wei Xing. "Abnormal Sex Ratios in Human Populations: Causes and Consequences." *Proceedings of the National Academy of Science of the United States of America* 103 (2006): 13271–275.

United States Central Intelligence Agency. *CIA World Factbook, 2013.* Washington, DC: U.S. Government Printing Office, 2013.

Natalie Wolchover. "Why Are More Boys Born Than Girls?" *livescience.com*, 2011. http://www.livescience.com/33491-male-female-sex-ratio.html.

Hunting and Gathering

Hunting and gathering is a process of sustenance by which people rely on wild animals and plants for survival. Hunting and gathering has been practiced by humans for at least several hundred thousand years, and it was the only means of human survival until the invention of agriculture some 10,000 to 12,000 years ago. Today, only a very few human societies continue to rely on hunting and gathering for survival.

As the name implies, hunters and gatherers survive by hunting wild animals and collecting wild plants and their fruits, nuts, roots, and other plant products. In order to hunt and gather successfully, members of hunting and gathering societies invented and used various types of tools. Spears, harpoons, blowguns, and other weapons were used to capture and kill wild animals. In coastal areas, hunters and gatherers used fishhooks, fishing nets, and bait to catch fish and other marine animals. Digging sticks were used to dig edible roots out of the ground.

Many hunting and gathering societies lived on the margins of survival. Hunters and gatherers depended on the availability of food. Declines in plant and animal populations caused food shortages, intensifying the risk of famine. Although the impact of hunting and gathering on the natural world was much less than is the case with human activities today, human activity did cause significant environmental change that forced hunting and gathering cultures to adapt to these changes. For example, many anthropologists believe that the extinction of North America's megafauna, including the woolly mammoth (*Mammathus primigenius*) and the giant ground sloth (*Megalonyx jeffersonii*), was caused or at least hastened by overhunting by ancestors of today's Native Americans.

Most hunters and gatherers were nomads who moved from place to place in order to follow the migration of wild animals or to be able to harvest fruits and nuts as they ripened in different environments. In general, unreliable food supplies meant that hunting and gathering could support only very small populations. Some anthropologists have estimated that the world's human population was only 10 to 20 million about 15,000 years ago, when all humans subsisted via hunting and gathering. The development of agriculture allowed rapid increases in population density, and larger, settled agricultural populations sometimes killed or enslaved hunters and gatherers or drove them to less hospitable environments. However, some societies may have been forced into hunting and gathering after having been forced by more powerful neighbors onto lands that were unsuitable for agriculture.

Although some hunting and gathering societies lived in isolation, many others maintained trade relationships with one another and/or with settled agriculture societies. In this way, these hunters and gatherers obtained tools and other artifacts that aided them in their search for food. Today, only a very few societies continue to survive through hunting and gathering. Although hunting and gathering is still practiced in some areas, most predominantly hunting and gathering societies today

The San people, who live in South Africa, Namibia, and Botswana, are among the indigenous peoples of the world whose cultures and economies have been transformed and in some cases threatened by globalization. This San man is teaching his grandchild to use a traditional San bow and arrow. (Nicole Duplaix/Photolibrary/Getty Images)

also practice agriculture, trade with other cultures, and have adapted and used modern technology.

See Also: Agriculture and Population; Famine; Food Production and Security

Further Reading

Hugh Brody. *The Other Side of Eden: Hunter-Gatherers, Farmers, and the Shaping of the World.* New York: North Point Press, 2001.

David J. Meltzer. *First Peoples in a New World: Colonizing Ice Age America.* Berkeley: University of California Press, 2009.

Catherine Panter-Brick, Robert H. Layton, and Peter Rowley-Conwy, eds. *Hunter-Gatherers: An Interdisciplinary Perspective.* New York: Cambridge University Press, 2001.

Illegal Immigration

Throughout the world, more than 200 million people today are believed to have migrated from their native countries to other countries. Although many immigrants move from one country to another in accordance with the destination country's laws and policies, many other immigrants move across international boundaries illegally. Illegal immigration has become a major political issue in the United States and many other countries. Millions of people throughout the world are illegal immigrants. Although it is difficult to estimate their numbers accurately, observers and government officials estimate that there are 10 to 12 million illegal immigrants living currently in the United States. Of these, more than half are believed to have moved to the United States from neighboring Mexico.

In general, decisions to migrate and where to migrate are dependent on push factors and pull factors. Because illegal immigrants often face the possibility of deportation or incarceration, they are often particularly motivated to migrate because incentives to move from a particular origin and/or to a specific destination are especially intense. In other words, migration to a specific destination is often associated with strong pull factors that encourage the immigrant to move to that destination despite the risk of punishment.

Many illegal immigrants are international labor migrants who move from less developed countries of origin to more developed destinations in search of employment. In developed countries, many illegal immigrants become part of the labor forces of the countries to which they have moved. In many cases, these immigrants take menial, low-paying jobs. Because such jobs pay poorly and often involve work that is dangerous or unpleasant, legal immigrants and native-born workers may refuse to work at these jobs. Thus illegal immigrants can provide the labor needed for such jobs to be filled.

Many other illegal immigrants are refugees who have very strong incentives to flee their native countries. While these refugees are fleeing their home countries because of fear of religious and/or political persecution, destination countries to which these refugees wish to move may refuse to accept them as legal immigrants. Some countries limit the number of refugees allowed to move into these countries and turn away others who exceed their quotas, and thus additional refugees above and beyond these quotas are regarded as illegal immigrants.

Illegal immigrants move between countries in different ways. Some cross international boundaries without reporting to immigration authorities. In order to curb such movement across international boundaries, some countries have constructed border fences to keep migrants from moving across their borders. For example, the United States has constructed a border fence along part of its boundary with Mexico, and India has built a border fence along its boundary with Bangladesh. In island countries or those with seacoasts, some illegal immigrants may arrive by boat. Other migrants may move to a destination country legally, but become illegal migrants eventually. For example, a person might move to another country on a temporary work visa that expires after a certain length of time, but not leave the destination country after the temporary work visa has expired. In the United States, it is believed that between 30 and 40 percent of illegal immigrants fall into this category.

Many illegal immigrants face severe problems in the countries to which they have moved. Employers may prefer to hire illegal immigrants because they can pay these immigrants lower wages and/or refuse to provide their illegal-immigrant employees with benefits. An illegal immigrant may be willing to work under such conditions because wages and working conditions are worse in their home countries. Moreover, illegal immigrants may be reluctant to complain about low wages and poor working conditions because they recognize that they could be deported or otherwise punished if they were to do so. Because illegal immigrants may fill these niches in a country's labor force, government officials in these countries may ignore laws against illegal immigration or enforce these laws only very loosely.

In addition to the possibility of substandard working conditions and low wages, illegal immigrants have been subject to many other forms of abuse and discrimination. Young women in particular have been tricked or forced into the sex trade, and their illegal status makes it more difficult for them to escape this exploitation. Illegal immigrants may also be forced into other types of criminal activity. They may also lack access to health care, education, and other government services because of their illegal status.

In the United States and other countries, the status of illegal immigrants is an important political issue. Some have argued that illegal immigrants should be deported upon apprehension. Others argue that their presence is beneficial over the long run and that they should be permitted to remain in the United States provided that they work and avoid participation in criminal activity.

The status of children who are brought to the United States with illegal-immigrant parents is also controversial. Beginning in 2001, the U.S. Congress has debated various proposals concerning the status of children of illegal immigrants residing in the United States. Such proposals have been termed the Development, Relief, and Education for Alien Minors (DREAM) Acts. Although the specifics of these proposals vary, the general principle is that children of illegal immigrants who complete a certain level of schooling and/or serve honorably in the armed forces will qualify for permanent residency in the United States, provided that they do not have a criminal record. Opponents of these proposals have argued that they provide additional incentives for people to move illegally to the United States.

See Also: Bangladesh; Border Fences; India; International Labor Migration; Mexico; Push Factors and Pull Factors; Refugees; States, Nations, and Population; United States of America

Further Reading

Gordon H. Hanson. "The Economics and Politics of Illegal Immigration into the United States." Migration Policy Institute, 2009. http://www.migrationpolicy.org/pubs/hanson-dec09.pdf.

Marie Friedman Marquart, Timothy Steigenga, Philip Williams, and Manuel Vasquez. *Living "Illegal": The Human Face of Unauthorized Immigration*. New York: The New Press, 2011.

Stanley Renshon. "The 11.7 Million-Person Question: What to Do about Illegal Aliens." Center for Immigration Studies, 2013. http://cis.org/renshon/117-million-person-question-what-to-do-about-illegal-aliens-pt-1.

Immigration and Nationality Act Amendments of 1965

The Immigration and Nationality Act Amendments of 1965 was a law that provided for comprehensive reform of immigration policy in the United States. Although it was regarded as landmark legislation, it technically extended the process of immigration reform that had begun with an overhaul of previous immigration laws in 1952. The 1965 amendments repealed the quota system for immigrants that had been put in place in 1921 and codified via the Johnson-Reed Act in 1924. The law is sometimes known as the Hart-Celler Act, after its principal sponsors, Senator Philip Hart of Michigan and Representative Emanuel Celler of New York. The bill was passed by the House of Representatives with a vote of 320 to 70 and by the Senate with a vote of 76 to 18. It was then signed into law by President Lyndon Johnson.

By the 1960s, the nativist sentiment that had pervaded many Americans during the early 20th century had waned. Support for immigration reform was fueled by recognition of the contributions to American life by immigrants and their descendants during and after World War II, as well as by attention called to the plight of European refugees displaced by the war, and later by the Cold War. As well, many countries in Africa and Asia were achieving independence, and some American leaders regarded the United States as hypocritical in that it was very difficult for people born in these Asian and African countries to immigrate to the United States.

The amendments fundamentally changed U.S. immigration law. The immigration quotas that had been imposed via the Johnson-Reed Act were eliminated. Instead, they were replaced by hemispheric quotas that overall increased the number of people who could immigrate legally into the United States. It also created a preference system such that persons who were related to U.S. citizens or permanent residents, or those who had needed skills, training, or ability were given priority. These relatives and "special" immigrants were not subject to hemispheric quotas. The amendments also allowed legal immigration from countries in the western hemisphere and Africa.

The impacts of the amendments in the United States were dramatic. During congressional debate over the merits of the amendments, some supporters predicted that they would have little overall impact on American life. Perhaps in order to placate opposition, they argued that the two key provisions of the bill were the clauses promoting family unification and allowing for "special" immigrants. The latter were seen as part of the brain drain and contributors to American science, technology, and the economy, whereas family reunification was seen as unlikely to affect the geographic distribution of immigrant origins. The number of new immigrants admitted to the United States under terms of the amendments was expected to be small. In testimony before the U.S. Senate Subcommittee on Immigration and Naturalization, Secretary of State Dean Rusk predicted, "The present estimate, based upon the best information we can get, is that there might be, say, 8,000 immigrants from India in the next five years. In other words, I don't think we have a particular picture of a world situation where everybody is just straining to move to the United States." However, Rusk's prediction proved to be inaccurate. Instead, levels of immigration from Latin America, Asia, the Middle East, and Africa skyrocketed after the act took effect. Today, the very large majority of American immigrants come from these areas of origin.

The text of that portion of the amendments repealing the immigration quotas can be found elsewhere in this encyclopedia. The complete text of the amendments can be found at https://www.govtrack.us/congress/bills/89/hr2580/text.

See Also: Asiatic Barred Zone; Johnson-Reed Act; Migration; United States of America

Further Reading

Roger Daniels. *Coming to America: A History of Immigration and Ethnicity in American Life.* 2nd ed. New York: Harper Perennial, 2002.

Laws.com. "Immigration and Nationality Act." Accessed July 30, 2014. http://immigration .laws.com/immigration-and-nationality-act$hash.bDbXjXJo.dpuf.

Jennifer Ludden. "1965 Immigration Law Changed Face of America." *NPR*, May 9, 2006. http://www.npr.org/templates/story/story.php?storyId=5391395.

Mary C. Waters and Reed Udea, eds. *The New Americans: A Guide to Immigration since 1965.* Cambridge, MA: Harvard University Press, 2007.

Indentured Servitude

Indentured servitude was a system by which persons would agree to work for a fixed number of years in a recently settled colony in exchange for transportation to that colony. Indentured servitude was an important source of population growth in the colonial United States and other European colonies.

An indenture was a legal contract binding upon the indentured servant, the servant's employer, and the captain of the ship upon which the servant was transported. Indentures were negotiated between the indentured servant and the ship's captain. The indentures were held by the captain, who sold them to farmers, plantation owners, and other employers once the ship arrived at the colony. Most indentures did not require the employer to pay the indentured servant, but the employer was required to provide the indentured servant with food, clothing, shelter, and other necessities. The indenture contract remained in force for a fixed term of years, after which the indentured servant became free to pursue his or her livelihood. Within this fixed term of service, indentures could be bought and sold by employers.

Newly settled colonies faced shortages of labor, and the purchase of indentures became a common source of labor for farm owners, business proprietors, and merchants. In the colonial United States, the majority of indentured servants worked as agricultural laborers. Others, especially those who were literate or had valuable skills, worked in various trades, including carpentry, bricklaying, tailoring, and blacksmithing. Many indentured servants pursued these trades after their terms of indenture expired, whereas those who were employed as farm laborers typically established their own farms. Often these farms were located on the frontiers of settlement as they existed at the time. For example, many settlers who moved to the foothills of Appalachia, west of areas where large-scale plantation agriculture occurred, were originally indentured servants.

Treatment of indentured servants varied from place to place and depended on the actions of the servants' employers. Some indentured servants were treated well, whereas others were treated badly by abusive masters. There is some evidence that employers imposed harsher treatment on indentured servants relative to slaves because indentured servants had limited terms of service fixed by their indenture contracts, whereas slaves were regarded as the master's property in perpetuity and masters had more incentive to keep their slaves healthy and productive.

DIVERSITY IN SURINAME

Suriname, a former Dutch colony located on the northern coast of South America, has one of the most diverse populations in the world. Suriname's cultural and ethnic diversity is a result of its history of slavery and indentured servitude.

During the 17th and 18th centuries, the Dutch imported numerous African slaves to work as agricultural laborers. After slavery was abolished, indentured servants and contract laborers were brought to Suriname from India. Today 37 percent of Suriname's people are of Asian Indian origin. The next largest ethnic group is the Surinamese Creoles, who are descended from West African slaves and Europeans and make up about 31 percent of the population. The third-largest ethnic group in Suriname consists of people of Javanese descent. Their ancestors also came to Suriname from present-day Indonesia as contract laborers. Most Javanese and some Indians are Muslims, and Suriname has the largest Muslim population by percentage (20%) of any state in the Americas. Dutch remains the official language of Suriname, but the most widely spoken language is Sranan, a language developed by African slaves in the 17th and 18th century.

Further Reading

Simon Romero. "In Babel of Tongues, Suriname Seeks Itself." *New York Times*, March 23, 2008. http://www.nytimes.com/2008/03/23/world/americas/23suriname.html ?pagewanted=all.

During the 17th and 18th centuries, most indentured servants who were transported to the western hemisphere came from the British Isles, Ireland, or present-day Germany. In theory, indenture was a free and voluntary contract. However, in practice, many indentured servants were transported involuntarily. Many were teenagers whose terms of indenture were negotiated by their fathers. Some were kidnapped into indentured servitude, and others were convicted criminals for whom indentured servitude became a form of convict transportation.

Indenture was very important to the rapid population growth of the 13 colonies prior to the independence of the United States. Historians estimate that as many as half of the white immigrants prior to the American Revolution arrived in the present-day United States as indentured servants. Indenture was especially commonplace in the southern and mid-Atlantic colonies, where large farms and plantations required large agricultural labor forces. Levels of indenture in the

United States declined rapidly in the 19th century, in part because the very high birth rates and the consequent high rate of natural increase reduced the demand for labor. However, an estimated 200,000 indentured servants from Japan were imported into Hawaii in the late 19th and 20th century. Today, people of Japanese ancestry make up about one-sixth of Hawaii's population.

Indenture was practiced not only in the United States but also in many other European colonies, including the Caribbean islands, Australia, and Africa. Although indenture had largely disappeared in the United States by the middle of the 19th century, the abolition of slavery in the British Empire resulted in increased demands for agricultural labor in other British colonies. Later indentured servants generally came from present-day India, China, Japan, and other Asian countries. Today, large numbers of descendants of these Asian Indian indentured servants live in Guyana, Trinidad and Tobago, Suriname, Fiji, and other countries, in which they form a majority or a large minority of these countries' populations. Many of these indentured servants were kidnapped or tricked into involuntary indentured servitude—a practice known commonly in Asia and Oceania as blackbirding. Although indenture is no longer practiced, it was an important factor in population growth and change in many parts of the world during the history of European expansion and colonization.

See Also: Blackbirding; China; Convict Transportation; India; Japan; Slavery; United States of America

Further Reading

David Galenson. "The Rise and Fall of Indentured Servitude in the Americas: An Economic Analysis." *Journal of Economic History* 44 (1984): 1–26.

Christopher Tomlins. "Reconsidering Indentured Servitude: European Migration and the Early American Labor Force, 1600–1775." *Labor History* 42 (2001): 5–43.

Indigenous Populations

Indigenous populations are groups of people who were the original inhabitants of the areas in which they once lived. Throughout the world, indigenous populations—some who lived in their homelands for hundreds or even thousands of years—have been displaced, exiled, or exterminated by conquerors. Many indigenous populations lived in Africa, Asia, Australia, and the western hemisphere prior to European colonization. In most cases, indigenous populations lacked the resources and technology to resist subjugation by Europeans. Although these indigenous populations were subject to persecution and even massacred in acts of

The Mayan empire dominated the Yucatan Peninsula of present-day Mexico and neighboring Belize and Guatemala more than 1,000 years ago. Although the Mayan empire collapsed about 900 A.D., millions of people of Mayan ancestry live in these regions today. (JOHAN ORDONEZ/Getty Images)

genocide, many survived. Today, descendants of these indigenous people continue to live in their ancestral homelands or elsewhere.

The history of indigenous populations and their fates after European conquest is typified by the experience of Latin America during and after its conquest by Spanish and Portuguese colonists. Before the Spanish and Portuguese conquest, Latin America was the home of several advanced civilizations, including the Maya, Aztec, and Inca.

The Mayan civilization was centered in the Yucatan Peninsula and nearby portions of present-day southeastern Mexico and northern Central America. Between 250 and 900 CE, the Mayans ruled this area while trading with other cultures in the Caribbean islands and on the mainland. The Mayans were well known for their intellectual and artistic achievements, including accurate predictions of the dates of eclipses and other astronomical observations. The Classic Maya civilization collapsed in approximately 900 CE for unknown reasons. Some anthropologists have speculated that the collapse of the Mayan civilization was due to a long-term drought that made it impossible to grow enough food to feed the population.

The Aztecs were the dominant civilization in present-day central and southern Mexico at the time of Spanish conquest in the early 16th century. The Aztec capital,

Tenochtitlan, was located near the site of present-day Mexico City. The population of the Valley of Mexico, which was the center of the Aztec empire, is believed to have declined by as much as 80 to 90 percent after the Spanish arrived. The Inca Empire dominated northwestern South America at the time of Spanish conquest. The Incas controlled much of present-day Ecuador, Peru, Bolivia, and northern Chile. After the arrival of the Europeans, many Aztecs and Incas were killed by European conquerors intent on taking control of the territories that these indigenous populations had inhabited. Many others were enslaved, and far more died of exposure to various European diseases to which they had no immunity. Similarly, large numbers of Native Americans or American Indians in the present-day United States were killed, died of exposure to European diseases, or were driven westward by British colonists beginning in the 17th century.

Outside of the western hemisphere, the experience of indigenous people is typified by the Ainu of Japan. The Ainu represent the largest indigenous population of present-day Japan, whose population is approximately 99 percent ethnic Japanese. Many anthropologists believe that the ancestors of the Ainu lived in Japan prior to the arrival of the ancestors of the modern Japanese. Gradually, the Japanese pushed the Ainu northwards into Hokkaido, where most Ainu live today. The Japanese government formally assumed control of Hokkaido in the late 19th century and encouraged people of Japanese nationality to move into Hokkaido. The indigenous Ainu were expected to adopt Japanese names and customs and to give up their traditional lifestyles. The use of the Ainu language was outlawed. The Japanese government did not formally recognize the Ainu as an indigenous population until 2008. The Ainu population in northern Japan and nearby Russian islands has been estimated at about 150,000.

The Ainu experience is typical in that many indigenous populations who survived initial contact and conquest were expected and in some cases forced to assimilate into the culture of the majority populations. Indigenous peoples were expected to abandon their traditional cultures and to adopt the languages, religions, and economic activities of the colonies or countries in which they resided. Persons who resisted this assimilation were subject to persecution and punishment.

Observing steady declines in the populations of indigenous peoples, by the end of the 19th century, many Western historians and anthropologists predicted that these indigenous people would die out entirely. These predictions proved incorrect, and the populations of many indigenous peoples have rebounded. Many residents of present-day Latin America are descended from the Mayas, Aztecs, Incas, and other indigenous peoples. A majority of Mexico's people are of *mestizo*, or mixed Spanish and Native American, ancestry. About 30 percent of Mexicans are of Native American ancestry only. Many of these people live in southeastern Mexico, including the states of Chiapas and Oaxaca. About 20 percent of Mexico's people

---

THE KHASIS OF INDIA

More than two-thirds of the world's indigenous people live in Asia, and India has the largest population of indigenous people in the world. The indigenous peoples of India are known collectively as Adivasis, or "Scheduled Tribes." In 2011, the census of India counted more than 104 million Adivasis, who make up nearly 9 percent of India's population. Adivasis are eligible for a variety of government-sponsored affirmative action programs. The largest concentration of Adivasis is found in northern and northeastern India, often near India's boundaries with Nepal, China, and Myanmar.

The Khasi people of northeast India typify the Adivasi population. About 1.3 million Khasi live in northeast India, with most in the Indian state of Meghalaya. The precise origin of the Khasi is unknown, but the Khasi language is closely related to the languages of Southeast Asia and is unrelated to most other Indian languages. As with other indigenous groups in India and elsewhere, cultural difference can impede relationships with central governments that are viewed as suppressing local culture. Khasi society is matriarchal, and land and property are passed from mothers to daughters. Thus Khasi men cannot inherit land, but foreigners who marry Khasi women can become landowners in Meghalaya.

Further Reading

Julien Bouissou. "Where Women of India Rule the Roost and Men Demand Gender Equality." *The Guardian*, January 18, 2011. http://www.theguardian.com/world/2011/jan/18/india-khasi-women-politics-bouissou.

---

speak Mayan or another Native American language as their first language. Some speak no Spanish at all, and others learn Spanish in school as a second language.

Other indigenous populations that have increased in recent years include Native Americans, who numbered about 1 million in 1900. Today, more than 5 million Americans identify themselves as having full or partial Native American ancestry. Similarly, the population of Australia's Aborigines was estimated at 93,000 in 1900, but has been estimated at more than 500,000 today. Generally, the rights and cultures of indigenous populations have become more accepted by majority populations, with efforts made to preserve indigenous cultures, languages, and histories. For example, a flag representing Aboriginal Australians was designed in 1971 and became recognized as an official flag by the Australian government in 1995. In 2008, the government of Guatemala formally recognized its Mayan people and their indigenous heritage. The government also launched a television network called TV Maya that began broadcasting in the Mayan language.

See Also: Climate Change and Population; Genocide; India; Japan; Mexico; States, Nations, and Population

Further Reading

Per Axelsson and Peter Skold, eds. *Indigenous Peoples and Demography: The Complex Relation between Identity and Statistics.* New York: Berghahn, 2013.

Josephine Flood. *The Original Australians: Story of the Aboriginal People.* Crows Nest, AU: Allen and Unwin, 2006.

Kim McQuarrie. *The Last Days of the Incas.* New York: Simon and Schuster, 2007.

Norimitsu Onishi. "Recognition for a People Who Faded as Japan Grew." *New York Times,* July 3, 2008. http://www.nytimes.com/2008/07/03/world/asia/03ainu.html?pagewanted=all.

Infant Mortality Rate

The infant mortality rate is the percentage of children in a given population who die before reaching their first birthdays. The infant mortality rate is calculated as a ratio of the number of infant deaths to the number of live births. Generally, it is expressed as the number of infant deaths per 1,000 live births. Thus, the infant mortality rate can be thought of as the age-specific death rate among people who are less than a year old.

Infants are much more likely to die from various causes than are older children and young adults. Newborn babies sometimes suffer from congenital medical conditions. In less developed countries, some die as a result of inadequate care and medical services during and after delivery. Older infants are sometimes susceptible to infectious diseases to which they may have little resistance. Especially in less developed countries, malnutrition and famine also contribute to infant mortality. Infants may also be susceptible to health-related issues associated with lack of sanitation, pollution, and environmental problems. Older children are more likely to survive episodes of disease, smog, famine, and other causes of infant death, and thus the age-specific mortality rate among infants is considerably higher than those among children more than a year old. In many countries, age-specific death rates among infants are higher than they are at any age before the forties and fifties.

Infant mortality rates vary considerably throughout the world, and are much higher in less developed countries than they are in developed countries. According to data compiled by the World Health Organization and published in the *CIA World Factbook,* as of 2013, the infant mortality rate in Japan was estimated at 2.17 per 1,000, giving Japan the lowest infant mortality rate in the world except for tiny Monaco. Among independent countries, Japan was followed by Singapore (2.59), Sweden (2.73), Iceland (3.17), Italy (3.33), France (3.34), Spain (3.35), Finland (3.38), Norway (3.47), and Germany (3.48). The infant mortality rate in the United States was 5.20 per 1,000, slightly higher than those of Hungary (5.16) and Greece (4.85).

The independent country with the highest estimated infant mortality rate as of 2013 was Mali, with 106.49 infant deaths per 1,000 live births. Mali was followed in order by

Somalia (101.91), the Central African Republic (95.04), Guinea-Bissau (92.66), Chad (91.94), Niger (87.95), Angola (81.75), Burkina Faso (78.30), Malawi (76.98), and Sierra Leone (74.95). All of the countries with the highest infant mortality rates are very poor countries located in sub-Saharan Africa. These very high infant mortality rates are related closely to malnutrition and to the absence of effective prenatal and postnatal care for mothers and their newborn infants. In some of these countries, infant mortality rates are increased because of civil war and political turmoil, in part because wartime conditions can make it difficult or impossible for food or medical supplies to be transported such that they can be used to treat infants who are seriously ill and in danger of dying. Worldwide, the infant mortality rate has been estimated at about 42 per 1,000, reflecting the fact that crude birth rates and total fertility rates are much higher in less developed countries than in developed countries.

Reflecting advances in medical knowledge, medical technology, and effective care for mothers and infants, infant mortality rates have declined throughout history. During the Middle Ages, it has been estimated that more than a third of newborn infants failed to survive until their first birthdays. In other words, infant mortality rates at that time may have exceeded 333 per 1,000, or more than three times higher than those of Mali and other countries that have the highest infant mortality rates in the world today. Even in the past 50 years, infant mortality rates have declined steadily. Between 1960 and 1965, for example, Sweden had the lowest infant mortality rate in the world, at 15.15 per 1,000. It declined to about 10.5 per 1,000 in the early 1970s, 6.7 per 1,000 in the early 1980s, 5.27 per 1,000 in the early 1990s, and 3.33 per 1,000 in the early 2000s before dropping to its current rate of about 2.73 per 1,000. Thus Sweden's infant mortality rate today is less than a fifth of what it was 50 years ago. In the United States, the infant mortality rate has declined from 25.38 per 1,000 in the early 1960s to about 5.2 per 1,000 today, again a decline of about 80 percent.

Infant mortality rates have also declined sharply in less developed countries. During the 1960s, Afghanistan's infant mortality rate of 245.44 per 1,000 was the highest in the world. Sierra Leone, Burkina Faso, Guinea, Angola, Liberia, Yemen, and Guinea-Bissau all reported infant mortality rates of more than 190 per 1,000. The infant mortality rates in these countries have, for the most part, declined steadily since the 1960s. For example, the infant mortality rate of Sierra Leone was 226.71 in the early 1960s, second only to Afghanistan. However, Sierra Leone's infant mortality rate declined to 194.70 per 1,000 in the 1970s and 135.32 in the early 1980s. It rose to 165.60 in the early 1990s, at which time Sierra Leone was embroiled in a bloody civil war. However, it dropped again to 133.27 in the early 2000s and has been estimated at 74.95 today.

See Also: Age-Specific Death Rate; Crude Birth Rate; Crude Death Rate; Total Fertility Rate

Further Reading

Marian F. MacDorman and T. J. Mathews. "The Challenge of Infant Mortality: Have We Reached a Plateau?" *Public Health Reports* 124 (2009): 670–81. http://www.ncbi.nlm.nih .gov/pmc/articles/PMC2728659/.

Eduardo Porter. "New Front in the Fight with Infant Mortality." *New York Times*, October 22, 2013. http://www.nytimes.com/2013/10/23/business/health-law-is-a-new-front-in -the-fight-against-infant-mortality.html?_r=0.

United States Central Intelligence Agency. *CIA World Factbook 2013*. Washington, DC: U.S. Government Printing Office, 2013. https://www.cia.gov/library/publications/the-world -factbook/fields/2054.html.

International Adoption

International adoption occurs when infants and children are adopted formally by adoptive parents living in other countries. Adopted children become permanent and legal residents of the countries in which their adoptive parents reside.

Many parents in developed countries have adopted children from less developed countries in recent years. Cross-cultural adoption has become controversial in that some critics have argued that the practice denies children the opportunity to be part of the cultures in which they were born. This child, born in impoverished Haiti, has been adopted by French parents. (Thierry Esch/Paris Match/Getty Images)

Usually, children born in less developed countries are adopted by parents from developed countries. More than half of all international adoptions are done by citizens of the United States. In 2007, the leading countries of child origin included China, Guatemala, Russia, Ethiopia, and South Korea. The strong preference for sons in Chinese culture has meant that over 90 percent of China-born children adopted by American parents are girls. Attitudes toward adoption in countries of birth vary considerably, and international adoption is forbidden in some countries. In 2012, Russia's president, Vladimir Putin, signed into law a ban on adoption of Russian-born children by American parents.

International adoption is regulated by the Hague Convention on International Adoption. The Hague Convention was drafted in 1993. As of 2014, 90 countries, including the United States and the countries of the European Union, had signed the Hague Convention. The principles underlying the Hague Convention include ensuring that international adoptions take place in the best interests of the child and with respect for the child's rights under international law, along with efforts to prevent the abduction, kidnapping, or sale of infants and children across international boundaries. This underlying concept is spelled out in the Protocol to the Hague Convention, which reads in part that "intercountry adoptions are made in the best interests of the child and with respect for his or her fundamental rights, and to prevent the abduction, the sale of, or traffic in children." As a general principle, adoptive parents must abide by adoption regulations of both their own country of citizenship, and those of the country from which the child comes. These regulations include questions about the child's citizenship after his or her adoption. Under U.S. law, an international child adopted by a U.S. citizen qualifies automatically for U.S. citizenship. The text of the Hague Convention is found elsewhere in this encyclopedia and can be accessed at http://www.hcch.net/index_en.php?act=conventions.text&cid=69.

Despite the convention, experts on international adoption express concern about corruption in the adoption process. Although the Hague Convention explicitly condemns the kidnapping and sale of children, child trafficking continues. Concerns have also been raised that birth parents are being coerced into giving up their children for adoption. Some experts have also addressed the issue of kinship and culture, in that children adopted by parents from another country can be deprived of an opportunity to develop relationships with their relatives and with the cultures of their countries of origin. These concerns, along with bans on international adoptions imposed in Russia and elsewhere, have likely contributed to the fact that the number of international adoptions has been declining. The number of international adoptions by Americans declined from nearly 23,000 in 2004 to less than 9,000 in 2012.

See Also: China; States, Nations, and Population; United States of America

Further Reading

Alissa de Carbonnel. "Putin Signs Ban on U.S. Adoption of Russian Children." *Reuters*, December 28, 2012. http://www.reuters.com/article/2012/12/28/us-russia-usa-adoptions-putin-idUSBRE8BQ06K20121228.

Eric Eckholm. "Eager to Adopt, Evangelicals Find Perils Abroad." *New York Times*, June 1, 2013. http://www.nytimes.com/2013/06/01/us/moved-to-adopt-evangelicals-find-children-and-pitfalls-abroad.html?nl=todaysheadlines&emc=edit_th_20130601&_r=0.

Kelly Ensslin. "Fixing the International Adoption Mess." *Global Post*, May 20, 2012. http://www.globalpost.com/dispatches/globalpost-blogs/commentary/fixing-the-international-adoption-mess.

Rachel L. Swarns. "American Adoptions from Abroad at Their Lowest Level in Years." *New York Times*, January 24, 2013. http://www.nytimes.com/2013/01/25/world/us-adoptions-from-abroad-decline-sharply.html?_r=0.

International Labor Migration

International labor migration refers to movement across international borders associated with the search for employment. Many of the more than 200 million persons around the world who have moved between countries are international labor migrants.

International labor migrants are motivated by both push factors and pull factors. In general, they move in response to push factors such as poverty and lack of economic opportunity, and in response to pull factors such as employment along with the opportunity to advance economically. Educational opportunity and better health care also attract many international labor migrants.

Most international labor migrants come from less developed countries and move to developed countries. Within these developed countries, many international labor migrants move to places where relatives and/or persons from their countries of origin are living already. Thus international labor migration is often associated with channelized migration. Because many international labor migrants move from rural communities in countries of origin to cities in destination countries, the process of international labor migration is associated also with rural-to-urban migration and urbanization.

In many countries, a substantial percentage of people are international labor migrants. It has been estimated that about 8 percent of people residing in Germany were born outside of the European Union. In the United States, more than 20 million people are regarded as international labor migrants or members of these migrants' families. Many international labor migrants immigrate legally, following the immigration laws of their countries of destination. However, many other international labor migrants are illegal immigrants.

In developed countries, the presence of international labor migrants is often seen in both positive and negative terms. On the one hand, international labor migrants are an important source of labor. Many work at unskilled or semiskilled jobs. Many accept jobs that are low paying, dangerous, dirty, or unpleasant, and are therefore unattractive to native-born citizens of destination countries. On the other hand, international labor migrants are sometimes seen as competition for scarce jobs. In general, international labor migrants are more welcome when jobs are plentiful, and are more likely to be received poorly during periods of recession and high unemployment. Provision of education, health care, and other public services to international labor migrants can be expensive and burdensome to destination countries in part because these international labor migrants generally earn low wages and therefore contribute relatively little to the destination country's tax base. Some evidence suggests that volumes of international labor migration fluctuate in accordance with changing economic conditions in destination countries. For example, migration from Mexico to the United States declined after 2008, when the U.S. economy entered a recession and unemployment rates increased.

International labor migration affects countries of origin as well as destination countries. A majority of international labor migrants are young adults, many of whom have more education and job skills than do other residents of their origin communities. A majority are males, and thus countries such as the United Arab Emirates and Kuwait that have attracted large numbers of international labor migrants have high human sex ratios, with far more men than women in these countries' populations. Thus persons who do not migrate are more likely to be women, children, and/or people who are elderly, disabled, or poorly educated. However, many international labor migrations send remittances to relatives and friends in their native countries, thus providing an important source of income to these communities, although remittances may not fully replace the lack of local labor productivity in origin communities.

Laws regarding international labor migration vary from country to country. These differences include issues such as migrants' rights, whether they have the right to reside permanently in their countries of destination, and whether they can qualify eventually for citizenship. Some countries have strict requirements limiting the rights of international labor migrants. In Singapore, for example, immigration law distinguishes between foreign workers and foreign talents. International labor migrants who hold unskilled or semiskilled jobs are regarded by law as foreign workers. Singapore maintains strict controls of its foreign workers. Most live and work in Singapore on fixed-term contracts and are required to leave Singapore once their contracts have expired. Other countries provide higher levels of protection to international labor migrants. For example, United States law allows all legal immigrants to achieve permanent residency and citizenship provided that various criteria, including length of residence, have been met. Whether these rights should be extended to illegal immigrants remains a matter of intense political debate. The United Nations, however, recognizes the rights of international labor migrants as a human rights issue. International Migrants Day is celebrated on December 18 of each year to call attention to issues faced by international migrants worldwide.

See Also: Human Sex Ratio; Illegal Immigration; International Migrants Day; Migration; Push Factors and Pull Factors; Refugees; Remittances; Rural to Urban Migration; States, Nations, and Population

Further Reading

Jon Goss and Bruce Lindquist. "Conceptualizing International Labor Migration: A Structuration Perspective." *International Migration Review* 29 (1995): 317–51.

Robert E. B. Lucas. "International Labor Migration in a Globalizing Economy." Carnegie Endowment for International Peace, 2008. http://carnegieendowment.org/files/international_migration_globalizing_economy.pdf.

Martin Ruhs. *The Price of Rights: Regulating International Labor Migration*. Princeton, NJ: Princeton University Press, 2014.

International Migrants Day

International Migrants Day is a day designated by the United Nations and set aside by the international community to call attention to issues associated with international migration. It is observed annually on December 18.

December 18 was designated by the United National General Assembly as International Migrants Day in 2000. The date was selected in order to commemorate the 10th anniversary of the adoption by the UN General Assembly of the United Nations' International Convention on the Rights of Migrant Workers and Their Families on December 18, 1990. Today, more than 230 million people, or about 3 percent of the world's population, consists of international migrants. The number of international migrants continues to increase, as indicated in the UN's declaration of International Migrants Day:

Throughout human history, migration has been a courageous expression of the individual's will to overcome adversity and to live a better life. Today, globalization, together with advances in communications and transportation, has greatly increased the number of people who have the desire and the capacity to move to other places. This new era has created challenges and opportunities for societies throughout the world. It also has served to underscore the clear linkage between migration and development, as well as the opportunities it provides for co-development, that is, the concerted improvement of economic and social conditions at both origin and destination.

International Migrants Day is observed informally in many countries and by various governmental and nongovernmental organizations that address human rights issues associated with international migration. In the United States, Assistant Secretary of State for Population, Refugees, and Migration Affairs Anne Richard gave remarks representing the U.S. position on the human rights of international migrants. (The text of Secretary Richard's remarks is found elsewhere in this encyclopedia.) The United Nations maintains a Web site associated with International Migrants Day that can be accessed at http://www.un.org/en/events/migrantsday/index.shtml.

See Also: International Labor Migration

Further Reading

Office of the United Nations High Commissioner for Refugees. "International Convention on the Protection of the Rights of All Migrant Workers and Members of Their Families," December 18, 1990. http://www2.ohchr.org/english/bodies/cmw/cmw.htm.

Anne Richard. "Migrants Need Protection." U. S. Department of State, Bureau of Population, Refugees, and Migration," December 18, 2013. http://www.state.gov/j/prm/releases/remarks/2013/219010.htm.

Azadeh Shahshahani. "The Unfulfilled Promise of International Migrants Day." *Huffington Post*, December 18, 2013. http://www.huffingtonpost.com/azadeh-shahshahani/the-unfulfilled-promise-o_b_4468447.html.

International Organization for Migration

The International Organization for Migration (IOM) is a global nonprofit organization that addresses questions associated with international migration. Its mission statement is based on the premise that "humane and orderly migration benefits migrants and society." Its goals include protecting the rights of migrants, undertaking research and technical support for migration-related issues, promoting the development and enhancing the effectiveness of migration policy, and monitoring adherence of migration policies to international law.

As with the Office of the United Nations High Commissioner for Refugees, IOM was founded in response to the displacement of millions of European refugees during and after World War II. It was founded in 1951 as the Provisional Intergovernmental Committee for the Movement of Migrants from Europe. The word "provisional" was dropped from its name in 1952, reflecting its permanent status. During the 1950s, the Intergovernmental Committee provided for the resettlement of hundreds of thousands of European migrants. The Intergovernmental Committee became the Intergovernmental Committee for European Migration in 1980. Since that time, IOM expanded from Europe to other areas of the world, and in recognition of its global mission, it adopted its present name in 1989.

Today, IOM is involved in numerous projects involving migration worldwide. IOM continues to address issues faced by refugees. Over many years, it has addressed international migration associated with wars and natural disasters. IOM works with governments, other nongovernmental organizations, and the private sector on promoting "humane and orderly" responses to migration-related questions. Its focus now includes child labor and forced migration and human trafficking, particularly of women and children. With respect to human trafficking, IOM's vision is as follows:

> Building on its individual commitment and global presence, IOM strengthens the capacities of its partners in government and civil society and sets operational standards to achieve sustainable results that will provide protection and empower trafficked women, men, girls and boys; raise awareness and understanding of the issue; and bring justice to trafficked persons.

Another major concern of the IOM is the rights of international labor migrants.

IOM publishes the *International Migration Journal* along with annual reports about the state of migration and migration policy throughout the world. Currently, 151 countries are members of the IOM.

See Also: International Labor Migration; Migration; Natural Disasters; Natural Resources and Population; Refugees; United Nations High Commissioner for Refugees

Further Reading

International Organization for Migration. "History." N.d. http://www.iom.int/cms/en/sites/iom/home/about-iom-1/history.html.

International Organization for Migration Web Site. www.iom.int.

Irish Potato Famine

The Irish Potato Famine, which took place between 1845 and 1850, was the last major famine to have occurred in the developed Western world. The famine is believed to have caused between 500,000 and 1,000,000 fatalities and induced another 1 to 2 million people to leave Ireland. As a result, Ireland's population declined by more than 25 percent in less than 10 years.

A funeral taking place in Skibbereen, County Cork, Ireland, at the height of the Irish Potato Famine in 1847. An estimated one million people died in Ireland during the famine, and as many as two million emigrated to the United States and other countries between 1845 and 1850. (Hulton Archive/Getty Images)

The potato is actually native to South America, but was introduced into Europe in the 17th century. Potatoes thrived in the cool, wet climate of Ireland, which was then part of the United Kingdom, and they allowed the production of more food production per acre than did grain crops. By 1700, the potato had become a staple crop for day-to-day sustenance. As Irish peasants increased their consumption of potatoes, Irish potato production increased, and Ireland's population grew very rapidly between 1700 and 1845. Many Irish potato farmers were tenant subsistence farmers, and many had very small farms. The small size of these Irish farms was due in part to a UK law requiring that landholdings be divided equally among male heirs. Over several generations this made many farms too small to be sustainable. However, much of Ireland's agricultural land was given over to production of grains and livestock for export. Considerable amounts of land in Ireland were given over to raising cattle to meet England's demands for beef.

Potato crop failure was not unusual in pre-famine Ireland. Between 1728 and 1840, more than 40 potato crop failures were reported in various parts of Ireland. Most of these, however, were localized and short-term crop failures. However, a blight caused by a fungus destroyed most of Ireland's potato crop each year between 1845 and 1849. The blight caused potatoes to turn black on the vine and rot, making them inedible. Recently, scientists have identified the pathogen responsible for this unique and devastating blight.

Because of the crop failure, people could not eat the potatoes that they cultivated and people had little or no money to buy food. Contemporary observers as well as historians today fault the British government for slow and inadequate response to the famine, especially given that grain crops and livestock continued to be exported out of Ireland during the famine years. Historians recognize that the famine and its devastating effects on Ireland triggered Irish nationalists and protests against British rule. These anti-British actions culminated eventually in the independence of the Republic of Ireland after World War I.

Ireland in 1845 had about 8 million people. Between 500,000 and 1 million died between 1846 and 1849. At least a million other people emigrated, many to the United States. According to the U.S. census of 1850, a quarter of the residents of Boston, New York, Philadelphia, and Baltimore were born in Ireland; 37,000 immigrants from Ireland arrived in Boston in the year 1847 alone, and in that sense the large-scale movement of Irish people to Boston and other American cities can be regarded as a diaspora. Many Irish immigrants were victims of discrimination. Businesses refused to hire Irish immigrants, posting signs reading "No Irish Need Apply." Many faced unsanitary living conditions, and lived in expensive, dangerous houses and apartments owned by unscrupulous landlords. During the 1850s, 60 percent of Irish American children in Boston died before reaching the age of six.

Despite these difficulties faced by Irish emigrants, out-migration continued throughout the remainder of the 19th century, and by 1900, Ireland's population had declined to about 4 million. Only in recent years has Ireland's population begun to approach its pre-famine levels. Today, about 6 million people live on the island of Ireland, including the Republic of Ireland and British Northern Ireland.

See Also: Diaspora; Famine; United Kingdom; United States of America

Further Reading

James S. Donnelly. *The Great Irish Potato Famine*. Stroud, UK: Sutton Publishing, 2005.
Christine Kinealy. *This Great Calamity: The Irish Famine 1845–52*. London: Gill and Macmillan, 1994.

Johnson-Reed Act

The Immigration Act of 1924 imposed quotas on immigration into the United States for the first time in U.S. history. The act is often known as the Johnson-Reed Act, after its primary sponsors, Representative Albert Johnson of Washington and Senator David Reed of Pennsylvania. Both Johnson and Reed were members of the Republican Party. The act was passed with little opposition by both Houses of Congress and signed into law by President Calvin Coolidge.

The Johnson-Reed Act was one of a series of anti-immigrant laws passed by the United States Congress in the early years of the 20th century, following the Asiatic Barred Zone. However, the specific target of the Johnson-Reed Act was immigration from Southern and Eastern Europe. Throughout most of the 19th century, the majority of immigrants into the United States had arrived from the United Kingdom, Ireland, Germany, Scandinavia, and other areas of origin in Northern and Western Europe. However, by the 1890s, levels of migration from these traditional areas of origin had declined, and migrants from Northern and Western Europe were outnumbered by those from Italy, Poland, Russia, Hungary, and other sites in Southern and Eastern Europe.

These immigrants from Southern and Eastern Europe were distrusted by many native-born Americans, for several reasons. By this time, free or cheap agricultural land was no longer available, and most Southern and Eastern Europeans flocked to cities where they took jobs in manufacturing industries. Thus some native-born Americans saw them as competition for jobs and a cause of depressed wages. As well, the large majority of native-born Americans at the dawn of the 20th century were Protestants. However, most Southern and Eastern European immigrants were Roman Catholics, Jews, or members of Eastern Orthodox churches. In part because of these religious differences, it was assumed that it would be more difficult for them to assimilate into the majority American culture. This distrust was magnified by the fact that many radicals and anarchists at that time were of Southern or Eastern European origin. Some supporters of the act were also proponents of eugenics who believed that unassimilated immigrants were less intelligent, lazier, and less able to contribute to the American economy or to American culture.

The Johnson-Reed Act addressed the question of immigration of persons from Southern and Eastern Europe by imposing quotas on the number of immigrants who were allowed to move to the United States each year. The quota system had been initiated in 1921 but was formalized and codified as part of the Johnson-Reed Act. Under terms of the act, each country of origin was assigned a quota, with its quota determined by the number of people who were of that country's nationality. Thus the largest quotas were assigned to the United Kingdom, Ireland, and Germany because these countries had sent large numbers of immigrants into the United States since the early 19th century. However, countries such as Italy and Russia were assigned much smaller quotas because they had sent significant numbers of immigrants only since 1890.

For the first three years of the act's existence, the annual quota was set at 2 percent of the total number of people whose nationality was that of each country of origin. This 2 percent quota system was to remain in effect for three years, after which the total number of immigrants was to be limited to 150,000 per year. Specific numbers for each country of origin would be determined by the number of people of each nationality according to census data. Thus the percentage of immigrants from each country remained approximately the same although overall numbers dwindled. The restriction to 150,000 immigrants annually was originally intended to go into effect in 1927, but was later postponed until 1929.

Exceptions were made to accommodate immigrants who were spouses, children, or parents of earlier immigrants, or who were regarded as skilled in agriculture or various trades.

The implementation of the Johnson-Reed Act had many significant impacts on the United States above and beyond the implementation of immigration quotas. Before the act took effect, major manufacturers in the Northeast and Great Lakes had relied heavily on immigrant labor to produce goods in their factories. With the flow of workers now cut off, these employers began to look toward the American South as a new source of labor. Beginning in the 1920s, millions of white and African American workers moved from the rural South to the cities and factories of the North.

The nativist sentiment that had led to the enactment of the Johnson-Reed Act subsided during and after World War II. During the war, the conscription of millions of Americans into the armed services created a shortage of labor that could no longer be filled by immigrants. Moreover, the contributions of American immigrants and their descendants to the war effort, both as military personnel and as civilians, were recognized by most Americans by the end of the war. No longer was it believed uncritically that immigrants from Southern and Eastern Europe were incapable of assimilating into American life. Also, Americans had become aware of the plight of European refugees who had been displaced during World War II and in the early stages of the Cold War. As a result, the act was modified substantially in 1952. The quota system that had formed the framework of the Johnson-Reed Act was eliminated following passage of the Immigration and Nationality Act of 1965.

The text of that portion of the Johnson-Reed Act dealing specifically with immigration quotas is presented elsewhere in this encyclopedia. The complete text of the act can be accessed at http://tucnak.fsv.cuni.cz/~calda/Documents/1920s/ImmigAct1924.html.

See Also: Asiatic Barred Zone; Immigration and Naturalization Act Amendments of 1965; Migration; Refugees; United States of America

Further Reading

John Bodnar. *The Transplanted: A History of Immigrants in Urban America.* Bloomington: Indiana University Press, 1987.

Steven G. Koven and Frank Gotzke. *American Immigration Policy: Confronting the Nation's Challenges.* New York: Springer, 2010.

Justinian Plague

The Justinian Plague, sometimes referred to as the Plague of Justinian, was one of the first documented epidemics in history. The Justinian Plague affected the Eastern

Roman Empire in 541 and 542 CE. It was likely caused by a strain of the organism responsible for the Black Death in Europe during the Middle Ages. Its short-term and long-term impacts on affected populations are believed by some historians to have been comparable to those of the Black Death more than 800 years later. It is named for Justinian I (c. 482–565 CE), who ruled the Eastern European Empire from 527 CE until his death. Justinian is believed to have contracted the plague himself, but survived his infection.

The Justinian Plague was centered in Constantinople (present-day Istanbul), which was the capital of the Eastern Roman Empire. The Roman Empire, which had dominated Europe, the Middle East, North Africa, and southwest Asia for hundreds of years, began to weaken by the third century CE. In 285 CE, the Roman Empire split between the Western Roman Empire, centered on the city of Rome itself, and the Eastern Roman Empire or Byzantine Empire, which was centered in Constantinople and controlled present-day Turkey, southeastern Europe, the coast of the eastern Mediterranean Sea, and Egypt. The Western Roman Empire collapsed in 476 CE, leaving the Byzantines as the most powerful empire in the Mediterranean region.

At this time, the Nile Valley in Egypt was a major source of grain and other foodstuffs consumed in the Byzantine Empire. Numerous ships loaded with grain crossed the eastern Mediterranean between Egypt and the port of Constantinople. Historians believe that the Justinian Plague was brought to Constantinople by rats on board these grain ships, and that organisms similar to those responsible for the Black Death caused the plague. From Constantinople, the plague spread throughout the Byzantine Empire. At around the same time, similar plagues affected India, Central Asia, and North Africa. Some historians have suggested that the plague originated in East Asia.

There are no reliable records or estimates of the mortality rate associated with the Justinian Plague. However, some estimates suggest that as many as 5,000 people in Constantinople died each day at the height of the plague. A quarter or more of the people of the Byzantine Empire may have perished as a result of the Justinian Plague, especially in the eastern Mediterranean region between the Nile Delta in Egypt and Constantinople. Worldwide, the Justinian Plague may have been responsible for as many as 25 million fatalities.

The plague had many indirect impacts on the Byzantine Empire and other parts of Europe and the Middle East as well. Many farmers died as a result of the plague. The loss of agricultural labor caused a reduction in crop yields, forcing food prices to rise. Reduced agricultural production reduced trade, therefore reducing the Byzantine Empire's tax base.

The plague may have affected Justinian's efforts to expand the empire. During the early years of his reign, Justinian was intent on reclaiming territories that had been part of the now-defunct Western Roman Empire in order to re-establish a unified Roman Empire under his rule. Justinian's troops conquered Italy and made efforts to reclaim the coastlands of the western Mediterranean. However, fatalities associated with the plague reduced the number of available troops. Declining tax revenues made it much more difficult for Justinian and his military leaders to provide their remaining soldiers with food and other necessities. Western Europeans, less affected by the plague, were better able to resist Justinian's efforts. Shortly after Justinian's death, Italy and other conquered areas along the western and central Mediterranean broke away from Byzantine rule and Justinian's dream of a re-established Roman Empire never came to fruition. Instead, Western and Central Europe continued to be fragmented politically, as they were for more than 1,000 years thereafter.

The Justinian Plague subsided after about 542 CE, although smaller and less virulent outbreaks of the disease continued intermittently for the next 300 years. After about 850 CE, the plague did not re-emerge until the onset of the Black Death in the 14th century. Scientists have expressed concern that a new form of the plague could emerge, with potentially devastating consequences given the fact that the world's population is much larger and more concentrated in urban areas than was the case during Justinian's days.

See Also: Black Death; Egypt; Epidemics; Italy; Turkey

Further Reading

William Rosen. *Justinian's Flea: Plague, Empire and the Birth of Europe*. New York: Viking, 2007.

Science Daily. "Plague or Black Death Could Re-Emerge: Cause of One of the Most Devastating Pandemics in Human History Revealed." January 27, 2014. http://www .sciencedaily.com/releases/2014/01/140127193741.htm?utm_source=feedburner &utm_medium=email&utm_campaign=Feed%3A+sciencedaily+%28Latest+Science+ News+—+ScienceDaily%29.

Kuznets, Simon

Simon Kuznets (1901–1985) was an American economist and demographer whose research on economic history had a major influence on understanding historical and contemporary relationships between economic development, technological changes, and population change throughout the world.

Kuznets was born in Pinsk, which was then part of the Russian Empire, in present-day Belarus and immigrated to the United States with his family in 1922. He earned his BS degree from Columbia University in 1923, followed by an MA in 1924 and a PhD in 1926, also from Columbia. He became a researcher with the National Bureau of Economic Research in 1927. In 1936, he became a professor of economics at the University of Pennsylvania, where he taught until 1954. He then taught at Johns Hopkins University from 1954 to 1960 and at Harvard University beginning in 1961. He remained at Harvard until he retired in 1970. He was awarded the Nobel Memorial Prize in Economic Sciences in 1971.

Kuznets's research was based on analysis of quantitative, historical economic data, establishing economics as an empirical as well as a theoretical discipline. He analyzed data associated with income, wealth, employment, savings, trade patterns, and demographic information as these variables changed over time. This analysis allowed Kuznets and others to make predictions about changes in economic growth and to make inferences about what caused these changes.

Kuznets's analysis showed that a country's economic growth is associated with changes in its economic structure. This analysis challenged the conventional wisdom of the time that suggested that countries go through systematic stages of growth. Under that view, less developed countries would develop along the same lines experienced already by developed countries. Instead, Kuznets showed that these paths to possible development differed, in part because of existing relationships between developed and less developed countries. He postulated what would become known as the "Kuznets curve," in which economic inequality in a society increases as a country develops but then declines.

Kuznets's analysis is related closely to population growth and change. For example, he pointed out that large-scale immigration from Europe to the United States contributed to economic growth in both places. Immigration provided needed labor to the United States while allowing surplus labor to leave Europe, reducing competition within European countries for limited resources and jobs. He noted that in the modern world there were very few opportunities for large numbers of people to resettle elsewhere, although his ideas anticipated the importance of international labor migration to the global economy today.

Kuznets also noted the impacts of demographic transition on economic development. Developed countries such as the United States had achieved high levels of economic development before undergoing demographic transition. However, during the middle of the 20th century, the crude birth rates of less developed countries remained very high. Thus, less developed countries had to provide needed goods and services for rapidly expanding populations. As Kuznets stated in his Nobel Prize lecture in 1971, "[N]o currently developed country had to adjust to the very high rates of natural increase of population that have characterized many less developed countries over the last two or three decades."

See Also: Demographic Transition Model; History of World Population; International Labor Migration

Further Reading

Simon Kuznets. "Modern Economic Growth: Findings and Reflections." Nobel Memorial Prize in Economic Sciences lecture, 1971. http://www.nobelprize.org/nobel_prizes /economic-sciences/laureates/1971/kuznets-lecture.html.

Simon Kuznets. *Population, Capital, and Growth.* New York: W. W. Norton, 1973.

Simon Kuznets. *Toward a Theory of Economic Growth*. New York: W. W. Norton, 1968.

Erik Lundberg. "Simon Kuznets' Contributions to Economics." *Swedish Journal of Economics* 73 (1971): 444–59.

Life Expectancy

Life expectancy is the number of additional years that the average person of a given age is likely to live. Usually, life expectancies are calculated from birth. However, life expectancies can be calculated for any age.

Life expectancies at birth vary throughout the world. Worldwide, life expectancy at birth was estimated at 67.2 years in 2010. However, country-by-country life expectancy varies from less than 50 years to more than 80 years. Life expectancies are considerably greater in developed countries than in less developed countries. The countries with the highest estimated life expectancies at birth in 2011 were Monaco (89.7 years), Japan (83.9), Singapore (83.8), San Marino (83.1), Andorra (82.5), Australia (81.9), Italy (81.9), Liechtenstein (81.5), Canada (81.5), France (81.3), and Spain (81.3). All of these are wealthy, highly urbanized, and highly developed countries. The life expectancy at birth in the United States is 78.5 years.

THE ELDERLY POPULATION OF JAPAN

Throughout the developed world, life expectancy is increasing while crude birth rates remain low. Hence the number of elderly people as a percentage of the overall population in many developed countries is increasing. Japan is believed to have the highest proportion of elderly persons in the world, in part because Japan's life expectancy of over 80 years is the highest of any large country in the world. As of 2006, more than 20 percent of Japanese citizens were over 65.

Japan's increasing elderly population has had ripple effects throughout Japanese society. The dependency ratio is decreasing, and a smaller cohort of working-age adults is responsible for the support of Japan's growing elderly population. More and more government income is being spent on medical care and social services for the elderly. Although Japanese culture has traditionally emphasized the role of young people in caring for older people, more and more of the elderly are left to fend for themselves. In 2013, one Japanese politician stirred up controversy by stating that elderly people should "hurry up and die."

Further Reading

Kanoko Matsuyama. "In Japan, the Rising Cost of Elder Care—And Dying Alone." *Business Week*, February 28, 2013. http://www.businessweek.com/articles/2013-02-28/in-japan-the-rising-cost-of-elder-care-and-dying-alone.

Justin McCurry. "Let Elderly People 'Hurry Up and Die,' Says Japanese Minister." *The Guardian*, January 22, 2013. http://www.theguardian.com/world/2013/jan/22/elderly-hurry-up-die-japanese.

The countries with the lowest estimated life expectancies in the world in 2011 were Chad (48.7 years), Guinea-Bissau (49.1), South Africa (49.4), Swaziland (49.4), Afghanistan (49.7), the Central African Republic (50.5), Somalia (50.8), Zimbabwe (51.8), Lesotho (51.9), and Mozambique (52.0). Although South Africa is one of the wealthiest countries in Africa, its low life expectancy at birth relative to other African countries has been attributed to the prevalence of the HIV/AIDS virus, which has caused the deaths of many young adults. HIV/AIDS is also a factor in the low life expectancies in Swaziland, Lesotho, and other southern African countries.

Life expectancies have also increased over time. The life expectancy of the United States, for example, has increased by more than 25 years between 1900 and 2000. Increased life expectancies in the United States and other developed countries have been attributed to improvements in medical care, better understanding of the causes and treatments for various diseases, reduced infant mortality, and improved public health. However, some experts believe that life expectancies in the United States are no longer increasing and may be stable or even decreasing. This change has been attributed in part to increased obesity.

Life expectancies vary by gender. In most countries today, women live longer than men. Historically, life expectancies for men were often higher than those for women because many women died in childbirth. As deaths in childbirth have declined throughout the world, female life expectancy has increased relative to male life expectancy. Some of the difference between female and male life expectancy has been attributed to the fact that men are more likely than women to die from accidents, violence, drug abuse, and diseases associated with cigarette smoking and alcohol abuse. In the United States, the life expectancy for women is about five years longer than for men. In 2009, female life expectancy in the United States was approximately 80.7 years, and male life expectancy was approximately 75.7 years.

Life expectancies can also be calculated for subsets of populations. For example, life expectancies are calculated for various ethnic groups within countries. In the United States, life expectancies among European Americans and Asian Americans are several years longer than they are for African Americans and Latinos. However, gaps in life expectancy between whites and nonwhites have been declining. Life expectancies in the United States also vary from state to state. Wealthier and more urbanized states have higher life expectancies than poorer states. In 2011–2012, the states with the highest life expectancies were Hawai'i (81.5 years), Minnesota (80.9), California (80.4), New York (80.4), and Connecticut (80.2). The lowest life expectancies were found in Mississippi (74.8 years), West Virginia (75.2), Alabama (75.2), Louisiana (75.4), and Oklahoma (75.6).

See Also: Demographic Transition Model; HIV/AIDS; Infant Mortality Rate; Japan; United States of America

Further Reading

Elizabeth Lopatto. "Life Expectancy in the U.S. Declines for the First Time since 1993." *Bloomberg News*, December 9, 2010. http://www.bloomberg.com/news/2010-12-09/life-expectancy-in-the-u-s-drops-for-first-time-since-1993-report-says.html.

United States Central Intelligence Agency. *World Factbook*, 2012. Washington, DC: U.S. Government Printing Office, 2012. https://www.cia.gov/library/publications/the-world-factbook/rankorder/2102rank.html.

Jennifer Warner. "Racial Gap in Life Expectancy Shrinking." *WebMD*, June 5, 2012. http://women.webmd.com/news/20120605/racial-gap-in-life-expectancy-shrinking.

Malthus, Thomas

Thomas Malthus (1766–1834) was a British economist, scholar, and clergyman who put forth the argument that continued population growth, if unchecked, will lead eventually to famine, disease, and war and cannot be sustained. Malthus's *Essay on the Principle of Population*, which was first published in 1798, remains in print and remains a highly influential work in population studies even today.

Malthus was educated at Jesus College of Cambridge University, from which he also earned an MA degree in 1791. He took holy orders in the Church of England in 1797. After serving as an Anglican curate, he was appointed as professor of history and political economy at the East India Company College in 1805. He was appointed as a fellow of the Royal Society in 1818.

Malthus wrote extensively on demography, economics, and related subjects throughout his lifetime. His *Essay on the Principle of Population* was his first major work, and remains his most influential contribution to scholarship. See excerpts from the *Essay* elsewhere in this volume. Here Malthus set forth what he regarded as the "laws" of population. His basic argument was that increase in population is limited by "means of subsistence." Populations increase when means of subsistence are plentiful, but under conditions of scarcity, populations come to be limited by "misery and vice." The principles articulated in the *Essay* remain associated with Malthus, and are referred to today as the Malthusian view of the relationship between population and resources. The *Essay* went through six editions during Malthus's lifetime, and in each new edition Malthus updated his material and responded to critics of his ideas. Numerous editions of the *Essay* are in print today.

Malthus wrote in response to writers of the late-18th-century Enlightenment. These Enlightenment writers took a utopian view of human progress and argued that continued improvement in the human condition could be expected as populations increased. Malthus responded specifically to William Godwin (1756–1836) and Marquis Nicholas de Condorcet (1743–1794). In fact, the full title of the first edition of the *Essay* is *An Essay on the Principle of Population, as It Affects the Future Improvement of Society with Remarks on the Speculations of Mr. Godwin, M. Condorcet, and Other Writers.*

Godwin (who became the father-in-law of the poet Percy Bysshe Shelley) believed in the perfectability of humanity. As an anarchist, Godwin blamed political institutions for hindering human progress and he believed that eventually each person's action would benefit the community in which he or she lived. Condorcet, along with other Enlightenment authors, developed the idea of progress. He viewed scientific knowledge and technology as ongoing keys to a world of increasing wealth and influence, which in turn would generate political and economic equality. Like Godwin, Condorcet saw individual interest coinciding with community interest. On the other hand, in arguing that shortages of resources would eventually limit population, Malthus saw a profound disconnect between individual and community interest. In short, Malthus saw poverty as a necessary condition of society. In that sense, Malthus's work can be seen as a precursor of the tragedy of the commons. Malthus also influenced the work of Charles Darwin and Alfred Russel Wallace, who developed the theory of evolution and based the evolutionary process on the principle of natural selection, which was again dependent on competition for scarce resources.

Malthus's work was subject to a great deal of criticism during his lifetime. Some of this criticism was personal. He was criticized for discussing population-related issues without himself having children. This criticism stemmed from a mistaken belief that his holy orders required priestly celibacy. In fact, as an Anglican clergyman Malthus could and did marry, and he and his wife had three children. More serious criticism focused on Malthus's theories. Following Condorcet, some critics saw technology as eliminating the constraints of population pressure. This argument continues to be articulated today, although Malthus's contemporary critics no longer see technology as means to complete elimination of poverty and population pressure. Rather, debate centers on the extent to which technology can alleviate the impacts of population growth on society and, increasingly, on the natural environment. Meanwhile, Karl Marx viewed excess population in terms of creating an industrial reserve army seeking employment. Thus Marx regarded Malthus as an apologist for the excess of capitalism.

Many contemporary observers have claimed that Malthus saw resources as fixed entirely. In fact, Malthus recognized the possibility that human ingenuity can create resources. In the *Essay*, Malthus compared population under various means of subsistence. He wrote, "In the rudest state of mankind, in which hunting is the principal occupation, and the only mode of acquiring food, the means of subsistence being scattered over a large extent of territory, the comparative population must necessarily be thin." He saw society advancing from this "rudest state of mankind" to what he called a "society of shepherds" or nomads whose social structure enabled them to coordinate movements: "It is well known that a country in pasture cannot support so many inhabitants as a country in tillage, but what renders nations of shepherds so formidable is the power which they possess of moving all together and the necessity they frequently feel of exerting this power in search of fresh pasture for their herds."

In examining the progression of society from the "society of shepherds" to societies supporting themselves by settled agriculture, Malthus recognized that improved agricultural technology could result in an increased level of per-acre agricultural productivity. However, he saw this increase in agricultural productivity as arithmetic, whereas the increase in population associated with this increased agricultural productivity. In his words,

> The population of the Island is computed to be about seven millions, and we will suppose the present produce equal to the support of such a number. In the first twenty-five years the population would be fourteen millions, and the food being also doubled, the means of subsistence would be equal to this increase. In the next twenty-five years the population would be twenty-eight millions, and the means of subsistence only equal to the support of twenty-one millions. In the next period, the population would be fifty-six millions, and the means of subsistence just sufficient for half that number.

In other words, he was very doubtful as to whether technology could keep up with increased population.

Malthus's ideas influenced many later demographers and economists. Some challenged his view that technology could not keep up with population increases. Others, such as Richard Easterlin, rejected his view that what Malthus called "passion between the sexes," or the desire to bear children, was constant. Easterlin postulated that people are inclined to produce more children under favorable economic circumstances. However, Malthus's writings remain influential, and the debate generated by his theories continues today.

See Also: Agriculture and Population; Carrying Capacity; History of World Population; Marx, Karl; Nomads; Tragedy of the Commons

Further Reading

Thomas Robert Malthus. *An Essay on the Principle of Population*. London: Dover, 2007. (Note: Many other editions of the *Essay* are also in print.)

William Petersen. *Malthus*. Cambridge, MA: Harvard University Press, 1979.

Marx, Karl

Karl Marx (1818–1883) was a German-born economist and social scientist whose ideas on the relationships between capital, labor, and the economy have had profound influence on contemporary social science and economic theory. He believed that population growth and the impoverishment of surplus populations were the outgrowth of capitalist economies.

Marx was born in Trier, Germany, and educated at the University of Bonn and the University of Berlin. He became active in 19th-century radical movements and moved to Paris, where he wrote articles for radical newspapers. Marx moved to London, where he lived for the remainder of his life, in 1849. In London, Marx remained active in support of socialist movements and continued writing for various radical publications. He also completed and published his most influential works, including the *Communist Manifesto* and *Das Kapital*. *Das Kapital* was published in three volumes. The second and third volumes were published after Marx's death, after being edited by his friend and collaborator Friedrich Engels.

Marx viewed history in terms of what he called "class struggle" between capital and labor. He believed that capitalists, who accumulated capital through ownership of means of production, profited from the exploitation of labor because labor contributed by workers provided capitalists with their sources of profit. Thus capitalists see the value of labor, like the value of goods and services, as a commodity. Over time, technological progress would reduce the costs of production, generating prosperity for society. However, the surplus value or the difference between the value of the worker's productivity and the worker's wages is held by the capitalist, thus reducing the

Karl Marx (1818–1883) developed the economic theory of class conflict, in which he interpreted history in terms of ongoing struggles between labor and capital. Marx's ideas influenced governmental processes around the world in the twentieth century. (Georgios Kollidas/Dreamstime.com)

purchasing power of workers. As the real value of wages declines, workers become poorer, and an increasing number of workers compete for scarce work opportunities, further depressing wages and contributing to poverty, hunger, and human misery. Marx believed that workers who continued to be oppressed would eventually rebel and work to overthrow capitalism, replacing it with a socialist economy.

Marx's views, while highly controversial and criticized frequently, have had great influence on the development of modern social science and economics. His work included analysis of population-related issues. He argued that population growth was an outgrowth of the capitalist system itself. In his view, more people provided more labor, giving an economy the opportunity to produce more and more food to support higher populations. Thus, in contrast to Thomas Malthus, Marx regarded technology as a means of creating resources and he did not regard population growth as limited by a fixed resource base. Rather, increased populations were seen as desirable to capitalists in that a larger number of potential workers allowed capital to exploit workers further. He regarded these increased populations as what he called an "industrial reserve army," whose numbers reduced and depressed wage levels and kept workers closer to the margins of survival. Increased food production allowed more and more workers to survive, although these workers were impoverished and continued to be exploited.

See Also: Malthus, Thomas

Further Reading

Vincent Barnett. *Marx*. London: Routledge, 2009.

David Harvey. *The Limits to Capital*. London: Verso, 2006.

Karl Marx. *Das Kapital*. Vol. I. Hamburg: Verlag von Otto Meisner, 1867. (Published in German. Volumes II and III were published posthumously in 1885 and 1894, respectively. Many modern English-language editions of *Das Kapital* are available.)

Karl Marx. *A Contribution to the Critique of Political Economy*. New York: International Publishers, 1975. Originally published in German in 1859.

Median Age

The median age of the population of any country or place is that age at which half of the population is older and half is younger. For example, suppose a country has a population of 20 million and a median age of 30 years. This means that 10 million people in the country are 30 years old or older, and that the other 10 million are less than 30 years of age. As with other population measures, the median age can be estimated for subsets of populations, for example by gender, ethnicity, religion, or region within a country.

Median ages are associated closely with crude birth rates, crude death rates, life expectancy, and rates of natural increase. As a general rule, higher median ages are associated with lower crude birth rates and lower crude death rates. Lower median ages are associated with higher crude birth rates and higher crude death rates. Thus, median age is correlated with life expectancy. In places where people live longer, median ages are higher. Over the last 200 years, median ages throughout the world have risen because of increases in life expectancy. These increases, in turn, are associated with advances in medicine and improved medical care and public health. High median ages are associated also with low or negative rates of natural increase in that places whose birth rates are lower than their death rates will have older populations.

As of 2011, the median ages of the populations of countries throughout the world ranged from less than 16 years to nearly 45 years. The 10 countries with the lowest median ages were Uganda (15.1 years), Niger (15.2), Mali (16.3), Zambia (16.5), Chad (16.8), Ethiopia (16.8), Mozambique (16.8), Burundi (16.9), Burkina Faso (16.9), and the Republic of the Congo (17.0). In these countries, barely half of the population has reached childbearing age. The total fertility rates of these countries are very high. However, even if the total fertility rate were to drop to two children per mother immediately, the population would continue to increase until the younger half of the current population became too old to have children. Thus, a low median age is a signal that a country's population is likely to continue to rise into the foreseeable future. The list also illustrates the relationship between rapid population growth and low levels of economic development in these and other less developed countries.

MEDIAN AGES IN THE UNITED STATES

As in many other developed countries, the United States has a relatively high median age. According to the 2010 census, the median age in the U.S. was 37.2 years. However, this median age varied from less than 30 years in three states to more than 42 years in Maine, the state with the highest life expectancy.

Life expectancies vary for several reasons, including out-migration of the young and in-migration of the elderly. Thus, Florida's median age is well above the national average because it is a popular migration destination. On the other hand, Maine and other rural and/or industrial states such as Pennsylvania, West Virginia, and Iowa have relatively high median ages because many young people are leaving in search of opportunities elsewhere. The three states with the lowest median ages were Texas, Utah, and Idaho. Immigration is a major factor contributing to Texas's low median age in that immigrants tend to be young and have larger families than do native-born Americans. The low life expectancy of Utah and Idaho may be due to the large Mormon populations of these states, given that Mormons tend to have more children than do non-Mormons.

Further Reading

Les Christie. "Where People Are Oldest—Maine Tops Florida." *CNNMoney*, May 27, 2011. http://money.cnn.com/2011/05/26/real_estate/americas_oldest_states/.

Not including very small countries and territories, the 10 states with the highest median ages in 2011 were Germany (44.9 years), Japan (44.8), Italy (43.5), Austria (43.0), Finland (42.5), Greece (42.5), Slovenia (42.4), Belgium (42.3), Sweden (42.0), and Bulgaria (41.9). In these and other developed countries, high median ages imply low birth and death rates. Rates of natural increase are negative, and deaths exceed births. Over the long run, this implies that the populations of these countries are likely to decrease in the years ahead. Only through immigration can these countries expect to retain their current populations. The median age of the United States, with its relatively high birth rate and immigration rate relative to most of Europe, was 38.9 years. More generally, median ages throughout the world are expected to increase as total fertility rates decline and as more and more people live longer.

See Also: Crude Birth Rate; Crude Death Rate; Demographic Transition Model; Life Expectancy; Rate of Natural Increase; United States of America

Further Reading

The Economist. "Median Age of the Population." March 6, 2003. http://www.economist .com/node/1622427.

United States Central Intelligence Agency. *CIA World Factbook 2013*. Washington, DC: U.S. Government Printing Office, 2013. https://www.cia.gov/library/publications/the-world -factbook/fields/2054.html.

Megacities

Megacities are very large metropolitan areas. Megacities include central cities and their suburbs. Some are centered on a single central city, whereas others include two or more large central cities located adjacent to one another. Many megacities, especially in developing countries, face ongoing issues with poverty, lack of infrastructure, and inability to cope with very rapid population increases.

There is no formal definition of a megacity. However, many definitions of megacities use a population threshold to identify megacities relative to other cities. One commonly used definition of a megacity is a metropolitan area with a population of 10 million or more. As of 2013, 29 metropolitan areas throughout the world met this criterion according to the Population Reference Bureau. The largest is Tokyo, with a population of about 35 million. The megacities of Guangzhou, Shanghai, Jakarta, and Seoul also have populations in excess of 25 million. Sixteen of the 29 megacities recognized in the Population Reference Bureau's list are located in Asia. In this encyclopedia, separate entries describe population trends and problems in each of the 29 megacities in the world with populations greater than 10 million.

Seoul is the capital of South Korea. With a population of more than 25 million, the Seoul metropolitan area is the third-largest metropolitan area in the world. Nearly half of all South Koreans live in the Seoul region, which is far more densely populated than are most megacities in developed countries. (Tatiana Grozetskaya/Dreamstime.com)

Within the context of history, megacities are recent phenomena. Megacities have arisen in response to very rapid rates of urbanization during and after the Industrial Revolution. In 1800, only about 3 percent of the world's people lived in cities. By 1950, the percentage of people living in cities increased to approximately one-third. At this time, New York became the world's first megacity, with more than 10 million people living in the city and its suburbs. New York is at the center of the American Megalopolis, the area between Boston and Washington within which more than 35 million people live today.

During the late 19th and early 20th centuries, the percentage of people world-wide who reside in cities has increased to nearly 50 percent today and has been projected to exceed 60 percent by 2050. Much of this growth has taken place in megacities. Many megacities are primate cities that serve as the political, financial, and cultural centers of their countries. Especially in less developed countries, megacities have experienced numerous difficulties in coping with rapid population increases. City and state governments have generally lacked the financial resources needed to provide housing, transportation, medical care, sanitation, and other services for their quickly growing populations. As a result, many megacities are experiencing high levels of poverty, homelessness, traffic congestion, and environ-mental pollution. In many, millions of residents live in squatter settlements that lack electricity and running water. Some governments have enacted policies intended to discourage migration into their megacities.

Economist Edward Glaeser has identified a paradox associated with the rapid growth of megacities. Historians and contemporary observers generally recognize that urbanization is associated with promoting economic development and with increased opportunity on the part of urban residents to create wealth. However, many megacities in developing countries remain impoverished.

Glaeser offers two potential reasons to explain this paradox. First, he argues that the development of cities has been associated historically with trade linkages between these cities and nearby rural hinterlands that supply food and other necessities to urban residents. Today, this relationship has become much weaker, in part because globalization has reduced a megacity's dependence on locally produced food and other resources. Instead, residents of megacities can purchase these commodities on global markets, thus reducing the income-generating potential of local rural areas and encouraging increased levels of migration to megacities. This in turn creates more population pressure in the urban areas, further limiting the opportunity for officials in the megacities to address ongoing problems with poverty and lack of infrastructure that could help the megacities' residents to lift themselves out of poverty.

MEGACITIES VULNERABLE TO ENVIRONMENTAL CHANGE

Megacities throughout the world are coping with rapid increases in population, which have strained their ability to provide the infrastructure, housing, and social services needed to support their rapidly growing numbers of people. But many of the world's megacities are at high risk of natural disasters, which could have significant short-run and/or long-run impacts on their populations.

What megacities are most at risk of natural disasters? According to one study, many of the most vulnerable megacities are located in Asia. Tokyo, which is the largest megacity in the world, was identified as the most at risk of a natural disaster. Tokyo is located in one of the most earthquake-prone areas of the world, and offshore earthquakes can trigger tsunamis. Further to the south, megacities such as Manila, Guangzhou, and Shanghai are susceptible to earthquakes as well as to intense typhoons originating in the Pacific Ocean. Typhoons, which are known as cyclones in South Asia, have also devastated Kolkata on several occasions. Potential natural disasters may have especially strong impacts on Kolkata and other poorer megacities such as Jakarta in that these cities lack the resources to plan for and protect themselves against these disasters.

Further Reading

Harrison Jacobs. "The 10 Cities Most at Risk of Being Hit by Natural Disasters." *Business Insider*, March 28, 2014. http://www.businessinsider.com/cities-most-at-risk-of-natural-disasters-2014-3.

According to Glaeser, a second explanation for the ongoing poverty of mega-cities involves the nature of migration to megacities itself. In many countries, a disproportionate percentage of people who move from rural areas to urban centers within their countries choose to move to the largest megacity within that country. Thus cities such as Cairo, Jakarta, Mexico City, and other megacities draw natives of rural areas at much faster rates than do smaller cities. In some countries, policy efforts are being made to divert these rural-to-urban migrants away from mega-cities and toward smaller cities that are growing less rapidly and are more likely to have the resources to combat poverty.

See Also: Globalization; Megalopolis; Primate City; Rural to Urban Migration; Squatter Settlements; Tokyo

Further Reading

Richard Florida. "Why So Many Emerging Megacities Remain So Poor." *Atlantic Cities*, January 16, 2014. http://www.theatlanticcities.com/jobs-and-economy/2014/01/why-so -many-mega-cities-remain-so-poor/8083/.

Edward L. Glaeser. "A World of Cities: The Causes and Consequences of Urbanization in Poorer Countries." National Bureau of Economic Research, NBER Working Paper 19745, December 2013. http://www.nber.org/papers/w19745.

Frauke Kraas, Surinder Aggarwal, Martin Coy, and Gunter Mertins, eds. *Megacities: Our Global Urban Future*. Dordrecht, NL: Springer, 2013.

Population Reference Bureau. *2013 World Population Data Sheet*. http://www.prb.org /pdf13/2013-population-data-sheet_eng.pdf.

Megalopolis

A megalopolis is an agglomeration of large cities located near one another that have histories as separate cities but over the course of time have coalesced into heavily populated and interdependent urban regions. The term originally was coined to refer to the cities of the northeastern United States, but has since been applied to large metropolitan areas in other parts of the world. Many megalopolises today are centered upon megacities, or individual cities and their suburbs with populations of 10 million or more.

In the 1950s, geographer Jean Gottmann recognized the concentration of popu-lation and increased population density in the cities of the eastern seaboard of the United States. He used the term "Megalopolis" to refer to the region between Boston to the northeast and Washington, D.C., to the southwest. Megalopolis is centered on the megacity of New York, and also includes the large metropolitan areas of Boston,

Philadelphia, Baltimore, and Washington. The size of this region is evident from the fact that Boston and Washington are separated by more than 400 miles. Megalopolis also includes smaller cities such as Trenton, New Haven, Hartford, and Providence that are located also within this region. This region has the highest population density of any place within the United States. The states of Rhode Island and New Jersey, both of which are located within the region and between the major cities of Megalopolis, have the highest population densities of any U.S. states.

As is the case with megacities, a megalopolis can be defined on the basis of population thresholds. Some experts have suggested that a region must have a population of at least 25 million to qualify as a megalopolis. Interdependence, including ease of access, is also important to the definition of a megalopolis. For example, the major cities of Megalopolis in the United States are connected closely to one another by air, rail, and road.

The concept of megalopolis has been applied to urban agglomerations in many other parts of the world. Many of the most populous urban agglomerations in the world are located in China. These include the Pearl River Delta region in southeastern China, including Hong Kong, Guangzhou, and Shenzhen. This region contains more than 60 million people in an area of less than 20,000 square miles, less than the size of the U.S. state of South Carolina. Another and even larger megalopolis is the Yangtze River Delta region, which is centered on Shanghai and includes the nearby large cities of Nanjing and Hangzhou. Between 80 and 100 million people, depending on the precise geographic definition of the area, live in the Yangtze River Delta region.

In other parts of the world, the areas centered on Tokyo in Japan and Seoul in South Korea are identified as megalopolitan regions. Some have extended the concept to southeastern Brazil, whose major cities of Sao Paulo and Rio de Janeiro are separated by only about 200 miles. Throughout the world, these very large urban agglomerations continue to face problems associated with congestion, environmental degradation, poverty, and assimilation of the large number of migrants who move into these places.

See Also: China; Megacities; New York; United States of America

Further Reading

Jean Gottmann. *Megalopolis: The Urbanized Northeastern Seaboard of the United States.* New York: Twentieth Century Fund, 1961.

Edward Soja. *Postmetropolis: Critical Studies of Cities and Regions.* Oxford: Basil Blackwell, 2000.

Migration

Migration is movement between places. For purposes of examining population and demography, migration refers to long-distance, permanent, or relatively permanent moves. A migrant is a person who moves from one community to another. In that sense, someone who moves from house to house on a city block, or within a neighborhood in a city, is not considered a migrant. Along the same lines, migrants move with the intention of remaining in their new residences on a permanent rather than a temporary basis. Thus the definition of migration excludes tourists, vacationers, or people on temporary work assignments.

In the 19th century, Ernst Ravenstein formulated what he termed "the laws of migration." Ravenstein's first law of migration postulates that people are more likely to move short distances as opposed to long distances. This principle is encapsulated in the gravity model, in which migration is seen as a function of the size of the origin, the size of the destination, and the distance between these places.

International borders also affect migration levels. In the world today, the great majority of migrations occur within rather than between countries. In most countries throughout the world, more than 90 percent of people born in a given country continue to live in that country as adults. Well over 98 percent of persons born in the United States live there as adults, and less than 2 percent are expatriates. Even countries with long histories of repression and/or economic deprivation such as Cuba and Haiti report that over 80 percent of people born in these countries continue to live there as adults. For purposes of this discussion, this entry focuses on people who migrate between as opposed to within countries.

Worldwide, the United Nations has estimated that about 3 percent of the world's population consists of international migrants, or people who live in a country different than their country of birth. Most recent estimates suggest that there are between 210 and 240 million international migrants today. However, the rate of migration from less developed countries to developed countries is considerably higher than the rate of migration from developed countries to less developed countries. About 9 percent of residents of developed countries are international migrants, as compared to less than 1.5 percent in less developed countries. Many international labor migrants remain in close touch with family and friends in their countries of origin, and many support their relatives and friends via remittances.

International migrants can be grouped into three broad categories: international labor migrants, brain drain migrants, and refugees. International labor migrants are people who migrate in search of employment opportunities. Usually, international labor migrants come from less developed countries and move to developed countries. International labor migration has become a major political issue in many countries throughout the world, including the United States. In many countries, a substantial percentage of people are international labor migrants. It has been estimated that about 8 percent of people residing in Germany were born outside of the European Union. In the United States, more than 20 million people can be considered international labor migrants or members of their families. Millions more international labor migrants are illegal immigrants.

Not all international migrants are impoverished natives of less developed countries. Many are well-educated persons including engineers, scientists, and physicians who move from less developed countries to developed countries in order to practice their professions. This phenomenon is known as the brain drain.

Some of these highly educated persons are victims of religious and/or political persecution in their home countries. These people also qualify as refugees. A refugee is a person who is forced to leave his or her native country and move elsewhere in response to political or religious persecution. Refugee migration is monitored by the Office of the United Nations High Commissioner for Refugees. Current estimates suggest that about 10 to 15 million people around the world can be categorized as refugees.

Generally, migration is regarded as a voluntary process. In deciding whether to move and in choosing a place to which to relocate, the prospective migrant identifies and evaluates push factors and pull factors. Push factors are characteristics of a prospective migrant's home country that might encourage migration to another country. These may include poverty, environmental degradation, or religious and political persecution. Pull factors refer to characteristics of potential migration destinations. Examples of pull factors include jobs, economic opportunity, presence of friends and relatives, a desirable physical environment, and freedom from religious and political persecution.

Although migration is analyzed usually as a voluntary process, in fact many migrants are coerced into moving. Historically, much of this involuntary migration involved slavery. Millions of Africans, for example, were kidnapped and transported to the western hemisphere between the 16th and 19th centuries. Even after slavery was abolished in most parts of the world during the 19th century, many people were kidnapped and transported to other countries as laborers. In Australia and various islands in the Pacific Ocean, this practice was known as blackbirding.

Diasporas represent another form of forced, involuntary migration. People belonging to particular nationalities or religious communities were forced to move in large numbers away from their homelands. The term applied originally to the forced movement of Jews from their homeland in and near present-day Israel in the first century CE. The expulsion of Armenians from present-day Turkey during and after World War I is another example of a diaspora. The term can also be applied to forced migration of indigenous people from their ancestral lands throughout the world. For example, European settlement of the western hemisphere resulted in the displacement of Native Americans, many of whom were forced to live on reservations.

See Also: Brain Drain; Expatriates; Illegal Immigration; Indigenous Populations; International Labor Migration; Push Factors and Pull Factors; Refugees; Slavery; States, Nations, and Population

Further Reading

John Haywood. *The Great Migrations: From the Earliest Humans to the Age of Globalization.* Frederick, MD: Quercus Press, 2009.

Russell King. *Atlas of Human Migration.* Boston, MA: Firefly Press, 2007.

Patrick Manning. *Migration in World History.* New York: Taylor and Francis, 2005.

Natural Disasters

Natural disasters are catastrophic events caused by various natural processes on the earth's surface, in the atmosphere, or below the surface. Natural disasters can be caused by hurricanes, tornadoes, earthquakes, volcanic activity, tsunamis, floods, droughts, and other natural phenomena. Throughout history, natural disasters have had frequent and sometimes very dramatic impacts on the populations throughout the world.

The 2010 earthquake in Haiti caused more than 200,000 deaths and reduced thousands of buildings to rubble. Here a girl scavenges through rubble in the Haitian capital city of Port au Prince. (AP Photo/The Canadian Press/Ryan Remiorz)

Not all potentially catastrophic events caused by natural processes qualify as natural disasters. Such events qualify as natural disasters only to the extent that they affect human populations. For example, an earthquake striking an isolated or very sparsely populated area will have no impact on populations. On the other hand, an earthquake of the same intensity striking a large city could cause thousands of fatalities, numerous injuries, and millions upon millions of dollars in property damage.

Also, in many cases catastrophic events that cause natural disasters cannot be separated from human activity. For example, global climate change is believed to be associated with sea-level rise. As a result, cities located on low-lying land near the coast such as Kolkata and Lagos are more likely to experience coastal flooding. Many climatologists believe that climate change could also result in more intense tropical storms, increasing the likelihood that such powerful storms will affect populated coastal areas.

Various types of potential natural disasters are more prevalent in some areas than in others. More than 80 percent of the world's earthquakes take place along the Ring of Fire, which stretches around the Pacific Ocean from Indonesia northward and eastward through the Philippines, eastern China, and Japan, northward to the east coast of Russia. The Ring of Fire continues through southern Alaska, along the west coast of the United States, and along the western coast of South America. More than 75 percent of the world's active volcanoes are also found along the Ring of Fire, whose location is associated with the movement of tectonic plates under the surface of the earth. The Ring of Fire is located where the large Pacific Plate, which underlies most of the Pacific Ocean, collides with other tectonic plates along the ocean's margins.

Intense tropical storms, which are called hurricanes in the United States, typhoons in East Asia, and cyclones in South Asia and Africa, occur primarily on the eastern coasts of all continents and along south-facing coasts in the northern hemisphere. Thus China, the Philippines, Vietnam, India, Bangladesh, the United States, and countries in Central America are especially susceptible to these storms. Droughts are most likely to occur in semi-arid regions, and floods occur most often in places that experience heavy rainfall and/or are located along major rivers.

Natural disasters vary in intensity. Some cause very large numbers of fatalities, injuries, and property damage whereas others cause relatively little damage. Various types of scales have been developed to measure the strength of natural catastrophes. For example, the Richter scale is used to measure the intensity of earthquakes, with high numbers associated with stronger earthquakes. Thus the Richter scale is a measure of the magnitude, or strength, of a natural catastrophe. Similarly, hurricanes are classified between Category 1 (the weakest) and Category 5 (the strongest) on the basis of their wind speeds. High-magnitude events occur relatively infrequently, but are generally associated with very high impacts on population. On the other hand, smaller events occur much less often but cause much more damage and destruction. Thousands of earthquakes occur under the earth's surface every day, but most are not strong enough to be noticed by people and most cause no damage. However, major earthquakes such as the Haitian earthquake of 2010 and the Fukushima earthquake off the coast of Japan in 2011 occur rarely, but have highly devastating consequences when they do occur. In other words, high-magnitude events occur with less frequency than do low-magnitude events.

THE HAITIAN EARTHQUAKE OF 2010

One of the most devastating natural disasters in recent history occurred in Haiti on January 12, 2010, when an earthquake measuring 7.0 on the Richter scale occurred not far from Haiti's capital city of Port-au-Prince. More than 150,000 persons lost their lives, and hundreds of thousands of others were injured or became homeless. Nearly 300,000 houses and other buildings are believed to have been destroyed or damaged heavily by the earthquake. The tragedy was exacerbated and relief efforts were hampered by Haiti's inadequate infrastructure, insufficient hospital facilitites and medical supplies, poor transportation, and shoddy building construction.

Following the earthquake, an epidemic of cholera broke out, causing another 10,000 deaths. Thousands of people left Haiti for the United States and other countries as environmental refugees, and others who lost their homes were still living in tents and other makeshift housing. Since the earthquake, Haiti, with the help of international disaster recovery organizations, has been able to rebuild much of its lost infrastructure. However, progress remains slow, especially given that Haiti is one of the most impoverished countries in the world.

Further Reading

Peter Granitz. "Four Years after Earthquake, Many in Haiti Remain Displaced." *NPR*, January 12, 2014. http://www.npr.org/2014/01/12/261723409/four-years-after -earthquake-many-in-haiti-remain-displaced.

Richard Kurin. "Since the Earthquake of Four Years Ago, Helping Hands Make a World of Difference." *Smithsonian*, January 8, 2014. http://www.smithsonianmag.com /smithsonian-institution/haitian-earthquake-four-years-ago-helping-hands-made -world-difference-180949297/?no-ist.

Examination of the impacts of natural disasters on populations is also associated with questions of risk and vulnerability. The risk of a natural disaster is a measure of the probability that a catastrophic event will occur. Seismologists often calculate the likelihood that earthquakes will occur at points along the Ring of Fire and elsewhere. Vulnerability represents the potential effect of a natural disaster should it occur. Generally speaking, vulnerability is highest in less developed countries and in areas with very high population densities. For example, Bangladesh is a poor country with a very dense population, and many Bangladeshis live on or near the coast of the Bay of Bengal. Hence, tropical storms and floods can and do have devastating impacts when they take place. Illustrating this point, a major cyclone struck Bangladesh in 1970, causing as many as 300,000 fatalities. Bangladesh's low-lying land, its poverty, and its high risk of floods and intense cyclones make it very highly vulnerable to natural disasters.

Bangladesh has been identified as one of the most vulnerable countries to disasters. Other highly vulnerable countries include neighboring India, Pakistan, the Philippines, and Vietnam. Less developed countries are usually much more vulnerable to natural disasters than are developed countries for several reasons. Their populations are generally growing rapidly. Because of their poverty and rapid rates of population growth, most do not have the resources to prepare for the eventuality of natural disasters. Houses and public buildings may not be constructed to withstand floods, tropical storms, or earthquakes. As well, warning systems are often inadequate, making it difficult to convey danger to people at risk of experiencing a natural disaster. People may not know about the impending arrival of a cyclone or typhoon and may therefore not be able to evacuate their properties in time. This problem is especially acute in places where large numbers of people are illiterate and/or do not have access to television, radio, or social media to learn about these catastrophic events.

As a result, individual natural disasters generally have much stronger impacts when they occur in less developed countries, as compared to those occurring in developed countries. For example, an earthquake measuring 7.0 on the Richter scale struck Haiti in 2010. This earthquake resulted in more than 200,000 fatalities. On the other hand, the much stronger Fukushima earthquake occurred off the coast of Japan in 2011. Although this earthquake was far stronger, measuring 9.0 on the Richter scale, it caused less than 20,000 fatalities. However, it devastated the nearby Fukushima nuclear power plant, leaving open the possibilities that many more people will be affected in the future by nuclear radiation entering the atmosphere.

Over the long run, some experts predict that the impacts of natural disasters on populations will increase. On the other hand, the impacts of these disasters could be mitigated with improved planning and warning systems. Yet many impoverished countries do not have the financial resources to implement such plans, leading to the likelihood that these countries will become even more vulnerable to natural disasters in the future.

See Also: Agriculture and Population; Bangladesh; Climate Change and Population; Japan; Population Density

Further Reading
Susan W. Kieffer. *The Dynamics of Disaster*. New York: W. W. Norton, 2011.

Robin McKie. "Climate Change: Melting Ice Will Trigger Wave of Natural Disasters." *The Guardian*, September 5, 2009. http://www.theguardian.com/environment/2009/sep/06/global-warming-natural-disasters-conference.

John Vedal. "Philippines Rockets Up List of Countries Most Vulnerable to Disaster." *The Guardian*, November 14, 2013. http://www.theguardian.com/global-development/2013/nov/14/philippines-disaster-vulnerable-haiyan.

Ben Wisner, Piers Blaikie, Terry Cannon, and Ian Davis. *At Risk: People's Vulnerability and Disasters*. New York: Routledge, 2004.

Natural Resources and Population

Population and population change are tied closely to the global economy, which involves the extraction of raw materials, the processing of these raw materials to manufacture finished products, and the distribution of these finished products. The raw material from which all finished products are made, from handicrafts to highly sophisticated computers and aircraft, are natural resources. Throughout the history of the world, populations have been affected by the presence or absence of natural resources, and by conflict over their use and control.

Throughout the world, population growth has been affected by the availability of natural resources. Wells such as this one in West Texas pump millions of barrels of oil per day. However, oil is a non-renewable resource and shortages or price increases could have profound impacts on populations in the future. (Scott Hales/Dreamstime.com)

A natural resource is a substance that is found in nature and that can be transformed into a product of value, or a substance that is useful in the operation of products of value. Many minerals are natural resources. Agricultural products are also natural resources when used to produce food or other items of value such as automobile tires. Other frequently used natural resources include wood, domestic or wild plants and animals, air, and water. However, it is important that not all substances of potential value are natural resources. For example, while petroleum found in the United States, Saudi Arabia, and Russia is a natural resource, an oil deposit under the ice cap in Antarctica would not be a natural resource. The cost of drilling through a thick ice cap under extreme weather conditions to extract the oil, followed by the cost of shipping the oil to markets, would be far greater than the value of the oil to those undertaking the drilling project. Thus drilling for this oil in Antarctica is not cost effective.

The hypothetical example of Antarctica illustrates that a substance is regarded as a natural resource only if it is useful under current economic and technological conditions. Countries often identify natural resource reserves. Reserves such as proven oil reserves represent the amount of a resource that is available again under current economic and technological conditions. The amount of reserves of a particular resource will increase if the price of a resource increases and/or if new technologies reduce production costs. A substance once deemed worthless can also become a natural resource if that substance can be put to valuable use.

As a general principle, the price of a natural resource is determined by supply and demand. Thus the price of a natural resource increases under conditions of reduced supply and/or increased demand. Most natural resources can be found only in limited areas. Thus, an organization or country that controls the sources or supply of a valuable natural resource can profit considerably. For example, petroleum is a highly valuable resource that is found in significant countries in only a relatively few parts of the world. The Arabian Peninsula is a large supplier of petroleum, and oil-rich countries such as Saudi Arabia, Kuwait, and the United Arab Emirates are among the wealthiest countries in the world on a per capita basis. However, in recent years petroleum production outside the Middle East has been increasing, and Russia now leads the world in annual oil production. The long-run prosperity of Middle Eastern countries may be threatened if oil production elsewhere increases and/or if global petroleum prices decline.

Oil is one of many natural resources that are located only in certain areas of the world. Most minerals have limited availability. For example, more than 75 percent of all the uranium produced in the world today comes from five countries—Kazakhstan, Canada, Australia, Niger, and Namibia. Many valuable fruits and vegetables cannot tolerate frost and can therefore be grown only in the tropics. More than 60 percent of cocoa, which is used to make chocolate, comes from West Africa.

Natural resources have affected populations in many ways for thousands of years. Because supplies of natural resources are finite and often limited geographically, various cultures have long contested for control over places where natural resources were believed to be available. The opportunity to search for gold and silver motivated European explorers to cross the Atlantic to present-day North America and South America during the Age of Exploration. At that time, it was commonly believed that wealth could be measured in terms of how much gold and silver one possessed. Spanish and Portuguese explorers discovered large deposits of these minerals in South America and present-day Mexico.

The largest and most lucrative Spanish mining operation was located at Potosí in present-day Bolivia. Large deposits of silver in the areas near Potosí were known to the Incas prior to the arrival of the Spanish. The Spanish founded Potosí in 1546. By 1600, the city had a population of 200,000 and was the largest in the Western Hemisphere. It has been estimated that at that time as many as 15 percent of all Spanish colonists in Latin America were involved in the mining operations at Potosí. Labor was provided originally by indigenous persons, many of whom were enslaved and many of whom died of exposure to European diseases, from overwork associated with forced labor, and from mercury poisoning contracted while mining and processing the ore. Thousands of African slaves were brought into the area to work the mines, but they also succumbed in large numbers to diseases, exposure to toxic chemicals, and inhumane working conditions. The silver mines began to become depleted by about 1800, but silver mining operations in the area continue there today.

The Potosí example illustrates how the measurement of value of a natural resource underwent a fundamental shift after gold and silver deposits such as those near Potosí were identified and mined. During the Age of Exploration, wealth was measured in terms of possession of gold, silver, and other precious commodities. However, by the 18th century it came to be recognized that value must be measured in terms of supply and demand, as Adam Smith articulated. Thus the value of gold, silver, and other commodities came to be based on how much others were willing to exchange for these commodities, rather than on how much of these commodities one possessed.

This point helps to illustrate one reason why North America became much more prosperous than Latin America during the 19th century. Explorers searching for gold and silver in North America were disappointed. However, other resources including high-quality agricultural land, plentiful supplies of fish, and wood were discovered in abundance. These substances could be transformed into necessary items such as food, clothing, and shelter. Thus the potential use for a natural resource became an important value in determining its value.

Potosí was one of many places in which forced labor and slavery were used in resource extraction. Throughout history, the discovery of natural resources has resulted in major changes in population distributions. Large numbers of people migrate to places in which these natural resources are found in order to obtain wealth. However, obtaining this wealth often requires large inputs of labor. Many of the great forced migrations in history, including the movement of African slaves to the western hemisphere, were undertaken in order to provide labor in mines or on plantations. The minerals, agricultural products, and other resources generated by these slaves and forced laborers were generally exported, bringing wealth to those owning the mines and plantations who exploited the laborers. However, the workers themselves received very little if any benefits from their labor. Rather, as in the case of Potosí, large numbers of slaves suffered from abuse, and many died because of disease, overwork, harsh treatment, and violence.

Forced migration associated with resource extraction continues today. For example, thousands of West African children and teenagers are forced to work on cocoa plantations in countries such as Côte d'Ivoire and Ghana. Most of these laborers come from other Africa countries. In effect, these children are slaves. Their jobs involve hard physical labor, sometimes require the use of dangerous tools and machinery making them highly subject to injury, and require long hours of work. Very few have the opportunity to attend school.

Populations are also affected indirectly by political conflict over control of resources. Throughout history, many wars have been fought over control of territory known to be rich in natural resources. Such wars have resulted in many fatalities. Not only are soldiers killed in battle, but civilians are affected also. Civilians may be killed or enslaved. Their homes and farms are often destroyed or burned, and many civilians are forced into refugee status. It is no accident that the largest concentrations of refugees in the world are found in places facing civil or international wars.

Populations are also affected by environmental problems associated with natural resource extraction. Mining and refining of many minerals cause pollution and other environmental effects. An extreme example is the Siberian city of Norilsk, which is located in the richest nickel-mining area in the world. Air and water pollution associated with mining and smelting nickel is so severe that life expectancy in Norilsk is nearly 10 years less than in Russia as a whole. About two-thirds of Niger's export income is generated by uranium mining in the northern part of the country. However, the local Tuareg people complain that most of the revenues are used in other, more densely populated areas of Niger while the environmental costs of uranium extraction, including radioactivity and pollution, must be borne locally.

Water resources are another source of conflict, especially in desert or semidesert areas of the world. Conflicts over water resources are expected to intensify in the 21st century in light of climate change and increasing population pressure, especially in less developed areas of the world. Large areas of the earth's surface receive an average annual precipitation of less than 400 millimeters, or 16 inches, of rainfall per year. This is illustrated by recent conflict over access to the Tigris and Euphrates River in southwestern Asia. Both rivers rise in Turkey and flow through Syria into Iraq, where they empty into the Persian Gulf. For thousands of years, the people of present-day Iraq have relied on the Euphrates and the Tigris as a vital source of water.

In the 1970s, Turkey developed the Southeastern Anatolia Project, whose purpose was to promote economic development in this historically impoverished region. The purpose of the Southeastern Anatolia Project was to use the Euphrates and Tigris Rivers to irrigate the arid regions of southeastern Turkey. Dams were constructed and water from the rivers was diverted for irrigation. However, the diversion of water from the rivers into Turkey meant that less water was available for use downstream in Syria and Iraq, restricting food production in these countries. Iraq has accused Turkey of diverting the water in the Tigris and Euphrates illegally.

The overriding issues involving the relationships between natural resources and population are associated with questions of overpopulation and carrying capacity. Although many natural resources such as wood and agricultural products are renewable, the overall resource base of the world is necessarily finite. Demand for natural resources will continue to increase as populations continue to grow. As these demands increase, the number of resource-related conflicts will also increase, with more and more impacts on local and global populations. The large question becomes how many people can be supported given the world's finite resource base, and the extent to which we can rely on technology to resolve these problems and to identify and create new resources.

See Also: Climate Change and Population; Indigenous Populations; Migration; Overpopulation; Refugees; Slavery

Further Reading

Daniel D. Charos and John P. Reganold. *National Resource Conservation: Management for a Sustainable Future*. New York: Benjamin Cummings, 2009.

Suzanne Goldenberg. "Why Global Water Shortages Pose Threat of Terror and War." *The Observer*, February 8, 2014. http://www.theguardian.com/environment/2014/feb/09/global-water-shortages-threat-terror-war/.

Geoff Hiscock. *Earth Wars: The Battle for Global Resources*. New York: Wiley, 2012.

Nomads

Nomads are people who have no fixed residence. Rather, they are members of societies that move from place to place. Many nomads do not live in houses; they live in temporary shelters that are used for only part of the year and in some cases are transported from place to place. Nomadism has been practiced widely historically, but is much less common today in part because organized state governments have pressured nomads to give up their nomadic lifestyles and live in settled

Bedouins have inhabited southwestern Asia for thousands of years. Although the Bedouins were tradiionally nomads, many have given up their nomadic lifestyles and moved to cities and towns such as Petra, Jordan. (lvinst/iStockphoto.com)

communities. Nevertheless, an estimated 35 to 40 million people worldwide continue to practice nomadism. In some countries, nomads continue to make up a significant proportion of the population.

Many nomads are pastoral nomads who raise cattle, camels, sheep, goats, and other livestock. Pastoral nomadism is generally practiced in and near deserts, where the lack of rainfall makes agriculture impossible. Some nomads live in other areas that are unsuitable for agriculture. For example, the Sami (Lapp) people of northern Scandinavia live in a tundra environment in which the growing season is too short to permit farming. Typically, many nomads move with their livestock between places over the course of the year. Some move their flocks to cooler, wetter upland or mountainous areas in the summer and to drier, warmer lowlands in the winter.

Historically, nomads used their animals for subsistence in many ways. Milk and meat from the animals were used as food, whereas their bones and hides were used for clothing and in the construction of temporary shelters. Livestock and animal products were also traded with people living in settled communities in exchange for foodstuffs, tools, weapons, and other goods otherwise unavailable to the nomadic communities. Some nomadic cultures used their knowledge of the inhospitable environments in which they lived to guide pilgrims, merchants, and other travelers across these places. For example, for centuries, Bedouin nomads living in present-day Saudi Arabia used their knowledge of the Arabian desert environment to guide Muslim pilgrims to and from the holy city of Mecca.

Today, many governments discourage nomads from continuing to practice their traditional lifestyles. State authorities often find it easier to administer settled populations, facilitating collection of taxes, provision of services, and conscription of young men into military service. The historic migration routes of many nomadic communities cross international borders. In such cases, state governments have even stronger incentives to discourage or eliminate nomadism.

The Bedouin are a nomadic culture whose traditional lifestyles have been impacted by the modern state system. About 20 million Bedouin people live in North Africa and southwestern Asia, including about 4 million in and near the Arabian and Sinai Peninsulas. Bedouins have been recorded in the Sinai Peninsula region for more than 7,000 years.

The traditional migration routes of the Bedouin living in this region extend across parts of Egypt, Israel, Jordan, and Saudi Arabia. However, the independence of Israel in 1948, followed by ongoing tension and war between Israel and its neighbors, placed sharp limitations on the movement of local Bedouins, who found it difficult to move across now-enforced international boundaries. Many were forced to identify themselves as citizens of one of the countries across which their traditional migration routes had been located.

Historians estimate that about 65,000 Bedouins lived in the Negev Desert region of southern Israel when Israel became independent in 1948. Of these, about 11,000 chose to remain in Israel and become Israeli citizens. The Israeli government pressured their Bedouin citizens to give up their nomadic lifestyles. Many moved to cities or towns and began working in factories or other enterprises for wages. The government encouraged Bedouin migration to urban communities through the construction of housing and provision of services to Bedouin citizens. Today, the Bedouin population of Israel is estimated at about 120,000. Although these Bedouin have full citizenship rights, rates of poverty and unemployment are much higher among the Bedouins relative to Israelis as a whole.

See Also: Agriculture and Population; Egypt; Food Production and Security; Hunting and Gathering; Saudi Arabia

Further Reading

Ghazi Falah. "Israeli State Policy towards Bedouin Sedentarization in the Negev." *Journal of Palestine Studies* 18 (1989): 71–91.

Jibrail S. Jabbur, Suhayl J. Jabbur, and Lawrence I. Conrad. *The Bedouins and the Desert: Aspects of Nomadic Life in the Arab East*. Albany: State University of New York Press, 1995.

Nikolay N. Kradin. "Nomadism, Evolution, and World-Systems: Pastoral Societies in Theories of Historical Development." *Journal of World-System Research* 8 (2002): 368–88.

One-Child Policy

The one-child policy was an initiative imposed by the government of China to limit crude birth rates and total fertility rates by limiting families to having only one child. In large part because of this policy, China's total fertility rate dropped from about 2.6 in 1980, when the policy was implemented, to about 1.6 in 2008 to about 1.4 today. In other words, China's total fertility rate is now below replacement-level fertility. The policy also caused a decline in China's rate of natural increase. Between 2000 and 2010, China's total population increased by about 75 million, with a rate of natural increase of about 0.5 percent per year. Thus the policy has been successful in reducing China's population growth. However, the one-child policy has been highly controversial since its inception and it has had many important ramifications for Chinese society ever since.

The one-child policy represented a reversal of traditional Chinese policy that encouraged high levels of fertility. However, by the 1970s many Chinese officials came around to the view that continued population increases would jeopardize China's efforts to become an economic power. In 1979, the government formally

Concerned about its rapid population growth, in the 1980s China instituted its controversial one-child policy in which most families were restricted to having only one child. Although birth rates in China declined, implementation of the policy has resulted in a considerable imbalance in the number of boys and girls given the tradtional culture preference in East Asia for sons over daughters. (Peter Charlesworth/LightRocket/Getty Images)

developed and imposed what it called the Family Planning Policy. The policy was implemented the following year. It required Han Chinese people, who comprise more than 90 percent of the country's population, to limit their fertility to a single child per couple. Uighurs, Tibetans, and other ethnic minorities were and continue to be exempt from the policy. Under terms of the policy, couples who have a second child without formal government permission can be fined as much as thousands of U.S. dollars. There have been numerous reports of forced sterilization or forced abortions performed on women who become pregnant for a second time. The policy is enforced strongly in most Chinese cities, but tends not to be enforced as rigidly in rural areas of China. Over the years, the government has granted many types of exceptions to the policy. For example, in 2008 a severe earthquake measuring 8.0 on the Richter scale struck the Chinese province of Sichuan, resulting in more than 70,000 fatalities, including thousands of children. Parents who had lost their only child in this disaster or other natural disasters were then permitted to have another child.

The Chinese government has argued that its one-child policy is beneficial to the Chinese people. A report published by the government in 1995 stated,

> China's reform and opening to the outside world as well as its economic development have created a favourable socioeconomic environment for family planning, while the achievements of family planning have in turn created a favourable population environment for the continuous development of the economy, the improvement of the people's living standards as well as the overall progress of society. . . . In vigorously promoting family planning, China strives to make the speed of population growth much lower than the speed of growth in the gross national product, thus gradually raising the per-capita level. Apart from the reform and opening to the outside world, family planning has been a factor for the sustained economic development of China and the steady improvement of its people's living standards over the past ten years and more.

The controversial policy has had several demographic impacts. Among these is gender imbalance in the population. In Chinese culture, there is a strong preference for sons to pass on the family name and inherit property. Given the traditional East Asian preference for sons, there is considerable evidence of abortion of female fetuses and infanticide of female babies. Many baby Chinese girls are given up for international adoption. Well over 90 percent of Chinese children adopted by American parents are girls. In response to this concern, China's government began to allow families whose first child was a girl to have a second child.

Despite this change, the human sex ratio of China increased. By 2010, it was estimated that China's population contained about 119 males for every 100 females. This imbalance is especially prevalent among children and young adults who were born after the policy was implemented. As evidence of abortion of female fetuses, the human sex ratio of newborn infants has remained at about 120 boys for every 100 girls since the early 1990s.

Strict adherence to the policy would also eliminate extended families. An only child of two only children will have no aunts, uncles, or cousins. In some parts of China, parents who are themselves only children are allowed to have more than one child. In the long run, however, a smaller younger generation may be responsible for supporting larger older generations. The term "4-2-1" has been used in China to describe this responsibility. Another concern associated with the policy has been an upsurge in kidnapping young Chinese boys in urban areas. The kidnapped boys are stolen from their parents and sold to parents in other areas of China who are desperate for male heirs.

The one-child policy has remained highly controversial, both within and outside China. Agencies and officials of the government of the United States have been especially critical of the policy. In 2004, Assistant Secretary of State Arthur Dewey testified before a House of Representatives committee that the United States government regarded the policy as violating human rights. Dewey called attention in particular to evidence of forced abortion and sterilization, as well as sex-selective abortion and abandonment of infant girls. (See the text of this statement elsewhere in this encyclopedia and at http://2001-2009.state.gov/g/prm/rls/39823.htm.) In 2008, the United States Congressional-Executive Committee on China, a bipartisan committee, prepared a statement that also condemned coercive measures associated with the one-child policy. (See the text of this statement elsewhere in this encyclopedia.)

Some Chinese government officials believe that the population of China today contains about 300 to 400 million fewer people than might have been the case without the policy. China's total fertility rate has dropped to about 1.4, or well under replacement-level fertility. However, some observers have argued that the total fertility rate might have dropped below replacement level anyway as a result of demographic transition, regardless of the policy and its social and gender implications. Human rights activists in the United States and elsewhere continue to call attention to forced abortion, forced sterilization, and infanticide associated with strict adherence to the policy. In part because of these considerations, and in part because wealthier Chinese people in particular can obtain exceptions to the policy, some experts predict that China will abandon the one-child policy in the foreseeable future.

See Also: China; Crude Birth Rate; Demographic Transition Model; Gender and Population; Human Sex Ratio; Rate of Natural Increase; Replacement-Level Fertility

Further Reading

Congressional-Executive Committee on China. "2008 Annual Report," 2008. http://www
.cecc.gov/publications/annual-reports/2008-annual-report.

Therese Hesketh, Li Lu, and Zhu Wei Xing. "The Effects of China's One-Child Family Policy
after 25 Years." *New England Journal of Medicine* 353 (2005): 1171–76.

Information Office of the State Council of the People's Republic of China. "Family Planning
in China," 1995. http://www.china.org.cn/e-white/familyplanning/13-3.htm (in English).

Jonathan Kaiman. "Time Running Out on China's One-Child Policy after Three Decades."
January 31, 2014. http://www.theguardian.com/world/2014/jan/31/time-running-out
-china-one-child-policy-exemptions.

Overpopulation

Are there too many people in the world today? Can we expect that there will be too
many in the foreseeable future? Those who pose and consider these questions are
asking questions about overpopulation, or populations too large to support with
sustainability.

Demographers and scientists who examine the question of overpopulation do so
in the context of carrying capacity. The carrying capacity of a given environment is
the maximum number of organisms that can be sustained in that environment.
This concept applies to animals as well as people. For example, what is the maximum number of cattle that can thrive on a pasture of a given size? The tragedy of
the commons model uses this carrying capacity as a metaphor, illustrating the possibility that individual decisions to bring more cattle onto the pasture will lead
eventually to the cattle population's exceeding the pasture's carrying capacity and
causing the cattle to starve. In other words, a question of whether there are too
many people in a given environment, or worldwide, becomes a question as to
whether the environment can support that number of people without exceeding its
carrying capacity, at present or in the future.

As indicated elsewhere in this volume, information needed to consider questions of overpopulation is generally accessible and is at least reasonably accurate.
Most countries conduct regular censuses or counts of their populations. This information is used to calculate crude birth rates, crude death rates, and rates of natural
increase. From this information, it is possible to make predictions or projections
about the future of a population. Such predictions can be made at all geographic
scales from the very local, such as a city, to the global scale. On the basis of
this information, it is known that the world's population (as of 2014) is about
7.2 billion and that it is increasing by between 120 and 150 million every year. In
other words, the total number of humans alive on the earth is rising worldwide by

about 2 percent annually. Conceptualized in terms of carrying capacity, the question becomes whether the earth can sustain this steadily increasing number of people. At what point can the necessarily finite natural resources of the earth no longer sustain the world's population?

Over the course of history, there have been many cases in which specific places became overpopulated. As a result, populations of these places declined suddenly and rapidly, suggesting that local carrying capacities had been exceeded. For example, the ancient Classic Mayan civilization dominated the Yucatan region of present-day southeastern Mexico, along with neighboring areas of what is today Guatemala and Belize, for hundreds of years beginning about 200 CE. Around 900 CE, however, the Classic Mayan civilization suddenly declined. Populations dropped quickly, although millions of people descended from the Mayas of more than 1,000 years ago still live in the region. Anthropologists and archaeologists do not know what caused the decline in the Mayan population. However, many speculate that the environment's carrying capacity had been exceeded. Long-run climate change, drought, and/or natural disasters may have affected the carrying capacity of the region, with catastrophic impacts on the Mayan population.

The Mayan civilization and others that suffered rapid population declines during ancient or medieval times lived in relative isolation. Unlike societies today, these populations did not have the technology to increase their environment's carrying capacities. Nor did they have the opportunity to trade with other societies in order to obtain food and other supplies necessary for sustenance. Today, of course, people have far more ability to increase carrying capacity. For example, global food production continues to increase at a rate faster than world population growth in part because of the Green Revolution. Modern transportation technology allows for rapid transportation of food needed to alleviate the possibility of famine. In fact, most famines today are the result of political and economic conflicts rather than the result of natural causes such as floods, droughts, and other disasters. In short, globalization has had the effect of increasing the earth's carrying capacity enormously.

Thus, a key point in the debate over whether the world is becoming overpopulated is the role of technology in increasing carrying capacities, locally and globally. Can we rely on technology to continue to support larger and larger numbers of people? This question has been an ongoing subject of debate since the late 18th century, when Thomas Malthus postulated that populations would increase at a much faster rate than would agricultural and industrial productivity. Hence, Malthus believed that overpopulation was inevitable unless efforts were made to halt or slow population growth. Today, of course, the earth supports far more people than in Malthus's day, in large part because of agricultural, industrial, and medical technologies.

Of course, increased global populations have had many environmental impacts, which in turn affect the number of people that can be sustained at a given time. For example, it is well established that human activity is contributing to global climate change. Continued global warming may have long-run negative impacts on the earth's ability to support its population, given the possibilities that sea levels will rise and that warmer, drier weather will no longer allow for productive agriculture in various parts of the world. Many doubt that these impacts of environmental change can be influenced by technology sufficiently to allow for continuing increase in carrying capacity. And, although technologies have allowed for the creation and use of more and more natural resources, the natural resource base of the earth is necessarily limited and finite.

Demographers have widely divergent opinions as to the long-run carrying capacity of the world. Some believe that we have already exceeded carrying capacity, suggesting that the earth can reliably support only as few as 4 or 5 billion people. Others suggest that the carrying capacity may be much larger, and because of continued technological advances the planet could sustain as many as 10 to 15 billion people. Those who argue that the earth's environment has not reached carrying capacity are generally more confident that technology can continue to develop in such a way as to support larger and larger numbers of people. Julian Simon and others saw human ingenuity, coupled with technology, as an opportunity to provide the means to support higher populations.

Still others suggest that the question of overpopulation should not be addressed solely in terms of relationships between the number of people on the planet and the ability of the earth's environment to sustain that population. Rather, some would argue that these questions need to be addressed in terms of overconsumption. On this view, questions of whether carrying capacities have been exceeded are related to questions as to whether individuals and societies consume too many resources. Those supporting this view argue that the effects of increasing numbers of people on the environment can be mitigated by decreasing individual as well as societal consumption of food, energy, and natural resources. Doing so could reduce the rate of global climate change and could curtail short-run and long-run environmental degradation. Nevertheless, questions about whether the world has become overpopulated, or will become overpopulated in the foreseeable future, continue to dominate discussion of population policies and their impacts on societies and economies throughout the world.

See Also: Carrying Capacity; Climate Change and Population; Green Revolution; History of World Population; Malthus, Thomas; Natural Resources and Population; Tragedy of the Commons

Further Reading

Lester R. Brown. *World on the Edge: How to Prevent Environmental and Economic Collapse.* New York: Norton, 2011.

Joel E. Cohen. *How Many People Can the Earth Support?* New York: W. W. Norton, 1996.

Erle C. Ellis. "Overpopulation Is Not the Problem." *New York Times*, September 13, 2013. http://www.nytimes.com/2013/09/14/opinion/overpopulation-is-not-the-problem.html?_r=0.

Physiological Density

Physiological density is the number of people per unit area of *arable* land in a given place. Arable land is land that is under cultivation, or has the potential to support cultivation. Thus physiological density differs from population density, which is the number of people per unit area of all land in that place.

About 11 percent of the world's land surface is considered arable. Other land areas are too dry, too cold, too steep, or otherwise unsuitable for cultivation. However, the percentage of land that is arable varies considerably between countries. In Bangladesh, Denmark, Moldova, and Ukraine, more than half the land surface is arable. Of course, not all arable lands are actually used for agriculture. Metropolitan areas such as Dhaka, Copenhagen, and Chicago are located on land that could be cultivated but is no longer farmed because of ongoing urbanization. In other countries, only a small percentage of land is arable. In Colombia, Egypt, Libya, Mongolia, Norway, Peru, and Saudi Arabia, less than 3 percent of the land surface in each country is arable.

In countries such as these, physiological density is much greater than population density. This divergence is illustrated by Egypt. The only arable land in Egypt is located in the valley of the Nile River, and in a few oases scattered throughout the country. The rest of Egypt is located in the Sahara Desert, is unsuitable for agriculture, lacks water, and is generally uninhabited. Overall, only about 3 percent of Egypt's land is arable. Thus the physiological density of Egypt is more than 30 times its actual population density. Egypt has a population of more than 80 million in a land area of more than 380,000 square miles. Its population density is slightly more than 200 per square mile. However, its physiological density is more than 6,700 per square mile.

The difference between population density and physiological density is reflected in the distribution of population throughout Egypt. More than 90 percent of Egypt's people live in the densely populated valley of the Nile, with 20 percent in the metropolitan area of Cairo alone. Because Egypt's population is so concentrated on only a small percentage of its land, physiological density is a more effective measure of the degree to which Egypt has become increasingly crowded.

Although physiological density is often a better measure of population pressure than is basic population density, the concept can be misleading given differences between countries in the quality and productivity of their arable lands. Two countries might have the same physiological density, but one could support a larger population than the other because its lands are of better agricultural quality and/or because they are farmed more effectively or intensively. Nevertheless, physiological density is a good measure of how many people can be supported in a given area. If the physiological density of a place is high, as in the case of Egypt, the ability of that place to provide food to support additional people is limited. However, a place with a relatively low physiological density has more potential to produce food that could support a larger population.

See Also: Agriculture and Population; Climate Change and Population; Egypt; Food Production and Security; Population Density

Further Reading

Mona Khalifa, Julie DaVanzo, and David M. Adamson. "Population Growth in Egypt—A Continuing Policy Challenge." RAND Corporation, 2000. http://www.rand.org/pubs/iss ue_papers/IP183/index2.html.

Nationmaster.com. *Geographic Statistics: Arable Land (Most Recent) by Country*, 2012. www .nationmaster.com/graph/geo_lan_use_ara_lan-geography-land-use-arable.

Population Association of America

The Population Association of America (PAA) is a scholarly organization devoted to research on demography and population-related issues. Its members include researchers and scholars from a wide variety of academic disciplines and in government service.

The PAA was founded in 1930 through the efforts of Henry Pratt Fairchild (1880–1956), who was a professor of sociology at New York University. At that time, Fairchild was the president of the American Eugenics Society. The well-known birth control and eugenics advocate Margaret Sanger participated in the initial meetings that led to the organization of the PAA. Fairchild was a friend of Sanger, but his colleagues insisted that Sanger should not be invited to serve on the board of directors of the newly formed organization on the grounds that she was an activist rather than a researcher. Fairchild became the PAA's first president. In 1936, the PAA established its headquarters at Princeton University under the sponsorship of the nonprofit Milbank Memorial Fund. The PAA has maintained its headquarters at Princeton ever since. During World War II, it collaborated with the League of Nations to initiate studies on potential postwar demographic planning for war-torn countries of Europe and elsewhere.

The PAA publishes the scholarly journal *Demography* and sponsors annual professional meetings at which population-related research is presented and discussed. Currently, PAA has about 3,000 members.

See Also: American Eugenics Society; Population Reference Bureau; Sanger, Margaret

Further Reading

David Lam. "How the World Survived the Population Bomb: Lessons from 50 Years of Extraordinary Demographic History." *Demography* 48 (2011): 1231–62.

Population Association of America Web Site. http://www.populationassociation.org/.

Population Connection

Population Connection is a nonprofit organization based in the United States that advocates the stabilization of world population. According to its mission statement, "Overpopulation threatens the quality of life for people everywhere. Population Connection is the national grassroots population organization that educates young people and advocates progressive action to stabilize world population at a level that can be sustained by Earth's resources."

Population Connection was founded as Zero Population Growth in 1968. Its leaders were inspired by Paul Ehrlich's book *The Population Bomb*. Ehrlich was one of the founders of Zero Population Growth, whose goal was to educate people on the impacts of population growth and to persuade people to have fewer children. The organization's original name was drawn from the idea that population would stabilize when crude birth rates were reduced to the level of crude death rates—in other words, to a point at which the rate of natural increase dropped to zero. As awareness of environmental degradation became more widespread in the early 1970s, Zero Population Growth worked to educate the public on linkages between overpopulation and environmental quality. The organization's name was changed to Population Connection in 2002.

Population Connection's activities focus on advocacy and education. It is active in promoting support for policies that it views as having potential to reduce global population growth. These policies include support for family planning and birth control. It publishes the magazine *Population Connection* and also rates members of the U.S. Congress on their voting records on bills associated with population issues. Population Connection also prepares educational materials that can be used by educators wishing to teach population-related concepts to their students.

See Also: Crude Birth Rate; Crude Death Rate; Ehrlich, Paul; Population Association of America; Rate of Natural Increase

Further Reading

Paul R. Ehrlich. *The Population Bomb*. Cutchogue, NY: Buccaneer Books, 1968.

Population Connection. "30 Years of Population Growth," 1998. http://www.populationcon nection.org/site/DocServer/1219thirtyyears.pdf?docID=261.

Population Connection Web Site. http://www.populationconnection.org.

Population Density

Population density refers to the number of people living in a particular place per unit area. Normally, population density is expressed as the number of people per square mile or per square kilometer. The population density is determined by dividing the number of people in a particular place by its land area.

In early 2013, the world's population was estimated at about 7.1 billion or 7,100 million. The world's land area is about 58 million square miles. Thus the world's population density is 7,100/58 or about 122 people per square mile. However, the world's 58 million square miles of land include the uninhabited continent of Antarctica. Excluding Antarctica, the world's population density is approximately 135 people per square mile.

The world's population is distributed very unevenly. Many places, including large metropolitan areas, are very densely populated. The most densely populated large areas of the world are in East Asia, including eastern China, Japan, South Korea, and Taiwan; in South Asia, including much of India, Bangladesh, and Pakistan; in Southeast Asia, including parts of Thailand, Vietnam, Singapore, and Indonesia; and in Western Europe, including an area located within a triangle connecting London, Paris, and Berlin. Other areas of the world, including much of Siberia, the interior of Australia, and the Sahara Desert, are virtually uninhabited. Places lacking agricultural potential because of desert climates, recurrent drought, cold weather, or other reasons tend to have very sparse populations.

Comparing different countries throughout the world according to national censuses between 2008 and 2012, the highest population densities were found in Monaco (48,003 people per square mile), Singapore (18,513), Bahrain (4,263), Malta (3,424), and Maldives (2,686). All of these are very small countries by land area and only Singapore and Bahrain have populations of more than a million. Among the larger countries of the world, those with at least 15 million people, those with the largest population densities were Bangladesh (2,497 people per square mile), Taiwan (1,676), South Korea (1,261), the Netherlands (1,046), India

(953), Japan (873), Sri Lanka (798), the Philippines (795), Vietnam (671), and the United Kingdom (660). All of these countries are located within the large population clusters of South Asia, East Asia, Southeast Asia, or Western Europe.

Other countries have large land areas but sparse populations. The least densely populated fully independent countries were Mongolia (1.9 people per square mile), Namibia (6.7), Australia (7.8), Iceland (8.0), Suriname (8.3), Mauritania (8.3), Botswana (8.8), Canada (9.1), Guyana (9.1), and Libya (9.3). All of these countries contain large areas of virtually uninhabited territory including very cold and inhospitable areas in Iceland and Canada, dense and poorly accessible tropical rainforests in Suriname and Guyana, and large deserts in the others.

The population density of the United States is about 85 people per square mile. However, population densities vary substantially within the United States. The most densely populated area of the United States is the northeast, and in particular the Megalopolis region extending from Boston southwestward through New York, Philadelphia, Baltimore, and Washington. On a state-by-state basis, the highest population densities are found in New Jersey (1,119 per square mile), Rhode Island (1,006), Massachusetts (840), Connecticut (739), and Maryland (596). All of these states are located in the Megalopolis corridor. The lowest population density among the 50 states is found in Alaska, with 1.3 persons per square mile. The next most sparse population densities are found in Wyoming (5.8 persons per square mile), Montana (6.9), North Dakota (9.9), and South Dakota (10.9). In America's highly urbanized society, all of these states stand out as lacking in significant metropolitan populations.

Population density is related to carrying capacity. Demographers attempt to predict the total number of people who can be sustained in a certain place at a given time, although their analyses vary considerably. Such analysis can be carried out at the local, regional, and national or international levels. Although individual demographers may not agree as to whether Earth has reached its carrying capacity of population, most agree that continued population growth will mean eventually that its carrying capacity will be reached eventually and that the quality of life will begin to decline more and more rapidly if populations continue to grow.

See Also: Bangladesh; Carrying Capacity; China; India; Japan; Singapore

Further Reading

M. Shahidul Islam. "Bangladesh's High Population Density: Opportunity amongst Anxiety." *South Asian Soundings*, November 19, 2010. http://blog.nus.edu.sg/southasiansoundings /2010/11/19/bangladesh%E2%80%99s-high-population-density-opportunity-amidst -anxiety/.

United States Central Intelligence Agency. *World Factbook 2012*. Washington, DC: U.S. Government Printing Office, 2012.

Population Pyramid

A population pyramid is a graphic illustration of the structure of a population distributed by age and gender. Population pyramids are bar graphs. Each bar represents the number of people in a certain age group. Usually, the number of males in each age group is shown separately from the number of females in that age group. The bar graphs are positioned such that the number of males in an age group is shown on the left and the number of females in that age group is shown on the right. Thus, a population pyramid is actually a pair of bar graphs positioned such that the male and female age cohorts match up with each other.

The age cohorts in a population can vary in length from 1 year to 10 years or more. Most frequently, however, each age cohort is five years in length. Thus, individual bars represent the number of people aged 0 to 4, the number of people aged 5 to 9, the number of people aged 10 to 14, and so on. The bars are placed on the graph such that the youngest age cohorts are on the bottom and the oldest age cohorts are on the top. In growing populations, there are more people in younger age cohorts than in older age cohorts. Thus the bars for young age cohorts are longer than those for older age cohorts and the pair of graphs resembles a pyramid. On the other hand, in developed countries with relatively low crude birth rates, the population pyramid resembles a bottle in that there are roughly the same number of people in each age cohort except for the elderly.

The shape of a population pyramid illustrates the impacts of total fertility rates and rates of natural increase on populations. In countries in which rates of natural increase are positive, crude birth rates exceed crude death rates. Thus there are many more children than there are older adults, and the bars at the bottom of the graph are much longer than those at the top of the graph. Such is the situation in Niger, Somalia, and other less developed countries that have high crude birth rates and high total fertility rates. On the other hand, a country with a total fertility rate of approximately 2 will have about the same number of people in each of the younger age cohorts. In other words, the number of people aged 0 to 4 will be approximately the same as those between 25 and 29. The bars become shorter as ages increase, as more and more people die after reaching old age. Thus, a population pyramid in a country with replacement-level fertility will be shaped more like a bottle than like a triangle. These countries have reached the fourth stage of demographic transition, such that birth rates have declined to the level of death rates.

In countries whose total fertility rates are considerably lower than two, there are fewer children than there are adults. In such cases, the population pyramid is narrow at the bottom, widens in early adulthood, and narrows again among the elderly. Such is the case in Japan, Singapore, and many other developed countries. The degree to which the population pyramid narrows as ages increase depends on life expectancy. Population pyramids for places such as Japan, with its very high life expectancy, will be higher at the top than will be the case in countries with lower life expectancies.

See Also: Age-Specific Death Rate; Crude Birth Rate; Crude Death Rate; Demographic Transition Model; Life Expectancy; Rate of Natural Increase; Replacement-Level Fertility; Total Fertility Rate

Further Reading

Martin de Wulf. "Population Pyramids of the World from 1950 to 2100" (visualization), 2010. http://populationpyramid.net/.

Population Action International. "World Age Structure 2005." http://populationaction.org/Publications2/Data_and_Maps/Shape_of_Things_to_Come/Summary.php. (Interactive map showing population pyramids by country in 1975, 2005, and projected to 2025.)

Population Reference Bureau

The Population Reference Bureau (PRB) is a nonprofit organization whose purpose is to undertake research on global population trends and to use this information to inform governments and policy-making efforts on policy-related issues. According to its Web site, one of its objectives is to "[build] coalitions and conduct workshops around the world to give our key audiences the tools they need to understand and communicate effectively about population issues." It also "works to ensure that policymakers in developing countries and in the United States rely on sound evidence, rather than anecdotal or outdated information, when creating population, health, and environmental policies." The core themes of the PRB's research include "Aging; Children and Families; Family Planning and Reproductive Health; Gender; Global Health; Inequality and Poverty; Migration and Urbanization; Population and the Environment; and Youth."

The PRB was founded in 1929, and for many years its activities were linked closely with those of the Population Association of America (PAA). However, the PAA has always been a scholarly organization, whereas PRB has played a more activist role centered on the use of information in policy efforts. Thus the PRB conducts workshops for government officials and journalists in order to promote understanding of population-related issues.

The headquarters of the PRB are located in Washington, D.C. Its work is supported by a variety of government agencies, foundations, and nonprofit organizations. It maintains the World Population Clock, which provides a continuously updated estimate of the world's population. The PRB also collects data from government censuses taken throughout the world. It publishes the *World Population*

Data Sheet along with periodic reports of population issues related to its core themes as observed in various countries worldwide.

See Also: Population Association of America

Further Reading

Carl Haub. "How Many People Have Ever Lived on Earth." Population Reference Bureau, 2011. http://www.prb.org/Publications/Articles/2002/HowManyPeopleHaveEverLived onEarth.aspx.

Population Reference Bureau. "2013 World Population Data Sheet." 2013 (published annually). http://www.prb.org/Publications/Datasheets/2013/2013-world-population-data -sheet.aspx.

Population Reference Bureau Web Site. http://www.prb.org.

Primate City

A primate city is a city that is simultaneously the economic center, political capital, and cultural center of the country in which it is located. Tokyo, Mexico City, Bangkok, Manila, Paris, and London are primate cities. Throughout the world, many primate cities are megacities with more than ten million residents in their metropolitan areas.

Most primate cities are much larger in population than other cities in their countries. For example, Bangkok's population in 2010 was nearly 8.3 million, with nearly 15 million in the Bangkok metropolitan area. Thus more than 20 percent of Thailand's people live in the Bangkok metropolitan area. Thailand's second-largest metropolitan area, Chiang Mai, had less than 1 million residents in 2010, with less than 150,000 in the city proper. Similarly, the population of the Paris metropolitan area is about 12 million, as opposed to about 1.5 million in France's second-largest metropolitan area, Marseille.

Many primate cities developed initially as centers for trade and commerce. Thus many of them, including Manila, Jakarta, and Bangkok, are ports. Others are located inland but have easy maritime access. Examples include London and Tokyo.

Not all countries have primate cities. Countries that lack primate cities include the United States, Canada, Germany, Italy, India, Australia, and South Africa. In many of these countries, the absence of a primate city reflects a deliberate decision to separate political and economic power from each other within these countries. For example, the First Congress of the United States, meeting in 1790, made a decision not to locate the capital city of the newly independent country in either of its two largest financial centers, New York and Philadelphia. This decision led to the

Paris is the capital and primate city of France. As with other megacities in the developed countries of the world, Paris is characterized by great ethnic diversity. Tension between immigrants and the native-born French population is evident in and near Paris. (Julian Elliott Photography/Getty Images)

establishment of Washington, D.C., as the capital of the United States. Similarly, Canada decided to locate its capital at Ottawa in part because Ottawa is roughly equidistant between Canada's two major economic centers, Montreal and Toronto. Australia chose to build its capital city at the site of what would become Canberra so that neither of its two largest cities, Sydney and Melbourne, would be able to dominate the country's government and economy.

Most primate cities, especially in less developed countries, are growing very rapidly in population. Because of primate cities' importance to their countries, they tend to be magnets for people who had lived in other parts of these countries. Many primate cities are experiencing significant problems associated with rapid population growth, including traffic congestion, rapidly increasing housing prices, air and water pollution, and burgeoning slums and squatter settlements. In some countries, efforts have been made to decentralize populations and otherwise reduce the size and influence of primate cities relative to other areas. For example, Nigeria moved its capital from Lagos to the new city of Abuja in the 1990s. Indonesia has used its transmigration program to encourage people on the densely populated island of Java to move to other Indonesian islands rather than to Jakarta.

See Also: Bangkok; Jakarta; London; Megacities; Paris; Tokyo

Further Reading

Stanley D. Brunn. *Cities of the World*. Boulder, CO: Rowman and Littlefield, 2003.

Michael Pacione. *Urban Geography: A Global Perspective*. 2nd ed. London: Routledge, 2005.

Push Factors and Pull Factors

Push factors and pull factors are reasons associated with an individual's decisions concerning migration. Push factors are reasons why the potential migrant chooses to leave one place of residence to move elsewhere, and pull factors are reasons why the migrant chooses a particular destination.

Analysis of push factors and pull factors is often based on an assumption that the decision *whether to move* is separated from the decision *where to move*. In reality, of course, these decisions are often made conjointly. This conceptual framework is based on an assumption that the migration decision is made individually, whereas in fact groups of people, and sometimes entire communities, make and act on a migration decision as a group. It is also based on human experience in the contemporary world, not considering the extensive migrations made by humans settling the entire planet over hundreds of thousands of years. However, the conceptual distinction between deciding whether to move and deciding where to move provides a useful context for understanding migration choices. The decision of whether to move involves push factors, and the decision of where to move involves pull factors.

With particular respect to long-distance international migration, push factors often include economic, social, political, cultural, or environmental considerations. In pre-industrial societies, people often moved away from places whose environments were less favorable to sustenance, for example from drought-prone areas to climates better suited to agriculture. Natural disasters can also trigger migration. Today, many people move away from areas characterized by poverty, unemployment, or lack of economic opportunity. For many others, migration is induced by political or religious persecution and/or government efforts to impose undesirable restrictions on individuals' freedom of religion, political expression, or cultural practices.

Major pull factors include economic opportunity as well as political and religious freedom. All of these were important pull factors associated with the migration of millions of people from Europe to North America in the 18th and 19th centuries. In the United States, the availability of vast amounts of free or very cheap land attracted millions of immigrants from Germany, Scandinavia, the Netherlands, and other densely populated and increasingly crowded European countries. Freedom and economic opportunity remain important pull factors today.

Countries including the United States, Australia, Canada, and European nations have long histories of attracting large immigrant populations, and all of these countries are also characterized by long histories of economic opportunity and freedom from persecution. Many of these immigrants moved to places where relatives, friends, and others from the same area of origin were living already, creating channelized migration. In some countries, however, policies of countries receiving large numbers of immigrants have discouraged or impeded immigration. Immigration remains a highly significant political issue in the United States and many European countries.

Push and pull factors apply to all three major types of international migration. International labor migrants are often driven to move by poverty or lack of opportunity in their homelands, and/or move to other places, especially large cities, in search of employment or economic opportunity. Those highly educated people who are part of the brain drain are often motivated to move by political and religious oppression on the part of autocratic governments, some of which have cracked down on intellectuals, regarding them as threats to their regimes. Highly educated natives of less developed countries are often drawn to more developed destinations by professional opportunity as well as religious and/or political freedom. Refugees are forced to move because of overt political or religious persecution in their home areas.

Analysis of push factors and pull factors presumes that a potential migrant can make choices about whether to move and where to move. Of course, many migrants have little or no choice about where to move. Historically, slaves were often forced to move long distances, in the process being separated from their families. Even today, victims of forced labor and sex trafficking have no opportunity to make decisions concerning where to live. Children usually have little or no say in a migration decision, and especially in developed countries, migration decisions for very elderly people in poor health are often made by family members in consultation with physicians and other health professionals. Nevertheless, analysis of push factors and pull factors is often a useful indicator of the impacts of migration on population change in particular places.

See Also: Brain Drain; Channelized Migration; Gravity Model; Illegal Immigration; International Labor Migration; Ravenstein, Ernst; Refugees

Further Reading

Lawrence A. Brown and Eric G. Moore. "The Inter-Urban Migration Process: A Perspective." *Geografiska Annaler: Series B, Human Geography* 52 (1970): 1–13.

Patrick Manning. *Migration in World History*. New York: Macmillan, 2005.

Julian Wolpert. "Behavioral Aspects of the Decision to Migrate." *Papers in Regional Science* 15 (1965): 159–69.

Rate of Natural Increase

The rate of natural increase is the difference between the crude birth rate and the crude death rate. For example, if a country has a crude birth rate of 21 per 1,000 and a crude death rate of 10 per 1,000, its rate of natural increase will be 11 per 1,000. Generally, rates of natural increase are expressed in percentage terms. In this hypothetical example, the rate of natural increase would be 1.1 percent. Of course, the overall population change in any country is affected also by the volume of in-migration and the volume of out-migration. But with no migration, the country's population would be growing at 1.1 percent per year.

The definition of the rate of natural increase implies that if the crude birth rate and the crude death rate are equal, then the rate of natural increase will be zero. If the crude death rate is higher than the crude birth rate, then the rate of natural increase will be negative. Such is the case in several European countries and in Japan today.

Worldwide, the rate of natural increase is the difference between the crude birth rate of 19.1 per 1,000 and the global crude death rate of 8.9 per 1,000. In other words, the rate of natural increase throughout the world is 10.2 per 1,000 or 1.02 percent. This implies that the world's population is growing by slightly over 1 percent, or about 70 million people, each year. However, rates of natural increase vary considerably throughout the world. In 2010, the *CIA World Factbook* estimated that the highest rates of natural increase in the world were found in Niger (3.7% per year), Uganda (3.6%), Ethiopia (3.2%), Zambia (3.2%), Burundi (3.2%), Mali (3.1%), Burkina Faso (3.1%), the Democratic Republic of the Congo (3.1%), Sao Tome and Principe (3.1%), and Madagascar (3.0%). All of these countries are located in Africa and all have very high crude birth rates. Because of poor medical care and inadequate public health, these countries' crude death rates are higher than the worldwide average but are still much lower than their very high birth rates.

The countries with the lowest rates of natural increase in 2010 were Haiti (-0.7%), Ukraine (-0.6%), Russia (-0.5%), Bulgaria (-0.5%), Serbia (-0.5%), Belarus (-0.4%), Latvia (-0.4%), Estonia (-0.3%), Hungary (-0.3%), and Italy (-0.3%). Haiti's low rate of natural increase in 2010 can be explained by the devastating earthquake of January 12, 2010, in which more than 300,000 Haitians lost their lives. The next eight countries are former Soviet satellites or former Eastern bloc countries. During the Cold War, these countries' Communist governments strongly encouraged high birth rates, including providing financial incentives to women who bore more children. Once the Communist governments were overthrown in the late 1980s and early 1990s, these incentives were removed and birth rates declined rapidly. Hence, rates of natural increase rose.

LATVIA'S DECLINING POPULATION

While the world as a whole continues to grow in population at a rate of nearly 2 percent a year, some countries have been losing population. One such country is Latvia, whose population has declined by more than 20 percent since the early 1990s.

Latvia is located on the Baltic Sea, west of Russia. It was absorbed into the Soviet Union in 1940, but regained its independence when the Soviet Union collapsed in 1991.

At the time of independence, Latvia's population was about 2.65 million. However, the population began to decline in the early 1990s, and has decreased steadily ever since to about 2 million people today. Thus its population has been declining at a rate of about 0.4 percent per year since independence. Latvia's decline in population is the result of several factors, including a very low crude birth rate, a low total fertility rate of 1.34, negligible rates of immigration, and substantial out-migration by skilled workers, part of the brain drain, due to high unemployment. Estimates suggest that 80 percent of people leaving Latvia are less than 35 years old. Currently, the government is developing policies intended to slow emigration and increase the birth rate.

Further Reading

France24.com. "Latvia Struggles with 'Demographic Disaster.'" May 22, 2012, http://www.france24.com/en/20120522-latvia-emigration-population-brain-drain-economy/.

Worldwide, 24 countries experienced negative rates of natural increase in 2010. These included 22 European countries, Haiti, and Japan. The rate of natural increase in the United States was estimated at 0.5 percent, about half of the worldwide rate of natural increase and comparable to the rates of natural increase estimated for China and Australia.

See Also: Crude Birth Rate; Crude Death Rate; Demographic Transition Model; Replacement-Level Fertility; Total Fertility Rate

Further Reading

Michael Balter. "100,000 Years of Dramatic Population Changes." *Discover Magazine*, October 18, 2012. http://discovermagazine.com/2012/oct/100-000-years-of-dramatic-population-changes#.UgKhuW0piQE.

United States Central Intelligence Agency. *CIA World Factbook 2010*. Washington, DC: U.S. Government Printing Office, 2010. https://www.cia.gov/library/publications/the-world-factbook/fields/2054.html.

Ravenstein, Ernst

Ernst Georg Ravenstein (1834–1913) was a German-born British geographer and cartographer. Ravenstein is best remembered today for having formulated a theory of migration that became the basis of the contemporary analysis of migration and migration policy.

Ravenstein was born in Frankfurt, Germany. He moved to England in 1852 and later became a naturalized British citizen. Ravenstein spent much of his career working for the British War Office. He was a member of the Royal Geographical Society and the Royal Statistical Society.

During the 1880s, Ravenstein examined internal migration within the United Kingdom using data obtained from the British censuses of 1871 and 1881. Based on his analysis of these data, Ravenstein postulated that a majority of migrants move short distances. He also noted that migration flows between pairs of places are associated with return flows between these places. In other words, a larger flow of migration in one direction generally occurs in conjunction with a larger flow in the other direction. These observations were later quantified in terms of the gravity model, which states that migration flows are related directly to the size of places and related inversely to the distance between them.

Ravenstein also observed rural-to-urban migration by noting that people are most likely to move from rural areas to urban areas rather than vice versa. He also noticed that longer migration flows tended to move to large cities. Thus, urban centers had more pull factors, while rural areas of origin were associated with push factors that encouraged people to leave rural areas for urban centers. Ravenstein also noticed that a disproportionate number of migrants were young adults, and that young adults were more likely to move overseas than were families with children. Because birth rates in rural areas were higher than in cities, he also observed that population increases in cities were associated in large part by in-migration, as opposed to natural increase. All of these observations have been verified empirically using data from many parts of the world ever since. Ravenstein's Laws of Migration, as set forth in his 1885 article, are as follows:

1. Most migrants move only a short distance.
2. There is a process of absorption, whereby people immediately surrounding a rapidly growing town move into it and the gaps they leave are filled by migrants from more distant areas, and so on until the attractive force (pull factors) is spent.
3. There is a process of dispersion, which is the inverse of absorption.
4. Each migration flow produces a compensating counter-flow.
5. Long-distance migrants go to one of the great centers of commerce and industry.

6. Natives of towns are less migratory than those from rural areas.
7. Females are more migratory than males.
8. Economic factors are the main cause of migration.

See Also: Gravity Model; Migration; Push Factors and Pull Factors

Further Reading

Ernst G. Ravenstein. "The Laws of Migration." *Journal of the Statistical Society of London* 48 (1885): 167–235.

Waldo Tobler. "Migration: Ravenstein, Thornthwaite, and Beyond." *Urban Geography* 16 (1995): 327–43.

Refugees

Refugees are persons who are forced to migrate to a different country in light of religious and/or political persecution. Most refugees come from less developed countries. Although many come to the United States and other developed countries, most move to countries close to their original homelands. Both the departure and arrival of refugees have had significant impacts on the populations of many countries.

In 1950, the United Nations established the United Nations High Commissioner for Refugees (UNHCR). The original intent of the UNHCR was to aid refugees in Europe who had been displaced during World War II. In 1951, UNHCR defined a refugee as

> a person who is outside his/her country of nationality or habitual residence; has a well-founded fear of persecution because of his/her race, religion, nationality, membership in a particular social group or political opinion; and is unable or unwilling to avail himself/herself of the protection of that country, or to return there, for fear of persecution.

This definition originally applied to people who had become refugees during World War II. In 1967, the United Nations extended this definition to apply to refugees throughout the world.

The Office of the United Nations High Commissioner for Refugees collects and distributes data on the origins and destinations of refugees throughout the world. These data provide a broad picture of refugee flows worldwide. The majority of refugees are victims of religious and political persecution in war-torn countries. In 2006, the UNHCR counted about 9.9 million refugees throughout the world. At

In 2014, rebels associated with the Islamic State of Iraq and Syria (ISIS) seized control of portions of these countries. Thousands of the ISIS regimes opponents have been tortured and/or murdered. Kurds in cities such as Mosul, shown here, live in fear of ISIS brutality and seek safety in refugee camps such as this one. (AP Photo/Sebastian Backhaus/NurPhsoto/Sipa)

that time, Afghanistan, Iraq, Burma (Myanmar), Sudan, and Palestine were the countries of origin of the largest numbers of refugees.

At the end of 2012, the estimated number of refugees worldwide had increased to 15.4 million who had yet to be resettled. The total number of refugees, including those who have been resettled in other countries, is estimated now at over 45 million people As in 2006, more refugees came from Afghanistan than from any other country, followed by Somalia and Iraq. Syria, which had generated only a negligible number of refugees in 2006, had jumped to fourth place in light of the outbreak of civil war in that country in 2012. Other countries with the largest numbers of unresettled refugees in 2012 were Sudan, the Democratic Republic of the Congo, Myanmar, Colombia, Vietnam, and Eritrea. The plight of these large and increasing numbers of refugees throughout the world has been recognized by the United Nations via the establishment and celebration of World Refugee Day on December 18 of each year.

Some refugees move to the United States and countries in the European Union. However, the large majority of refugees move to nearby countries. Many lack the resources to travel longer distances. In 2012, Pakistan hosted the largest number of refugees, followed by Iran. Most of these persons were refugees from neighboring

Afghanistan. Kenya, Ethiopia, Chad, and Jordan have also hosted large numbers of refugees. The main source countries of refugees moving into these countries were Somalia, Eritrea and Somalia, Sudan, and Sudan respectively. Many of these countries hosting refugees are themselves poor and lack the resources and infrastructure to provide for their refugee populations. Thus many refugees live in refugee camps, where conditions can be squalid; they may lack food, water, and basic services. Among the developed countries, Germany hosts the most refugees. The United States has granted refugee status to about 2.6 million refugees since 1980, although the number of refugees per year has dropped steadily. In 2012, about 27,000 refugees entered the United States.

REFUGEE ADMISSION TO THE UNITED STATES

Most refugees throughout the world move to neighboring countries. However, many are resettled in the United States and other developed countries.

Currently, U.S. law allows for the admission of 70,000 to 80,000 refugees per year, with quotas determined on a regional basis on the basis of historical and contemporary circumstances that are associated with political and religious persecution. In 2012, more than half of these refugees arrived from the Middle East or from South Asia, including Iran, Pakistan, Afghanistan, and Iraq, with the latter two affected by long-lasting civil wars. About 18,000 Southeast Asian refugees were admitted, with the majority coming from Myanmar. In Africa, the leading sources of refugees were Somalia, Eritrea, and the Democratic Republic of the Congo. Thus the leading sources of refugees worldwide were less developed countries affected by war and violence, continuing a long-standing trend. In 2012, the U.S. government allocated more than $750 million to support the resettlement of these refugees.

Further Reading

Rozanne Larsen. "U.S. Refugee Admissions and Resettlement Policy." journalistsresou rce.org, April 2, 2012. http://journalistsresource.org/studies/government/immigrat ion/us-refugee-admissions-resettlement-policy#.

Some refugees seek political asylum in other countries. A person seeking political asylum is seeking the right to be recognized as a refugee and to receive legal protection and material assistance. During the first decade of the 21st century, about half of these people who sought political asylum did so in one of six countries: France, the United Kingdom, Germany, the United States, Switzerland, and Canada.

The term "refugee" is now being applied to people who may be subject to displacement because of climatic and environmental change. These people have been termed environmental refugees or climate refugees. For example, residents of low-lying island countries risk the possibility that their homelands will be inundated by rising sea levels. The Maldives in the Indian Ocean and Kiribati in the Pacific Ocean are countries that suffer from this threat. In other countries, people are expected to be displaced because of flooding and/or drought. For example, ongoing drought in Niger and other countries in the Sahel region of Africa are being forced to leave because their drought-prone lands can no longer support agriculture and food production.

See Also: Democratic Republic of the Congo; Environmental Refugees; Migration; United Nations High Commissioner for Refugees; World Refugee Day

Further Reading

Alexander Betts. *Forced Migration and Global Politics*. London: Wiley-Blackwell, 2009.

United Nations High Commission for Refugees. *State of the World's Refugees*. New York: Oxford University Press, 2012.

United Nations High Commission for Refugees. "UNHCR Population Statistics," 2013. http://popstats.unhcr.org/?_ga=1.81994704.796117561.1388072212.

Remittances

Remittances are transfers of money from migrants to relatives and friends in their native countries. Usually, remittances come from people who have moved from less developed countries to developed countries to obtain employment and send some of their earnings to relatives and friends in their countries of origin. In many parts of the world, remittances provide a significant source of income and development capital. In some countries, remittances represent more than a quarter of their entire gross domestic products.

Remittances are increasing dramatically, in part because of the reduced cost and greater security of transferring money over long distances. The overall volume of remittance income throughout the world has been estimated at more than $400 billion per year. Most of this income is transferred to less developed countries. In Africa, the largest recipient of remittance income in 2010 was Nigeria, which received about $10 billion in remittance income. Other African countries with more than $1 billion in remittance income were Sudan ($3.2 billion), Kenya ($1.8 billion), Senegal ($1.2 billion), and South Africa ($1.0 billion). Thus Nigeria's remittance income is nearly $60 per capita per year, with $86 per capita in much smaller Senegal. Per capita remittance income is even greater in Latin America, given its proximity to the United States. For example, El Salvador has a population of about 8.5 million, many of whom live and work abroad. Its remittance income has been estimated at $3.4 billion, or about $400 per capita per year.

REMITTANCES TO EL SALVADOR

The economy of the Central American country of El Salvador has been affected considerably by remittance income. About 8.5 million people live in El Salvador. However, as many as 3 million Salvadorians live and work abroad, including more than 1 million in the United States. Most can be classified as international labor migrants. Many of these persons left El Salvador during and after a civil war in the 1980s while others emigrated for economic reasons. A recent study estimated remittances to El Salvador at about $2.8 billion U.S. dollars per year (or nearly $1,000 per migrant per year). This figure represented about 13 percent of El Salvador's total gross domestic product, and about 22 percent of Salvadorian households received remittance income. Thus remittances are an important source not only of income, but also of potential development capital. An ongoing challenge for El Salvador's government is to plan how to use this remittance income productively as an agent of sustainable economic development.

Further Reading

Jacinta Escudos. "El Salvador Depending on Remittances for Its Economic Survival." futurechallenges.org, July 1, 2011. https://futurechallenges.org/local/el-salvador -depending-on-remittances-for-its-economic-survival/.

Although remittances represent very important sources of income in many less developed countries, some critics have pointed out that reliance on remittance income can stifle local efforts to promote economic development. As well, dependence on remittance income can make the receiving country highly vulnerable to changes in the global economy. Remittances from the United States and the European Union to people in less developed countries have declined in conjunction with downturns in the world economy. For example, in 2008, the Inter-American Development Bank conducted a survey of Latin American immigrants living in the United States. The survey indicated that only half of Latin American immigrants to the United States remitted money regularly to their native countries in 2008 after the U.S. economy went into a recession, whereas 74 percent did so in 2006. The overall amount of money remitted to Latin America increased from $15 billion in 2001 to $45 billion in 2006, but between 2006 and 2008, the overall amount of money remitted stayed the same.

See Also: Channelized Migration; International Labor Migration; Migration; Push Factors and Pull Factors; Rural to Urban Migration

Further Reading

Adolfo Barajas, Ralph Chami, Connel Fullenkamp, Michael Gapin, and Peter Montiel. "Do Workers' Remittances Promote Economic Growth?" IMF Working Paper WP/09/153, 2013. http://www.iadb.org/intal/intalcdi/pe/2009/03935.pdf.

Jacinta Escudos. "El Salvador Depending on Remittances for Its Economic Survival." *Future Challenges*, July 1, 2011. http://futurechallenges.org/local/el-salvador-depending-on-remittances-for-its-economic-survival/.

Replacement-Level Fertility

Replacement-level fertility is the level of fertility associated with maintaining a population over time. Over the long run, replacement-level fertility implies one birth for each death. Replacement-level fertility also implies a rate of natural increase of zero. In other words, under replacement-level fertility the crude birth rate and the crude death rate are equal to each other.

Replacement-level fertility is associated with a total fertility rate of slightly higher than two children per woman over the course of her lifetime. If each woman were to have two children, then there will be one birth for every death. Because some girls do not survive to adulthood and other women are unable to or choose not to have children, however, the total fertility rate must be slightly higher than two to ensure that the population replaces itself over the long run.

Demographers have estimated that on a global scale, replacement-level fertility implies a total fertility rate of about 2.1, again taking into account that some women never have children. However, replacement-level fertility in less developed countries is higher because of higher rates of mortality among children and young adults of childbearing age. The total fertility rate worldwide is about 2.52. Thus births continue to outnumber deaths and the world's population is expected to continue to increase during the foreseeable future.

See Also: Crude Birth Rate; Crude Death Rate; Demographic Transition Model; Rate of Natural Increase; Total Fertility Rate

Further Reading

Thomas J. Espenshade, Juan Carlos Guzman, and Charles F. Westoff. "The Surprising Global Variation in Replacement Fertility." *Population Research and Policy Review* 22 (2003): 575–83.

Tim Searchinger, Craig Hanson, Richard Waite, Brian Lipinski, Sarah Harper, and George Leeson. "Creating a Sustainable Food Future, Installment Three: Achieving Replacement Level Fertility." World Resources Institute, July 2013. http://www.wri.org/publication/achieving-replacement-level-fertility.

Rockefeller, John D.

John D. Rockefeller (1839–1937) was an American industrialist, business executive, and philanthropist. His long-standing interest in population issues helped to encourage him to create the Rockefeller Foundation, whose projects include research and analysis of population-related questions.

Rockefeller was born in Richford, New York. He spent his childhood in upstate New York and then in Cleveland, Ohio, where he became a bookkeeper. In the late 1860s, he helped to found the Standard Oil Company, which soon dominated the oil-refining industry in Cleveland. Standard Oil soon expanded and bought out most of its competitors. By 1880, Standard Oil controlled nearly 90 percent of U.S. oil production. The company expanded to control many aspects of the oil industry, including extraction, refining, and distribution. By this time Rockefeller was a millionaire, and by the beginning of the 20th century, he was regarded as one of the world's richest men.

Rockefeller's activities as the dominant figure in the world oil industry, along with actions of other individuals and corporations who controlled major commodity production and distribution, led to "trust-busting" actions by governments to reduce their power. These laws included the creation of the Interstate Commerce Commission in 1887 and the enactment of the Sherman Antitrust Act in 1890. These laws forced Standard Oil and other companies to reduce monopoly power by separating stages of production such as refining and transportation from one another. In 1911, the U.S. Supreme Court ruled that Rockefeller's reconstituted company, Standard Oil of New Jersey, operated in violation of the Sherman Antitrust Act. The Court's ruling forced Standard Oil to break up into several smaller companies, many of which, including ExxonMobil, Chevron, and Pennzoil, remain active today.

Rockefeller retired from the oil business in the early 20th century and turned his interests toward philanthropy, focusing especially on education and health. He was a major benefactor of the University of Chicago and established the Rockefeller Institute for Medical Research, which later became Rockefeller University, in New York.

In 1913, Rockefeller endowed the Rockefeller Foundation, whose mission was to "promote the well-being of mankind throughout the world." Many of the foundation's major projects have involved medical research, health, and population-related issues. The foundation was instrumental in making public health a field of academic study and research, establishing Johns Hopkins and Harvard Schools of Public Health. Research sponsored by the Rockefeller Foundation and the Rockefeller Institute was critical in efforts to eradicate malaria and hookworm.

The foundation was also instrumental in the development of the Green Revolution, promoting increased agricultural production in impoverished and less developed countries. The foundation established the Mexican Agriculture Project, which sponsored the Cooperative Wheat Research Production Program in conjunction with the government of Mexico. The program's staff included Norman Borlaug, who was known subsequently as the "Father of the Green Revolution." However, in its early years, the foundation was also involved in the eugenics movement, including research that was used by the Nazi government of Germany to justify the Holocaust and other forms of genocide.

See Also: American Eugenics Society; Eugenics; Green Revolution

Further Reading

Ron Chernow. *Titan: The Life of John D. Rockefeller, Sr.* New York: Random House, 1998.

David Crary. "The Rockefeller Foundation Reflects on Successes, Controversies 100 Years On." *Time*, May 12, 2013. http://www.huffingtonpost.com/2013/05/13/rockefeller-found ation-100-years_n_3265983.html.

Raymond Fosdick. *The Story of the Rockefeller Foundation*. New York: Transaction Books, 1989.

Rural to Urban Migration

Over the past two centuries, rural to urban migration has had profound impacts on the distribution of population throughout the world. Large-scale rural to urban migration is associated closely with the process of urbanization. Especially in less developed countries, the process has been a major contributor to the explosive population growth of megacities such as Jakarta, Lagos, and Mexico City. Generally, demographers use the term rural to urban migration to refer to migration within countries as opposed to international migration.

As with all types of voluntary migration, rural to urban migration is associated with important push factors and important pull factors. Push factors generally include a lack of economic opportunity in rural areas of origin. In many places, lack of economic opportunity is exacerbated by rapid population growth, which results in a shortage of farmland relative to the population. Local agricultural opportunities may be affected also by environmental degradation, pollution, and desertification. They may also be affected by droughts and natural disasters.

At the same time, cities are powerful magnets for migrants. Perceived economic activities are pull factors that draw many migrants, although the sheer volume of rural to urban migration often reduces the number of available economic opportunities. Often, large cities do not have the resources to provide basic necessities such as shelter, electricity, and running water to rural to urban migrants. Thus many are forced into squatter settlements, most of which are characterized by squalid and overcrowded living conditions. For other migrants, cities represent political freedom and escape from the restrictive cultural strictures of rural areas.

Rural to urban migration also involves major changes in lifestyle as well as location. Migrants lose immediate access to the social and cultural environments and resources of rural areas of origin. Many are forced into anonymity and experience the impersonal social structures of the city, as opposed to more informal, kinship-based social networks of the countryside. It may be difficult for the rural to urban migrant to cope with the diversity of the city, which contains people from a large variety of cultural backgrounds who speak different languages and practice different religions. In order to replicate these informal social structures as much as possible, many rural to urban migrants gravitate to places in which relatives, friends, and former residents of their home communities are already living.

Despite these abrupt changes in lifestyle, many rural to urban migrants remain in close contact with people in their native communities. Many visit relatives in their native rural areas frequently. Others send remittances on a regular basis to people in their home communities. As with international labor migration, large-scale rural to urban migration can result in demographic imbalances in rural areas because the large majority of rural to urban migrants are relatively well-educated and skilled young adults. Thus a disproportionate percentage of people remaining in rural areas are very young, elderly, or disabled people who are unable to contribute to the local economy.

See Also: International Labor Migration; Migration; Remittances; Squatter Settlements

Further Reading

Chukwuedozie K. Ajaero and Patience C. Onokala. "The Effects of Rural-Urban Migration on Rural Communities of Southeastern Nigeria." *International Journal of Population Research*, 2013: 1–10.

Tom Miller. *China's Urban Billion: The Story behind the Biggest Migration in Human History*. London: Zed Books, 2012.

Sachs, Jeffrey

Jeffrey Sachs (1954–) is an American economist who is the Quetelet Professor of Sustainable Development at Columbia University and Director of Columbia's Earth Institute. He has worked extensively on issues involving economic development and environmental sustainability.

Sachs was born in Detroit and earned his BA, MA, and PhD degrees from Harvard University. He joined the economics faculty at Harvard in 1980 and remained at Harvard until 2002, when he assumed his present position at Columbia. He has served as an advisor on economic development to governments in Latin America, Eastern Europe, and Africa. In 2002, he founded the United Nations Millennium Project, whose intent is to promote economic development in less developed countries, including reduction of their infant mortality rates. Since 2006, Sachs has also served as the director of the United Nations' Sustainable Development Solutions Network.

Much of Sachs's work is focused on the possible alleviation of poverty in Africa. Through the Millennium Project, as well as in his academic research, Sachs has promoted local economic development as a means to reduce poverty. He has argued that two keys to promoting development include promoting agricultural production by small landholders and encouraging investment in locally based primary health care in order to reduce the effects of disease on local productivity and initiative. In Sachs's view, the costs of disease far outweigh the costs of investment in preventing disease. For example, he has argued that malaria costs Africa more than $12 billion annually in light of fatalities, medical care, and reduced labor productivity. However, he claims that these costs can be eliminated with investment of less than $3 billion in various prevention efforts.

Sachs has also advanced the argument that agricultural production can be increased with the use of improved technology; thus, his arguments parallel those that had been used historically in support of the Green Revolution in Africa and elsewhere. However, some of Sachs's critics point out that his proposals require large-scale foreign investment, and that countries such as China and India that have made significant economic strides in recent years have done so without dependence on large amounts of aid from developed countries. Other critics argue that Sachs's policy proposals create dependence on developed countries, rather than promoting self-sufficiency.

See Also: Agriculture and Population; China; Green Revolution; India

Further Reading

Jeffrey Sachs. *Common Wealth: Economics for a Crowded Planet*. New York: Penguin, 2008.

Jeffrey Sachs. *The End of Poverty: Economic Possibilities for Our Time*. New York: Penguin, 2005.

Sanger, Margaret

Margaret Higgins Sanger (1879–1966) was a strong advocate for population control and family planning during the early 20th century. She coined the term

Margaret Sanger (1879–1966) was a strong proponent of birth control and family planning. However, she remains a controversial figure today because of her support for eugenics. (Keystone-France/Gamma-Keystone/Getty Images)

"birth control" to describe contraception, and she was the founder of Planned Parenthood.

Sanger was born in Corning, New York, and trained as a nurse in White Plains. Moving to New York, Sanger became active in the radical bohemian movement centered on New York City. She frequently nursed poor women who had undergone multiple pregnancies, often at the expense of their own health. She treated many women who died following self-induced abortions. At that time, sex education for women was virtually unknown and most women had little opportunity to control their fertility.

Sanger's nursing experiences convinced her to devote her efforts to promoting birth control and empowering women to limit their pregnancies. She published several controversial but influential articles and pamphlets advocating birth control. These publications were regarded by many as radical and obscene, and in 1914 she was prosecuted for violating obscenity standards. These charges were dropped, but in 1916, Sanger opened a birth control clinic in New York City at which contraceptive devices were advocated and distributed. Her actions violated a New York State law that forbade contraception, and she was once again arrested and tried. Her conviction was eventually overturned by an appellate judge who ruled that physicians had the right to prescribe contraception to their patients. In 1936, the courts expanded this ruling to allow physicians to obtain contraceptives to distribute to their patients.

In 1921, Sanger founded the American Birth Control League, and she gave numerous speeches and published additional articles in support of birth control and family planning. She founded Planned Parenthood in 1946, and served as its president until 1959. A year before her death in 1966, the U.S. Supreme Court, in *Griswold v. Connecticut* (381 U.S. 479), overturned a Connecticut law prohibiting contraception on the grounds that prohibiting contraception violated a woman's right to privacy. The *Griswold* decision legalized birth control throughout the United States. Sanger was also active in global efforts to promote population control. In 1927, she organized the first World Population Conference in Geneva, Switzerland, to discuss the global problem of overpopulation. She also participated in efforts to create the Population Association of America, but she was denied a seat on the association's board of directors on the ground that she was an activist as opposed to a scholar, as the purpose of the association was to promote scholarly research on population-related concerns.

Sanger's views and actions were highly controversial, both during her lifetime and since her death. She was a supporter of eugenics, and argued for strict limits on immigration and compulsory sterilization of those women considered "unfit" for motherhood. Nevertheless, Sanger is regarded today as a key figure in global efforts to promote contraception and eventually to limit total fertility rates throughout the world.

See Also: American Eugenics Society; Eugenics; Population Association of America

Further Reading

Jean H. Baker. *Margaret Sanger: A Life of Passion.* New York: Macmillan, 2011.

Madeline Gray. *Margaret Sanger: A Biography of the Champion of Birth Control.* New York: Richard Marek Publishers, 1979.

Sex Trafficking

Sex trafficking is the illegal kidnapping and movement of persons for the specific purpose of prostitution and coerced sexual activity on the part of its victims. In that sense, sex trafficking is a form of slavery. Thus victims of sex trafficking are among a larger set of persons who are victims of coerced sexual activity. Over the course of history, many young women have been kidnapped and forced to provide sexual favors for soldiers. Forced marriage, including the kidnapping of women as brides for men elsewhere, is also a form of sex trafficking.

Sex trafficking can occur across international boundaries as well as within countries, although the term is used most frequently to refer to the forced migration of people across international boundaries for sex purposes. A large majority of victims of sex trafficking are girls and women, and it has been estimated that more than a third are less than 18 years of age including children forced into pornography. Because sex trafficking is illegal, it is very difficult to estimate the number of people who are affected by the practice. The United Nations International

Each year, millions of young women and girls are trafficked as sex slaves. Many young girls such as these in the Czech Republic are kidnapped, transported across international boundaries, and forced into prostitution. (Sean Gallup/Staff/Getty Images)

Children's Emergency Fund (UNICEF) estimated that about 2 million persons worldwide had been trafficked and forced involuntarily into the international sex trade. However, other experts regard these estimates as very conservative. Some estimates suggest that as many as 15 to 20 million women and girls are sex slaves, or victims of the sex trade, and the actual number may be even greater.

Sex trafficking occurs throughout the world. In 2006, a United Nations report identified Thailand and Japan as the countries that were the most common destinations for victims of sex trafficking. Other frequent destinations included the United States, Germany, Turkey, Italy, the Netherlands, and Belgium. Many of these victims come from relatively less developed countries, including China, Nigeria, Ukraine, and Belarus. The majority of sex slaves in Thailand come from southwestern China or from the poorer countries of Southeast Asia, including Myanmar, Cambodia, and Laos. India is a frequent destination of children who are victims of sex trafficking, with one report suggesting that there are more than a million child prostitutes in the country. However, it is believed that a large majority of India's child prostitutes come from within India rather than from other countries.

Determining the number of victims of sex trafficking is often difficult because authorities may be prone to underreport its occurrence. Police and other authorities may refuse to prosecute cases of alleged sex trafficking, in some situations because of bribery. Many victims of sex trafficking are kidnapped or abducted. Others are sold into sex slavery by parents and relatives, especially in countries where young girls and women are seen as economic burdens by their families. Victims of sex trafficking suffer from many types of problems. Large numbers of prostitutes are exposed to HIV/AIDS and other sexually transmitted diseases. Victims, especially children, are often subject to physical and psychological abuse, including beatings and other physical punishments if they refuse to work in the sex trade or if they do not bring in enough money to satisfy their owners. Many victims of sex trafficking are transported to distant countries. It is very difficult or impossible for these victims to return home. However, in some cultures those who are able to return home are stigmatized or even ostracized, in part because their experience as sex slaves may make them undesirable to other local residents as potential marriage partners.

Sex trafficking is regarded universally as a violation of human rights. In 2002, the International Criminal Court was established. Its jurisdiction includes four core crimes, including genocide, war crimes, crimes of aggression, and crimes against humanity. In this context, sex trafficking is regarded as a crime against humanity. However, given the prevalence of prostitution worldwide, there is little evidence that this designation or other international efforts to reduce sex trafficking have had a significant impact on its prevalence throughout the world.

See Also: Gender and Population; Slavery

Further Reading

BBC News. "UN Highlights Human Trafficking." March 26, 2007. http://news.bbc.co.uk/2/hi/6497799.stm.

CNN Asia. "Official: More Than 1m Child Prostitutes in India." May 11, 2009. http://www.cnn.com/2009/WORLD/asiapcf/05/11/india.prostitution.children/index.html.

Siddharth Kara. *Sex Trafficking: Inside the Business of Modern Slavery.* New York: Columbia University Press, 2010.

Simon, Julian

Julian L. Simon (1932–1998) was an American economist. Simon is best known for his argument that the quality of life is enhanced, rather than diminished, by increased populations. Thus his arguments challenged Thomas Malthus's view that population is limited by resources.

Simon was born in Newark, New Jersey. He earned a BA degree from Harvard University in 1953 and a PhD in business economics from the University of Chicago in 1961. He was a member of the faculty at the University of Illinois for many years until moving to the University of Maryland, where he taught and did research on population, resources, and related subjects for the remainder of his life.

Simon's theories of population were published in his major book, *The Ultimate Resource*, which was published in 1981. Simon argued that technological development, ingenuity, innovation, and the accumulation of wealth would increase society's resource base. Thus, he argued against Malthus's view that continued population growth would cause resource scarcity and declining economies. Rather, population increases would result in reducing the cost of resources. Reduced resource costs would promote the search for natural resources that had previously been too expensive to extract. Market forces would also promote innovation in order to alleviate temporary shortages of resources.

Simon examined long-run historical trends in resource costs in support of his theory. He noted that the costs of various metals in real dollars had declined steadily over the course of history. In support of his argument, he won a highly publicized bet with fellow economist Paul Ehrlich about the cost of mineral resources over a 10-year period, predicting that the costs of these metals would decline, whereas Ehrlich predicted that the prices would increase. Simon also observed that although the world's population had increased substantially over the course of his lifetime, the average person had more food available and the risk of starvation decreased. Thus his views are consistent with observations about the impacts of the Green Revolution on relationships between food supply and population change.

Although many criticized Simon's views, he has been credited with reopening the debate about the validity of Malthus's ideas by focusing on the relationships between populations, resources, and prosperity. Today, many recognize that human ingenuity and innovation may have increased the carrying capacity of the earth with respect to human populations, although ultimately the quantity of natural resources is inevitably finite.

See Also: Carrying Capacity; Ehrlich, Paul; Malthus, Thomas

Further Reading

Julian L. Simon. *A Life against the Grain: The Autobiography of an Unconventional Economist*. Piscataway, NJ: Transaction Publishers, 2003.

Julian L. Simon. *The Ultimate Resource*. Princeton, NJ: Princeton University Press, 1981.

Slavery

Slavery is the practice of treating humans as property, usually using them as sources of forced labor. Throughout history, the practice of slavery has resulted in the long-distance, usually involuntary movement of millions of people.

Although the slave trade was abolished formally in the developed countries in the nineteenth century, millions of workers continued to be transported over long distances to provide agricultural labor. Some agricultural workers in the late nineteenth century were slaves, while others were blackbirded and were kidnapped or tricked into becoming agricultural laborers on plantations. This engraving of slaves and contract laborers working on a sugar plantation was done in 1882. (traveler1116/iStockphoto.com)

Slavery has been practiced and documented for thousands of years. Anthropologists recognize that slavery became commonplace when societies began to give up hunting and gathering in favor of settled agriculture. Farming supported much larger populations than did hunting and gathering, and thus the amount of labor required to produce steady food supplies increased dramatically. Slaves were captured and forced to work in the fields to produce these needed food supplies. Many ancient societies including the Israelites, Greeks, and Romans recognized slavery as an established institution, with slaves captured and used to perform agricultural labor. Historians have estimated that as many as a quarter of all inhabitants of these and other ancient and medieval societies, including empires in precolonial Africa and Asia, were slaves.

Slaves were obtained in a variety of ways. Frequently, inhabitants of conquered territories or members of conquered tribes were forced into slavery. Some were enemy soldiers captured in battle. Others, especially women and children, were captured after their homelands were captured by enemy combatants. Generally, slaves were regarded as property that could be bought and sold, and their children were also slaves. Although many slaves were forced to work in farming, others were forced into other occupations such as mining and transportation. Many of these occupations involved long hours of hard physical labor, often requiring dirty and dangerous activities. Other slaves, especially women, became part of the practice of sex trafficking.

Slaveholding societies had legal codes involving the practice of slavery. Laws regulated the purchase and sale of slaves. In many societies, it was illegal to help slaves to escape from slavery. Other societies, including Southern states in the pre–Civil War United States, forbade teaching slaves to read and write or assembling in large numbers. These laws were intended to impede slaves' efforts to rebel against their slave status.

Slavery often involved forced migration. Many slaves were transported over long distances, in part in order to make it more difficult for slaves to escape from slavery and return home. The largest and most significant slave trade involved the capture of Africans, who were sold into slavery generally in North America and South America. Slavery was practiced in Africa well before the arrival of Europeans, with local Africans captured and sold into slavery in nearby African empires and across the Sahara Desert into the Middle East. However, the slave trade expanded rapidly after Europeans began to colonize the coast of West Africa. Several major cities of contemporary West Africa, including Lagos and Dakar, were founded originally as slave-trading ports.

The trans-Atlantic slave trade followed European colonization of the Americas during the 16th and 17th centuries. In South America and Mexico, Spanish and Portuguese conquerors sought forced labor to supply themselves with food and minerals to export back to Europe. Originally, local Native Americans were captured and forced into slavery. However, these indigenous people had no immunity to European diseases, and large numbers died from these diseases and/or from overwork and harsh treatment. The Europeans turned to Africa as a source of forced labor, greatly expanding the already flourishing African slave trade.

Although precise figures do not exist, it is estimated that 12 to 15 million Africans were captured and brought to the Americas, with the largest number of these Africans sold into slavery in Brazil. Between 600,000 and 750,000 Africans were brought across the Atlantic to the present-day United States. Descendants of these African slaves form a large percentage of the populations of both countries and several other North and South American countries, notably in the Caribbean, where majorities in Jamaica, Haiti, the Bahamas, Barbados, and other countries are descended from African slaves. About 40 million African Americans, many of whom have slave ancestry, live in the contemporary United States.

Slavery as an institution began to disappear in the 19th century. The Constitution of the United States specified that the importation of slaves into the country would cease 20 years after the Constitution was ratified (that is, in 1808), although slavery itself was not banned in the United States until the end of the Civil War in 1865. Slavery was outlawed in Britain and throughout the British Empire in 1834. After slavery ended in the British Empire and other European colonies, plantation owners and others seeking cheap labor turned to the practice of indenture in order to obtain agricultural workers. Some were kidnapped and sold into slavery, following a practice known as blackbirding. Many other countries throughout the world also abolished slavery in the 19th and 20th centuries. Mauritania was the last country in the world to outlaw slavery, in 2007.

SLAVERY TODAY

Most Americans know about the history of slavery in the United States, but many fail to realize that slavery remains an ongoing problem today in many parts of the world. An Australian-based nonprofit organization known as Walk Free conducted a study of slavery worldwide. In 2013, Walk Free issued a report indicated that nearly 30 million people around the world live as slaves. Modern slavery takes many forms, including forced labor and human trafficking. Many of the world's slaves are women or children, with a large number of female slaves forced into the sex trade. Child labor is commonplace in some countries, with children and teenagers kidnapped and forced to work on farms, on plantations, or in mines.

According to Walk Free, nearly half of the world's contemporary slaves live in India. The highest rate of slavery is found in Mauritania, where some have estimated that as many as 15 to 20 percent of the population consists of slaves, despite the fact that slavery became illegal there in 2007. Many slaves are illiterate or poorly educated, and many are transported long distances. Thus many are unable to return to their home areas or to escape lives of forced labor.

Further Reading

Michael Curtis. "Slavery in the World Today." *The American Thinker*, October 25, 2013. http://www.americanthinker.com/2013/10/slavery_in_the_world_today.html.

Although slavery is illegal throughout the world today, observers have estimated that as many as 25 million people or more worldwide today are slaves. Many contemporary slaves, including women victimized by sex trafficking, continue to be transported forcibly across international boundaries.

See Also: Blackbirding; Convict Transportation; Indentured Servitude; Indigenous Populations; Sex Trafficking

Further Reading

Milton Meltzer. *Slavery: A World History.* Cambridge, MA: Da Capo Press, 1993.

Junius P. Rodriguez. *Slavery in the Modern World: A History of Political, Social, and Economic Oppression.* Santa Barbara, CA: ABC-CLIO, 2011.

Smith, Adam

Adam Smith (1723–1790) was a Scottish economist and philosopher who is regarded as one of the founders of modern economics. Smith is best known for developing his theory of how economic prosperity results from the "invisible hand" of rational self-interest and competition through the market process. However, Smith's ideas also encompassed population changes, and in that sense his work can be linked to that of his near-contemporary Thomas Malthus.

Smith was born in Kirkcaldy in County Fife and was educated at the University of Glasgow and Oxford University. He returned to the University of Glasgow as a professor in 1751, remaining until he resigned to become a tutor and later the Scottish commissioner of customs. He was a founding member of the Royal Society of Edinburgh, which included Scotland's leading intellectuals in science, social science, and the arts.

Smith's most important work, *The Wealth of Nations*, was originally published in 1776. The book sold well and confirmed Smith's reputation as one of Europe's leading intellectuals. Smith argued in *The Wealth of Nations* that while individuals are self-interested, markets allow the interactions of self-interested persons to promote the common good. Thus he argued that society benefits from self-interest, and that it benefits from allowing people to exchange goods and services with one another without being directed by governments or other authorities. Free markets, he argued, promoted the common good by reducing prices whereas monopoly or directives by autocrats caused prices to increase, thus resulting in declining demand and reduced prosperity.

Smith also developed the ideas of economies of scale and division of labor. Economies of scale refer to the fact that the cost of production per unit declines as overall amounts of production increase. The more produced, the less it costs to produce each unit. Economies of scale result in part from the division of labor. With a larger labor force, the production process can be divided in such a way that each worker specializes in one component. Hence factory production is more efficient and cheaper than craftsmanship in which one worker is responsible for producing the entire product.

Smith recognized relationships between economies of scale, division of labor, and population change. Over time, with decreasing prices the size of the market for a given product would increase, creating further economies of scale. This process would intensify with increasing population growth. However, more people would also mean a larger potential labor force. Like Thomas Malthus, Smith believed that population growth rates were controlled by the opportunity of a population to feed itself. As available resources exceeded these limits, populations would increase and wages would also increase. Yet further division of labor and increased economies of scale could reduce employment opportunities, depressing wages and therefore contributing to decreased populations. He recognized that technological change affected these relationships in general, but did not consider the direct impacts of technology on population change itself.

Today, Adam Smith is recognized as the founder of modern economic theory. His views on labor supplies and consumer markets have impacted later analysis of population growth and its relationships to economic change.

See Also: International Labor Migration; Malthus, Thomas

Further Reading

Ian Simpson Ross. *The Life of Adam Smith*. Oxford: Oxford University Press, 2005.

Adam Smith. *An Inquiry into the Nature and Causes of the Wealth of Nations*. Chicago: University of Chicago Press, 1977. Originally published in 1776. (Many other modern editions of this book are available.)

Spanish Flu

The Spanish flu epidemic of influenza, which occurred in 1918 and 1919, was the most deadly disease of the 20th century and possibly the most deadly epidemic in history. As many as half a billion people around the world are believed to have been infected with the disease, and an estimated 30 to 50 million people or nearly 5 percent of the world's population died as a result of the epidemic. In part because modern antibiotics and other treatments had yet to be discovered, the mortality rate from the Spanish flu was unusually high.

The Spanish flu is believed to have been caused by an unusually virulent strain of the H1N1 virus, which also caused a major epidemic of influenza in 2009. The epidemic is believed to have originated in Europe. However, there is no evidence that the disease originated in Spain, despite its name. Rather, early reports of its incidence originated in Spain, which was neutral during World War I, rather than other European countries that were embroiled in the war.

The history of the Spanish flu is intertwined closely with that of World War I. During the war, millions of soldiers fighting for both the Central Powers and the Allies were engaged in trench warfare. They were living in close proximity to one another, often in outdoor trenches, with poor sanitation and often inadequate food. Given Western Europe's cool and damp climate, the soldiers themselves were often cold and wet. Because influenza viruses thrive under cold and wet conditions, the Spanish flu virus spread quickly among these troops. In contrast to most influenza viruses, this particular strain of virus also affected young adults, including soldiers, much more strongly than it affected children or the elderly.

World War I ended with the signing of the armistice on November 11, 1918. After the peace agreement was signed, troops from both sides demobilized and returned to their homes. The disease spread quickly back to the soldiers' home countries. Death tolls have been estimated at more than 250,000 in the United Kingdom and 400,000 in France. Thousands of American troops boarded ships and sailed across the Atlantic Ocean back to the United States, and the disease spread quickly to civilians. Historians believe that about a quarter of the U.S. population contracted the disease, and estimates suggest that at least half a million perished. However, the epidemic also spread to other parts of the world that were not affected directly by the war, including Japan, present-day Indonesia, New Zealand, and some islands in the South Pacific Ocean. Fortunately, although the epidemic spread quickly it also subsided quickly. By 1920, death rates had declined to previous levels.

Over the long run, the Spanish flu epidemic may have spurred research on efforts to cure future flu victims and to promote public health measures to prevent future pandemics. The Spanish flu is believed to have caused more fatalities than the Black Death or the HIV/AIDS epidemic, both of which took place over much longer periods of time.

See Also: Crude Death Rate; Epidemics; France; United Kingdom; United States of America

Further Reading

John M. Barry. *The Great Epidemic: The Epic Story of the Deadliest Plague in History.* New York: Viking Penguin, 2004.

Nancy K. Bristow. *American Pandemic: The Lost Worlds of the 1918 Influenza Epidemic.* New York: Oxford University Press, 2012.

Alfred W. Crosby. *Epidemic and Peace.* Westport, CT: Greenwood Press, 1976.

Squatter Settlements

Squatter settlements are communities that consist of makeshift dwellings that are inhabited by local residents who generally do not have formal legal title to the land on which they live. Most squatter settlements are located in and near megacities and other large cities in less developed countries. The term "squatter" refers to the fact that most residents do not legally own the land upon which their dwellings are located, and hence are living on this property illegally. Squatter settlements are often called "shanty towns," referring to the fact that many residents live in hastily constructed, flimsy houses built from plywood, sheet metal, plastic, and other cheap and locally available building material.

Squatter settlements known as favelas are found in and near large cities throughout Brazil. This favela is located in the city of Salvador da Bahia. (AP Photo/Marcus Brandt/picture-alliance/dpa)

Conditions in squatter settlements are often squalid. Population densities are usually very high. Many squatter settlements lack electricity, running water, sewage treatment, sanitation, or other basic services. Lack of sanitation along with crowded living conditions often causes the rapid transmission of infectious diseases. Residents of squatter settlements have little or no access to public transportation, education, or medical care. Police and fire protection are often lacking, and fires are major hazards in squatter settlements given the very dense housing stock made primarily from highly flammable building materials. Unemployment rates are high, and many economic transactions are undertaken via the informal sector, bargaining, or the black market. Crime and drug trafficking are often commonplace.

Squatter settlements have arisen as a result of large-scale rural to urban migration. State and municipal governments lack the resources to accommodate large numbers of people who flock to cities. Hence the housing stock is insufficient to meet the needs of rapidly growing populations, and municipal authorities are unable to provide even basic services to impoverished newcomers. When possible, governments have made efforts to improve living conditions and/or to discourage migrants from moving into squatter settlements.

THE FAVELAS OF BRAZIL

Squatter settlements in and near the cities of Brazil are known as *favelas*. Although *favelas* have existed in Brazil since the 19th century, most of Brazil's contemporary *favelas* have come into existence during and since the 1970s. By 2010, the Brazilian census estimated that 11 million people, or about 6 percent of the country's population, lived in *favelas*. About 20 percent of the people of the Rio de Janeiro metropolitan area live in the city's more than 600 *favelas*. The growth of Brazil's *favelas* is attributed to large-scale rural to urban migration.

Favelas in Brazil and their residents face many problems above and beyond the lack of sanitation, electricity, and running water that plagues squatter settlements around the world. Many are located on hillsides and are subject to landslides and mudslides during rainy weather. The government lacks direct control of some *favelas*, which are ruled effectively by criminal gangs that are often involved in illegal drug trafficking. Violence is commonplace, and *favela* residents often have very little opportunity to participate in the mainstream of Brazilian culture.

Further Reading

Suketu Metha. "Inside the Violent Favelas of Brazil." *The New York Review of Books*, August 15, 2013. http://www.nybooks.com/articles/archives/2013/aug/15/violent-favelas-brazil/.

Estimating the population of squatter settlements is often difficult, and many residents of squatter settlements are uncounted in their countries' censuses. However, in some countries it has been estimated that a quarter or more residents of these metropolitan areas live in squatter settlements. For example, it has been estimated that 12 million or more people live in squatter settlements near Rio de Janeiro and São Paulo in Brazil, where these communities are known as *favelas*. There are approximately 600 *favelas* in the Rio de Janeiro area. Even higher percentages of people residing in many large cities in less developed areas of Asia and Africa live in squatter settlements. The movie *Slumdog Millionaire* depicts conditions in the squatter settlements of Mumbai.

See Also: Megalopolis; Mumbai; Rio de Janeiro; Rural to Urban Migration

Further Reading

Robert Neuwirth. *Shadow Cities: A Billion Squatters, a New Urban World*. New York: Routledge, 2005.

Jane Perlman. *Favela: Four Decades of Living on the Edge in Rio de Janeiro*. New York: Oxford University Press, 2010.

States, Nations, and Population

The contemporary world is divided into approximately 200 independent countries, or *states*. Each state has legal jurisdiction over specified territory, although some territories are contested among two or more states. The contemporary system of states is very important to the study of population because each state has the right to enact and enforce demographic policies within the territory under its legal jurisdiction.

The words "state" and "nation" are often used interchangeably. However, from the point of view of population policy, these terms have distinct meanings. A nation is a group of people who share a common cultural, ethnic, linguistic, or religious heritage. A state is a political unit whose legal existence and whose right to control territory are recognized by the international community. According to this definition, Americans, Swedes, Chinese, French, and Japanese are nations. The United States, Sweden, China, France, and Japan are states.

In many parts of the world, nations and states are linked closely. For example, most Japanese people live in Japan, and most residents of the state of Japan are Japanese nationals. However, many countries include people of multiple nations. For example, the large and diverse states of India and Nigeria each contain over 100 distinct nations, each of which has a distinct cultural and linguistic heritage. Many nations extend across two or more states. Examples include the Arabs and Kurds of the Middle East, and the Basques of Spain and France.

A state must have a territory, a population, an economy, a government, and a system of infrastructure including transportation, education, and communications. Thus places such as Antarctica, with no permanent resident population, are outside of the international system of states. These requirements lead to the concepts of citizenship and sovereignty. Citizenship links individuals to the state and represents the rights and responsibilities linking a person to the state. In the United States and many other countries, citizenship is related to the state, and is independent of nationality. To become a naturalized U.S. citizen, one must pass a test demonstrating knowledge of U.S. history and government. A person who does so is eligible for citizenship regardless of national origin. In other countries, national origin is an important criterion for citizenship. For example, it is difficult for someone who cannot prove that he or she has German ancestry to become a German citizen. Often, citizens of particular countries have rights, such as the right to vote, not held by noncitizens living in these countries.

Sovereignty is recognition by the international community of a state's right to rule its territory. Sovereignty also implies the right of a country's government to rule over people and places within its territory. As a general principle, state governments do not possess the legal right to interfere in one another's internal affairs.

States as we know them today evolved from territories controlled by particular rulers. The word "territory" is derived from the Latin word "territorium," a conjunction of "earth" or "land" with "belonging to" or "surrounding." During ancient and medieval times, territories were often fluid. However, the idea of a state as having formal control of territory derives from the Peace of Westphalia, which was a set of treaties signed in 1648 to end the Thirty Years' War in central Europe. The Peace of Westphalia stated that rulers of individual territories had the right to determine the religion of the areas under their control. These rulers could choose among Roman Catholicism, Lutheranism, and Calvinism.

The principle underlying the Peace of Westphalia was soon extended to secular as well as religious matters. Thus the Peace of Westphalia established the principle of state sovereignty over territory on the earth's surface. The establishment of state sovereignty and its linkage with territory meant that territories had to be mapped in order to identify the geographic limits of formal government authority. Boundaries were delineated in order to identify the geographic limits of sovereignty. Since that time, many international disputes have involved disagreement over the locations of boundaries between states.

Historically, some boundaries were drawn without knowledge of local conditions. For example, the European powers divided Africa into European colonies by delineating boundaries through the African interior without direct knowledge of what nations and resources would be separated by these boundaries. Today, boundary delineation is undertaken with such knowledge. For example, India was separated from Pakistan, including present-day Bangladesh, on the basis of religions, with most Hindu-majority areas placed in India and most Muslim-majority areas placed in Pakistan.

In accordance with international law, each state has the right to enact laws and policies that are binding upon its citizens and other residents. Many of these policies involve population-related issues. Historically, some states have encouraged population growth, for example by rewarding mothers who bear large numbers of children. Others have enacted policies intended to reduce population growth. An example is China's controversial one-child policy.

Other policies involve immigration. Some states have encouraged immigration, while others have forbidden or discouraged immigration. States that have discouraged immigration have enacted policies making it difficult for noncitizens to immigrate legally. Recognizing that much migration in the contemporary world is illegal immigration, other states, including the United States, have constructed border fences in order to keep illegal immigrants out. In some countries, point systems have been established in order to prioritize potential immigrants on the basis of education, professional training, job market needs, and other criteria. For example, Singapore divides potential immigrants into foreign talents and foreign workers. Foreign talents are generally highly educated professionals, including physicians, scientists, and engineers. Foreign talents are encouraged to move to Singapore and are given priority in obtaining citizenship. On the other hand, foreign workers hold low-skill and menial jobs and their rights as residents of Singapore are circum-scribed strictly.

In general, population policy throughout the world is associated closely with the state, sovereignty, and territory. Thus the state system is crucial to issues involving population change, migration, and other aspects of demography today. In this en-cyclopedia, separate entries describe population-related issues for the world's larg-est states by population, including all states that have populations greater than 40 million, along with several other states whose population trends and issues are im-portant for understanding the demography of the contemporary world.

See Also: Border Fences; Illegal Immigration; International Labor Migration; Migration

Further Reading

Colin Flint and Peter Taylor. *Political Geography: World Economy, Nation-State, and Locality.* 6th ed. London: Routledge, 2011.

Fred M. Shelley. *Nation Shapes.* Santa Barbara, California: ABC-CLIO, 2013.

Total Fertility Rate

The total fertility rate of a country is the average number of children born to a woman over the course of her lifetime.

The total fertility rate is related closely to the rate of natural increase. A total fertility rate of 2 implies that the crude birth rate is equal to the crude death rate. Because the rate of natural increase is defined as the difference between the crude birth date and the crude death rate, a total fertility rate of 2 implies that the rate of natural increase will be around zero and that the population will be stable. Thus, a total fertility rate of 2 is known as replacement-level fertility. The more the total fertility rate exceeds 2, the higher the rate of natural increase. Total fertility rates below 2 imply that crude death rates exceed crude birth rates. In this case, over the long run, a population will decrease in the absence of immigration from other places.

The world total fertility rate is about 2.5, but rates vary considerably between countries. High total fertility rates are found in less developed countries, where birth rates remain high. As of 2012, the countries with the highest total fertility rates were Niger (7.52), Uganda (6.65), Mali (6.35), Somalia (6.26), Burundi (6.08), Burkina Faso (6.07), Ethiopia (5.97), Zambia (5.90), Afghanistan (5.64), and the

Republic of the Congo (5.58). All of these countries have very low median ages and are experiencing high rates of population growth. In these and other countries with high total fertility rates, many women face cultural pressures to marry and begin having children at very young ages. Large families are encouraged because children can provide labor and can provide care for their parents in their old age. Many of these women are illiterate or have very limited educations, giving them few alternatives to bearing large numbers of children. Access to contraception may be lacking or limited as well.

On the other hand, many countries now have total fertility rates well below 2. As of 2012, the 10 countries with the lowest total fertility rates were Singapore (0.78), Taiwan (1.16), South Korea (1.23), Lithuania (1.27), Czech Republic (1.27), Belarus (1.27), Bosnia and Herzegovina (1.28), Ukraine (1.29), Romania (1.30), and Poland (1.31). All of these countries, and others with low total fertility rates, face the possibility of long-run population declines unless total fertility rates increase. Low total fertility rates also imply aging populations, with the elderly forming a larger and larger percentage of the population.

The total fertility rate in the United States in 2012 was 2.06. This implies that the rate of natural increase in the United States is slightly above zero. This illustrates that most of the population growth in the contemporary United States is due primarily to immigration, rather than to natural increase.

See Also: Crude Birth Rate; Crude Death Rate; Demographic Transition Model; Population Pyramid; Rate of Natural Increase

Further Reading

Lee Kuan Yew. "Warning Bell for Developed Countries: Declining Birth Rates." *Forbes*, October 16, 2012. http://www.forbes.com/sites/currentevents/2012/10/16/warning-bell -for-developed-countries-declining-birth-rates/.

United States Central Intelligence Agency. *CIA World Factbook 2012*. Washington, DC: U.S. Government Printing Office, 2012. https://www.cia.gov/library/publications/the-world -factbook/fields/2054.html.

Tragedy of the Commons

The tragedy of the commons is a conceptual framework used to model the divergence between individual self-interest and the common good. It has been applied to overpopulation as well as many other situations involving natural resources.

The principles underlying the tragedy of the commons were articulated by Thomas Malthus, Adam Smith, and other leading thinkers of the 18th and 19th centuries. Its contemporary formulation was articulated by American biologist

Garrett Hardin, who illustrated the concept using an example of farmers who own a large area of pasture land in common. Suppose that each farmer owns a herd of cattle that graze on the commonly held pasture. The income of each herder depends on the size of his or her herd; the larger the herd, the more money the herder earns. Thus, it is in the interests of each herder to add more cattle to his or her herd. However, if too many cattle are added to the common pasture, the pasture becomes overgrazed. In environmental terms, this means that the carrying capacity, or the number of cattle that can be sustained on the pasture under current environmental conditions, would be exceeded. In that case the cattle starve, and everyone's income is lost.

At any given time, each farmer is faced with a choice—should the herder add another cow to his or her herd, or not? An individual farmer faced with this choice is likely to reason that one additional cow will have little impact on the overall cattle population. As a simple example, suppose that there are 100 herders with 50 cattle each using the common pasture. Thus the total cattle population is 5,000. An individual herder reasons that his or her adding another cow will increase the total cattle population from 5,000 to 5,001. The 5001st cow is a "drop in the bucket" and is very unlikely to cause pasture-wide overgrazing. However, if everyone adds a cow, and continues to add cows, overgrazing will result and will harm everyone. Thus pursuit of individual interest leads to a situation in which everybody acting in his or her own self-interest suffers.

The tragedy of the commons has many real-world applications involving the management of common-property resources, including rainforest depletion, overgrazing, overfishing, and many others. For example, rainforest depletion is a major environmental problem in the Amazon River basin of South America and many other tropical environments throughout the world. Farmers cut down rainforests in order to convert the land to cropland or grazing land. An individual farmer may reason that cutting down a few acres of rainforest in order to plant crops on the land will have little impact on the vast rainforest. However, as more and more farmers cut down rainforests, depletion intensifies. Experts have estimated that about 25,000 square miles, or an area about the size of West Virginia, is converted from rainforest to other uses in the Amazon basin every year. As applied to overpopulation, the tragedy of the commons model illustrates divergence between an individual's interest in having more children and society's interest in preventing overpopulation.

What can be done to alleviate the conflict between individual and collective interest, especially as applied to population-related issues? Communication is often a key to overcoming the tragedy of the commons. Farmers facing the tragedy of the commons could meet and agree upon a set of ground rules to govern managing the common-property resource. The rules would likely include penalties for those violating the rules. In the contemporary world, rules are imposed by population policies. In some countries, such as India, population policy involves voluntary incentives to discourage large families. In other countries, such as China, with its one-child population policy, rules are more coercive.

At least in the short run, the impacts of the tragedy of the commons have been alleviated, or at least postponed, by technological change. As an illustration, what if researchers were able to buy or breed more "productive" cows that would require less grass in order to survive, or would produce more milk or beef per pound? In this case, the number of cows that the pasture could support without exceeding carrying capacity would increase. As applied to population, this increased-productivity strategy is the strategy of the Green Revolution, in which technology was used in order to increase per-acre crop yields in Africa, India, and other parts of the world in order to alleviate hunger problems associated with overpopulation. Over the long run, however, it is recognized that Earth's carrying capacity is finite, and that continuing population growth will result eventually in large-scale environmental impacts.

See Also: Agriculture and Population; Carrying Capacity; Ehrlich, Paul; Green Revolution; Hardin, Garrett; Natural Resources and Population; Overpopulation

Further Reading

Garrett Hardin. "The Tragedy of the Commons." *Science* 162 (1968): 1243–48.

Elinor Ostrom. *Governing the Commons: The Evolution of Institutions for Collective Action.* Cambridge: Cambridge University Press, 1990.

United Nations Commission on Population and Development

The United Nations Commission on Population and Development is an agency of the United Nations charged with advising the UN on issues associated with population, migration, and economic development.

In 1946, the UN established the United Nations Population Commission. Recognizing close linkages between questions involving population and those involving economic development, the commission's name was changed to the United Nations Commission on Population and Development in 1994. The commission's charge is to inform the UN on questions associated with population and economic development, including population trends, development policies, and the implementation of "population and development strategies."

The commission's membership consists of representatives of 47 UN member states. Members are selected by the Economic and Social Council of the United

Nations, to which the commission reports. Each member of the commission serves for a term of four years, and each is expected to have expertise in demography and development-related issues. The commission has met annually since 1994.

The work of the commission is supported by the United Nations Population Division. The Population Division's work includes compilation and dissemination of demographic data and the preparation of population projections. It also evaluates new methods for demographic analysis and projecting population trends, and it is responsible for undertaking research in preparation for the commission's annual meetings. For example, the Population Division provided information considered by the UN General Assembly in its High-Level Dialogue on International Migration and Development, held in October 2013. The purpose of the High-Level Dialogue was to identify and consider "concrete measures to strengthen coherence and cooperation at all levels, with a view to enhancing the benefits of international migration for migrants and countries alike and its important links to development, while reducing its negative implications." The text of the dialogue can be accessed at http://daccess-dds-ny.un.org/doc/UNDOC/GEN/N13/439/69/PDF/N1343969.pdf?OpenElement.

See Also: Demography; Gender and Population; Migration

Further Reading

Barbara Crossette. "At the UN, Twenty Years of Backlash to 'Women's Rights Are Human Rights.'" *The Nation*, March 5, 2013. http://www.thenation.com/article/173203/un-twenty-years-backlash-womens-rights-are-human-rights#.

United Nations Commission on Population and Development Web Site. http://www.un.org/en/development/desa/population/commission/index.shtml.

United Nations High Commissioner for Refugees

The Office of the United Nations High Commissioner for Refugees (UNHCR) is an agency of the United Nations that is charged with providing support for refugees throughout the world.

The status of refugees has been an important concern of the international community since the end of World War I. After that war ended, millions of persons had become refugees and many others were former prisoners of war. Under the leadership of the noted Norwegian Arctic explorer Fridtjof Nansen, hundreds of thousands of refugees were repatriated or resettled elsewhere under the auspices of the League of Nations by the early 1920s. The League of Nations established a high commission for refugees. Nansen, who was awarded the Nobel Peace Prize in 1922, became the head of the commission. After Nansen died in 1930, the commission was renamed the Nansen International Office for Refugees. However, its activities foundered with the rise of Nazi Germany and the onset of World War II.

Millions of Europeans were displaced from their countries of birth and became refugees during World War II. Recognizing the issues faced by these refugees, the ad hoc United Nations, consisting of the Allied powers, founded the United Nations Relief and Rehabilitation in 1944. This agency addressed problems faced by these European refugees. After the war, and after the UN came into formal existence, the UN established the International Refugee Organization (IRO) in 1947. The IRO became operative in 1948. However, the IRO soon ran into problems. The IRO's charge specifically excluded residents of Germany who had been displaced as refugees during the war. As well, by the late 1940s, the Cold War was in full swing. By this time, the "Iron Curtain" separated Western Europe from Eastern Europe, which was dominated politically and economically by the Soviet Union. The Soviets refused to participate in the activities of the IRO and did not allow the IRO to operate in these Soviet-dominated areas.

In 1949, the UN authorized the formation of UNHCR as a direct subsidiary organization of the General Assembly. UNHCR was established formally in December 1950, and began its operations on January 1, 1951. It was authorized originally to operate for three years, but later became a permanent agency of the UN. In 1951, UNHCR worked with UN member countries to establish the Convention Relating to the Status of Refugees. (The full text of the convention can be accessed at http://www.unhcr.org/protect/PROTECTION/3b66c2aa10.pdf.) The convention defines refugee status and also describes rights of individuals who request and are granted political asylum.

The original intent of the convention was to address questions associated with European refugees who had been displaced during World War II. By the 1960s, however, it had become evident that these European refugees were far outnumbered by refugees displaced from other parts of the world. Much of this displacement was associated with worldwide decolonization, when numerous former European colonies in Africa and Asia achieved political independence. Recognizing the growing number of refugees outside Europe, UNHCR expanded its scope formally to include refugees worldwide in 1967. Today, nearly all of UNHCR's efforts take place in less developed countries throughout the world.

The formal activities of UNHCR include short-term and long-term assistance to individual refugees, responses to emergency refugee crises, and efforts to promote the long-run well-being of refugees, asylum seekers, and internally displaced persons. It collects and disseminates data on the status of refugees worldwide, and it produces period reports on the state of the world's refugees. UNHCR employs over 7,600 staffers who work in 125 countries throughout the world. It was awarded the Nobel Peace Prize in 1954 and 1981.

See Also: Bureau of Population, Refugees, and Migration; Germany; Refugees; Russia

Further Reading

Office of the United Nations High Commissioner for Refugees. "The State of the World's Refugees: A Search for Solidarity." 2012. http://www.unhcr.org/4fc5ceca9.html.

Office of the United Nations High Commissioner for Refugees. "The State of the World's Refugees: Human Displacement in the New Millennium." 2006. http://www.unhcr.org/4a4dc1a89.html.

United Nations High Commission for Refugees Web Site. http://www.unhcr.org/cgi-bin/texis/vtx/home.

United Nations Population Fund

The United Nations Population Fund (UNFPA) is an agency of the United Nations. Its mission, according to its Web site, is to "[deliver] a world where every pregnancy is wanted, every birth is safe, every young person's potential is fulfilled." In support of this mission, UNFPA's goals include "achieving universal access to sexual and reproductive health (including family planning), promoting reproductive rights, reducing maternal mortality, . . . improving the lives of youths and women by advocating for human rights and gender equality and by promoting the understanding of population dynamics."

UNFPA was founded as the United Nations Fund for Population Activities in 1967 and was placed under the auspices of the UN General Assembly in 1971. Its current name was adopted in 1987, but its original acronym is still used. In providing input to the General Assembly, UNFPA is guided by a Programme of Action prepared in conjunction with the UN-sponsored International Conference on Population and Development, which took place in Cairo in 1994. The preamble to the Programme of Action reads in part,

> The world as a whole has changed in ways that create important new opportunities for addressing population and development issues. Among the most significant are the major shifts in attitude among the world's people and their leaders in regard to reproductive health, family planning and population growth, resulting, inter alia, in the new comprehensive concept of reproductive health, including family planning and sexual health, as defined in the Programme of Action. . . . [S]ustained economic growth in the context of sustainable development will enhance the ability of countries to meet the pressures of expected population growth; will facilitate the demographic transition in countries where there is an

imbalance between demographic rates and social, economic and environmental goals; and will permit the balance and integration of the population dimension into other development-related policies.

The complete text of the preamble and the remainder of the Programme of Action can be accessed at http://www.iisd.ca/Cairo/program/p00000.html.

UNFPA regards reproductive health as at the "very heart" of its mandate. It sees reproductive health as

> an issue that lies at the intersection of human rights, gender equality and population dynamics. Lack of access to reproductive health and rights, including the ability to freely choose the number and spacing of births, places a disproportionate burden on two groups in particular: women and young people, especially those who are marginalized by poverty or other circumstances. (http://www.unfpa.org/issues/)

In support of this mission, UNFPA has established several specific goals, including a 75 percent reduction in maternal mortality, reduced infant mortality, universal access to reproductive health services, and increased life expectancy. UNFPA produces annual reports on global populations under the title of "State of the World's Population."

UNFPA is funded by governments, nongovernmental organizations (NGOs), foundations, and private donors. Currently, about 175 member countries of the United Nations support UNFPA. However, on several occasions the United States has withheld financial support for UNFPA. Funds were withheld during the administrations of Presidents Ronald Reagan, George H. W. Bush, and George W. Bush. The United States' refusal to support UNFPA financially has been linked to concerns that UNFPA's policies and programs support forced abortion and sterilization. In 2004, Undersecretary of State Arthur Dewey testified before a House of Representatives committee that the George W. Bush administration was withholding support for UNFPA on the grounds that the fund's activities implied support for China's one-child policy, including coerced sterilization and forced and sex-selective abortion. (Excerpts from the text of Undersecretary Dewey's testimony are found elsewhere in this encyclopedia.) However, upon taking office in 2009, President Barack Obama restored American funding to UNFPA.

See Also: Gender and Population; One-Child Policy; Overpopulation

Further Reading

United Nations Population Fund. "State of the World's Population 2011: People and Possibilities in a World of 7 Billion." 2011. http://www.unfpa.org/webdav/site/global/shared /documents/publications/2011/EN-SWOP2011-FINAL.pdf.

United Nations Population Fund. "State of the World's Population 2012: By Choice, Not by Chance: Family Planning, Human Rights, and Development." 2012. http://www.unfpa .org/webdav/site/global/shared/swp/2012/EN_SWOP2012_Report.pdf.

United Nations Population Fund. "State of the World's Population 2013: Motherhood in Childhood: Facing the Challenge of Adolescent Pregnancy." 2013. http://www.unfpa .org/webdav/site/global/shared/swp2013/EN-SWOP2013-final.pdf.

United Nations Population Fund Web Site. http://www.unfpa.org.

United States Bureau of the Census

The United States Bureau of the Census is the agency of the U.S. federal government that is charged with conducting a census of the nation's population each decade along with the collection of other data about American demographics, economy, and society. The bureau also prepares projections and estimates of the United States population and its demographic characteristics.

The Constitution of the United States mandates that a census of the American people be conducted every 10 years for purposes of allocating seats in the U.S. House of Representatives among the states on the basis of population. As stated in Article I, Section 2, "The actual Enumeration shall be made within three Years after the first Meeting of the Congress of the United States, and within every subsequent Term of ten Years, in such Manner as they shall by Law direct." The first such census was conducted in 1790, and a census has been conducted every 10 years since then.

At first, censuses were overseen formally by the nation's secretary of state. In practice, however, the data collection was conducted under the auspices of U.S. marshals supervised by the judicial branch of the government. Beginning with the census of 1880, however, they have been overseen by the executive branch of the federal government. The Census Office was established in 1902 as a permanent agency under the jurisdiction of the U.S. Department of the Interior. In 1903, it was renamed the United States Bureau of the Census and was placed under the jurisdiction of the newly established Department of Commerce and Labor.

In 1913, the Department of Commerce and Labor was split into the Department of Commerce and the Department of Labor, with the bureau becoming part of the Department of Commerce. Although the Bureau of the Census is not an independent agency, its director is appointed by the president, subject to confirmation by the U.S. Senate. The bureau's headquarters are located in Suitland, Maryland, and it employs more than 5,000 people on a permanent basis, with many others hired temporarily to assist in the collection of census data each decade. In addition to the formal census itself, the bureau conducts numerous surveys on population, housing, crime, government activity, trade, income, and other activities. Data gathered from the census as well as from these surveys are used widely by government agencies and in the private sector for allocation of revenues and planning purposes.

See Also: Census; United States of America

Further Reading

United States Bureau of the Census. "About Us," 2013. http://www.census.gov/aboutus/.

United States Bureau of the Census. "History and Organization," 2000. http://www.census.gov/history/pdf/cff4.pdf.

United States Bureau of the Census Web Site. http://www.census.gov.

War and Population

Wars have occurred throughout history, resulting in millions of fatalities. Increased death rates have been a direct consequence of war throughout the world. However, wars also have many indirect consequences with respect to populations. In many wars, the number of military casualties has been exceeded by civilian casualties.

Although warfare has affected populations throughout history, more soldiers and civilians have lost their lives in wars in the 20th century than in all previous centuries combined. The deadliest war in world history was World War II, which took place between 1939 and 1945. Estimates suggest that more than 60 million people throughout the world lost their lives. Of these casualties, more than two-thirds were civilians. An estimated 7 million Soviet troops and 5.3 million German troops were killed in battle. About 420,000 American military personnel were killed during the war.

In addition to these battle deaths, large numbers of civilians in the Soviet Union, Germany, and other countries lost their lives as a result of famine, genocide, and large-scale bombing of cities and other civilian targets, including the dropping of atomic bombs in the Japanese cities of Hiroshima and Nagasaki in 1945. Overall, between 2 and 3 percent of the world's population lost their lives during World War II.

World War I, fought between 1914 and 1918, also caused large numbers of military and civilian casualties. Between 9 and 10 million soldiers were killed during the war, with the largest number of military casualties suffered by Germany and Russia, with about 2 million battle deaths each. Nearly 120,000 American soldiers were also killed during World War I. Throughout the world, an estimated 7 million civilians lost their lives. Moreover, World War I was followed immediately by the global epidemic of Spanish flu, which is believed to have killed more than 50 million people and was the most deadly epidemic in global history. Soldiers returning home from battlefields after the end of the war are believed to have contributed to the worldwide spread of this epidemic. Very large numbers of soldiers and civilians lost their lives in both world wars because of the scope of the conflicts, which involved large numbers of countries around the world, and because of the increased destructive power of military technology relative to that available in previous centuries.

Above and beyond direct military and civilian casualties, wars have had many impacts on populations. Wars have contributed to demographic imbalances within populations because the very large majority of those killed in battle are young men. As a result, postwar populations include a relatively large number of children, elderly people, and women. In addition, the young men killed in battle would be approaching their peak earning years as civilians. Hence the overall amount of income brought into communities is reduced substantially, lowering the overall productive capacity of populations.

Not only are very large numbers of people killed directly during wars, but wars generally cause large-scale displacement of surviving populations. Millions of people have been forced to leave their home countries as refugees. About 40 million Europeans became refugees before, during, and after World War II. Controversy and discord over the treatment of these refugees led directly to the establishment of the United Nations High Commissioner for Refugees in 1950. More recently, large numbers of refugees have been displaced by conflicts in Vietnam, Iraq, Syria, Sudan, the Democratic Republic of the Congo, and many other countries. At any given point in time, the number of people who become displaced as refugees is greatest in those countries facing international or civil wars.

Wars have also contributed to famines and food shortages at many junctures throughout history. Famines and food shortages have occurred in many cases because food supplies are reduced for a variety of reasons. In some cases, enemy troops burn or otherwise destroy crops and livestock. Roads, railroads, and other supply lines are cut, making it more difficult to transport food to people facing food shortages. In addition, the productive capacity of agricultural land is diverted to provide food for soldiers and other persons involved directly in battle, reducing food supplies available to local civilians. Famine occurring as a result of warfare can intensify the impacts of epidemic disease, in that people lacking sufficient food have weakened resistance to disease and are therefore more likely to succumb to epidemic diseases as they occur. Overall, the demographic consequences of wars have had long-lasting impacts on populations that continue for long periods of time after the actual wars have come to an end.

See Also: Berlin Wall; Border Fences; Democratic Republic of the Congo; Epidemics; Famine; Genocide; Refugees; Spanish Flu; Vietnam

Further Reading

Kenneth Hill. *War, Humanitarian Crises, Population Displacement, and Fertility: A Review.* Washington, DC: National Academies Press, 2008.

Bradley A. Thayer. "Considering Population and War: A Critical and Neglected Aspect of Population Studies." *Philosophical Transactions of the Royal Society* 364 (2009): 1081–92.

World Refugee Day

World Refugee Day is a day designated by the United Nations and set aside by the international community to call attention to issues associated with refugees. It is observed annually on June 20.

The plight of refugees has been recognized by the international community since the period following the end of World War I. During and after that war, millions of people throughout Europe were displaced. In 1921, the League of Nations established the Commission on Refugees, which worked to resettle persons who became refugees during the war and its aftermath. As the successor organization to the League of Nations, the United Nations carried on the league's work on behalf of

The United Nations has designated June 20 of each year as World Refugee Day. The idea of World Refugee Day is to call the world's attention to the often squalid conditions faced by millions of refugees throughout the world. This photograph shows refugee women from Afghanistan in Islamabad, Pakistan. (Anadolu Agency/Getty Images)

refugees. The UN established the International Refugee Organization in 1947, and in 1950 its functions were transferred to the Office of the United Nations High Commissioner for Refugees (UNHCR). In 1951, UNHCR spearheaded the drafting and ratification of the Convention Relating to the Status of Refugees. This convention applied originally to European refugees, but it was extended to encompass the entire world in 1967.

The history and activities of UNHCR provide context for World Refugee Day. In 2000, the United Nations General Assembly passed Resolution 76/55, which called attention to the fiftieth anniversary of the establishment of UNHCR and of the Convention Relating to the Status of Refugees. This resolution called also for the establishment and recognition of World Refugee Day. The date of June 20 was chosen because the Organization of African Unity (now known as the African Union) had already recognized June 20 as African Refugee Day. Governments and individuals are encouraged to organize and participate in events associated with awareness of the plight of refugees throughout the world.

In the United States, the Department of State hosts an annual World Refugee Day Event. At the 2013 event, Secretary of State John Kerry gave an address concerning the meaning and importance of World Refugee Day to Americans. The full text of Secretary Kerry's remarks can be found elsewhere in this encyclopedia.

See Also: Bureau of Population, Refugees, and Migration; Refugees; United Nations High Commissioner for Refugees

Further Reading

John Kerry. "Remarks at the World Refugee Day Event," June 20, 2013. http://www.state.gov/secretary/remarks/2013/06/210935.htm.

United Nations General Assembly. Resolution 76/55: Fiftieth Anniversary of the Office of the United Nations High Commissioner for Refugees and World Refugee Day, December 4, 2000. http://www.un.org/en/ga/search/view_doc.asp?symbol=A/RES/55/76&Lang=E.

Part II: Countries

China

China, known formally as the People's Republic of China, is the largest country in the world by population, with more than 1.3 billion people. About 18 percent of the world's people live in China, and a large majority of them live in the eastern half of the country. With a land area of about 3.7 square miles, China is the fourth-largest country in the world by land area, behind Russia, Canada, and the United States. However, China's population density is much greater than those of the three larger countries by land area.

Many of the more populated areas of China were unified politically more than 2,000 years ago. The Han Dynasty (which gave its name to the modern Han Chinese population) controlled most of present-day eastern China for more than 400 years beginning around 206 BCE. A succession of dynasties ruled China until the early 20th century. During the early 19th century, European colonial powers, and later the United States and Japan, began to establish trading centers on the Chinese coast. Britain established a port at Hong Kong, and Portugal established a port at Macau. Both Hong Kong and Macau are located on the southeastern coast of China, and both have now been incorporated into the Chinese state.

With about 24 million people, Shanghai is the largest city in China as well as China's major financial and economic center. Thus Shanghai has become a focal point for China's rapid economic growth, and it is a magnet for millions of natives of rural China. (Yunhao Zhang/Dreamstime.com)

In 1912, reformers overthrew the last Chinese empire and proclaimed the Republic of China, establishing what would become known as the Nationalist government. The Nationalists were challenged by Communist insurgents during the 1930s, and they were also threatened by imperial Japan. The Nationalists and the Communists worked together to expel the Japanese during World War II, but resumed hostilities against each other after the war ended. In 1949, the Communists, under Mao Zedong (1893–1976), established control over the entire Chinese mainland and established the People's Republic, and the Nationalists established control of Taiwan. The Communist Party has maintained control over China ever since.

The People's Republic isolated itself from the rest of the world during the 1950s and 1960s, attempting to create a self-sufficient Communist state. These efforts to maintain self-sufficiency were largely unsuccessful, and the Great Chinese Famine between 1958 and 1962 resulted in more than 40 million fatalities. In the early 1970s, China began to open itself to more foreign trade. In the late 1970s, China began to move away from its strict policy of collective ownership of means of production and began to encourage private enterprise. China has since emerged as one of the largest economies in the world.

Throughout its history, China has been one of the most heavily populated places in the world. Historical estimates suggest that China's population was over 80 million during the Han Dynasty, and reached 110 million by 1500 and over 400 million by 1900. Censuses taken by the government of the People's Republic counted about 582 million in 1953, 695 million in 1964, and just over 1 billion in 1982. However, this large population is distributed unevenly. More than 90 percent of China's people live in the eastern half of the country. About a third of China's people live in rural areas. The government is promoting migration from eastern to western China. It has also been encouraging people to move from rural to urban areas, although it is also trying to steer people away from China's largest megacities, such as Shanghai and Beijing, and instead toward smaller cities and metropolitan areas.

The last half of the 20th century saw rapid declines in China's crude birth rate. The crude birth rate of China has declined from about 37 per 1,000 in 1950 to about 12 per 1,000 today. Crude death rates have also declined, from 18 per 1,000 in 1950 to 7.1 per 1,000 today. The rate of natural increase has slowed over the past several decades to about 0.5 percent per year today. The total fertility rate of 1.40 is well below replacement-level fertility.

The decline in China's rate of natural increase has been due in large part to China's one-child policy, which has been an initiative on the part of China's government to reduce China's population growth by limiting fertility to one child per couple. The policy was one of the most far-reaching efforts to control population at a large scale in history. Although crude birth rates, total fertility rates, and rates of natural increase have declined substantially since the Chinese government instituted its one-child policy, the controversial initiative has had far-reaching effects on China's society and economy.

China is currently experiencing ethnic conflict. About 91 percent of China's people are Han Chinese, and the others belong to one of more than 50 government-recognized ethnic minority groups. The largest of these ethnic groups are the Uighurs of northwestern China and the Tibetans, who live on the Tibetan Plateau in the Himalayas of western China. The Uighur language is related to Turkish, and most Uighurs are Muslims. Thus the Uighurs have much closer cultural ties to the populations of Central Asia than they do to the Han Chinese. Similarly, the Tibetans speak a distinctive language unrelated to Chinese and practice a form of Buddhism far different than the Buddhist and Confucianist religion practiced historically by many Chinese people.

CHINA—NOT ENOUGH NAMES TO GO AROUND?

One implication of China's immense population has become a shortage of both surnames and given names. Large numbers of people share the same name. For example, the surname Ma is the 13th most common family name in China, and it is shared by about 17 million people. More than 250 million Chinese are named Wang, Li, or Zhang, and about 85 percent of Chinese people have one of the 100 most common surnames in China. By contrast, 90 percent of Americans have one of 70,000 surnames.

In part to eliminate confusion, the Chinese government has mandated that every Chinese citizen must carry a computer-readable state identification card. However, the computers are programmed to read only about 32,000 Chinese characters. About 60 million Chinese citizens have given names that contain characters that are not readable by these computers. In order to facilitate issuing identification cards, Chinese government officials are strongly encouraging these people to change their names.

Further Reading

Sharon LaFraniere. "Name Not on Our List? Change It, China Says." *New York Times,* April 20, 2009. http://www.nytimes.com/2009/04/21/world/asia/21china.html? pagewanted=all&_r=0.

Members of both groups have agitated for political independence, in part because of linguistic, religious, and cultural differences between the Han Chinese and themselves. China's government has encouraged Han Chinese to move to Xinjiang Province, where most Uighurs live, or to Tibet. In 1949, about 95 percent of Xinjiang's residents were Uighurs, whereas Uighurs comprise only about half of Xinjiang's people today. Uighur and Tibetan activists accuse the Chinese government of working actively to dilute their cultures and imposing Han Chinese culture on their territories and people.

Immigration has had a negligible impact on the Chinese population, as only about 1.1 million expatriates (about 0.08% of the population) live permanently in China. Of these, about half have moved from Hong Kong, Macau, or Taiwan (which China continues to claim). South Korea, the United States, and Vietnam are the next largest sources of migrants into China. Historically, large numbers of Chinese natives have left the country. These emigrants are known as Overseas Chinese. Overseas Chinese people form a majority of the population of Singapore and are found in significant numbers in many other countries throughout East and Southeast Asia, including Indonesia, Thailand, and Malaysia.

See Also: Beijing; Census; Crude Birth Rate; Crude Death Rate; Great Chinese Famine; Indonesia; Japan; Megacities; One-Child Policy; Population Density; Rate of Natural Increase; Replacement-Level Fertility; Russia; Shanghai; Singapore; South Korea; Thailand; United Kingdom; United States of America

Further Reading

Josh Chin. "Chinese Scholars Call for Revision of One-Child Policy." *Wall Street Journal*, July 6, 2012. http://online.wsj.com/article/SB1000142405270230396230457750906266 0508548.html.

Ian Johnson. "China's Great Uprooting: Moving 250 Million into Cities." *New York Times*, June 15, 2013. http://www.nytimes.com/2013/06/16/world/asia/chinas-great-uprooting -moving-250-million-into-cities.html?_r=1&.

Feng Wang. "China's Population Density: The Looming Crisis." *Brookings Institution Research*, September 2010. http://www.brookings.edu/research/articles/2010/09/china -population-wang.

Feng Wang, Yong Cai, and Baochang Gu. "Population, Policy, and Politics: How Will History Judge China's One-Child Policy?" *Population and Development Review* 38 (2012): 115–29.

India

India, formally known as the Republic of India, is the second-largest country in the world by population, with more than 1.2 billion inhabitants, or more than one-sixth of the world's people. Only China has more people. However, India's land area of about 1.3 million square miles is only one-third of that of China, and therefore India's population density is nearly three times that of China. India shares the Indian subcontinent in South Asia with Pakistan and Bangladesh, which are also among the 10 most populous countries in the world. The Indian subcontinent is one of the most densely populated large areas in the world. Many demographers predict that India's population will surpass that of China by 2025 or 2030.

Present-day India has been inhabited by settled agricultural civilizations for more than 5,000 years. Most of what is now India, Pakistan, and Bangladesh was united by the Mughal Empire in the 16th century. During the 18th century, the British East India Company began to take over port cities on the Indian coast, including Mumbai and Kolkata. The East India Company extended its control over interior India gradually, and in 1858, the Indian subcontinent was placed under direct British control as part of the British Empire.

British India was granted independence in 1947. The colony was divided into two countries on the basis of religion, with most Hindus placed within India and most Muslims placed within Pakistan (which then included present-day Bangladesh). A democratic government took power at the time of independence, and India has been the world's largest functioning democracy ever since.

India's population has more than tripled since independence. The first official census, taken after independence in 1951, counted about 361 million people. Between 1951 and 2001, the population of India increased by more than 20 percent per decade, or more than 2 percent per year. The population passed 1 billion in 2001, and increased an additional 17.6 percent to 1.21 billion in 2011. India's highest population densities are found in the northern part of the country, especially in the valleys of the Ganges and Brahmaputra Rivers. Rural population densities are somewhat lower in the Indian peninsula to the south and in desert or mountainous areas in the western, northern, and eastern portions of the country.

India has undergone considerable demographic transition. In 1955, its crude birth rate was 43.3 per 1,000. The birth rate fell to 30.0 by 1995, and has declined more quickly since then, to 23.1 in 2010. The crude death rate has also fallen steadily, from 25.5 in 1955 to 10.2 in 1995 to 8.3 in 2010. Thus the current rate of natural increase is about 1.5 percent per year. As with other countries undergoing demographic transition, the total fertility rate has also declined, from 5.9 in 1955 to 2.73 in 2010. However, India's total fertility rate remains considerably higher than that of China. India's population is relatively young, with a median age of about 25.

Historically, India has experienced considerable net out-migration. After the abolition of slavery in the British Empire in the 19th century, large numbers of Indian natives relocated to other areas of the world as agricultural laborers and indentured servants. Today, people of Indian ancestry form a significant component of the populations of Fiji, Guyana, Trinidad and Tobago, and other countries to which their ancestors moved in the late 19th or early 20th centuries.

More recently, people have moved from India to destinations around the world. About 4 million people of Indian ancestry live in the United States, and many others live in the United Kingdom and elsewhere in Europe. Many are highly educated physicians, scientists, educators, and other professionals who are part of the worldwide brain drain. Millions of other Indians work as contract laborers or merchants on a temporary or permanent basis in the United Arab Emirates, Singapore, and other wealthier countries of the Middle East and Asia. However, India has also experienced substantial in-migration in recent years. Hindus from Pakistan and present-day Bangladesh moved across the border into India following the 1947 partition of British India. More recently, thousands of Bangladeshis have crossed from crowded, impoverished Bangladesh into India in search of employment and land. In order to stem the flow of migrants from Bangladesh into India, India has constructed a border fence that extends along much of the boundary separating the two countries. As the only stable democracy in South Asia, India has also attracted and housed substantial populations of refugees from Tibet, Afghanistan, Sri Lanka, and other nearby war-torn countries and regions.

In recent years, India's government has actively promoted programs to reduce fertility by encouraging contraception and voluntary sterilization. However, critics have argued that the government's policies discriminate against women in that husbands push their wives to undergo sterilization procedures in order to get financial incentives offered by the government. Sex-selective abortion is common in India, although not as prevalent as it is in China. Nationwide, there are 110 males under age 15 for every hundred females under 15. Nevertheless, the rate of population growth in India has dropped considerably since the 1980s. Although India's rate of population growth has slowed somewhat, demographers predict that India will surpass China as the most populous country in the world by 2030.

See Also: Bangladesh; Border Fences; Brain Drain; Census; China; Crude Birth Rate; Crude Death Rate; Demographic Transition Model; Indentured Servitude; Kolkata; Median Age; Mumbai; Pakistan; Population Density; Rate of Natural Increase; Slavery; Total Fertility Rate; United Kingdom; United States of America

Further Reading

Soutik Biswas. "Is India's Population Policy Sexist?" *bbc.co.uk*, July 12, 2011. http://www.bbc .co.uk/news/world-south-asia-14117505.

Daily Mail Online. "India Set to Overtake China as World's Most Populated Country after Adding 180m People in a Decade." March 31, 2011. http://www.dailymail.co.uk/news /article-1371996/India-set-overtake-China-worlds-populated-country-adding-180m -people-decade.html?ito=feeds-newsxml.

Daniel Naujoks. "Emigration, Immigration, and Diaspora Relations in India." Migration Information Service, October 2009. http://www.migrationinformation.org/feature /display.cfm?ID=745.

United States of America

The United States of America is the third-largest country in the world by population, with about 317 million people. Thus the United States is the third-largest country in the world by population following China and India. With a land area of nearly 3.7 million square miles, the United States is the fourth-largest country in the world, behind Russia, Canada, and China.

Anthropologists believe that between 1 and 4 million Native Americans lived in what is now the United States at the time when European exploration of the Americas began in the late 15th century. In the 16th century, Spaniards settled St. Augustine in present-day Florida and several communities along the Rio Grande in present-day New Mexico.

During the 17th century, European powers, including Spain, the United Kingdom, France, the Netherlands, and Sweden, contested control of territory along the Atlantic Ocean coast of what is now the United States. The Dutch, who settled present-day New York State and established what would become the city of New York, were expelled from North America following an agreement signed by the two countries in 1664. By 1700, the British controlled the Atlantic coastline of the present-day United States from Georgia to Maine, a region that comprised the original 13 colonies.

As the 13 colonies grew rapidly in population during the 18th century, American colonists began to push for political independence. The American Revolution broke out in 1775 and ended in 1781. In 1783, the United Kingdom agreed to the Treaty of Paris and recognized the United States as an independent country. The newly independent United States was surrounded by territory controlled by European colonial powers. The British maintained control of Canada to the north. The territory west of the Mississippi River, which formed the western boundary of the United States, was controlled by Spain until it was ceded to France in 1798. Spain also controlled Florida to the south.

During the 19th century, the United States expanded to encompass all of its present territory. The United States obtained new territory with the Louisiana Purchase, including most of the territory between the Mississippi and the Rocky Mountains, from France in 1803. Florida was purchased from Spain in 1819. Between 1845 and 1853, the United States obtained Texas, California, and most of the Southwest from Mexico as Spain's successor state. Alaska was bought from Russia in 1867, and Hawaii was annexed in 1898.

The population of the United States has increased steadily since independence, both because of natural increase and immigration. The U.S. Constitution mandates that a census be conducted every 10 years. The first census, taken in 1790, counted nearly 4 million residents of the United States. The population increased to 23 million in 1850 and 76 million in 1900. It grew to 106 million in 1920, 151 million in 1950, and nearly 250 million in 1980.

The United States underwent most of its demographic transition in the 19th century. During the Great Depression of the 1930s, the crude birth rate of the United States was approximately 19 per 1,000. It increased to 25 per 1,000 during the baby boom of the late 1940s and 1950s, then dropped again after 1964 and declined to between 15 and 16 during the late 1970s and 1980s. It rose slightly in the 1990s, and then declined to its current rate of 12.6 per 1,000. The crude death rate has remained low throughout the 20th century, but dropped slightly from 10 per 1,000 in the late 1930s and the 1940s to about 8 per 1,000 today.

Because births have exceeded deaths throughout its history, the United States has a positive rate of natural increase, which has declined slowly over several decades. Today the rate of natural increase is about 0.45 percent per year. The total fertility rate was slightly above 2 during the Great Depression and World War II, rose to 3.7 in the late 1950s, and declined to 2.5 in the late 1960s. It dropped below 2, or below replacement-level fertility, for the first time in 1973. Since then the total fertility rate has hovered around 2, with a 2012 level of 1.87. Thus population growth in the contemporary United States is driven by immigration, as opposed to natural increase.

Throughout its history, the United States has been a country of immigrants. Nearly 99 percent of Americans are immigrants or are descended from immigrants from Europe, Asia, Africa, the Middle East, or Latin America. The major sources of immigrants have varied over the years. Before independence and until 1890, the large majority of immigrants came from northwestern Europe, including the United Kingdom, Ireland, Germany, the Netherlands, and Scandinavia. Before 1808, millions of slaves were captured and transported involuntarily to the United States from Africa.

After 1890, the major source of immigrants shifted from Northern and Western Europe to Eastern and Southern Europe, including Italy, Poland, Russia, Hungary, and Bohemia. U.S. policy allowed unrestricted immigration until 1917, when U.S. law banned nearly all immigration from Asia in what was designated as the Asiatic Barred Zone. The Asiatic Barred Zone included most of present-day South, Southeast, and East Asia. In 1924, the Johnson-Reed Act placed severe restrictions on immigration from other parts of the world, with particular impacts on migration from Eastern and Southern Europe. The restrictive immigration policies were repealed in 1965, and immigration levels once again increased. Today, the major sources of immigration into the United States are Latin America, especially Mexico, and Asia. About 13 percent of Americans are immigrants themselves, and an additional 86 percent are descended from immigrants from Europe, Asia, Africa, or Latin America.

Because immigrants into the United States have arrived from all areas of the world, the ethnic diversity of the United States is the highest of any developed country in the world. Today, birth rates among most immigrant populations and American nonwhites are relatively high. Hence demographers have estimated that by the early 2040s, less than half of the U.S. population will be of European ancestry. Already, whites comprise a minority of the populations of several U.S. states, including Hawaii, California, New Mexico, and Texas.

Immigration has become a highly controversial issue within the United States, especially given the large numbers of illegal immigrants living in the United States. In 2011, the U.S. government estimated that 11 to 14 million illegal immigrants were residing in the United States, with more than half coming from Mexico. In order to stem the flow of illegal immigrants from Mexico, the U.S. government began to construct a border fence. Today this controversial fence extends across about a third of the boundary.

See Also: Baby Boom; Census; China; Crude Birth Rate; Crude Death Rate; Demographic Transition Model; Demography; France; Germany; Illegal Immigration; India; Italy; Mexico; Migration; Rate of Natural Increase; Replacement-Level Fertility; Russia; Slavery; Total Fertility Rate; United Kingdom

Further Reading

Steven A. Camarota. "Immigrants in the United States: A Profile of America's Foreign-Born Population." Center for Immigration Studies, 2012. http://www.cis.org/sites/cis.org/files/articles/2012/immigrants-in-the-united-states-2012.pdf.

Hope Yen. "Census: White Majority Gone by 2043." *U.S. News and World Report*, June 6, 2013. http://usnews.nbcnews.com/_news/2013/06/13/18934111-census-white-majority-in-us-gone-by-2043?lite.

Indonesia

Indonesia is the fourth-largest country by population in the world, following China, India, and the United States, with more than 240 million people. Indonesia is located off the coast of mainland Southeast Asia. It represents the world's largest archipelago, and includes more than 17,500 islands, of which about 6,000 are inhabited. Overall, the land area of Indonesia is roughly 735,000 square miles, or slightly less than three times the land area of Texas and about a fifth of that of the United States. Thus its population density is more than five times greater than of the United States.

Archaeologists and anthropologists believe that the islands of Indonesia have been inhabited by humans for at least 50,000 years. As long as 2,500 years ago, Indonesian traders established trade routes connecting the islands with China, India, and East Africa. In 1602, the Dutch East India Company was established in order to promote trade between Europe and present-day Indonesia. The Netherlands took formal control of Indonesia, which it named the Dutch East Indies, in the early 19th century. Indonesian leaders declared Indonesia to be independent at the end of World War II, and the Netherlands recognized Indonesia as formally independent in 1949.

The overall population of Indonesia has increased steadily since before Indonesia achieved independence. The Dutch estimated the population of the Dutch East Indies at about 43 million in 1900. In 1950, shortly after independence, the population was 75 million. It doubled to about 150 million by 1980. Since that time, Indonesia's rate of population growth has slowed. It population was estimated at 180 million in 1990, 206 million in 2000, and 231 million in 2010.

The slowdown in Indonesia's rate of population growth in recent years reflects the fact that Indonesia has undergone substantial demographic transition since independence, especially after 1970. Indonesia's crude birth rate was estimated at 42.7 in 1955. It remained above 40 until 1970, after which it began to decline steadily. Over the next 40 years, it dropped by more than 50 percent, falling to 19.1 by 2010. Indonesia's total fertility rate has declined from 5.5 in 1955 to about 2.6 in 2010. The crude death rate also declined from 24.7 in 1950 to 7.2 in 2010.

Indonesia's population is distributed very unevenly. About 60 percent of Indonesia's people live on the island of Java, which contains the capital city of Jakarta. Java is the most densely populated large island in the world, with more than 135 million people living in an area roughly the size of Illinois. Thus Java contains about 2,500 people per square mile. Despite Indonesia's reduced total fertility rate, Java continues to grow because of migration to Jakarta and other large cities on Java from outlying islands of Indonesia.

During the 1970s and 1980s, the Indonesian government attempted to alleviate overcrowding on Java by implementing a policy of transmigration. The government encouraged people to leave Java and its crowded neighbors, Bali and Madura, and resettle on less densely populated islands, including Sumatra, Sulawesi, and the Indonesia portions of Borneo and New Guinea. About 2.5 million transmigrants were resettled during the 1970s and 1980s. The government's goal was not only to alleviate overcrowding on Java, but also to promote economic development on the outlying islands. Another goal was to promote the creation of an Indonesian national identity, as opposed to identity with individual islands. In some areas, transmigrants and their descendants now outnumber the local populations.

The transmigration program has been criticized on several grounds. Some critics argued that transmigration diluted local cultures by encouraging in-migration by Javanese people. In some places, conflict between transmigrants and local residents led to violence. For example, riots in 2001 led to the deaths of more than 500 transmigrants, and an unknown number of indigenous Dayaks, in the Indonesian province of Central Kalimantan on the island of Borneo. Environmental issues were also raised by critics of the transmigration program. Increased populations accelerated rates of deforestation and resulted in overgrazing and other overuse of natural resources. For example, nearly 100 percent of the island of Borneo was covered in dense forest in 1950. According to estimates, however, about half of Borneo's land surface will be deforested by 2020. Although transmigration is no longer pursued as actively in the past, about 15,000 families a year continue to be resettled under the program today.

ACEH AND THE INDIAN OCEAN TSUNAMI OF 2004

On December 26, 2004, a powerful earthquake measuring 9.2 on the Richter scale struck in the Indian Ocean. The earthquake and the resulting tsunami cost more than 220,000 lives worldwide. However, more than half of these fatalities occurred in the Indonesia province of Aceh, located close to the epicenter. Because of the short distance between the epicenter and the Aceh coast, there was very little time to warn people about the oncoming tsunami.

The disaster also affected relationships between Aceh and the government of Indonesia. Aceh has long regarded itself as culturally and economically distinct from the rest of the country, resisting efforts to integrate it into Indonesian society. Its people practice a much more conservative form of Islam than do other Indonesians. For decades, a guerilla organization known as the Free Aceh Movement pushed to make Aceh independent. However, after the earthquake, many Aceh residents interpreted the disaster as a sign that they were insufficiently pious. The Free Aceh Movement signed a peace accord with the Indonesian government in 2005, and today Aceh is the only Indonesian province that is allowed to enforce partial sharia law; for example, women in Aceh are now required to wear headscarves in public.

Further Reading

Nic Borgese. "Aceh Separatists Roll Out Sharia Law." *newmatilda.com*, February 17, 2014. https://newmatilda.com/2014/02/17/aceh-separatists-roll-out-sharia-law.

The Indonesian government has also promoted family planning in order to reduce the country's total fertility rate, encouraging couples to have fewer children and providing contraception. The goal of the program was to reduce the total fertility rate to 2.1, or replacement-level fertility, during the second decade of the 21st century. Although the total fertility rate has declined steadily, some Indonesian officials remain critical of the program because its targets have not been achieved.

See Also: China; Crude Birth Rate; Crude Death Rate; Demographic Transition Model; India; Jakarta; Population Density; Replacement-Level Fertility; United States of America

Further Reading

Sarah V. Harlan. "Why Focus on Family Planning in Indonesia?" *Knowledge for Health*, February 11, 2013. http://www.k4health.org/blog/post/why-focus-family-planning-indonesia.

Lesley Potter. "New Transmigration Paradigm in Indonesia: The Case of Kalimantan." *Asia Pacific Viewpoint* 53, no. 3 (2012): 272–87.

Brazil

Brazil, officially the Federative Republic of Brazil, is the fifth-largest country in the world by population, behind China, India, the United States, and Indonesia with nearly 200 million people. It is also the fifth-largest country by land area in the world, behind Russia, Canada, the United States, and China. It is the second-largest country by population in the western hemisphere. Relative to most Asian and African countries, Brazil's population density is low. However, the population distribution of Brazil is uneven, with the large majority of Brazilians living in São Paulo, Rio de Janeiro, and other areas along and near the Atlantic coast. Most areas of the Brazilian interior, including much of the Amazon River basin, are sparsely populated.

What is now Brazil has been inhabited by numerous indigenous peoples for at least 10,000 years. The coast of Brazil was settled by Portuguese colonists beginning in the early 16th century. The city of Rio de Janeiro, which would be Brazil's capital city for nearly 400 years, was founded in 1565. As the Portuguese developed Brazil's agricultural and mining activities, they imported millions of African slaves to work in the fields and in the mines. Today, Brazil has one of the most heterogeneous and diverse populations in the world, including people of European, African, Asian, indigenous, and mixed-race ancestry.

Brazil became independent in 1822. After more than a century of autocratic rule, Brazil became a democracy after World War II except for the period between 1964 and 1985, when it was governed by a military dictatorship. Since the restoration of democracy, Brazil's economy has boomed, and it is regarded by the United Nations as the sixth-largest economy in the world.

The government of Brazil has conducted a formal census for more than 140 years. The first official census, taken in 1872, counted nearly 10 million people. The population tripled to about 30 million in 1930, and reached 70 million by 1960. It doubled over the next three decades, with nearly 147 million people counted in the 1991 census. According to the most recent census, taken in 2010, the population of Brazil was about 192.8 million. Projections suggest that the population will level off at around 205 to 210 million between 2030 and 2050.

Both crude birth rates and crude death rates in Brazil have fallen steadily since the 1950s. The birth rate was 44.1 in 1955, and dropped to 32.5 in 1980 and 16.4 by 2010. The death rate in 1955 was 15.5, declining to 9.0 in 1980 and 6.4 in 2010. Thus the rate of natural increase has also decreased from 2.9 percent per year in 1955 to 0.9 percent per year in 2010. The total fertility rate has also declined from 6.15 in the 1950s to 1.90 by 2010. Experts attribute this decline to much higher levels of education and increasing participation of women in the work force, and not particularly to efforts on the part of the government. Total fertility rates are higher in rural areas and among immigrants and rural to urban migrants, while they are lower in large cities.

Throughout its history, Brazil's population has been influenced by the arrival of large numbers of immigrants. Immigration was common throughout the 19th century and peaked in the early 20th century. At that time, most immigrants moving to Brazil came from Europe, and especially from Portugal, Spain, Italy, and Germany. Immigration levels declined between the 1930s and the 1980s, but began to increase again in the late 20th century. Portugal remains the largest source of Brazilian immigrants, but many other immigrants today come from Asia and elsewhere in South America.

See Also: Census; China; Crude Birth Rate; Crude Death Rate; India; Indonesia; Rate of Natural Increase; Rural to Urban Migration; Russia; São Paulo; Slavery; Total Fertility Rate; United States of America

Further Reading

Ernesto Friedrich Amaral and Wilson Fusco. "Shaping Brazil: The Role of International Migration." Migration Information Service Country Profiles, June 2005. http://www.migrationinformation.org/Profiles/display.cfm?ID=311.

Lael Brainard and Leonardo Martinez-Dias, eds. *Brazil as an Economic Superpower? Understanding Brazil's Changing Role in the Global Economy*. Washington, DC: Brookings Institution Press, 2009.

Juan Ferero. "Brazil's Falling Birth Rate: A 'New Way of Thinking.'" *npr.org*, January 15, 2012. http://www.npr.org/2012/01/15/145133220/brazils-falling-birth-rate-a-new-way-of-thinking.

Pakistan

Pakistan, known formally as the Islamic Republic of Pakistan, is the sixth-most populous country in the world, with a population of over 180 million. Pakistan's land area is 307,374 square miles, or about the size of Texas and Louisiana combined. Thus Pakistan's population density is about 600 persons per square mile.

Afghanistan has been beset by civil war since the early 1980s, and millions of Afghans have been displaced as refugees. This girl is one of an estimated 1.6 million Afghan refugees who live in neighboring Pakistan. (AP Photo/Muhammed Muheisen)

Given that much of Pakistan's land area consists of deserts and/or rugged mountains unsuitable for farming, its physiological density is considerably higher than its overall population density.

Pakistan is located in the western part of the Indian subcontinent. Many of the country's people live in or near the valley of the Indus River, which is the site of one of the oldest civilizations in the world. Archaeologists have discovered that the Indus Valley Civilization arose about 6,000 years ago, and the valley has been inhabited continuously ever since. Present-day Pakistan was controlled by various empires from the Middle East, Persia, and India before it was conquered by the Mughal Empire in 1526.

In the 19th century, the British East India Company deposed the Mughals and established control over present-day Pakistan. The territory became part of the colony of British India in the late 19th century. In the 20th century, efforts within British India to achieve independence were complicated by the question of whether to divide the colony into separate countries on the basis of religion. Many Muslims in British India supported partition, given that a large majority of people throughout the colony were Hindus. However, most people living in present-day Pakistan were Muslims.

After World War II, the decision was made to divide British India into two independent countries: India, with a Hindu majority, and Pakistan, with a Muslim majority. The two countries became independent in 1947. After partition, Pakistan included two portions separated by 1,000 miles of Indian territory. These were present-day Pakistan, then known as West Pakistan, and present-day Bangladesh, which was then known as East Pakistan. Bangladesh seceded from Pakistan and became an independent country in 1971.

Pakistan has seen very rapid population growth since it became independent. In 1950, three years after independence, the population of present-day Pakistan (not including present-day Bangladesh) was estimated at about 37.5 million. The population more than doubled in the next 30 years, reaching 80 million by 1980. In 2000, the population was approximately 145 million. The population of Pakistan is distributed very unevenly. The large majority of Pakistanis live in the Indus River valley, extending from the Indian border in northeastern Pakistan to the country's largest city of Karachi on the Arabian Sea coast. Arid and mountainous northern and western Pakistan are sparsely populated.

Pakistan has undergone partial demographic transition, with a sharp decline in its crude death rate since independence and a more recent decline in its crude birth rate. The crude birth rate of Pakistan remained nearly constant at about 42 or 43 births per 1,000 people between 1950 and 1990. After 1990, the birth rate began to decline, reaching 28 per 1,000 by 2010. The total fertility rate of Pakistan was above 6.3 between 1950 and 1990 but dropped to 3.65 by 2010. The total fertility rate is higher among less educated, rural Pakistani women relative to more educated urban residents. Pakistan's crude death rate was 23.8 per thousand in 1950 but dropped to 7.7 in 2010. The rate of natural increase was about 2 percent per year in 1950. It rose to 3.1 percent by 1990, but has since dropped to less than 2 percent per year today.

Most of Pakistan's population growth has occurred because of natural increase, although the United Nations has estimated that Pakistan's population includes about 3.5 million people, or 2 percent, who were born in other countries. The largest community of immigrants consists of refugees from neighboring, war-torn Afghanistan. Pakistan's government regards these Afghan refugees as temporary residents who will return eventually to Afghanistan if and when armed hostilities cease, although many of these refugees express a preference to remain in Pakistan. Pakistan also contains large populations of international labor migrants, most of whom come from poor Asian and Middle Eastern countries, including Bangladesh, Myanmar, and Tajikistan, and many of whom work at unskilled jobs.

Although Pakistan's rate of natural increase is slowing, Pakistan's population continues to grow at a much faster rate than do other large Asian countries including India, Bangladesh, China, and Indonesia. Some Pakistani government officials regard continuing population growth as a potentially serious problem for Pakistan.

These officials and other experts have called for stepped-up efforts to promote reduced fertility. Those promoting fertility reductions also see linkages between population growth and unemployment, environmental degradation, and incentives to promote terrorism. In 2010, Pakistan's government established a comprehensive national population policy. Whether it will be successful in promoting further reduced birth rates in Pakistan remains to be seen.

See Also: Bangladesh; China; Crude Birth Rate; Crude Death Rate; Demographic Transition Model; India; Indonesia; International Labor Migration; Karachi; Physiological Density; Population Density; Rate of Natural Increase; Refugees; Total Fertility Rate

Further Reading

Dawn.com. "Afghan Refugees in Pakistan Resist Pressure to Return." December 26, 2012. http://dawn.com/2012/12/12/afghan-refugees-in-pakistan-resist-pressure-to-return/.

Myra Imran. "Pakistan's Rapid Population Growth 'Crushing Burden on Economy.'" *Pakistan International News*, May 3, 2013. http://www.thenews.com.pk/Todays-News-6 -175010-Pakistans-rapid-population-growth-crushing-burden-on-economy.

Nigeria

Nigeria, which is known formally as the Federal Republic of Nigeria, is by far the largest country in Africa by population. The country is located on the coast of the Gulf of Guinea, which is part of the Atlantic Ocean. Nigeria's population of approximately 175 million is more than twice that of Ethiopia, which is the second largest African country by population. Nigeria's largest city and former capital of Lagos is the largest city by population in sub-Saharan Africa. However, about half of all Nigerians live in rural areas and about 30 percent of Nigeria's workers are farmers.

Nigeria's land area is about 367,000 square miles, making its land area slightly smaller than Texas and New Mexico combined. Nigeria's population density of about 480 people per square mile is third among mainland African countries, trailing only the much smaller countries of Rwanda and Burundi. Population densities are highest in the southern third of Nigeria near the Gulf of Guinea coast, although they are greater than 100 people per square mile in every Nigerian state.

Nigeria's current territory has been contested by various kingdoms, empires, and chieftaincies over more than 2,000 years. In the early 18th century, Europeans began to establish settlements, including Lagos, along the Nigerian coast. These settlements were centers for the slave trade until slavery was banned by the British government in 1834. In 1861, Britain annexed the Lagos area as the Lagos Colony.

The coastal region east of Lagos was governed by the British-backed Niger Coast Protectorate beginning in 1891. The protectorate was merged with the Niger Colony in 1906. What is now northern Nigeria was recognized as a British sphere of influence following the Congress of Berlin, at which Africa was divided into European colonies. In 1914, this region was merged with the southern coastal regions to form the colony of Nigeria, named for the Niger River that flows through the country. Nigeria became independent in 1960.

As is the case throughout Africa, Nigeria has experienced rapid and continuing population growth over the course of the 20th and 21st centuries. In 1950, a census commissioned by the British government counted about 38 million people in what is today Nigeria. The population was estimated at 52 million in 1965, when the first census of Nigeria was taken by the government of the newly independent country. The population grew to about 77 million in 1980 and 124 million in 2000. Nigeria's population continues to grow at about 3 percent annually.

Nigeria's rapid population growth is due in part to continuing high crude birth rates. In contrast to many less developed countries, the crude birth rate in Nigeria has dropped only slightly since the 1950s, falling from 46.5 in 1955 to 40.1 in 2010. However, the crude death rate in Nigeria has dropped more rapidly, from 27.7 in 1955 to 15.1 in 2010. Hence Nigeria's rate of natural increase has risen over the past half-century. Nigeria's high crude birth rates are associated with its high total fertility rate of 5.6, down only slightly from 6.35 in the 1950s and 1960s. Nigeria's high total fertility rate has contributed to the fact that the country's population is very young. Its median age of about 18 years is the lowest of any large country in the world.

Nigeria has a very diverse population. More than 250 distinct ethnic groups are recognized. However, about two-thirds of Nigerians are members of the Hausa and Fulani, Yoruba, or Igbo people. About half of Nigerians are Christians and a quarter of them are Muslims. Ethnic and religious conflict has plagued Nigeria since independence. In particular, conflict between Muslims, who dominate the northern half of the country, and Christians, who dominate the southern half, has erupted into violence on many occasions. In order to reduce this sectarian conflict, and also to slow the rate of population growth in densely populated Lagos, the government of Nigeria moved its capital city from Lagos to the new city of Abuja, near the geographic center of the country, in 1991. The site of Abuja was chosen in order to promote development of the interior, and it was also located in an area between the Muslim-dominated north and the Christian-dominated south with the idea of trying to stem religious discord.

In the foreseeable future, Nigeria's population is expected to continue to increase rapidly. If current growth rates continue, the country's population will reach 300 million by 2040. Even if total fertility rates were to decrease quickly, the fact that there is a very large number of young people in Nigeria's population means that population will continue to grow over the next few decades. Nigeria faces many problems common to crowded countries with rapidly increasing populations including high levels of unemployment, inadequate infrastructure, insufficient numbers of schools to educate the country's very large number of children, and environmental damage associated with population growth. Government officials have initiated efforts to promote family planning and otherwise discourage people from having large families, but these efforts have been hindered by local opposition on religious and cultural grounds.

See Also: Census; Crude Birth Rate; Crude Death Rate; Ethiopia; Lagos; Median Age; Population Density; Rate of Natural Increase; Total Fertility Rate

Further Reading

Elisabeth Rosenthal. "Nigeria Tested by Rapid Rise in Population." *New York Times*, April 14, 2012. http://www.nytimes.com/2012/04/15/world/africa/in-nigeria-a-preview-of-an-ov ercrowded-planet.html.

Good Wilson. "Nigeria's National Population Policy and Its Implications for Sustainable Development." *LWATI: A Journal of Contemporary Research* 8, no. 4 (2012): 255–71.

Bangladesh

Bangladesh, known formally as the People's Republic of Bangladesh, is located in the northeastern part of the Indian peninsula in South Asia. It is the eighth-largest country in the world by population, with more than 160 million people. With a land area only slightly larger than Iowa, Bangladesh has a population density of approximately 2,700 people per square mile. It is the most densely populated large state in the world. Although the urban populations of Bangladesh are increasing, a majority of Bangladeshis live in small villages in rural areas. Population densities are high throughout the country.

Most of Bangladesh is located within the fertile valleys of the Ganges and Brahmaputra Rivers, whose combined delta comprises nearly half of the country's land area before the rivers empty into the Bay of Bengal. The large majority of Bangladesh's people are ethnic Bengalis who speak the Bengali language and practice Islam. In 1858, present-day Bangladesh became part of British India, a part of the British Empire along with present-day India and Pakistan.

The British granted independence to British India in 1947. At that time, the British decided to divide British India into two countries on the basis of religion, creating the two independent states of India and Pakistan. Pakistan included those areas of British India with predominantly Muslim populations. Present-day Bangladesh was known as East Pakistan, which was nearly 1,000 miles from West

Pakistan by air. Tensions between East Pakistan, which contained a majority of the population, and West Pakistan, which controlled the government, intensified during the 1950s and 1960s. In 1971, East Pakistan seceded from Pakistan and became the independent country of Bangladesh.

Bangladesh's population has grown very rapidly since it became independent from the British Empire. In 1951, a census taken by the government of Pakistan estimated about 42 million people living in what was then East Pakistan. The population doubled over the next 30 years, reaching 87 million in 1981. Since that time, it has nearly doubled again. Bangladesh's population increases have been due largely to its high rate of natural increase, although its rates of natural increase have declined in recent years. According to United Nations estimates, the rate of natural increase in Bangladesh has declined from about 2.8 percent in the 1950s to about 1.5 percent today. Much of this increase has been due to a decline in Bangladesh's total fertility rate, which has dropped from about 6.4 in the 1950s to about 2.4 today.

Changing demographics in Bangladesh are evident in historical trends in crude birth rates and crude death rates. The crude birth rate of present-day Bangladesh in the early 1950s, shortly after Pakistan became an independent country, was estimated at about 48 per 1,000. It remained above 40 per 1,000 until the 1980s and has declined ever since. The current crude birth rate is about 20 per 1,000. The crude death rate in the 1950s was nearly 20 per 1,000. It dropped consistently through the 1960s, 1970s, and 1980s except for a brief spike in the early 1970s following transition to independence and a series of natural disasters. The crude death rate dropped below 10 per 1,000 in the early 1990s, and has continued to decline to about 6 per 1,000 today.

Many Bangladeshis have emigrated in recent years in search of better economic opportunities. Most of these emigrants are international labor migrants. Hundreds of thousands have moved to oil-rich countries such as Saudi Arabia, the United Arab Emirates, and Qatar in order to find jobs. However, many more Bengalis have moved across the border into less densely populated India. Many of these immigrants are illegal immigrants and the issue of immigration policy has become highly controversial in both countries. In an effort to control illegal immigration, India is completing work on a border fence that will extend along the entire border of more than 2,000 miles between the two countries.

Bangladesh's large population has also been subjected to devastating natural disasters. Several of the most devastating tropical cyclones in world history have made landfall in or near Bangladesh via the Bay of Bengal. A typhoon that struck present-day Bangladesh in 1970 is believed to have caused more than 400,000 fatalities. Another typhoon struck in 1991, with a death toll of about 140,000. As well, half of Bangladesh's land surface is less than 30 feet, or 10 meters, above sea level. This low-lying land is especially vulnerable to potential rises in sea levels resulting from global climate change. Bangladesh's vulnerability to destructive tropical storms, flooding, and food shortages given its immense population leaves open the possibility that its crude death rate may increase at least in the short run in the foreseeable future.

See Also: Border Fences; Crude Birth Rate; Crude Death Rate; India; International Labor Migration; Pakistan; Population Density; Rate of Natural Increase; Total Fertility Rate

Further Reading

Scott Carney, Jason Miklian, and Kristian Hoelscher. "Fortress India," *Foreign Policy*, July/August 2011. http://www.foreignpolicy.com/articles/2011/06/20/fortress_india?page=full.

Atiqar Rahman Khan and Mufaweza Khan. "Population Programs in Bangladesh: Problems, Prospects, and Policy Issues." populationcommons.org, 2010. http://www.populationcommunication.com/Medias/Bangladesh_report.pdf.

William Alex Litchfield. "Climate Change Induced Extreme Weather Events and Sea Level Rise in Bangladesh Leading to Migration and Conflict." *ICE Case Studies* 229 (2010). http://www1.american.edu/ted/ice/Bangladesh.html.

Russia

Russia, known formally as the Russian Federation, is by far the largest country in the world by land area. Its land area is 60 percent greater than that of Canada, and it is almost twice as large as the United States and China. With about 143 million people, Russia ranks ninth in the world by population. Russia's population density is much lower than are the population densities of any of the world's other highly populated countries. The large majority of Russians live in the European portion of the country. Eastern Russia, especially to the north, is very sparsely inhabited.

What is now western Russia was settled by Slavs from Eastern Europe nearly 2,000 years ago. These early settlers were joined by newcomers from Scandinavia, including the Rus people for whom Russia was named. The Rus, whose capital was at Kiev in present-day Ukraine, became the dominant power in northeastern Europe until their regime was deposed by Mongol invaders in the 13th century. The Mongols were overthrown in the 14th century, and the Grand Duchy of Moscow, centered on that city, achieved political power. Ivan IV, known also as Ivan the Terrible, became the first Tsar of Russia in 1547.

Between the 16th and the 19th century, Ivan's successors expanded the Russian state to the east, west, and south. Russia expanded into territory controlled previously by Poland, Lithuania, and Finland. To the east, Russia established control of

Russia's population has declined since the collapse of the Soviet Union in 1991 because of high rates of emigration, very little immigration, and very low birth rates. Population declines are especially notable in outlying areas such as the town of Chersky in northern Siberia. This man is riding a snowmobile along the main street of Chersky, which lost more than half of its population between 1991 and 2010. (AP Photo/Arthur Max)

sparsely populated Siberia. The Russian state also expanded to the Black Sea and the Caspian Sea in Central Asia.

The last Tsar of the Russian Empire, Nicholas II, was deposed in 1917 as the Russian Revolution broke out. After World War I ended, civil war between the Bolsheviks and the Mensheviks, two rival factions of the Russian Revolution, broke out. The Bolsheviks defeated the Mensheviks and gained control of Russia and neighboring areas by the early 1920s. In 1922, they established the Union of Soviet Socialist Republics (USSR). Within the USSR, present-day Russia became the Russian Soviet Federative Socialist Republic (RSFSR). The RSFSR was the largest of the 15 Soviet republics, which were delineated on linguistic and cultural lines, by both population and land area. It contained about 75 percent of the Soviet Union's land area and about half of its population.

The USSR collapsed in 1991, and each of the 15 former Soviet republics became an independent state. The RSFSR became the independent Russian Federation and began a transition from Communism to a market-based democracy. Since then, the former RSFSR has experienced a steady decrease in its population due to emigration, low birth rates, and substandard public health.

Russia's population grew modestly during the country's seven decades of Communist rule, and has declined since then. The population of the RSFSR was estimated at 100 million in 1930 and rose to about 110 million on the eve of World War II in the late 1930s. According to a census taken by the USSR in 1946, the RSFSR's population was about 98 million. The decline in Russia's population during World War II was caused by large numbers of military and civilian casualties, including victims of widespread famines, occurring during the war. After the war, Russia's population rebounded to about 120 million in 1960 and to about 148.5 million at the time of the USSR's collapse in 1990. Since that time, Russia's population declined each year between 1991 and 2008, rebounding slightly since that time.

Russia's population declines were associated partly with a declining rate of natural increase. Its crude birth rate dropped from about 26 per 1,000 in the 1950s to between 15 and 18 each year between 1970 and 1988. After the collapse of Soviet Communism, the birth rate began to drop rapidly. It reached a low of 8.5 in 1997, but then increased slowly to 13.3 in 2012. These declines in the birth rate occurred in part because the Soviets had encouraged large families and provided material rewards to mothers who bore large numbers of children, but these incentives ended once the Soviet Union dissolved. This decline is also reflected in Russia's declining total fertility rate. The total fertility rate hovered around 2, or replacement-level fertility, during the 1970s and 1980s but dropped to 1.2 by 2000. Since then, it has rebounded to about 1.7 in 2012. This increase may reflect the fact the current Russian government is once again promoting higher levels of fertility.

While Russia's birth rate has declined since the early 1990s, its crude death rate has increased. The crude death rate in the RSFSR was below 12 per 1,000 each year between 1948 and 1990. However, it rose to 14.3 in 1993 and has remained above 13 every year since then. Thus, Russia's rate of natural increase has been negative every year since 1992. Increases in the death rate have occurred for several reasons, including extensive alcoholism, high levels of pollution associated with mismanagement of natural resources during the Soviet regime, and low quality of health care. Life expectancy declined below 65 years in the mid-1990s, but has increased to 70 years by 2012. However, life expectancy remains low in places associated with mining and other environmentally destructive practices. For example, the city of Norilsk north of the Arctic Circle is the world's largest nickel-mining center. Fumes and tailings from nickel smelters have destroyed almost all of the vegetation within a 30-mile radius of Norilsk, and life expectancy there remains 10 years less than the national average. There is a substantial gap in life expectancy between men and women, with women on average living more than 12 years longer than men. This gap is attributed in part to alcohol abuse, violence, and inadequate health care.

NORILSK

The city of Norilsk is a mining center in northern Siberia in Russia. Norilsk is located north of the Arctic Circle. Deposits of nickel, copper, cobalt, platinum, and other valuable minerals were discovered in the area near present-day Norilsk in the 18th century. These minerals were mined on a large scale beginning in the early 20th century. The city was founded in 1935 and built largely with forced and convict labor. Today, about one-fifth of the nickel produced in the world is mined in the area near Norilsk.

Decades of mining operations have devastated Norilsk, whose current population is estimated at about 175,000. In 2007, Norilsk was identified as one of the 10 most polluted cities in the world. Because much of the nickel mined near Norilsk is smelted there, all of the trees within 30 miles of the nickel smelter have been killed by sulfur dioxide and other emissions. It has been estimated that 1 percent of all of the sulfur dioxide emissions into the atmosphere of the entire earth comes from Norilsk. Life expectancy in Norilsk has been estimated as much as 10 years less than in the rest of Russia.

Further Reading

Coburn Dukehart. "Russians Adapt to a Freezing, Dark, and Polluted Place." *National Geographic Proof*, January 6, 2014. http://proof.nationalgeographic.com/2014/01/06/russians-adapt-to-a-freezing-dark-and-polluted-place/.

Russia's population changes since the early 1990s have been associated also with changing migration patterns. Within a few years after the collapse of the Soviet Union, many Russians moved to much wealthier and more developed Western Europe, the United States, Canada, or Israel. More recently, Russia has experienced positive net migration. Many in-migrants into Russia have moved there from former Soviet republics such as the now-independent countries of Central Asia such as Kazakhstan and Uzbekistan.

Russian president Vladimir Putin has noted that if current trends continue, Russia's population could drop to as few as 107 million by 2050. In response to these predictions, Russia's government is pursuing actively policies to encourage population increases by increasing the birth rate, lowering the death rate, and by promoting immigration. The policy is based on a premise that economic development will provide couples with more resources to have more children. The government has also mounted an active campaign to reduce alcoholism and drug abuse, which it has associated with despair over a sluggish economy and uncertain future. Russia's population has begun to increase slowly after years of decline, but whether this trend will continue or the degree to which these policies will contribute to changing demographics remains to be seen.

See Also: Census; China; Crude Birth Rate; Crude Death Rate; Famine; Population Density; Rate of Natural Increase; Replacement-Level Fertility; Total Fertility Rate; United States of America

Further Reading

Ivan A. Aleshkovski. "International Migration, Globalization, and Demographic Development of the Russian Federation." *Journal of Globalization Studies* 3 (2012): 95–110.

Julie DaVanzo and David Adamson. "Russia's Demographic Crisis: How Real Is It?" RAND Objective Analysis, Effective Solutions, Paper IP-162, 2010. http://www.rand.org/pubs/issue_papers/IP162/index2.html.

Fred Weir. "Putin Vows to Halt Russia's Population Plunge with Babies, Immigrants." *Christian Science Monitor*, February 14, 2012. http://www.csmonitor.com/World/2012/0214/Putin-vows-to-halt-Russia-s-population-plunge-with-babies-immigrants.

Japan

Japan is located off the coast of East Asia. Its closest mainland neighbors are South Korea and China. The Japanese archipelago includes the main islands of Hokkaido, Honshu, Shikoku, and Kyushu and more than 6,800 smaller islands. Japan's overall land area of about 145,000 square miles is slightly smaller than California. The largest of the four major islands is Honshu, which contains about 60 percent of Japan's land area and more than 80 percent of Japan's people. Honshu contains the metropolitan area of Tokyo, which is Japan's political capital, economic and financial center, and primate city. Tokyo is at the center of the largest metropolitan area in the world, with a population of more than 35 million. Population densities on the other islands, especially Shikoku and the northern part of Hokkaido, are considerably lower.

Archaeologists have confirmed that humans have lived in Japan for more than 30,000 years. The ancestors of most modern Japanese, or Yamato people, moved to Japan from the mainland between 2,500 and 3,000 years ago. In the 17th century, Japan isolated itself from the outside world by placing strict limits on trade with other countries and forbidding Japanese nationals to leave the country. In 1853, Japan's self-imposed isolation was ended when U.S. Navy commodore Matthew Perry forced Japan to open itself to trade with the United States and other Western powers.

Japan had been ruled by emperors for nearly 2,500 years, but for most of this period the emperor's role was largely ceremonial. In 1868, however, Japan's emperor gained real political power in what came to be known as the Meiji Restoration. Japan industrialized rapidly. In the early 20th century, Japan became a colonial power after seizing control of many areas of mainland East Asia, Southeast Asia, and islands in the Pacific. In the 1930s, Japan allied itself with Nazi Germany and fascist Italy. After Japan and its allies were defeated by Allied forces in World War II, Japan relinquished its colonial empire and remained sovereign over the Japanese archipelago only.

At that time, the Japanese emperor relinquished his power and Japan became a republic that was occupied by United States forces until 1952. Beginning in the 1950s, Japan's economy underwent rapid economic development. By the 1980s, Japan had become a highly developed country. Its per capita income and standard of living are comparable to those of the United States and most European countries.

Japan takes an official census of its population every five years. In October 2010, the official Japanese census determined that Japan's population was 128,057,352. Japan's population increased steadily during the 20th century. In 1910, Japan's population was about 51 million. This increased to about 73 million by 1940. The population declined slightly during World War II but began to increase again after 1945. It reached 83 million in 1950 and 117 million in 1980. After 1980, the rate of population increase slowed. The population was about 126.9 million in 2000. Thus, Japan's population in 2010 was less than 1 percent higher than it was in 2000. In 2012, Japan's official statistical agency estimated that Japan's population has begun to decline. According to this estimate, if current crude birth rates and crude death rates remain steady, Japan's population will decline by about a million people per year over the next several decades.

Japan's impending population declines are associated with very low birth rates and very low levels of immigration. Japan's total fertility rate, or number of children born to the average woman, was estimated at 1.39 in 2010. Thus, Japan's total fertility rate is considerably lower than replacement-level fertility.

The rate of population decline in Japan has been slowed by the fact that Japan's life expectancy is among the highest in the world. The current life expectancy for newborn babies in Japan is over 83 years. The high life expectancy in Japan is associated with a large elderly population. About 23 percent of Japanese citizens are over 65 years of age, and this percentage is expected to increase to as high as 35 percent by 2050. Japanese government officials have pondered difficulties associated with providing services to support Japan's aging population. With a low birth rate and an increasing elderly population, a smaller and smaller percentage of Japan's population remains in the labor force. The cost of providing pensions and medical care to the elderly continues to increase, with fewer resources available to cover these costs. More and more Japanese people continue to work into their old age in order to have the resources to support themselves and their families.

In many societies, the aging of the population and the increasing percentage of people who are elderly are offset by immigration. In Japan, however, the percentage of people who are immigrants is much lower than in the United States, Canada, Europe, or Australia. A very large percentage of Japan's people are of ethnic Japanese origin. As of 2010, Japan's population included about 2.2 million immigrants, or about 1.7 percent of its population. Relative to other developed countries, Japan has highly restrictive immigration laws. Although Japan has historically been hostile to immigration on the part of non-Japanese people, the Japanese government has recently initiated efforts to relax Japan's strict immigration standards in order to reduce the degree of Japan's historic antipathy toward immigrants. A few ethnic groups indigenous to the Japanese islands are recognized by the Japanese government. These include the Ainu, whose 150,000 people live primarily in northern Hokkaido, and the indigenous peoples of Okinawa and other islands south of the main portions of the Japanese archipelago.

See Also: Crude Birth Rate; Crude Death Rate; Germany; Italy; Life Expectancy; Primate City; Replacement-Level Fertility; Tokyo; Total Fertility Rate

Further Reading

Michael Birt. "Another Tsunami Warning: Caring for Japan's Elderly." National Bureau of Asian Research, 2011. http://www.nbr.org/research/activity.aspx?id=131.

Carl Haub. "Japan's Demographic Future." *Population Reference Bureau*, May 2010. http://www.prb.org/Articles/2010/japandemography.aspx.

Brian Salsburg, Clay Chandler, and Heang Chhor. *Reimagining Japan: The Quest for a Future That Works*. San Francisco: VIZ Publishing, 2011.

Mexico

Mexico, or the United Mexican States, is the 11th-largest country in the world by population, with about 115 million people. It is the third-largest country by population in the western hemisphere, following the United States and Brazil. Mexico is the largest country in which Spanish is the primary language. Its political capital and primate city, Mexico City, is one of the five largest cities in the world.

Present-day Mexico was inhabited by numerous Native American cultures for thousands of years prior to the arrival of Spanish colonists in the 16th century. The Olmec civilization flourished along the Gulf of Mexico coast of eastern Mexico approximately 3,000 to 3,500 years ago. For several centuries beginning around 200 CE, the Mayan civilization controlled the Yucatan Peninsula along with nearby areas of southeastern Mexico and northern Central America. The Mayan Empire collapsed between 900 and 1000 CE, for unknown reasons. Some anthropologists believe that the Mayan population exceeded the area's carrying capacity, and that environmental degradation and/or natural disasters decimated the population.

To the northwest, the Aztec Empire arose in the Valley of Mexico near the site of Mexico City. The Aztecs remained in control of central and southern Mexico before the regime was overthrown by Spanish conquistadors, who had established trading centers on the Gulf of Mexico coast, in 1521. Spanish conquest of the Aztecs was motivated by a search for gold and silver. Mining and export of these minerals became an important economic activity. Mexico soon was incorporated into the Spanish empire as the colony of New Spain.

Beginning in 1810, rebels against Spanish rule in New Spain began active guerilla efforts to overthrow Spanish rule. The Mexican War for Independence lasted 11 years, after which Mexican independence was recognized in 1821. During the 1840s and early 1850s, much of northern Mexico was ceded to the United States. Texas declared its independence from Mexico in 1836 and joined the United States in 1845. Three years later, the United States annexed California, Nevada, and most of Utah, Arizona, and New Mexico following the signing of the Treaty of Guadalupe Hidalgo ending the Mexican-American War. In 1853, the United States purchased southern Arizona and southern New Mexico, establishing the current boundary between the two countries.

Mexico's population has been estimated at about 6 million at independence in the early 1820s. The population doubled over the next 80 years and has been estimated at 13.6 million in 1900. Since that time, Mexico has grown steadily as the country has undergone demographic transition. It reached 20 million around 1940 and doubled to about 40 million by 1965. The population doubled again in the next 25 years, reaching 80 million around 1990. Since then Mexico has continued to grow, but at a slower rate, as birth rates and total fertility rates have declined steadily.

Mexico's rate of natural increase has declined in recent years in accordance with declining birth rates. During the first two-thirds of the 20th century, Mexico's death rate dropped quickly in accordance with reduced infant mortality and improved diagnosis and treatment of diseases in adults. The Green Revolution, which resulted in large increases of food production in Mexico during the years after World War II, also contributed to reduced death rates. The birth rate remained high until the late 20th century, however, when it began to decline. It has dropped from about 33 per 1,000 in the early 1990s to an estimated 22 per 1,000 by 2012. The total fertility rate has also declined from about 3.4 in 1990 to 2.1 in 2010. Some Mexican demographers predict that Mexico's total fertility rate will soon drop below replacement-level fertility, and therefore that Mexico's population will reach a peak and then begin to decline slowly beginning around 2040 or 2050.

Mexican's population density is uneven, and its physiological density is considerably higher than its overall population density because much of Mexico's land is mountainous and/or arid and unsuitable for agriculture. The Valley of Mexico, including Mexico City, is densely populated. This region, which was once the center of the Aztec empire, and neighboring portions of highland central Mexico contain about 40 percent of Mexico's people. Areas once dominated by the Mayans in southeastern Mexico also have fairly high population densities. Today, the fastest-growing region of Mexico includes the cities along the boundary of the United States, including Tijuana, Ciudad Juarez, Nuevo Laredo, and Matamoros. Many other areas of Mexico are sparsely populated, including the large and mountainous region between the heavily populated central highlands and the U.S. border.

Migration has had very large impacts on Mexico's population. Since the 1960s, Mexico has been the leading source of migrants to the United States. Most are international labor migrants and some are illegal immigrants. Some estimates suggest that as many as 6 to 8 million Mexicans have migrated illegally to the United States, with many more having migrated legally. Large-scale migration to the United States has impacted Mexican communities as well as American cities in that most who migrate are young working adults, leaving behind children, the elderly, and the disabled.

The status of these illegal immigrants, and other Mexican migrants, has been a significant political issue in both countries. Since about 2008, however, rates of legal and illegal migration from Mexico to the United States have dropped, as the U.S. economy went into a recession and Mexico's economy continued to improve, reducing both push factors and pull factors. Mexico has become an increasingly important destination for migrants leaving Central and South America.

See Also: Brazil; Carrying Capacity; Crude Birth Rate; Demographic Transition Model; Green Revolution; Illegal Immigration; Infant Mortality Rate; International Labor Migration; Mexico City; Natural Disasters; Physiological Density; Primate City; Push Factors and Pull Factors; Rate of Natural Increase; Replacement-Level Fertility; Total Fertility Rate; United States of America

Further Reading

Damian Cave. "In Mexican Villages, Few Are Left to Dream of U.S." *New York Times*, April 2, 2013. http://www.nytimes.com/2013/04/03/world/americas/new-wave-of-mexican -immigrants-seems-unlikely.html?pagewanted=all.

The Economist. "Mexico's Population: When the *Niños* Run Out." April 22, 2010. http://www .economist.com/node/15959332.

GeoMexico. "Mexico's Population Keeps Growing, but at a Slower Rate." May 5, 2011. http:// geo-mexico.com/?p=4039.

Philippines

The Republic of the Philippines is the 12th-largest country by population in the world, with a population of about 100 million. The country is an archipelago of about 7,000 islands. The 100 million residents of the Philippines live in an area slightly larger than the state of Arizona; hence the population density of the Philippines is among the highest of the largest countries in the world.

The largest island in the Philippines is Luzon, which contains half of the Philippines' population and a third of its land area. Luzon includes the city of Manila, which is the country's capital city and the 21st-largest metropolitan area in the world by population, with more than 15 million inhabitants. About 25 percent of the country's people live on the southern island of Mindanao, with the other 25 percent living on the other approximately 2,000 inhabited islands comprising the archipelago.

Archaeologists believe that the Philippines archipelago was first settled at least 50,000 years ago. The islands were divided among numerous small kingdoms and chiefdoms for at least 2,500 years before the Spanish navigator Ferdinand Magellan claimed the islands for Spain in 1521. In 1565, Spain began to establish permanent settlements on the islands, which were named in honor of King Philip II. Manila, which was already inhabited by indigenous Filipinos, was taken over by the Spanish and made the administrative center of the colony. The Spanish legacy continues in that a majority of Filipinos are Roman Catholics and the Spanish language continues to be spoken widely.

Spain remained in control of the Philippines until 1898, when sovereignty over the islands was transferred to the United States during the Spanish-American War. Between 1899 and 1901, the Americans rejected a Filipino independence claim and defeated Filipino insurgent forces. The islands remained under American administration until they were captured by Japan in 1942, during World War II. The United States regained sovereignty over the islands after the end of the war, and governed the colony briefly until the Philippines were granted formal independence in 1946.

As with many less developed countries, the Philippines have experienced rapid and steady population growth during the 20th and 21st centuries. The first official census of the Philippines was taken by the Spanish in 1877 and counted about 5.6 million residents. In 1903, the population was estimated by an American census at 7.6 million. The population was estimated at 17 million in 1941 and at 27 million according to the official census of 1960. Since then, the population of the Philippines has nearly doubled every two decades, reaching about 48 million in 1980 and nearly 77 million in 2000.

Other population trends in the Philippines are consistent with those of other developing countries. The crude birth rate has dropped by about 50 percent since the 1950s, from 48.6 babies per 1,000 people in 1955 to 25.9 per 1,000 in 2010. The crude death rate has also fallen steadily, from 13.3 in 1955 to 5.9 today. Hence the rate of natural increase has also declined. The current rate of population growth is about 2 percent per year. Life expectancy at birth is about 72 years, placing the Philippines below highly developed Asian countries such as Japan and Singapore but considerably higher than most other less developed countries throughout the world.

Population growth in the contemporary Philippines is due entirely to natural increase. For many years, the Philippines has experienced net out-migration. Since 2000, the annual net rate of migration has averaged slightly more than -1 per 1,000 people. The United States is a major destination for Filipino immigrants. In 2010, about 3.4 million Americans, or 1.1 percent of the U.S. population, claimed full or partial Filipino ancestry. California and Hawaii have the largest Filipino-American populations of the U.S. states, followed by New York, Illinois, and Texas. The metropolitan areas with the largest Filipino populations are Los Angeles, San Francisco, Honolulu, New York, and San Diego. Many other Filipinos have moved temporarily to other countries in search of employment. As of 2004, about half of Filipino labor migrants were working in the Middle East, with an additional 38 percent in Asia. Most Filipino migrants to the United States are permanent migrants, while most migrants to the Middle East or Asia move temporarily in search of work.

Population policy has been a contentious issue in Filipino politics. The Constitution of the Philippines decrees reproductive freedom, allowing couples to determine how many children they wish to have. However, various governments have initiated efforts to promote contraception and family planning. These efforts have been opposed by some Roman Catholic and Muslim leaders, as well as by officials concerned that a rapid decline in the birth rate will force the country to adjust to a rapidly aging population.

See Also: Crude Birth Rate; Crude Death Rate; Japan; Life Expectancy; Manila; Population Density; Rate of Natural Increase; Singapore

Further Reading

Maruja M. B. Asis. "The Philippines' Culture of Migration." *Migration Information Source*, January 2006. http://www.migrationinformation.org/feature/display.cfm?ID=364.

Nimja Ojema. "Population Stabilization: Philippine Case." *populationcommunication.com*, 2010. http://populationcommunication.com/Medias/Philippines_report.pdf.

Vietnam

Vietnam, known formally as the Socialist Republic of Vietnam, is located in mainland Southeast Asia along the South China Sea. It has an estimated population of about 90 million. Its land area is 128,565 square miles, slightly larger than New Mexico. Thus Vietnam has the highest population density of any country in mainland Southeast Asia. However, Vietnam's population is concentrated in two areas. These include the area around the capital city of Hanoi in the valley of the Red River to the north. The valley of the Mekong River to the south is even more densely populated. This area includes Ho Chi Minh City, which was formerly known as Saigon and is Vietnam's largest city. However, central Vietnam and the mountainous regions throughout the country have relatively low population densities.

The early history of Vietnam is linked closely to that of China, its neighbor to the north. Chinese rulers controlled northern Vietnam for more than 1,000 years beginning in the second century BCE. An indigenous Vietnamese regime ousted Chinese rule in 938 CE. Vietnamese dynasties ruled the region more than 950 years until 1885, when France incorporated Vietnam along with neighboring Laos and Cambodia as its colony of French Indochina.

In 1954, France granted independence to Vietnam, which was soon divided into North Vietnam and South Vietnam. North Vietnam was governed by a Communist regime backed by China and the Soviet Union, while South Vietnam was ruled by a regime dominated by rulers who were loyal to the pre-independence French. Beginning in the late 1950s, a guerilla organization known as the Viet Cong initiated efforts to overthrow the South Vietnamese government. Civil war broke out, with the Viet Cong supported by North Vietnam and China and the South Vietnamese regime supported by the United States.

The war ended in 1975, after the United States withdrew its troops and the Viet Cong captured the South Vietnamese capital city of Saigon (now known as Ho Chi Minh City). The North Vietnamese regime took control of the entire country, which was reunited as a socialist autocracy in 1976. As the Communist regime consolidated its control of Vietnam, hundreds of thousands of refugees, many of whom were South Vietnamese military personnel or government officials and their families, left the country; many relocated to the United States. As of the 2010 United States census of population, nearly 1.8 million Americans claimed full or partial Vietnamese ancestry.

Since the end of French colonial rule, Vietnam's population has increased steadily. Its overall population (including both North Vietnam and South Vietnam) has been estimated at about 31 million at the time of independence in 1954. The population increased to about 45 million in 1970 and 54 million in 1980, thus continuing to increase despite military and civilian casualties and the exodus of refugees during the war years. After the war, the population began to increase at a higher rate. More recently, Vietnam's population has begun to rise at a slower rate as the country has undergone demographic transition.

Vietnam's crude birth rates and crude death rates have also fallen steadily. The crude birth rate has been estimated at about 45 per 1,000 at the time of independence. It declined to 39.3 in the early 1970s and remained above 30 for the next two decades. Since then, it has fallen to about 17 as of 2010. The crude death rate fell from about 24 per 1,000 in the early 1950s to about 18 in the early 1970s. With the reunification of the country, the death rate began to decline more rapidly, dropping below 6 by the late 1990s. Today, the death rate is estimated at about 5 per 1,000.

These changes have affected Vietnam's rate of natural increase, which remained steady at between 2 and 2.5 percent per year from the 1950s until the 1990s, but has since declined to about 1.2 percent today. The total fertility rate, which was above 6 births per woman between the 1950s and the 1970s, has dropped to slightly over 2 by the 1990s. It has been below 2, or below replacement-level fertility, since 2000.

Following China's lead, in the 1960s North Vietnam imposed a policy limiting fertility to two children. The policy was imposed upon the entire country after reunification, but rescinded in 2003. Recently, concerns about continued population growth have induced government officials to revisit the effectiveness of the policy. As efforts to enforce the two-child policy have been stepped up, sex-selective abortion has increased.

During its history as an independent country, Vietnam's net migration rate has generally been negative, as more people have left the country relative to the number of immigrants. Emigration peaked as large numbers of people fled during and after the Vietnamese civil war. More recently, large numbers of Vietnamese workers have moved as international labor migrants to Australia, Thailand, and other more prosperous countries. Remittances from Vietnamese natives have become a major source of development capital in Vietnam. In recent years, Vietnam's economy has improved and rates of emigration have declined while people who had emigrated previously have returned to the country.

See Also: Census; China; Crude Birth Rate; Crude Death Rate; Demographic Transition Model; International Labor Migration; Migration; Population Density; Rate of Natural Increase; Refugees; Replacement-Level Fertility; Total Fertility Rate; United States of America

Further Reading

English News. "Vietnam's Population Reaches 88.78 Million in 2012, More Female Than Male," *Englishnews.cn*, December 28, 2012. http://news.xinhuanet.com/english/world /2012-12/28/c_132069155.htm.

Nguyen Khac Trung. "Vietnam to Enforce Two-Child Policy." *BBC Asia*, April 8, 2011, http://thegioithitrung.com/2011/04/vietnam-to-enforce-two-child-rule-bbc-asia/.

Nguyen Viet Cuong and Daniel Mont. "Economic Impacts of International Migration and Remittances on Household Welfare in Vietnam." *International Journal of Development Issues* 11: 144–63.

Ethiopia

Ethiopia, whose formal name is the Federal Democratic Republic of Ethiopia, is the second-largest country in Africa by population, with about 85 million residents. Only Nigeria among African countries has more people. It has a land area of about 426,000 square miles, roughly the size of Texas, New Mexico, and Oklahoma combined. Much of Ethiopia consists of well-watered highlands that are drained by the Blue Nile River. Most of Ethiopia's people live in this region, with relatively few in drier areas to the north and the southeast.

Homo sapiens is believed to have evolved in what is now Ethiopia and nearby Kenya 2 to 4 million years ago. During ancient times, societies in present-day Ethiopia maintained trade relationships with the empires of Egypt and the Arabian peninsula as well as with the Roman Empire. In contrast to most of Africa, Ethiopia retained its independence throughout the 19th century. Ethiopia rebuffed an Italian effort to take it over in 1896, but Italian troops invaded and captured Ethiopia in 1935. Allied forces expelled the Italians during World War II. In 1944, Ethiopia and Britain signed an agreement to guarantee Ethiopian independence. Emperor Haile Selassie I (1892–1975) was restored to power, and he remained Ethiopia's head of state until he was deposed in a

These children are citizens of Ethiopia, whose population is approaching 100 million and which is the second-largest country in Africa by population. As with many countries in sub-Saharan Africa, Ethiopia has a high birth rate, a low median age, and a young population. (Hadynyah/Getty Images)

military coup d'état in 1974. The country became a multiparty democracy in the 1990s, with the first multiparty elections held in 1998.

Ethiopia's population has more than quadrupled since the end of World War II. The population was estimated at 18.4 million in 1950. It doubled to about 35 million in 1980, and was estimated at nearly 66 million in 2000. The rapid rate of population growth in Ethiopia is associated with the fact that the country has not fully undergone demographic transition. Crude death rates have fallen, having dropped from 29.9 per 1,000 people in 1950 to 20.6 in 1975. The death rate hovered at about 20 for the next two decades, a period in which Ethiopia was involved in ongoing civil wars and international conflicts. It then started downward again in the 1990s, dropping to 10.5 by 2010.

On the other hand, Ethiopia's crude birth rate has dropped significantly only in the past two decades. The birth rate remained nearly steady for 50 years, going from 49.4 per 1,000 in 1950 to 47.5 in 2000. It began dropping more significantly as the 21st century began, reaching 33.3 in 2010. Because the birth rate has not decreased quickly, rates of natural increase have not dropped as has been the case in many other less developed countries. Ethiopia's high rate of natural increase is associated with its total fertility rate, which remains high relative to other parts of the world at 4.60 in 2010. Ethiopia's population is very young, with a median age of 16.8 years as of 2010. The high total fertility rate and low median age ensure that Ethiopia will continue to experience rapid population growth in forthcoming decades.

The majority of international migrants moving into and out of Ethiopia in recent years have been refugees. Many Ethiopians left the country after the collapse of the monarchy and the period of military rule in the 1970s and 1980s. Some moved across Ethiopia's borders to neighboring countries, while others moved across the Red Sea to Yemen or to Europe or the United States. More recently, many refugees from war-torn Somalia and Sudan have crossed international boundaries into Ethiopia.

As Ethiopia transitioned from autocratic to more democratic governance, the government began to take a more proactive approach to reducing population growth. In 1993, the government issued a National Population Policy. Responding to concerns about environmental degradation, crop failure, and possible famine associated with continued increases in population, the government established several goals for Ethiopia's population. The specific goals included reducing the total fertility rate to 4.0 by 2015, reducing infant and maternal mortality, and encouraging rural development in order to reduce rural to urban migration and therefore to reduce urban unemployment. Policies to achieve these goals were designed to address public health issues, promote family planning, and provide more educational opportunities for women. To date, the policies have been reasonably successful, although the total fertility rate remains above the target figure of 4. Critics have argued that the policy has been less than successful because it has not been implemented systematically or as effectively as could be.

See Also: Crude Birth Rate; Crude Death Rate; Demographic Transition Model; Egypt; Famine; Italy; Median Age; Nigeria; Rate of Natural Increase; Refugees; Total Fertility Rate; United Kingdom

Further Reading

Sonja Fransen and Katie Kuschminder. "Migration in Ethiopia: History, Current Trends, and Future Prospects." Maastricht Graduate School of Governance, December 2009. http://mgsog.merit.unu.edu/ISacademie/docs/CR_ethiopia.pdf.

Government of Ethiopia. *National Population Policy of Ethiopia*, 1993. http://www.un.org /popin/regional/africa/ethiopia/policy/policy.htm.

Assefa Hailemariam, Solomon Alayu, and Charles Teller. "The National Population Policy (NPP) of Ethiopia: Achievements, Challenges and Lessons Learned, 1993–2010," in *The Demographic Transition and Development in Africa*, edited by Charles Teller and Assefa Hailemariam, 303–21. Berlin: Springer Science+Business Media, 2011.

Egypt

Egypt is the largest country by population in the Middle East, with nearly 85 million people. Egypt's land area is nearly 400,000 square miles, and thus its population is only about 200 people per square mile. Most of Egypt is located in Africa, with the Sinai Peninsula extending into southwestern Asia. African Egypt is located entirely in the Sahara Desert, which is the largest and driest desert in the world. Asiatic Egypt is located within the equally dry Arabian Desert.

For more than 5,000 years, Egyptians have lived in the valley of the Nile River, which is the only permanent river that crosses the Sahara. Today, well over 90 percent of Egypt's people live within 10 miles of the Nile, which has been a reliable source of water for crops for thousands of years. Thus Egypt illustrates clearly the distinction between population density and physiological density. Although Egypt's overall population density is fairly low, its physiological density is very high given that most of its people live in a very small portion of its overall land area. The Nile Valley has a population density of about 4,000 people per square mile, while much of the rest of Egypt's land is uninhabited. About 20 percent of Egypt's people live in the capital city and primate city of Cairo and its suburbs.

Anthropologists have documented human settlement along the Nile dating back to at least 6,000 years BCE. The populations of the Nile Valley were first unified politically in approximately 3150 BCE, and Egypt has remained unified politically ever since. Nearly 3,000 years of internal rule ended in 323 BCE, when it was conquered by the Macedonian general Ptolemy I. Ptolemaic rule ended when Egypt was conquered by the Roman Empire in 30 BCE. In the seventh century CE, Egypt became part of the Islamic Caliphate, which retained power until it became part of the Ottoman Empire in 1517.

Ottoman rule ended when an Ottoman general, Mehmet Ali Pasha, seized power in 1801 and took the name Muhammad Ali. Muhammad Ali's successors ruled Egypt until the monarchy was deposed in 1952. Between 1956 and 2011, Egypt was ruled successively by Gamal Abdel Nasser (1918–1970), Anwar Sadat (1918–1981), and Hosni Mubarak (1928–). In 2011, widespread protests against Mubarak's autocratic rule broke out. Elections were held, and Islamic fundamentalist parties secured a majority of seats in parliament. Mohammed Morsi, who was strongly supported by Islamic fundamentalists, was elected president of Egypt in 2012. After massive protests against Morsi's increasingly autocratic rule, the Egyptian army deposed him in July 2013.

The Nile Valley has been one of the most densely populated areas of the world since ancient times. Over the past three centuries, Egypt's population has increased very rapidly. Its population has been estimated at about 2.4 million in 1700, 3.9 million in 1800, and 10.2 million in 1900. The population doubled between 1900 and 1950. It tripled over the next half-century, reaching 67 million in 2000.

Egypt remains one of the fastest-growing countries in the world in part because its crude birth rate remains high relative to those in many other parts of the world. The crude birth rate was estimated at between 38 and 45 per 1,000 throughout the 1930s, 1940s, and 1950s. It remained above 35 per 1,000 into the late 1980s. Since then it has dropped below 30 per 1,000, although since 2011, it is believed to have rebounded above 30 per 1,000. The crude death rate dropped quickly, from more than 25 per 1,000 in the 1930s to less than 15 per 1,000 by the early 1970s. It fell below 10 per 1,000 in the 1980s and has been stable at between 6 and 6.5 per 1,000 since about 2000. Total fertility rates have been estimated at about 7 in 1960, 5.3 in 1980, 3.6 in 1995, and about 3 today.

Most of Egypt's population growth is taking place in and near Egypt's major cities. Egypt's capital city of Cairo has a metropolitan-area population of over 17 million, making it the largest city by population on the African continent. As is the case with other primate cities, it has been hard for Cairo's leaders and Egypt's government to provide adequate housing and basic services for its very large number of migrants from rural areas of Egypt. More than 99.6 percent of Egypt's people were born in Egypt. In contrast to nearby Saudi Arabia and the United Arab Emirates, immigration from other countries has had virtually no impact on the growth of Egypt's population.

The demographics of Egypt are typical of those of developing countries. According to the *CIA World Factbook*, as of 2011, the annual rate of natural increase in Egypt was 1.96 percent. The median age of Egypt's population was 24 years, and less than 5 percent of Egyptians are more than 65 years of age. However, continued population growth has raised the question as to whether Egypt can continue to feed and otherwise support itself. Per capita food production in Egypt has declined, and Egypt is a net importer of both food and energy. Currently, demographers and planners in Egypt are debating whether Egypt's population has reached unsustainable levels, given that population growth will continue for the foreseeable future despite recent declines in fertility.

See Also: Cairo; Crude Birth Rate; Crude Death Rate; Physiological Density; Population Density; Primate City; Total Fertility Rate

Further Reading

Mona Khalifa, Julie DaVanzo, and David M. Adamson. "Population Growth in Egypt: A Continuing Policy Challenge." RAND Corporation, Issue Paper IP-183, 2000. http://www.rand.org/pubs/issue_papers/IP183/index2.html.

Susan Kraemer. "Egypt's Conflagration Is an Advance Warning for an Unsustainable World." *greenprophet.com*, February 2, 2012. http://www.greenprophet.com/2011/02/egypt-warning-for-an-unsustainable-world/.

Germany

Germany, whose official name is the Federal Republic of Germany, has a population of about 81 million. It is the second-largest country by population in Europe, behind Russia, and is the largest country by population in the European Union.

Much of present-day southern and western Germany was part of the Roman Empire in the first two centuries CE. Beginning in the third century CE, however, Germanic tribes drove the Romans out of Germany and established numerous small kingdoms and principalities. The most powerful of these tribes were the Franks, who occupied present-day western Germany, eastern Belgium and the Netherlands, and northeastern France. The Frankish King Charles the Great, or Charlemagne, united the area and was crowned as Holy Roman Emperor by Pope Leo III in 800 CE. After Charlemagne's death, his empire was divided. The eastern part of the realm, including much of present-day Germany, retained the title of the Holy Roman Empire. Although the Holy Roman Empire remained a recognized power until 1806, it included hundreds of petty kingdoms, duchies, and principalities. Conflict among these political units intensified after the Reformation, which began in Germany and resulted in schism between the Roman Catholic Church and the Lutherans and other Protestants. In 1618, religious conflicts between Catholics and Protestants erupted in what would become known as the Thirty Years' War. The Thirty Years' War ended in 1648 with the signing of the Peace of Westphalia, which established the modern concept of state sovereignty and the need to delineate formal boundaries between neighboring states.

Present-day Germany remained divided politically until the 19th century. In 1815, the German Confederation was formed. The confederation included 39 German-speaking states including most of present-day Germany and Austria, but it was dominated by Prussia and Austria. Prussia defeated Austria in an 1866 war, and in 1871 Prussia's King William I proclaimed himself as the Kaiser, or Emperor of Germany. Germany opposed and was defeated by France and the United Kingdom during both World War I and World War II, after which it ceded territory to the Allies in both cases.

After World War II, Germany was divided into four occupation zones, administered by Britain, France, the United States, and the Soviet Union. The Soviets separated the Soviet occupation zone from the rest of Germany, establishing the German Democratic Republic, while the British, French, and American occupation zones were united as the Federal Republic of Germany. The two separate countries were known informally as East Germany and West Germany, respectively. After the Soviet-backed government of East Germany collapsed in 1989, Germany was reunified as East Germany became part of the Federal Republic. Millions of East Germans migrated to the much more prosperous former West Germany. The movement of East Germans to the west caused considerable tension between these migrants and immigrant communities because under German law, it was much more difficult for people of non-German ancestry to obtain German citizenship than it was for people of German ancestry living in the former East Germany and elsewhere.

Germany underwent demographic transition during the 19th and early 20th centuries and its population has risen only slowly over the past hundred years. In 1901, the population of Germany was estimated at 55 million. It increased to about 66 million in 1914, at the beginning of World War I. The population declined to 62 million in 1921, after the war ended. At the outset of World War II in 1939, the population had risen to about 69 million. Including both East Germany and West Germany, the population was about 64.3 million in 1946. It increased to almost 79 million at the time of reunification in 1990, peaked at 82.5 million in 2003, and declined to below 81.9 million in 2011. In interpreting these statistics, it should be noted that the territorial extent of the German state changed during 1918–1919, after World War I, and again in 1945–1946 after World War II.

Germany's crude birth rate has been estimated at about 35 per 1,000 during the first decade of the 20th century. It dropped to about 20 per 1,000 in the 1920s. After World War II, the birth rate declined to about 16. It remained steady at about 15 to 16 until the 1970s, when it dropped quickly to 10 per 1,000. Today, Germany's birth rate is about 8.4, one of the lowest birth rates in the world. The crude death rate declined from about 20 per 1,000 between 1900 and 1910 to about 12 in the 1920s. Since then it has dropped to about 10 per 1,000. Deaths have exceeded births each year since 1972, and the rate of natural increase has been negative throughout the last forty years. The total fertility rate was slightly over 2 in the 1950s and increased to about 2.4 in the 1960s. In 1971, it fell below 2 for the first time and thus Germany fell below replacement-level fertility. It continued to decline until reaching a low of 1.24 in 1994. It has rebounded slowly to 1.36 today, but remains one of the lowest in the world.

Germany's very low birth and total fertility rates, along with its negative rate of natural increase, implies that immigration is responsible for population growth in modern Germany. As one of the most prosperous countries of Europe, Germany has attracted millions of immigrants. During the 1950s, many immigrants from southern Europe, including Spain, Italy, and Portugal, moved to Germany. More recently, the primary source of immigrants into Germany has been the Middle East and Asia.

Today, an estimated 15 percent of Germany's people are of non-European ancestry. Legally, those who moved to Germany from outside Europe between the 1950s and 1980s were known as *Gastarbeiters*, or "guest workers." These international labor migrants tended to hold menial jobs and were regarded by law as temporary rather than permanent residents of Germany. The rights of *Gastarbeiters* and their descendants, including citizenship rights, have remained an issue of controversy within Germany.

See Also: Crude Birth Rate; Crude Death Rate; Demographic Transition Model; France; International Labor Migration; Italy; Migration; Rate of Natural Increase; Replacement-Level Fertility; Russia; Spain; Total Fertility Rate; United Kingdom; United States of America

Further Reading

James Angelos. "What Integration Means for Germany's Guest Workers." *Foreign Affairs* 90, 2011. http://www.mmg.mpg.de/fileadmin/user_upload/Publikationen/Pdf/What_Integration_Means.pdf.

Jim Russell. "Germany's Demographic Bust." *Pacific Standard*, June 14, 2013. http://www.psmag.com/business-economics/burgh-disapora/germanys-demographic-bust-60271/.

Iran

Iran is known formally as the Islamic Republic of Iran. In 2011, its population was estimated at about 75 million, and it may be approaching 80 million today. Iran's land area is about 636,000 square miles, making it slightly larger than Alaska. Its population is distributed unevenly. Much of Iran's land area is mountainous and/or dry, and for thousands of years settlement has been concentrated in valleys with fertile soil and ample water supplies. Today, most Iranians continue to live in these areas or in cities.

Anthropologists believe that present-day Iran may have been occupied by humans for more than 300,000 years. The recorded history of Iran dates back 6,000 years, when residents developed agriculture and began to inhabit settled communities. Given the dry climate, irrigation became important to the success of agriculture and remains so today.

Around 550 BCE, the Achaemenid or Persian Empire was established by Cyrus the Great. The Achaemenid Empire became the largest and most powerful empire in the world during the next two centuries. It extended northward to present-day Turkey, westward to the Mediterranean coast and the Nile Delta of Egypt, and eastward to present-day Pakistan and Afghanistan. The Achaemenids were overthrown by Alexander the Great in 333 BCE, and the area, then known as Persia, was ruled by the Parthian Empire for more than 450 years beginning in 238 BCE. The Parthians and the Roman Empires coexisted throughout this period, with occasional skirmishes and armed conflicts along their frontier. The Parthians were overthrown by the Sassanids in the third century CE.

The Sassanids were deposed by Muslim invaders from the Arabian Peninsula in the early seventh century, and by about 650 CE most of present-day Iran was controlled by Muslim rulers. The large majority of Persia's people converted to Islam over the next century. However, the Muslim community experienced a schism between the Shiite and Sunni branches of the faith during the late seventh century. Although a large majority of Muslims worldwide practice Sunni Islam, most Persians became Shiites. The schism between the Shiites and the Sunnis has affected relationships between Iran and its neighbors ever since.

Persia was ruled by a series of empires and kingdoms between the Muslim conquest and the early 20th century. Although Persia retained its independence and never became a European colony, the European colonial powers achieved considerable influence in the country, which became known formally as Iran in 1935. Under pressure from Britain and the Soviet Union during World War II, Shah Reza Khan was forced to abdicate and was replaced by his son, Mohammad Reza Shah Pahlavi. The Shah was overthrown in 1979, and a new government whose policies were based on the principles of Shiite Islam took power.

As has been the case with its Middle Eastern neighbors, Iran has undergone demographic transitions during the 20th century. The population of Iran was estimated at about 9 million in 1880. It rose slowly over the next 50 years to about 12 million in 1940. After World War II, the population rose more rapidly as the crude death rate began to decline. It reached 30 million by 1970 and was about 63 million in 2000. Demographers have estimated that Iran's population may reach 100 million by 2050, although the rate of natural increase has been declining.

Both the crude death rate and the crude birth rate have declined steadily since 1950. During the early 1950s, the crude death rate was estimated at about 28 per 1,000. It declined quickly to 12 per 1,000 in the late 1970s. The death rate spiked to 17 in the 1980s, when Iran was involved in a civil war as well as war with neighboring Iraq. The death rate declined once again after 1990, reaching a low of 5.4 per 1,000 by 2010.

The birth rate has also dropped during the past 60 years. It was about 50.6 per 1,000 in 1950 and declined slowly to 44.4 in 1980. After 1980, it began to decline more rapidly, reaching 21.1 in 2000 and 17.7 in 2010. The rate of natural increase was more than 2.6 percent annually between 1960 and 1990 but has since dropped to about 1.2 percent today. The declining birth rate has been associated with a decreasing rate of natural increase, which was more than 6 between 1950 and 1985 but has since dropped to about 1.8, or less than replacement-level fertility, by 2010. However, because Iran's population is relatively young, its rate of natural increase is likely to be positive during the foreseeable future.

As with other developing countries ruled by autocratic governments, Iran has experienced far more out-migration than in-migration. In 2010, the United Nations estimated that about 5 million Iranian natives have left the country, with a majority having moved to Europe or the United States. Many of these emigrants are highly educated, and hence Iran has been a major contributor to the brain drain. However, as many as a million refugees from nearby war-torn Afghanistan and Iraq have moved into Iran.

In 2011, the Iranian government initiated policies intended to encourage increased fertility. The government announced a series of financial incentives to couples with increased numbers of children. Proponents of these measures have argued that Iran should strive for a population of 150 million, in part in order to increase Iranian economic and military strength relative to Western Europe, Japan, and other highly developed countries. However, many couples have declined to have larger families in part because of Iran's struggling economy and continued autocracy.

See Also: Brain Drain; Crude Birth Rate; Crude Death Rate; Demographic Transition Model; Rate of Natural Increase; Refugees; Replacement-Level Fertility

Further Reading

Palash Ghosh. "Be Fruitful and Multiply: Iran's Program to Increase Its Population May Not Work." *International Business Times*, April 22, 2013. http://www.ibtimes.com/be-fruitful-multiply-irans-program-increase-its-population-might-not-work-1207351.

Behrouz Saba. "Brain Drain: Destroying Iran One University Graduate at a Time." *New America Media*, October 23, 2011. http://newamericamedia.org/2011/10/brain-drain-destroying-iran-one-university-graduate-at-a-time.php.

Turkey

Turkey, whose official name is the Republic of Turkey, is located between Europe and Asia along the shores of the Mediterranean and Black Sea. About 97 percent of Turkey's land area is located in the Asiatic portion of the country, which is separated from the European portion by the Bosporus, the Sea of Marmara, and the Dardanelles. Turkey's largest city of Istanbul straddles the two continents. The country's total population is estimated at about 75 million. Turkey's highest population densities are in the Istanbul area and along the Mediterranean and Black Sea coasts, and are generally lower in the interior except for the area near the capital city of Ankara.

Given its strategic location at the crossroads between Europe and Asia, the area comprising present-day Turkey has been contested among various powers since ancient times. In 330 CE, the Roman Emperor Constantine had an imperial residence constructed at Byzantium on the site of present-day Istanbul. The city was renamed Constantinople. When the Roman Empire was divided between the Western and Eastern Roman Empires, Constantinople became the capital of the Eastern Roman Empire, which was also known as the Byzantine Empire. Constantinople was captured by the Ottoman Empire in 1453, and the Ottomans controlled all of present-day Turkey by the 16th century. The Ottoman Empire was abolished after

About 30 million Kurds live in southeastern Turkey, northeastern Iraq, and adjacent areas of Iran and Syria. However, Kurds are an ethnic minority group in all four countries. Many Kurds support the creation of a fully independent Kurdish state. (AP Photo/Sipa)

World War I, and the Republic of Turkey was recognized formally as the successor state to the Ottoman Empire in 1923. The boundaries between Turkey and its neighbors were established at that time, and with only minor adjustments they remain in place today.

Turkey has undergone demographic transition during the 20th century, although its population has increased steadily. At the time of independence in 1923, the population of Turkey was estimated at 13 million. It doubled to about 26 million by 1960. Since that time, the country's population has increased by about 10 million per decade. The population reached 35.6 million in 1971, 45.5 million in 1981, 55 million in 1991, and 66.3 million in 2001. The current rate of natural increase is about 1.2 percent per year.

The crude birth rate and the crude death rate of Turkey have both declined steadily over the past 60 years. The crude birth rate fell from over 45 per 1,000 in the early 1950s to about 30 per 1,000 in the early 1980s to less than 18 today. The crude death rate was over 18 per 1,000 in the 1950s, and has since declined to less than 11 in the 1980s and to less than 6 today. Because the birth rate has dropped at a higher rate than the death rate, the rate of natural increase has also declined. The rate of natural increase was nearly 3 percent per year in the 1950s and fell to below 2 percent per year in the late 1980s, dropping below 1.5 percent per year by 2000. Consistent with other developing countries, Turkey has seen a substantial drop in its total fertility rate from over 6 in the 1950s to about 2.15 today.

In the years since World War II, millions of Turks have emigrated, primarily to Germany and other European Union countries. Tensions between local residents and Turkish immigrants have surfaced on many occasions, especially in Germany, where the law makes it very difficult for people who are not of German ethnic ancestry to attain German citizenship. More recently, however, Turkey has become a net importer of immigrants. More people are now moving to Turkey than out of Turkey. Turkey's economy has strengthened considerably in recent years, reducing the incentive for Turks to emigrate and encouraging Turkish natives who had moved to the European Union to return home.

As well, Turkey's strong economy and stable political system relative to much of the Middle East and South Asia have made Turkey a magnet for immigrants from Iran, Pakistan, Afghanistan, and other countries. Many of these immigrants are refugees. In 2012 and 2013, civil war in neighboring Syria drove hundreds of thousands of Syrian refugees across the international boundary. By 2012, Turkey ranked 10th in the world in overall number of refugees.

Turkey's demography has also been affected by conflict between the majority Turkish population and the minority Kurdish population. Kurds, who have a distinctive culture and language relative to the rest of Turkey, make up more than 20 percent of Turkey's population. Most of Turkey's Kurds live in rural southern and eastern Turkey, although many have moved to Istanbul and other large cities in search of employment opportunities. Many Kurds in Turkey and neighboring Iran, Iraq, and Syria have demanded independence or increased autonomy, although the Turkish government has actively resisted these demands. Currently, the birth rate and total fertility rate among Kurds are considerably greater than with the overall Turkish population, leading some observers to predict that Kurds may make up a majority of Turkey's population within the next 50 years.

See Also: Crude Birth Rate; Crude Death Rate; Demographic Transition Model; Rate of Natural Increase; Refugees; Total Fertility Rate

Further Reading

Palash Ghosh. "A Kurdish Majority in Turkey within One Generation?" *IBI Times*, May 6, 2012. http://www.ibtimes.com/kurdish-majority-turkey-within-one-generation-705466.

Hurriyet Daily News. "Turkey Refugee Ranking Skyrockets within a Year." June 15, 2013. http://www.hurriyetdailynews.com/turkey-refugee-ranking-skyrockets-within-a-year.aspx?pageID=238&nid=49106.

Philip Martin. "Turkey-EU Migration: The Road Ahead." *Perceptions*, 17 (2012): 125–44. http://sam.gov.tr/wp-content/uploads/2012/05/philip_martin.pdf.

Ibrahim Sirkeci, Jeffrey H. Cohen, and Pinar Yazgan. "Turkish Culture of Migration: Flows between Turkey and Germany, Socio-Economic Development, and Conflict." *Migration Letters*, 9 (2012): 33–46.

Democratic Republic of the Congo

The Democratic Republic of the Congo is sometimes known as Congo-Kinshasa, after its capital city, to distinguish it from the neighboring Republic of the Congo or Congo-Brazzaville. Most of the country is included within the drainage basin of the Congo River, from which the country was named. The Democratic Republic of the Congo is the largest country by land area in sub-Saharan Africa and the second largest on the African continent following Nigeria. Although estimates are not fully reliable, its population is estimated at between 68 and 75 million. Its most densely populated areas are scattered throughout the country, with many located near the Congo River. The interior, much of which consists of rainforests, is more sparsely populated.

The present-day Democratic Republic of the Congo was one of the last parts of Africa to be visited or settled by Europeans in the 19th century. It became a Belgian colony known as the Congo Free State in 1885. King Leopold II regarded the Congo Free State as his personal property, and he founded what is now the city of Kinshasa, which he named Leopoldville after himself. Large rubber plantations were established in the Congo Free State, and many indigenous Africans were forced to work on these plantations as slaves. As many as half of the Free State's indigenous African population is believed to have died by the early 20th century as a result of overwork and exposure to European diseases. In 1908, control of the Congo Free State was transferred to the Belgian government and the colony was renamed Belgian Congo. Belgian Congo became independent in 1960.

In 1971, military officer Joseph Mobutu seized control of the Congolese government, establishing an autocratic regime. Mobutu remained in power until he was deposed in 1997, after which a civil war broke out. During the next six years, an estimated 5 million Congolese military personnel and civilians are believed to have lost their lives as a result of warfare, disease, and famine. Millions more left the country as refugees. A peace agreement ending the war was signed in 2003, although violent clashes between government and rebel forces continue and as many as 3 million people in the Democratic Republic of the Congo died from war-related causes during the next decade.

As has been the case throughout sub-Saharan Africa, the population of the Democratic Republic of the Congo has grown rapidly since independence. At the time of independence in 1960, the population of the Democratic Republic of the Congo was estimated at 15.4 million. The population doubled to 31 million by 1985, and more than doubled again to 66 million by 2010. The rapid increase in the Democratic Republic of the Congo's population reflects a very high rate of natural increase. The crude death rate in the Democratic Republic of the Congo has declined from about 25 per 1,000 in the 1960s to about 17 per 1,000 today. However, the crude birth rate has remained constant over the past 50 years. It has been estimated at 47 per 1,000 in the 1950s, rose above 50 in the late 1980s and early 1990s, and fell slightly to 45 in 2010.

The slow decline in the crude birth rate relative to the crude death rate has meant that the rate of natural increase in the Democratic Republic of the Congo has risen. Currently, the rate of natural increase is about 2.8 percent per year. Total fertility rates also remain high. The total fertility rate was about 6 in the 1950s, rose above 7 in the 1990s, and has since dropped back to 6. The continued high rate of natural increase, high birth rates, and high total fertility rates illustrate that the Democratic Republic of the Congo has not completed fully the process of demographic transition.

The demographics of the Democratic Republic of the Congo have been affected by internal and international wars over many years. Especially during the period between 1997 and 2003, large numbers of Congolese left the Democratic Republic of the Congo as refugees. In 2012, the United Nations High Commission on Refugees estimated that nearly 500,000 refugees from the Democratic Republic of the Congo were residing in neighboring countries. More recently, refugees from the Central African Republic and other war-torn neighbors of the Democratic Republic of the Congo have moved into the country, which lacks the resources to provide adequate care and support for these refugees.

See Also: Crude Birth Rate; Crude Death Rate; Famine; Nigeria; Rate of Natural Increase; Refugees; Slavery; Total Fertility Rate

Further Reading

Mvemba Phezo Dizolele. "A Crisis in the Congo." *Foreign Policy*, December 14, 2011. http://www.foreignpolicy.com/articles/2011/12/13/a_crisis_in_the_congo.

Anatole Romaniuk. "Persistence of High Fertility in Tropical Africa: The Case of the Democratic Republic of the Congo." *Population and Development Review* 37 (2011): 1–28.

Jason K. Stearns. *Dancing in the Glory of Monsters: The Collapse of Congo and the Great War of Africa*. Madison: University of Wisconsin Press, 2012.

Thailand

The Kingdom of Thailand is the largest country by population in Southeast Asia, with about 68 million people. Its land area is about 200,000 square miles, slightly smaller than Colorado and Wyoming together and slightly smaller than neighboring Myanmar.

Thailand's population is distributed unevenly. As is the case in Myanmar, Vietnam, and other countries in Southeast Asia, most people live in fertile lowland valleys. Most Thai people live in the valley of the Chao Phraya River, which flows from north to south through the center of the country. The capital city of Bangkok is located not far from the mouth of the Chao Phraya. Bangkok is an extreme example of a primate city, and its metropolitan-area population is more than thirty times that of Thailand's second-largest city of Nonthaburi. Areas to the north, east, and west of the Chao Phraya are hilly, with much sparser populations. More than half of Thailand's people live in rural areas, although Bangkok in particular and other cities are growing rapidly in population.

Ancestors of the Thais are believed to have moved to the Chao Phraya valley from present-day southwestern China more than a thousand years ago. Present-day Thailand was ruled by a series of dynasties, many of which originated outside the Chao Phraya region, over the next several hundred years. At that time, the country was known as Siam. The Thai leader Rama I became one of the first native-born rulers of Siam in 1782. He established the Chakri dynasty, which continues to reign over the kingdom today. Thailand's current king, Rama IX, is a direct descendant of Rama I. The Chakris were absolute rulers of the country until the middle of the 20th century, when Thailand became a constitutional monarchy. In contrast to the rest of Southeast Asia, Thailand retained its independence since the accession of the Chakris and has no colonial history.

Thailand's population, like that of many developing and semideveloped countries, has grown quickly throughout its recent history. Its population was estimated at 20 million in 1950. It doubled to about 40 million in the mid-1970s and passed the 60 million mark in about 2000. Since then, the rate of population growth has slowed somewhat. Currently, Thailand's rate of natural increase is estimated at about 0.5 percent per year, down from about 3 percent per year in the middle of the 20th century.

Declining rates of natural increase in Thailand are associated with the process of demographic transition and are illustrated by changes in crude birth rates and crude death rates since the 1950s. Thailand's crude birth rate was about 42 per 1,000 in the early 1950s and remained above 40 per 1,000 until the early 1970s, when it began to decline. It dropped below 20 per 1,000 in the early 1990s and is about 12 per 1,000 today. Declining birth rates result in part from government efforts and policies to promote family planning and reduced fertility.

The crude death rate of Thailand has declined from about 15 per 1,000 in the 1950s to about 7 per 1,000 today. Thailand's total fertility rate was over 6 during the 1950s and 1960s, but dropped below replacement-level fertility in the 1990s. It is estimated at about 1.6 today. Thus, although Thailand's per capita income is well below that of other Asian countries, its demographic characteristics are approaching those of wealthier Asian countries such as Japan and South Korea although the population of Thailand is expected to continue to grow until people born before 1980 age beyond child-bearing years. If current trends continue, Thailand's population may begin to decline by the early 2020s. Some Thai officials predict that caring for a growing elderly population will become a significant issue in Thailand in the foreseeable future.

About three-quarters of Thailand's people are of Thai nationality. The largest minority group in Thailand is the Chinese, who represent about 14 percent of the population. Many ethnic minority groups in Thailand live in the mountainous regions of northern, eastern, and western China outside the Chao Phraya valley. Some including the Karen people of western Thailand and neighboring Myanmar have claimed discrimination by the Thai government and have agitated for political independence.

Thailand has become an important migration destination, especially for people from poorer Southeast Asian countries including Myanmar, Bangladesh, Laos, and Cambodia. An estimated 2 million legal immigrants live in Thailand, and it has been estimated that as many as 4 or 5 million illegal immigrants also live in the country. Recent Thai governments have attempted to curb illegal immigration, and Thailand has been criticized by international human rights organization for harsh treatment of illegal immigrants.

See Also: Bangkok; Crude Birth Rate; Crude Death Rate; Demographic Transition Model; Japan; Myanmar; Primate City; Rate of Natural Increase; Replacement-Level Fertility; South Korea; Vietnam

Further Reading

Nora McGann. "The Opening of Burmese Borders: Impacts on Migration." Migration Policy Institute, February 20, 2013. http://www.migrationpolicy.org/article/opening-burmese-borders-impacts-migration.

Dhara Ranasinghe. "This Asian Nation Faces a Growing Crisis from Aging." *CNBC*, October 23, 2013, http://www.cnbc.com/id/101119344.

France

France, whose official name is the French Republic, is the third-largest country by population in Europe behind Russia and Germany. France regards several overseas colonies including the islands of Guadeloupe and Martinique in the Caribbean and French Guiana in South America as part of the French Republic. It uses the term "Metropolitan France" to refer to those portions of France located in Europe, including the island of Corsica in the Mediterranean Sea. The land area of Metropolitan France is slightly larger than that of Germany, making France the largest country by land area in the European Union. About 63.5 million people live in Metropolitan France.

France, which was known in ancient times as Gaul, was part of the Roman Empire between the first century BCE and the fourth and fifth centuries CE, when the Roman Empire collapsed. After the Romans were overthrown, France was divided into numerous small kingdoms until the late eighth century CE, when most of present-day France along with neighboring areas of Belgium, Germany, and Italy were conquered and united by Charles the Great, or Charlemagne. After Charlemagne died, the empire was divided among his heirs. What would become western and central France was ruled by Charlemagne's grandson, Charles the Bald. This area became the core of the modern French state, which later expanded to the east and south. By the 16th century, the boundaries between France and its neighbors approximated those used today, although control of Alsace-Lorraine along the border between France and Germany was contested well into the 20th century.

Throughout much of its history, France was the largest country in Europe by population. Its population has been estimated at about 16 million, or one-quarter of Europe's entire population, at about 1200. The population increased to an estimated 20 million before the onset of the Black Death in the mid-14th century. It dropped back to about 16 million in 1450 and did not pass 21 million again until the 18th century. France's population began to increase more rapidly during the Industrial Revolution in the late 18th and early 19th centuries. It reached 36 million in about 1850. During the late 19th and earlier 20th century, population growth in France slowed down as the country underwent demographic transition. After World War II, the rate of population growth increased again, largely because of immigration. It was estimated at 55 million in the early 1980s, and passed 60 million in about 2003. Today only about 12 percent of Europe's population lives in France.

France's crude birth rate was estimated at 22.5 per 1,000 in 1901. It dropped to about 15 per 1,000 during the 1930s. After World War II ended, France underwent a baby boom similar to that experienced in the United States. France's birth rate spiked for about 15 years, reaching a high of 21.4 in 1948 and remaining above 15 until the mid-1970s. Since then, France's birth rate has dropped to 12.2 in 2011. France's birth rate is higher, however, than that of many other European Union members. France's crude death rate has also declined steadily, falling from about 20 per 1,000 in the first decade of the 20th century to about 9 per 1,000 today. Thus France's rate of natural increase has generally been positive, with the exception of the years of World War I and World War II when deaths greatly exceeded births. Today, the rate of natural increase is about 0.4 percent per year. The total fertility rate has dropped from about 3 in 1901 to about 2 by 2011. The high total fertility rate in France relative to other European Union countries is due in large part to the large number of immigrant women, who tend to have larger families than do native-born Europeans.

Immigration plays a very large role in French demography today. In 2011, it was estimated that more than 5 million French residents were born outside the European Union, and an additional 6.5 million were children of non-European immigrants. Thus, more than 15 percent of Metropolitan France's population consists of first-generation or second-generation immigrants. Many of these immigrants come from the North African countries of Morocco, Algeria, and Tunisia, which were French colonies until the early 1960s. More recently, an increasing number of immigrants have moved to France from former French colonies in sub-Saharan Africa including Senegal, Côte d'Ivoire, and Cameroon. Others come from Turkey and other Southwest Asian countries. Tensions between immigrants, many of whom live in highly segregated and impoverished neighborhoods in Paris and other large French cities, have escalated in recent years and have sometimes led to violence.

See Also: Baby Boom; Black Death; Crude Birth Rate; Crude Death Rate; Demographic Transition Model; Germany; Migration; Rate of Natural Increase; Russia; Total Fertility Rate; United States of America

Further Reading

Jonathan Laurence and Justin Vaisse. "Understanding Urban Riots in France." Brookings Institution, December 1, 2005. http://www.brookings.edu/research/articles/2005/12/01 france-laurence.

Zachary Propert. "Nationalism and Integration in France." *Fair Observer*, July 28, 2011. http://www.fairobserver.com/article/nationalism-and-immigration-france.

Audrey Vucher. "Fertile France Tops European Population Growth." *Mediapart*, July 10, 2012. http://www.mediapart.fr/journal/france/200111/fertile-france-tops-european-population-growth.

United Kingdom

The United Kingdom of Great Britain and Northern Island occupies the island of Great Britain, the northeastern part of the island of Ireland, and several smaller islands in the northeastern Atlantic Ocean. The islands are separated from the mainland of Europe by the English Channel and the North Sea. Great Britain is divided into the provinces of England, Scotland, and Wales. England is by far the largest of these provinces. England contains about 55 percent of the United Kingdom's land area and more than 80 percent of the United Kingdom's population of about 64 million. Overall, nearly 95 percent of the United Kingdom's people live on the island of Great Britain. The United Kingdom is the third-largest country by population in the European Union, after Germany and France. However, the United Kingdom's population density is much higher, given its much smaller land area of about 94,000 square miles, less than half of the land area of Germany and of France.

The history of the present-day United Kingdom is one of successive waves of migration from the European mainland. Great Britain was occupied by Celtic tribes, when much of present-day England was conquered by the Romans in the first century BCE. After the Romans were expelled in the fifth century CE, Anglo-Saxons moved to Great Britain from present-day Germany and Denmark in the sixth and seventh centuries. The Anglo-Saxons established several kingdoms in present-day southern and eastern England. Beginning in 793 CE, the coasts of Great Britain were raided by Vikings from Scandinavia.

The Kingdom of England, including present-day England and Wales, was established in 927 CE. In 1066, Normans from northern France invaded England and under William the Conqueror took over the English throne. England has been unified politically since that time. Wales was incorporated formally in 1535, and Scotland became part of the United Kingdom in 1707. Britain took control of the island of Ireland in the 16th century, and formally incorporated into the United Kingdom of Great Britain and Ireland in 1801. After more than a century of rebellion on the part of many in Ireland, the island was divided between independent Ireland and Northern Ireland, which remained part of the United Kingdom, in 1922. The name of the country was changed to the United Kingdom of Great Britain and Northern Ireland.

The United Kingdom underwent demographic transition in the 19th and early 20th centuries. Its population increased steadily throughout the 20th century, but the rate of natural increase has slowed since World War II. According to the census of 1901, the population of the United Kingdom was about 38.2 million. The population was about 50 million in 1951, 56.4 million in 1981, and 62.5 million in 2011. The crude birth rate in 1961 was 17.9 per 1,000. It declined to 13 per 1,000 in 1981 and dropped to 11.3 in 2001. Since then, it has rebounded slightly to 12.8 in 2011. The crude death rate declined from 12 per 1,000 in 1961 to 8.8 per thousand in 2011. The rate of natural increase was 0.6 percent in 1961, dropping to 0.25 percent in 1991 and rising to 0.4 percent in 2011. The United Kingdom's total fertility rate decreased from 2.8 in 1961 to 1.63 in 2001, increasing to 1.93 in 2011.

Given that the United Kingdom's total fertility rate is below replacement-level fertility, current population increases in the United Kingdom are the result of immigration. Immigrants into the United Kingdom have higher total fertility rates than do native-born residents of the country, and the presence of increasing numbers of immigrants explains recent increases in its crude birth rate and its total fertility rate. There are several major sources of immigration into the United Kingdom. Many immigrants have moved to the United Kingdom from former British colonies throughout the world including India, Pakistan, Bangladesh, South Africa, and Jamaica. Ireland has also been a major source of immigrants into the United Kingdom for several hundred years. More recently, many immigrants have moved to the United Kingdom from the Middle East and North Africa. The inclusion of several relatively impoverished Central and Eastern European countries into the European Union has allowed citizens of these countries to move to the United Kingdom and other Western European countries. As well, thousands of the United Kingdom's immigrants are refugees from war-torn countries outside of Europe. Many of these refugees have requested political asylum in the United Kingdom.

According to the census of 2001, about 5 million residents of the United Kingdom were born elsewhere. A majority of these immigrants are from non-European countries. Tension between these non-European immigrants and native-born United Kingdom residents has flared up on many occasions. A major issue involving the relationships between the United Kingdom and its immigrant population is the degree to which the immigrant population has been willing to assimilate into the mainstream culture of the United Kingdom. Government officials are also considering the extent to which immigration from outside the European Union is beneficial to the country's economy, and those who are skeptical of the benefits of immigration have advocated imposing limits on the number of immigrants and asylum seekers allowed to enter the country.

See Also: Bangladesh; Census; Crude Birth Rate; Crude Death Rate; Demographic Transition Model; France; Germany; India; Migration; Pakistan; Population

Density; Rate of Natural Increase; Refugees; Replacement-Level Fertility; South Africa; Total Fertility Rate

Further Reading

Mehdi Hasan. "In Defence of Britain's Multiculturalism." *Al Jazeera English*, August 2, 2012. http://www.aljazeera.com/indepth/opinion/2012/08/2012819528793336.html.

Steven Swinford. "Immigrants Create Overcrowding and Fuel Tensions." *Telegraph*, July 3, 2013. http://www.telegraph.co.uk/news/politics/10158678/Immigrants-create-overcrow ding-and-fuel-tensions-report-finds.html.

Divya Talwar. "Growing Use of Sharia by UK Muslims." *BBC News*, January 16, 2012. http:// www.bbc.co.uk/news/uk-16522447.

Italy

Italy, which is known formally as the Italian Republic, occupies the Italian Peninsula and territory north of the Peninsula bordering France, Switzerland, Austria, and Slovenia. Italy has a population of about 60.5 million and a land area of 116,346 square miles, or slightly smaller than Montana. Its land area includes the islands of Sicily and Sardinia, which are the largest islands in the Mediterranean Sea, along with many smaller islands. Italy's population densities are highest in the industrialized north and in central Italy in and near the capital city of Rome, and are lower in the south and the interior highlands.

After the collapse of the Roman Empire in the fifth century CE, what is now Italy consisted of small, independent city-states. The Roman Catholic Church provided linguistic and cultural unity to the Italian peninsula and held temporal sovereignty over what is now central Italy, which was then known as the Papal States. During the middle of the 19th century, northeastern Italy was controlled by Austria, and the rest of Italy was divided into three independent states with northwestern Italy ruled by Sardinia, central Italy controlled by the Papal States centered on Rome, and southern Italy being part of the Kingdom of Sicily.

The Austrians were expelled and Italy became a unified state in the late 19th century. The question of temporal sovereignty over the Papal States was settled with the signing of the Lateran Accords in 1929. Under the Lateran Accords, the church ceded temporal sovereignty over the Papal States to Italy. In exchange, Italy recognized the sovereignty of the church over Vatican City and acknowledged the spiritual authority of the church throughout Italy.

Italy's population increased steadily throughout the late 19th and early 20th centuries, and then only slowly after World War II as the country completed undergoing demographic transition. The first census taken after reunification, in 1871, estimated 27.3 million people. The population increased to about 33 million in 1901 and 50.6 million in 1951. It reached 56.6 million in 1981 and remained nearly constant over the next two decades, with 57 million in 2001. Between 2001 and 2011, however, Italy's population increased by more than 3 million.

The 1901 census estimated Italy's crude birth rate at about 33.5 per 1,000. It started to decline in the 1920s, falling to 20.5 in 1941. After several years of relatively low birth rates, it increased again after World War II and reached a postwar high of 23 in 1946. The birth rate remained between 17 and 20 over the next two decades and then began to decline. It fell below 10 for the first time in 1989, and since then it has remained steady at between 9 and 10 per 1,000.

The crude death rate of Italy was estimated at 22 per 1,000 in 1901. It spiked during and after World War I, reaching 35.3 in 1918 in part because of the global Spanish flu epidemic. After the war, the death rate declined to 14. After increasing temporarily during World War II, it dropped below 10 for the first time in 1950. It has remained between 9 and 10 ever since. The rate of natural increase has also declined. It was estimated at 1.1 percent in 1901 and continued between 0.8 percent and 1.2 percent for the next 50 years, with the exception of the war years. It then declined from 1.1 percent in 1946 to 0.3 percent in 1983. It dropped below 0 for the first time in 1993, and with one exception has remained negative since then. The total fertility rate also dropped from about 3.2 in 1931 to 2.11 in 1976. It dropped to 1.98 in 1977 and has remained below replacement level since that time, reaching a low of 1.18 in 1995 and rebounding to 1.43 in 2012.

Given its negative rate of natural increase, Italy's recent population growth is the result of substantial levels of immigration. Historically, Italy has been a country of emigrants. An estimated 24 million people left Italy for the United States, Argentina, and other countries between the 1870s and the 1970s. Beginning in the late 1970s, however, rates of immigration began to exceed emigration rates as Italy's economy underwent steady growth.

Many of these immigrants to Italy have come from North Africa. More recently, immigration from Eastern Europe has increased as Romania, Bulgaria, and other former Communist countries have joined the European Union, allowing their citizens to move freely within Europe. In 2011, an estimated 1 million Romanian natives were living in Italy. Today, more than half of Italy's immigrants come from elsewhere within Europe. The overall immigrant population increased from about 1.5 million in 2003 to almost 4.6 million in 2011, accounting for Italy's contemporary population increase. Most of these immigrants are young, in contrast to the aging population of native-born Italians. The presence of larger numbers of immigrants has resulted in political controversy and occasional violence within the country.

See Also: Argentina; Census; Crude Birth Rate; Crude Death Rate; Demographic Transition Model; Migration; Rate of Natural Increase; Replacement-Level Fertility; Rome; Spanish Flu; Total Fertility Rate; United States of America

Further Reading

Tom Kington. "Italy Wakes Up to the Realities of Immigration." *The Observer*, February 20, 2010. http://www.guardian.co.uk/world/2010/feb/21/italy-milan-race-riots.

Elisabetta Povoledo. "Italy Struggles with Immigration and Aging." *New York Times*, June 22, 2008. http://www.nytimes.com/2008/06/22/world/europe/22iht-migrants.4.13893156 .html?_r=0.

Myanmar

Myanmar, which is known formally as the Republic of the Union of Myanmar, is the third most populous country in Southeast Asia, after Vietnam and Thailand. Its population has been estimated at about 58 million. Myanmar's land area is slightly larger than that of neighboring Thailand. Despite its large population, Myanmar's population density is the lowest in Southeast Asia and is considerably lower than that of its neighbors, including India, Bangladesh, China, and Thailand. The majority of Myanmar's people live in and near the valley of the Irrawaddy River, which bisects the country from north to south. Hilly areas to the west, north, and east are sparsely populated.

Myanmar is referred to sometimes by its former official name of Burma, after its majority ethnic group. About two-thirds of Myanmar's people are Burmese, who are also known as the Bamar people. The population of Myanmar is distributed unevenly. The large majority of Myanmar's people live in the valley of the Irrawaddy River, which flows from north to south through the center of the country and flows through the capital and primate city of Yangon before emptying into the Bay of Bengal. Most people of Burmese ethnicity live in the Irrawaddy valley. The areas to the west, north, and east of the Irrawaddy are mountainous and are inhabited by people of non-Burmese ancestry. In some areas, notably along the rugged and heavily forested region along the boundary between Myanmar and Thailand, non-Burmese have engaged in ongoing guerilla activities against the government of Myanmar in an effort to gain more autonomy or eventual independence.

Anthropologists and historians believe that the ancestors of today's Burmese people moved southward from Yunnan in present-day southern China to the Irrawaddy valley between 1,200 and 1,500 years ago. The Burmese established the kingdom of Myanmar, whose name is commemorated in the present-day name of the country, in the ninth century CE. Over the next several hundred years, the

Myanmar is the largest country by land area in mainland Southeast Asia. Its population of approximately 58 million ranks third in the region behind Vietnam and Thailand, and it is the 24th largest country in the world by population. This photograph shows Kakku in Shan State, in which there has been considerable agitation for political independence. (Simone Matteo Giuseppe Manzoni/Dreamstime.com)

Burmese absorbed the earlier inhabitants of the region, or drove them into the nearby mountains. During the 19th century, Britain began efforts to establish colonies in the area. Three wars between British and Burmese forces took place between 1824 and 1885. After the third Anglo-Burmese War, the Myanmar monarchy was overthrown and Britain incorporated the region into British India. The British separated Myanmar from the rest of British India in 1935. The country became independent in 1948. Myanmar has been ruled by a series of dictators since the early 1960s, and its repressive governments have kept Myanmar relatively isolated from the rest of the world over the past half-century.

Population figures for Myanmar are notoriously unreliable. Although the best estimates of the country's population range from 55 to 60 million, some observers estimate less than 50 million and others estimate as many as 70 million. The lack of reliable information about Myanmar's population stems from the fact that the country's last official census was taken in 1983. Myanmar's population was estimated at about 20 million in the late 1950s, and so the population has grown steadily. Its demographic profile is similar to those of other developing countries in East and Southeast Asia. In 2011, the rate of natural increase was estimated at about 1 percent per year, and the median age was estimated at about 29 years. Life expectancy has been estimated at about 65 years. It should be reiterated, however, that these estimates are less meaningful than similar estimates for other countries, given the lack of reliable data.

Although the estimates are not fully reliable, the crude birth rate and the crude death rate of Myanmar have fallen steadily since the middle of the 20th century, in keeping with the process of demographic transition. In the early 1950s, the crude birth rate of Myanmar was estimated as 47.5 per 1,000. This declined to 31.5 in the early 1980s and to about 17.9 by 2010. The crude death rate was estimated at 28.6 per 1,000 in the early 1950s, and it declined to 19.2 in the early 1980s and to about 9 by 2010. Thus the rate of natural increase rose slightly during the 1960s and 1970s and fell once again after the 1980s. The country's total fertility rate has also declined steadily, from about 6 between 1950 and 1975 to about 2, or replacement-level fertility, today. The total fertility rate in Myanmar today is somewhat lower than that of India, Thailand, Bangladesh, and other neighboring countries. Some attribute the relatively low total fertility rate in Myanmar to Myanmar's poverty and economic hardship, resulting in delayed marriage, as well as to the Buddhist tradition of celibacy.

Myanmar is characterized by considerable ethnic diversity and is experiencing substantial ethnic conflict. The majority of Myanmar's residents are ethnic Burmese, most of whom live in the Irrawaddy River valley. Most people who live outside the valley live in more isolated mountainous areas. In some of these places, the national government has little control over local populations. Some of these indigenous peoples are actively resisting control by the Myanmar central government, and in some cases their activities are funded in part by illegal activities, including drug cultivation and production, smuggling, and poaching of wild animals.

Increases in Myanmar's population are due almost entirely to natural increase, as emigration away from Myanmar has far exceeded immigration into the country given Myanmar's history of autocratic government and its poverty relative to many of its neighbors. Large numbers of Myanmar's citizens leave the country temporarily or permanently. It has been estimated that more than 2 million Myanmar citizens live and work in more prosperous, democratic Thailand. Many are illegal immigrants. As many as 300,000 refugees, primarily non-Burmese, live across the borders in neighboring India and Thailand or in other countries.

See Also: Bangladesh; Census; China; Crude Birth Rate; Crude Death Rate; Illegal Immigration; India; Life Expectancy; Median Age; Population Density; Primate City; Rate of Natural Increase; Replacement-Level Fertility; Thailand; Total Fertility Rate; Vietnam

Further Reading

Gavin W. Jones. "Delayed Marriage and Very Low Fertility in Pacific Asia." *Population and Development Review* 33 (2007): 453–78.

Simba Shani Kamaria Rousseau. "Migrant Workers Face Tough Times in Thailand." *Inter-Press News Agency*, June 21, 2013. http://www.ipsnews.net/2013/05/migrant-workers
-face-tough-times-in-thailand/.

South Africa

South Africa, formally the Republic of South Africa, is located at the southern tip of the continent of Africa between the Atlantic Ocean to the west and the Indian Ocean to the east. South Africa has a population of about 52 million. This population is distributed relatively unevenly across the country, whose land area of about 476,000 square miles is roughly twice the size of Texas. Many South Africans live in the densely populated plateau region of northeastern South Africa, which includes the country's capital city of Pretoria and its largest city and economic center of Johannesburg. This area has the highest population density of any large area within South Africa. Other clusters of population are found in and near cities along the coast including Cape Town in the southwest and Durban in the southeast. Northwestern South Africa, which is located on the edge of the very arid Kalahari Desert, has very few inhabitants.

The Dutch established the first permanent European settlement in South Africa near present-day Cape Town in the 17th century. At that time, present-day South Africa was occupied by Bantu-speaking people who had moved into the region from the north about 1,500 years ago. Dutch farmers known as Boers settled in the area around Cape Town. Slaves from Madagascar, Indonesia, and East Asia were captured and imported to provide labor on these farms.

During the 18th and 19th centuries, Dutch settlement expanded eastward while Bantu peoples moved westward. Armed skirmishes, largely over control of land, broke out along the frontier between these two cultures. Meanwhile, Britain captured Cape Town in 1795 and established the Cape Colony in southern and western South Africa in the early 19th century. Britain abolished slavery in the Cape Colony in 1807. Afterwards, some Boers moved northward and eastward with their slaves to avoid British control and slave emancipation in what became known as the Great Trek. The Boers established the republics of Transvaal and the Orange Free State.

The discovery of valuable deposits of gold and diamonds in the late 19th century encouraged the British to seek expanded control of these republics. British forces defeated the Boers during the Boer War between 1899 and 1902. Transvaal and the Orange Free State were consolidated with the Cape Colony and the British province of Natal on the Indian Ocean to become the Union of South Africa, which became independent within the British Commonwealth in 1931.

The population of newly independent South Africa was highly diverse, including indigenous Africans, people of Boer and English ancestry, descendants of Dutch slaves, and a substantial population of South Asians who had moved to the area in the late 19th century. The population also included people of mixed-race ancestry, who were known as "coloured." People of European ancestry comprised a small minority of South Africa's population but controlled much of its land and wealth. However, a large majority of people in South Africa are of African ancestry. Today, about 80 percent of South Africa's people are of African ancestry, 10 percent are white, and 10 percent are either "coloured" or Asian.

In 1948, the white-dominated South African government imposed the policy of apartheid, which mandated racial segregation and consigned the nonwhite majority to the status of second-class citizens. Incomes among Africans were much lower, and poverty rates much higher, than among the white minority. Facing international pressure as well as vigorous opposition by the African minority, the government began to relax its apartheid policies in the late 1980s and repealed them entirely in the early 1990s.

South Africa's population has grown rapidly since independence. At first, population growth was due primarily to natural increase, and more recently it has been due increasingly to immigration. The first census of the Union of South Africa counted about 5.2 million people. The population increased to 11.4 million in 1946, shortly before the implementation of apartheid. It nearly doubled to 21 million in 1970, and nearly doubled again to 40.6 million in 1991.

South Africa has undergone considerable demographic transition, especially during the second half of the 20th century. The crude birth rate has been estimated at more than 40 per 1,000 during the 1950s. It dropped to about 34 per 1,000 in the early 1980s and to less than 22 by 2010. The crude death rate dropped from about 20 per 1,000 in the 1950s to 8.5 by the early 1990s. Since then, the crude death has risen and reached 15 by 2010. The recent increases in South Africa's death rate have been attributed to the HIV/AIDS epidemic and to a large influx of refugees from war-torn, impoverished countries. The total fertility rate has declined from over 6 in the 1950s to about 2.5 today. South Africa's current rate of natural increase is about 0.6 percent per year.

Although births continue to outnumber deaths in South Africa, much of South Africa's recent population growth is associated with immigration. Relative to its neighbors, post-apartheid South Africa is peaceful and prosperous. Immigrants have moved from throughout southern Africa in search of employment. South Africa also hosts large refugee populations, with the largest numbers of refugees coming from Zimbabwe, the Democratic Republic of the Congo, and Somalia. International observers have estimated that about 4 million immigrants, many of whom are illegal immigrants, live currently in South Africa. As in other countries, armed clashes between immigrants and native-born South Africans have occasionally resulted in fatalities and injuries. The question of repatriating refugees has become a significant political issue in South Africa.

See Also: Census; Crude Birth Rate; Crude Death Rate; Democratic Republic of the Congo; Demographic Transition Model; HIV/AIDS; Illegal Immigration; Indonesia; Migration; Population Density; Rate of Natural Increase; Refugees; Slavery; Total Fertility Rate; United Kingdom

Further Reading

Celia W. Dugger. "Breaking with Past, South Africa Issues Broad AIDS Policy." *New York Times*, December 1, 2009. http://www.nytimes.com/2009/12/02/world/africa/02safrica.html.

Erhabor Sunday Idemudia, John K. Williams, and Gail E. Wyatt. "Migration Challenges among Zimbabwean Refugees before, during, and post Arrival in South Africa." *Journal of Injury and Violence Research* 5 (2013): 17–27.

Mmanaledi Mataboge. "Zimbabwe Wants SA to Keep Its Citizens." *Mail and Guardian*, May 17, 2013. http://mg.co.za/article/2013-05-17-00-zimbabwe-wants-sa-to-keep-its-citizens.

South Korea

South Korea, which is formally known as the Republic of Korea, occupies the southern half of the Korean peninsula in northeastern Asia. South Korea's current population is estimated at about 50 million. Its land area is less than 40,000 square miles, and therefore its population density is well over 1,000 people per square mile. South Korea is highly urbanized, with nearly half of its residents living in and near the country's capital and primate city of Seoul.

Present-day South Korea and its present-day northern neighbor, North Korea, were contested among various small kingdoms for thousands of years until the entire peninsula was united under a single ruler in the seventh century CE. Korea remained a united kingdom under a succession of dynasties until the late 19th century, when its rulers were threatened by the expanding empires of both Russia and Japan. Japan annexed Korea formally as part of the Japanese Empire in 1910 and retained control of the peninsula until 1945.

The Japanese Empire was dismembered at the end of World War II by the United Nations. Under terms of this action, the United States occupied the southern half of the peninsula and the Soviet Union occupied the northern portion with the 38th parallel of north latitude as the boundary between the American and Soviet occupation zones. The United Nations' intention was that the two portions of the peninsula would be reunited as a single country. However, in 1950, the Soviet-backed government of northern Korea invaded the south, with the backing of the Soviet Union and the People's Republic of China. North Korea's intention was to reunite the entire peninsula under Communist rule. The United States intervened in support of the South Koreans, with the support of the United Nations. Over the next three years, about 400,000 Koreans, as well as more than 55,000 American troops, were killed in what would become known as the Korean War. A ceasefire was negotiated in 1953, and South Korea and North Korea came to be recognized as separate countries.

After the war ended, South Korea underwent rapid economic development. Per capita incomes today are now comparable to many European countries. During the same period, South Korea has undergone the process of demographic transition. In 1949, shortly before the Korean War began, the population of what is now South Korea was estimated at about 20 million. It doubled to slightly above 40 million according to a census taken in 1985. Since then, population growth in South Korea has slowed down significantly, rising to about 46 million in 2000. The current rate of natural increase in South Korea is about 0.5 percent per year.

Demographic transition in South Korea is evident from changes in its crude birth rate, crude death rate, and total fertility rate. The crude birth rate in the early 1950s, at the time of partition, was estimated at 36 per 1,000. It remained above 30 per 1,000 until the 1970s, and in the late 1980s dropped to about 15 per 1,000. Recent estimates suggest that the current crude birth rate in South Korea is about 10 per 1,000. The crude death rate was about 16 per 1,000 in the 1950s, dropped below 6 per 1,000 in the 1980s, and is estimated at 5 per 1,000 today. Reflecting declining birth rates, the total fertility rate in South Korea declined from nearly 6 in the 1950s to slightly over 2 in the 1980s. Since the late 1980s, South Korea's total fertility rate has been below the replacement-level total fertility rate of 2. The current total fertility rate is estimated at about 1.3. Thus, South Korea's population is expected to stabilize at 52 to 53 million people in the early 2020s and then begin to decline.

The rapid decline in South Korea's birth rate and total fertility rate is associated with economic development and government policy. As elsewhere in the world, total fertility rates have dropped with prosperity. During the early 1960s, moreover, South Korea's government began to enact policies intended to reduce birth rates. These policies included legalizing abortion, encouraging families to have only one child, and rewarding parents with small families while penalizing those with larger families.

These policies contributed to rapidly declining birth rates and total fertility rates in South Korea. However, as in other developed countries they have contributed to a rapidly aging population. By 2009, more than 10 percent of South Koreans were over 65 years of age. As currently middle-aged persons continue to age and as birth rates remain low, the percentage of elderly in South Korea's population is expected to continue to rise. The median age of South Korea is currently about 37, but some demographers predict that it may exceed 50 years in the foreseeable future if current trends in total fertility continue. As in China and Japan, a smaller number of people of working age will be expected to support a larger and larger number of elderly persons. An aging population is also expected to result in increased per capita health care costs.

South Korea is one of the most ethnically homogeneous countries in the world. More than 98 percent of South Korea's people are ethnically Korean. However, South Korea's recent prosperity has encouraged in-migration from elsewhere. By 2010, nearly a million residents of South Korea were born in other countries. Nearly half a million came from China, although many of these immigrants were Chinese citizens of Korean ancestry. Thousands of international labor migrants have also moved to South Korea. Most come from less prosperous Asian countries such as the Philippines, Thailand, and Vietnam or from Central Asia. Many refugees crossed from North Korea into South Korea in the 1950s after partition, and smaller numbers of people continue to escape North Korea and move southward today.

See Also: Census; China; Crude Birth Rate; Crude Death Rate; Demographic Transition Model; International Labor Migration; Japan; Median Age; Philippines; Population Density; Primate City; Rate of Natural Increase; Replacement-Level Fertility; Russia; Seoul; Thailand; Total Fertility Rate; Vietnam

Further Reading

The Economist. "The 54th Parallel: South Korea Needs to Make Better Use of Its Older Workers." October 26, 2013. http://www.economist.com/news/special-report/21588200-south-korea-needs-make-better-use-its-older-workers-54th-parallel.

Thomas Klassen. "South Korea: Ageing Tiger." *Global Brief*, January 12, 2010. http://globalbrief.ca/blog/2010/01/12/south-korea-ageing-tiger/.

Choe Sang-Hun. "In Changing South Korea, Who Counts as Korean?" *New York Times*, November 29, 2012. http://www.nytimes.com/2012/11/30/world/asia/demographic-shifts-redefine-society-in-south-korea.html.

Colombia

The Republic of Colombia has a population of about 48 million. It is the second-largest country by population in South America, following much larger Brazil. Its land area is nearly twice as large as that of the state of Texas. Thus it is slightly smaller by land area than Argentina and Peru, with a somewhat higher population density.

After present-day Colombia was occupied by settlers from Spain in the 16th century, it was governed as part of the Viceroyalty of Peru. In 1717, present-day Colombia along with present-day Venezuela, Ecuador, and Panama became the

Viceroyalty of New Grenada, which was governed from the present-day Colombian capital city of Bogota. In 1819, the Viceroyalty of New Grenada declared its independence under the name of Gran Colombia. However, Venezuela separated from Gran Colombia in 1829 and Ecuador followed suit in 1830. Present-day Panama remained part of Colombia until it declared independence in 1903, and Colombia recognized Panama as an independent country in 1921.

Colombia has experienced steady and rapid population growth since the 19th century. Its population was estimated at 3.9 million in 1900 and reached 12 million in the early 1950s. It passed the 25 million mark in the mid-1970s and has doubled again in the last three decades. Currently, Colombia's rate of natural increase is approximately 1.5 percent per year.

Although Colombia's population continues to increase, the country has undergone demographic transition as crude birth rates, crude death rates, and total fertility rates have declined steadily. Colombia's crude birth rate was estimated at 48 per 1,000 in 1950. However, it dropped to 41 per 1,000 by the late 1960s. Subsequently, it declined more rapidly to 28 per 1,000 in the late 1980s and to about 20 per 1,000 today. The crude death rate also declined from 16 per 1,000 in the early 1950s to 8 per 1,000 in the 1970s. The current crude death rate in Colombia is estimated at about 5.5 per 1,000. The country's total fertility rate was between 6 and 7 during the 1950s and 1960s, but has since dropped to below 3 in the 1990s and to about 2.5 today. Life expectancy has also increased from less than 55 years in the early 1950s to about 73 years currently.

Colombia has considerable population diversity and ethnic heterogeneity. Most people are descended from indigenous peoples who inhabited the area before Spanish conquest, from Spanish settlers, or from slaves brought to present-day Colombia from Africa prior to Colombian independence. Current estimates suggest that about half of Colombia's people are of mixed European and indigenous ancestry, with about a third of European ancestry. About 11 percent of Colombians have African ancestry, and nearly 4 percent are of indigenous ancestry. Smaller populations of persons from other parts of the world also live in Colombia, including several hundred thousand expatriates from North America and Europe. Many of these migrants are retirees.

Colombia has been affected by periods of civil war and political instability since the end of World War II. In the 1940s and early 1950s, a period of civil war and insurrection known as "La Violencia" claimed more than 200,000 lives. Political violence intensified again in the early 1980s, when a Marxist-Leninist guerilla organization known as the Revolution Armed Forces of Colombia (FARC) initiated efforts to take control of the government. International observers believe that FARC's activities were funded in part by the illegal drug trade.

Over the next 25 years, millions of Colombians left the country in search of economic opportunity or as refugees. Many of these refugees moved to Ecuador, whose government estimated that more than 200,000 Colombians were living in 2009 although some international observers believe that the actual number of Colombian refugees in Ecuador is much larger. Overall, nearly a million natives of Colombia live in the United States, which contains the largest number of Colombian migrants in the world. Other large communities of Colombian natives are found in Venezuela and in Spain. During the past few years, however, Colombia's rate of out-migration has subsided in light of reduced political violence and higher levels of prosperity.

See Also: Argentina; Brazil; Crude Birth Rate; Crude Death Rate; Demographic Transition Model; Expatriates; Life Expectancy; Population Density; Rate of Natural Increase; Refugees; Spain; Total Fertility Rate; United States of America

Further Reading

Myriam Berube. "Colombia: In the Crossfire." Migration Policy Institute, November 1, 2005. http://www.migrationpolicy.org/article/colombia-crossfire.

Tim Harcourt. "Can Young People Rebuild Colombia's Social Capital?" *Globalist*, March 25, 2013. http://www.theglobalist.com/can-young-people-rebuild-colombias-social-capital/.

ICMC Europe. "The Colombian Refugee Situation." 2013. http://www.resettlement.eu /page/colombian-refugee-situation.

Spain

The Kingdom of Spain, with a population of about 46 million, is the second-largest country in Europe by land area, following only France. However, Spain's population is smaller than those of France, Germany, Italy, and the United Kingdom, indicating its lower population density.

Spain was part of the Roman Empire and was later occupied by Germanic tribes before it was conquered by the Moors, who were Muslims who moved into Spain from Africa in the eighth century. The Moors controlled Spain until they were forced out by Christian kingdoms in the 14th and 15th century. The "Reconquista" was completed in 1492 and Spain has maintained its independence and territorial integrity ever since.

At the same time, Spanish explorers began to sail across the Atlantic Ocean. During the 17th and 18th centuries, Spain controlled an empire including present-day Mexico, most of Central America, and much of South America. At that time, Spain was perhaps the leading economic power in the world. Spain's power and influence declined after its colonies became independent in the early 19th century. It stagnated under dictatorial rule in the early 20th century, but more recently has

The Spanish enclave of Melilla is located on the Mediterranean coast of Africa and is surrounded by Moroccan territory. In order to keep immigrants from Morocco and other African countries out of Spain, the Spanish government constructed a border fence around Melilla. However, some Africans have been successful in climbing over the fence and crossing the Mediterranean into Europe. (AP Photo/Rex Features)

become prosperous as a democratic country and a member of the European Union.

Spain's population was estimated at 18.5 million in 1900. Its population grew slowly in the early 20th century, more rapidly between the 1950s and the 1980s, and more slowly once again since that time. The population has been estimated at 22 million in 1925, 28 million in 1950, and nearly 36 million in 1975. Spain's rates of natural increase have followed this general pattern. It averaged about 1 percent per year during the first half of the 20th century, except for 1918, when deaths exceeded births for the only time in recent Spanish history because of the global Spanish flu epidemic. The annual rate of natural increase exceeded 1.2 percent in 1958 and remained above 1.2 percent per year through 1967. It continued above 1 percent per year until 1977, but dropped below this figure in 1978 and has declined ever since. Today, Spain's annual rate of natural increase is estimated at about 0.1 percent. Its life expectancy is more than 82 years and is estimated to be the second highest in Europe.

As in most other countries throughout the world, Spain has experienced steady declines in its crude birth rates and crude death rates since the early 20th century. Spain's crude birth rate was estimated at 35 per 1,000 during the first decade of the 20th century. It declined slowly during the first half of the century, to about 22 per 1,000 in the 1930s. Between the 1930s and the late 1960s, it hovered at slightly more than 20 per 1,000. However, Spain's crude birth rate began to decline in the 1970s and 1980s, reaching about 10 per 1,000 in the late 1980s. The crude birth rate has remained steady at about 10 per 1,000 ever since. The overall declines in crude birth rates in Spain are reflected in declining total fertility rates. Spain's total fertility rate has dropped from about 4 in the 1920s to between 2.5 and 3 in the 1950s and 1960s. It dropped below replacement-level fertility, or below 2, in the early 1980s. Spain's current fertility rate is estimated at about 1.3.

Spain's crude death rate was estimated at about 25 per 1,000 between 1900 and 1910. It dropped slowly to about 20 per 1,000 by the mid-1920s, except for a brief spike to 33 per 1,000 during the Spanish flu epidemic of 1918. Spain's crude death rate began to decline quickly during and after World War II, dropping below 10 per 1,000 for the first time in 1952. It has remained relatively constant since that time, and is estimated at about 8.8 per 1,000 today.

That Spain's population is continuing to increase despite its low total fertility rates reflects the importance of migration. About 15 percent of Spain's people today are immigrants. Of these, nearly half come from former Spanish colonies in Latin America. More recently, substantial numbers of migrants have moved to Spain from Eastern Europe, especially after former Soviet satellites such as Romania and Bulgaria joined the European Union. Many other people moving to Spain are international labor migrants from Algeria, Nigeria, Morocco, and other countries in North and West Africa. Many of these immigrants are illegal immigrants who are encouraged by the fact that at its closest point, Spain's coast on the Mediterranean Sea is only nine miles from that of Morocco. Moreover, some illegal migrants enter Spain via the Spanish exclaves of Ceuta and Melilla along the Moroccan coast. In 2012, however, Spanish officials estimated that Spain's population dropped for the first time since 1918. This decline has been attributed to an economic slowdown in Spain, whose unemployment rate rose to more than 20 percent. This economic crisis has made Spain less attractive to immigrants and has also encouraged native-born Spaniards to move elsewhere in search of employment and economic opportunities.

See Also: Algeria; Crude Birth Rate; Crude Death Rate; France; Germany; Illegal Immigration; International Labor Migration; Italy; Mexico; Nigeria; Population Density; Rate of Natural Increase; Replacement-Level Fertility; Spanish Flu; Total Fertility Rate; United Kingdom

Further Reading

Jason DeParle. "Spain, Like U.S., Grapples with Immigration." *New York Times*, June 10, 2008. http://www.nytimes.com/2008/06/10/world/europe/10migrate.html?pagewanted=all.

Raphael Minder and Jim Yardley. "Desperation Fuels Trips of Migrants to Spain." *New York Times,* October 4, 2013. http://www.nytimes.com/2013/10/05/world/europe/as-desperation-mounts-more-migrants-cast-their-lot-on-a-troubled-sea.html.

UK Daily Mail Foreign Service. "Population of Spain Falls for the First Time as Foreigners Leave Because of the Eurozone Crisis." April 22, 2013. http://www.dailymail.co.uk/news /article-2313261/Population-Spain-FALLS-time-foreigners-leave-eurozone-crisis.html.

Ukraine

Ukraine is located in Eastern Europe, with a population of approximately 46 million. Its land area of about 233,000 square miles makes it slightly smaller than Texas.

Ukraine is the home of the Kievan Rus culture, which was centered near the present-day city of Kiev in central Ukraine more than 1,000 years ago. At its apex of power, the Kievan Rus controlled most of present-day Ukraine as well as portions of neighboring Russia and Belarus. Descendants of the Kievan Rus eventually moved northward and eastward into present-day Russia and became the ancestors of today's Russian people.

Since the 14th century, what is now Ukraine has been contested by various civilizations based in both Europe and Russia. During the 18th century, western Ukraine was controlled by the Austro-Hungarian Empire, while eastern Ukraine was part of the Russian Empire. Divisions between European-oriented western Ukraine and Russian-oriented eastern Ukraine affect Ukraine and its politics and economy today. At the outset of World War II, a secret agreement between the Soviet Union and Nazi Germany rendered Ukraine part of the Soviet sphere of influence. Both portions of Ukraine became the Ukrainian Soviet Socialist Republic, which was one of the constituent republics of the Soviet Union. The Soviets controlled Ukraine until the breakup of the Soviet Union in 1991, and during this period they encouraged people of Russian ancestry to move to the Ukrainian Soviet Socialist Republic. Ukraine became an independent country in 1991.

Ukraine's population grew steadily during most of the 20th century, but has since then been in decline. The population of what is now independent Ukraine was estimated at 25 million in 1900. It rose to about 34 million in 1914, but dropped to less than 25 million by 1920. Thus World War I had a major impact on Ukraine's population, with millions of Ukrainians dying as a result of warfare, disease, and famine. The population grew to about 41 million at the outset of World War II, but declined once again from about 41 million in 1939 to about 34 million in 1946. It grew once again after the war ended. A census taken by the Soviet government in 1960 counted about 42.5 million people in the Ukrainian Soviet Socialist Republic. The population peaked at about 52 million in 1993, shortly after Ukrainian independence. Since then, the population has declined steadily with a rate of natural increase of about -0.7 percent per year. If present trends continue, Ukraine's population may drop below 30 million by 2050.

These changes in Ukraine's population reflect changes in the country's crude birth rate and crude death rate. The birth rate in Ukraine was estimated at about 23 per 1,000 in 1950. It remained above 15 per 1,000 until shortly before the collapse of the Soviet Union, after which it began to decline more rapidly. Today, Ukraine's birth rate is estimated at about 10 per 1,000. Its total fertility rate is about 1.2, giving Ukraine one of the lowest total fertility rates in the world.

Meanwhile, the crude death rate of Ukraine has risen. It was estimated at about 10 per 1,000 in 1950 and at nearly 13 per 1,000 by 1991. Its current crude death rate is estimated at more than 15 per 1,000. The increase in Ukraine's crude death rate can be attributed to several factors including a legacy of substandard medical care during decades of Soviet rule. Alcoholism is a significant factor contributing to the death rate, especially among men. The crude death rate has been affected also by patterns of international migration. Especially since 1991, substantial numbers of young Ukrainians have emigrated, leaving older persons behind. At the same time, relatively few people have moved into Ukraine. Coupled with very low birth rates, lack of immigration and the prevalence of emigration have left Ukraine with a substantially older population. Crude death rates are higher in rural areas, whose populations are generally older than those in the cities. Life expectancy in Ukraine is estimated at about 68 years. As in Russia, life expectancy among men is more than 10 years less than life expectancy among women.

About 77 percent of Ukraine's people are ethnic Ukrainians, with about 20 percent ethnic Russians who usually speak Russian as their first language. Most ethnic Russians live in the eastern and southern portions of Ukraine, reflecting this area's historic ties to Russia. In contrast, many ethnic Ukrainians in the western and northern parts of the country have historic ties with Poland, Hungary, and other European countries that have become part of the European Union after the collapse of the Soviet Union. Many western Ukrainians favor increased ties between Ukraine and eastern and central Europe, including possible membership in the European Union. Differences between western and eastern Ukraine are evident in recent Ukrainian politics since independence and transition to democracy. In recent elections, pro-Western candidates have won large majorities of votes in western Ukraine whereas eastern Ukraine has given large majorities of votes to pro-Russian candidates. In early 2014, protestors in western Ukraine succeeded in toppling the pro-Russian government, and Russia has threatened to reassert its dominance of the country.

See Also: Census; Crude Birth Rate; Crude Death Rate; Famine; Germany; Rate of Natural Increase; Russia; Total Fertility Rate

Further Reading

Palash Ghosh. "No Country for Men: Ukraine Facing Grave Demographic Crisis." *International Business Times,* September 5, 2013. http://www.ibtimes.com/no-country-men-ukraine-facing-grave-demographic-crisis-1402966.

Oleksandr Kramar. "We Were 52 Million." *Ukrainianweek.com*, March 14, 2012. http://ukrainianweek.com/Society/43071.

World Population Review. "Ukraine Population 2013," 2013. http://worldpopulationreview.com/countries/ukraine-population/.

Tanzania

Tanzania, which is known formally as the United Republic of Tanzania, is located on the Indian Ocean coast of East Africa. It has a population of about 45 million and a land area of roughly 365,000 square miles, or about the size of Texas and New Mexico together. The country consists of two components: the territory of Tanganyika on the mainland and the islands of Zanzibar off the coast. About 98 percent of Tanzania's people live on the mainland, which contains about 98 percent of the country's total land area. Mainland Tanzania's rural population is distributed unevenly, with some areas densely populated and others supporting far fewer people.

Tanganyika has been occupied by a variety of peoples with different cultural and linguistic backgrounds over the past several thousand years. Many contemporary Tanzanians are descended from members of Bantu-speaking tribes who moved into present-day Tanganyika between 1,000 and 2,000 years ago. Others are descended from people who moved southward from the upper valley of the Nile River in present-day Ethiopia and Sudan. The Indian Ocean coast, including the islands of Zanzibar, has been a center for long-distance trade for many centuries. Anthropologists believe that traders from the Arabian Peninsula, India, and perhaps Southeast Asia conducted regular trade with Africa via its Indian Ocean ports.

After the Portuguese explorer Vasco de Gama became the first European to sight the coast of Tanganyika in 1498, Portugal claimed the territory. However, the Portuguese were expelled by Arabs from the southern Arabian Peninsula who established the Sultanate of Zanzibar and also controlled part of the mainland coast. In 1885, Tanganyika became a German colony under the auspices of the Congress of Berlin, via which Africa was divided into European colonies and spheres of influence. However, Germany was stripped of its colonies after World War I, and control of Tanganyika was transferred from Germany to the United Kingdom. Meanwhile, Zanzibar remained a nominally independent sultanate and a British protectorate throughout the first half of the 20th century. Tanganyika became independent of Britain in 1962. In 1963, the Sultan of Zanzibar was deposed in a coup d'état. The following year, Tanganyika and Zanzibar were merged into the present country of Tanzania.

Tanzania's population continues to grow at a rapid rate. In 1965, shortly after independence and the merger between Tanganyika and Zanzibar, the country's population was estimated at about 11.7 million. Its population reached 25 million in the late 1980s and was nearly 35 million in 2000. That Tanzania's population continues to grow quickly reflects the fact that birth rates in Tanzania have not declined as rapidly as they have in many other parts of the world. The country's crude birth rate was approximately 49 per 1,000 at the time of independence in the early 1960s and dropped only slightly to 41 per 1,000 by the first decade of the 21st century. The total fertility rate has also declined only slightly from about 6.8 in the 1960s to an estimated 5.6 today. As with many other countries, Tanzania's total fertility rate is higher in rural areas than in urban areas. It has dropped below 2 in Dar es Salaam, the country's largest city, economic, and commercial center, and former political capital. However, a majority of Tanzanians continue to live in rural areas of the country. In 2010, the government estimated a total fertility rate of 3.7 in urban areas and 6.1 in rural areas.

Population growth in Tanzania is also the result of more rapid declines in the country's crude death rate. The crude death rate was about 20 per 1,000 at independence and is about 11 per 1,000 today. Thus the rate of natural increase has held steady at between 2.5 and 3 percent annually over the past 50 years. Continued high rates of natural increase are associated with the fact that Tanzania has a very young population. Today only about 3 percent of Tanzania's people are over 65 years of age. Nearly 45 percent are less than 15 years old. Death rates are affected somewhat by the HIV/AIDS epidemic. An estimated 5 percent of Tanzanian adults are currently affected by the virus. The current life expectancy is estimated at 61 years.

Tanzania's population includes more than 100 recognized ethnic groups. Nearly 99 percent of Tanzanians are of African ancestry, with small communities of Europeans and Asians located primarily in Dar es Salaam and other cities. Relative to neighboring African countries, Tanzania has a recent history of economic growth and political stability. Hence hundreds of thousands of refugees have moved to Tanzania in recent years, with most coming from nearby African countries including the Democratic Republic of the Congo, Rwanda, Burundi, and Zimbabwe. It has been estimated that Tanzania may have the largest refugee population on the African continent. However, recently the Tanzanian government has become more reluctant to grant shelter to more refugees, and some have been repatriated to countries whose governments are at odds with the government of Tanzania itself.

See Also: Crude Birth Rate; Crude Death Rate; Democratic Republic of the Congo; Ethiopia; Germany; HIV/AIDS; Rate of Natural Increase; Total Fertility Rate; United Kingdom

Further Reading

BBC News Africa. "Why Has Tanzania Deported Thousands to Rwanda?" September 2, 2013. http://www.bbc.com/news/world-africa-23930776.

Joseph Metbe. "Tanzania Alarm over Expected Population Boom." *The East African*, January 1, 2013. http://www.theeastafrican.co.ke/news/Tanzania-alarm-over-expected-population-boom/-/2558/1655352/-/83jsmc/-/index.html.

World Population Review. "Tanzania Population 2013," 2013. http://worldpopulationreview.com/countries/tanzania-population/.

Kenya

The Republic of Kenya is located on the Indian Ocean coast of East Africa, immediately north of neighboring Tanzania. It has a population of about 43 million. Its land area of about 224,000 square miles makes it roughly the size of Texas. Thus Kenya's population density is somewhat larger than that of Tanzania.

Like Tanzania, Kenya has been home to many different cultures and civilizations for thousands of years. Arab traders are believed to have established the port of Mombasa on the Indian Ocean coast as much as 2,000 years ago. Britain took control of present-day Kenya as part of the East African Protectorate, whose boundaries correspond roughly with those of modern Kenya, in 1895. After World War I, the protectorate became the Colony of Kenya. Thousands of British citizens moved to Kenya during the 1920s and 1930s, and these white settlers controlled much of the economy and dominated the government. Following World War II, African nationalist movements began to agitate for independence and reduced European economic control. The colony became independent as the Republic of Kenya in 1963, and after independence, many British-born settlers and their descendants left the country.

The population of Kenya has grown nearly fivefold since independence. Shortly before independence, a 1962 census counted 8.6 million people. The first official census of postindependence Kenya was taken in 1969 and the population was estimated at 11 million. It nearly doubled to 21.5 million in 1989 and reached 38.6 million in the 2009 census. Kenya's crude birth rate has declined since independence, although it remains high relative to many other parts of the world. The crude birth rate of Kenya was about 51 per 1,000 in the 1950s and dropped to about 47 per 1,000 in the 1980s and about 38 per 1,000 today. Kenya's total fertility rate was more than 8 in the 1960s, and has since declined to less than 5. However, total fertility rates vary widely between urban and rural areas. According to the government's 2009 census, Kenya's fertility rate was 2.9 in urban areas and 5.2 in rural areas.

Crude death rates have declined over the course of Kenya's history. The crude death rate of the Colony of Kenya was estimated at about 23 per 1,000 in the 1950s. It dropped below 15 per 1,000 in the 1970s and to about 10 per 1,000 in the 1990s. Since then, it has risen slightly to about 11 per 1,000, in part because of HIV/AIDS and because of famines associated with persistent droughts. Kenya's rate of natural increase has remained high. It was above 3.5 percent annually throughout the 1960s, 1970s, and 1980s, but has begun to drop slightly. Current estimates suggest a rate of natural increase of about 2.6 percent per year. As is the case with Tanzania, Kenya has a very young population. Less than 3 percent of Kenyans are over 65 years of age, and well over 40 percent are less than 15 years old.

Kenya's population consists of numerous ethnic groups. Over 99 percent of Kenyans are of African ancestry, with very small communities of Europeans, Asian Indians, and Arabs. As a relatively stable and prosperous country surrounded by war-torn neighbors, Kenya has become home to several hundred thousand refugees. Neighboring Somalia, which has been plagued by ongoing political violence, civil war, and drought, is the leading source of refugees living in Kenya. The refugee camp at Dadaab, located in northeastern Kenya near the border between Kenya and Somalia, has been identified as the largest refugee camp in the world. Some have estimated that Dadaab currently houses more than 350,000 Somali refugees. War-torn Uganda, Sudan, South Sudan, and the Central African Republic have also sent large numbers of refugees and migrants to Kenya.

In 2012, the government of Kenya began implementing a new policy intended to reduce the country's total fertility rate from nearly 5 children per woman, as is the case today, to about 3 children per woman. This policy was part of an overall national development plan known as Vision 2030. The new policy emphasized public awareness of the importance of family planning, education, and involvement of local government and religious leaders while improving access to family planning services, especially in rural areas. Significantly, Vision 2030 is based on the premise that local individuals and leaders should be involved significantly in policy planning and implementation. Thus, Kenya's new policy stands in sharp contrast to China's approach to family planning, in which the controversial one-child policy was imposed by the national government from the top down.

See Also: Census; China; Crude Birth Rate; Famine; HIV/AIDS; Population Density; Rate of Natural Increase; Tanzania; Total Fertility Rate

Further Reading

Azad Essa. "Dadaab, the World's Biggest Refugee Camp." *Al-Jazeera*, July 11, 2011. http://www.aljazeera.com/indepth/features/2011/07/201171182844876473.html.

Wolfgang Fengler. "Demographic Transition and Growth in Kenya." World Bank, April 28, 2010. http://www.worldbank.org/en/news/opinion/2010/04/28/demographic-transition-growth-kenya.

Heidi Worley. "New Kenyan Population Policy a Model for Other Countries." Population Reference Bureau, 2014. http://www.prb.org/Publications/Articles/2014/kenyan-population-policy.aspx.

Argentina

Argentina is the second-largest country in South America by land area and the third-largest country in South America by population, behind Brazil and Colombia. Its population is about 41 million. With a land area of over 1.06 million square miles, Argentina is the eighth-largest country in the world by land area.

As with the rest of South America, present-day Argentina was inhabited by various Native American cultures before the arrival of explorers and conquistadors from Spain in the sixteenth century. The Spanish established a permanent settlement at Buenos Aires, which is Argentina's capital and primate city today, in 1580. In 1776, Spain made Buenos Aires the capital of the Viceroyalty de la Plata, which

In 2010, Argentina celebrated the 200th anniversary of the May Revolution against Spanish rule. The May Revolution led to formal Argentine independence in 1816. With a population of over 42 million, Argentina is the third-largest country in South America by population. (AP Photo/Natacha Pisarenko)

included most of present-day Argentina along with neighboring Paraguay, Uruguay, and parts of present-day Bolivia and Chile. The viceroyalty declared its independence from Spain in 1816, and present-day northern Argentina became united as the Argentine Confederation in 1829. In the late 19th century, Argentina extended its territorial control southward into Patagonia in southern South America.

Argentina's population has grown steadily since the 19th century, although its rate of population growth has slowed in the past few decades. Its population was estimated at 5.7 million in 1900 and rose to 12 million by 1930. The population doubled to nearly 24 million in 1975, reaching 35 million around 1996 and passing 40 million around 2010. Argentina's crude birth rate was estimated at about 38 per 1,000 in 1910. It remained above 30 per 1,000 into the 1930s, dropping to between 21 and 25 per 1,000 between the 1940s and the 1980s. Today, Argentina's crude birth rate is about 18 per 1,000. The total fertility rate has also declined, from slightly over 3 between the 1950s and the 1980s to about 2.25 today. Thus, Argentina's total fertility rate remains above replacement-level fertility.

Argentina's crude death rate has also declined consistently. The crude death rate was estimated at more than 18 per 1,000 in 1910. It dropped below 15 per 1,000 in the early 1920s and held steady between 10 and 12 per 1,000 during the 1930s and 1940s. It dropped below 10 per 1,000 in the early 1950s and has declined very slowly since that time. Today, Argentina's crude death rate is estimated at about 7.8 per 1,000. Life expectancy has increased from about 62 years in the early 1950s to more than 75 years today.

Argentina's population is diverse. In contrast to the populations of many other South American countries, however, the large majority of Argentina's people are of European ancestry, with relatively few people of mixed European and indigenous ancestry. About 1.5 percent of Argentines are of primarily indigenous descent. Many Argentines are descended from the original Spanish settlers who moved to present-day Argentina before independence. Others are descended from Europeans who moved to Argentina from other countries later.

During the late 19th century, Argentina's government actively promoted European immigration. Estimates have suggested that nearly 7 million Europeans immigrated to Argentina between the 1850s and the 1950s. Of these, more than 40 percent came from Italy. Today, it is believed that more than half of all Argentines have full or partial Italian ancestry. Other major sources of European immigration into Argentina include Germany, France, and Portugal. Historically, Germany has been the third-largest source of immigrants into Argentina, following Spain and Italy. More recently, a majority of people migrating into Argentina have come from elsewhere in South America. Today, the four leading countries of origin of migrants to Argentina include Paraguay, Bolivia, Chile, and Peru. An estimated 5 percent of Argentines today are believed to be immigrants.

See Also: Brazil; Buenos Aires; Colombia; Crude Birth Rate; Crude Death Rate; France; Germany; Italy; Life Expectancy; Primate City; Replacement-Level Fertility; Spain; Total Fertility Rate

Further Reading

Gaston Chillier and Ernesto Seman. "Argentina's Migration Solution." *American Quarterly*, Spring 2011. http://www.americasquarterly.org/node/2432.

Marcela Valente. "Argentina: The Promised Land for South American Neighbours." *Inter Press Service*, August 28, 2012. http://www.ipsnews.net/2012/08/argentina-the-promised-land-for-south-american-neighbours/.

Algeria

Algeria, whose formal name is the People's Democratic Republic of Algeria, is one of five countries in northern Africa that border the Mediterranean Sea. It is the second largest of these countries by population behind Egypt, with more than 38 million residents.

Algeria's land area of about 920,000 square miles makes it nearly twice the size of Alaska by land area. It is the 10th-largest country in the world by land area in the world and the largest in Africa, slightly larger than the Democratic Republic of the Congo. However, most of Algeria's land area is part of the Sahara Desert. Much of the Saharan portion of Algeria is uninhabited or very sparsely populated. Most Algerians who live in the Sahara Desert are nomads or live near oases. More than 90 percent of Algeria's people live within 150 miles of the Mediterranean coast in an area containing only about 10 percent of the country's total land area. As in the case of Egypt, Algeria's physiological density is much greater than its actual population density.

The coastal regions of present-day Algeria have been populated densely, relative to contemporary global standards, for at least 3,000 years. In the fifth and fourth centuries BCE, much of the present-day Algerian coast was controlled by the Carthaginian Empire, centered in nearby present-day Tunisia. The Carthaginian Empire was dismembered after a series of military defeats by the Roman Empire in the third and second centuries BCE, and the region was incorporated into the Roman Empire in about 24 BCE. Subsequently, the region was conquered by Muslims from the Arabian Peninsula during the seventh century CE. Coastal Algeria was taken over by the Ottoman Empire in the 16th century, and in 1830, the region was annexed to France.

The French regarded coastal Algeria as an integral part of the French state. After World War II, some Algerians began to agitate for political independence. Full-scale rebellion led to several armed clashes between supporters of Algerian independence and French troops during the 1950s. France recognized Algeria formally as an independent country in 1962. Algeria's population characteristics reflect its long history. The indigenous people of Algeria and neighboring states were Berbers, but many Arabs moved to coastal Algeria following its conquest by Muslim Arabs. Today, nearly all Algerians are of mixed Arab and Berber ancestry, and more than 97 percent are Muslims. Hundreds of thousands of people of French ancestry returned to France after Algeria became independent, with the result that the percentage of Muslims of Arab/Berber ancestry increased.

Algeria's population has grown very rapidly since the early 20th century, especially since independence. A census taken in 1901 counted about 4.7 million people. In 1948, Algeria's population was estimated at 8.7 million. However, it doubled to more than 16.5 million in 1975 and doubled again to over 35 million by 2010. Its population is estimated to exceed 38 million today. Algeria's rate of natural increase has held steady at slightly over 2 percent per year since the 1950s.

Crude birth rates in Algeria have fallen steadily over the past 50 years, although reliable data are available only since the 1980s. The crude birth rate of Algeria has been estimated at 50 per 1,000 in the mid-1960s, shortly after independence. It remained above 40 per 1,000 into the 1980s, and subsequently began to decline more rapidly. In 1993, it dropped below 30 per 1,000 for the first time and dropped to 20 per 1,000 by about 2000, although it has begun to increase slightly since then. Crude death rates have also fallen steadily, especially between the 1960s and the 1980s. The crude death rate has been estimated at 6 per 1,000 in 1990 and about 4.5 per 1,000 today. Thus Algeria's steady rate of natural increase reflects demographic transition, followed by a more recent upturn in the crude birth rate. Algeria's current total fertility rate is estimated at about 3.

As is the case with many countries that have undergone demographic transition in the second half of the 20th century, Algeria has a young population. Algeria's median age is estimated at about 27.5 years. The recent increase in Algeria's birth rate reflects in part the fact that there is a large cohort of people currently in their twenties and thirties who were born shortly before and during the time that the country's birth rate began to fall quickly. Less than 6 percent of Algerians are more than 65 years of age, as compared with more than 25 percent who are 14 and under. Life expectancy is now estimated at nearly 75 years. In part because of the relatively large population of young adults, unemployment has become a significant issue in the country.

Before independence in 1962, Algeria was considered part of the French state, and Algerians were free to relocate to France proper. Large-scale migration of Algerians to France continued into the 1970s, with many Algerians moving to the French city of Marseille on the north shore of the Mediterranean Sea. In the 1970s, this outflow of international labor migrants declined, in part because Algeria's economic situation improved as a result of increased revenues from the production and export of oil and gas. Even today, however, it is estimated that about 1 million Algerians live overseas. Of these, about three-quarters live in France and an additional 16 percent live in other countries in the European Union.

Algeria's recent prosperity, along with its location along the coast of the Mediterranean Sea, has been attracting a larger and larger number of migrants from other countries. Some migrants have moved to Algeria in search of employment, while others have moved to Algeria with the idea of seeking an opportunity to move across the Mediterranean into Europe. Algeria now harbors more than 100,000 refugees. The largest source of refugees currently living in Algeria is Western Sahara, a former Spanish colony located on the Atlantic coast south of Morocco. Morocco claims Western Sahara, while Algeria has supported rebels seeking independence for the territory. Algeria estimates that about 100,000 Western Saharan refugees live within Algerian territory, although Morocco claims that Algeria has deliberately overestimated the refugee population in order to promote international sympathy for the rebels' cause.

See Also: Census; Crude Birth Rate; Democratic Republic of the Congo; Demographic Transition Model; Egypt; France; International Labor Migration; Life Expectancy; Median Age; Nomads; Physiological Density; Population Density; Rate of Natural Increase; Refugees; Total Fertility Rate

Further Reading

Abdel Nasser Jaby. "The Impasse of Political Transition in Algeria: Three Generations and Two Scenarios." Arab Center for Research and Policy Studies, 2011. http://english.dohai nstitute.org/release/9d3fd57b-e368-42d5-bd7b-aadb74f9017e.

Migration Policy Institute. "Migration Profile: Algeria," 2013. http://www.migrationpolicy centre.eu/docs/migration_profiles/Algeria.pdf.

Paul A. Silverstein. *Algeria in France: Transpolitics, Race, and Nation.* Bloomington: Indiana University Press, 2004.

Niger

Niger, whose official name is the Republic of Niger, is an impoverished African country whose rate of natural increase is among the highest in the world. Landlocked Niger is located in north-central Africa, south of the Sahara Desert and north of Nigeria. Its land area is about twice as large as that of Texas, and its population is more than 17 million. Most of these people live in the southern quarter of the country, where rainfall is usually sufficient to support agriculture.

Niger was part of the French colony of French West Africa from the 1880s until it became independent in 1960. It is one of the poorest countries in the world. According to the *CIA World Factbook*, Niger's per capita gross domestic product was about $900, ranking it 220th among the 229 countries included in the ranking. More than two-thirds of Niger's people work in agriculture, and less than half of Niger's children attend school.

Niger's population has increased rapidly since independence. Its population was estimated by Nigerien government officials at 3.2 million in 1960. The population increased to 5.6 million in 1980, 10.5 million in 2000, and 15.2 million in 2010. A 2013 estimate placed Niger's population at nearly 17 million. Its annual rate of population growth is more than 3.3 percent per year. If current trends continue, it has been estimated that Niger's population will exceed 50 million by 2050.

Niger's demography is typical of less developed countries throughout sub-Saharan Africa. Niger's crude birth rate is among the highest crude birth rates in the world. In contrast to many less developed countries, Niger's crude birth rate has dropped only slightly over the past half century, from 55.5 per 1,000 in the early 1960s to 49.5 per 1,000 between 2005 and 2010. The crude death rate has dropped substantially, from about 25 per 1,000 in the 1960s to less than 14 per 1,000 today. The increasing difference between the crude birth rate and the crude death rate has generated Niger's high rate of natural increase.

Niger's high rate of natural increase is associated with its very high total fertility rate. Its total fertility rate has remained at about 7 children per woman since the 1960s. Between 2005 and 2010, the total fertility rate was estimated at 7.19. The fact that Niger's crude birth rate and its total fertility rate remain very high implies that Niger remains in the second stage of demographic transition. Niger's median age of 15.2 years is among the lowest in the world, and nearly 10 percent of infants born in the country die before reaching their first birthdays. The high rate of infant mortality contributes to Niger's low life expectancy of approximately 54 years.

Efforts to promote economic development in Niger have been impeded by the country's location in the semi-arid and drought-prone Sahel region of Africa. Northern Niger has too little rainfall to support farming, and there is little room for agriculture to expand into previously uncultivated areas of the country. Climatologists predict that the climate of the Sahel will become hotter and drier as global warming continues, further imperiling Niger's efforts to produce enough food to support its population.

Rapid population increases have also impeded domestic and international efforts to promote economic development. Beginning in 2007, Niger's government initiated efforts to promote family planning. Currently, nearly half of Nigerien women are married by the age of 15, but the government has proposed to increase the age of legal marriage to 18. The goal of these policies has been to reduce the total fertility rate to 5 by 2015, but whether this goal will be realized remains problematic. Niger's demographic circumstances illustrate the problematic relationships among poverty, rapid population growth, and environmental degradation.

See Also: Crude Birth Rate; Crude Death Rate; Demographic Transition Model; Infant Mortality; Life Expectancy; Median Age; Rate of Natural Increase; Total Fertility Rate

Further Reading

Integrated Regional Information Networks. "Niger: Population Explosion Threatens Development Gains." December 11, 2007. http://www.irinnews.org/Report/75801/NIGER-Population-explosion-threatens-development-gains.

Malcolm Potts, Virginia Gidi, Martha Campbell, and Sarah Zureick. "Niger: Too Little, Too Late." *International Perspectives on Sexual and Reproductive Health* 37 (June 2011). http://www.guttmacher.org/pubs/journals/3709511.html.

Saudi Arabia

Saudi Arabia, officially the Kingdom of Saudi Arabia, is one of the fastest-growing countries by population in the world. Its population has increased about sevenfold over the past 50 years. Saudi Arabia's rapid population growth is associated with a very high crude birth rate, a relatively low crude death rate, and substantial in-migration.

Saudi Arabia contains about 80 percent of the Arabian Peninsula in southwestern Asia, between the Red Sea to the west and the Persian Gulf to the east. Most of Saudi Arabia is desert. The southeastern portion of Saudi Arabia, known as the Rub Al-Khali or "Empty Quarter," is virtually rainless and is uninhabited. Saudi Arabia contains the city of Mecca, which is the holiest city of Islam.

The population of Saudi Arabia in 1960 has been estimated at about 4 million. It reached 10 million around 1980 and doubled to 20 million around 1998. In 2010, the Saudi census showed an overall population of more than 27 million, or an increase of about 30 percent in around 12 years. The increase in Saudi Arabia's population has been due to both natural increase and immigration. According to United Nations statistics, the number of deaths in Saudi Arabia has been stable at between 80,000 and 90,000 per year since the early 1950s, and the country has among the lowest crude death rates in the world. The very low crude death rate is the result of the country's large number of young temporary and permanent immigrants. However, the number of live births per year has increased steadily, from about 159,000 per year between 1950 and 1955 to nearly 500,000 per year in the 1980s and nearly 600,000 per year today. Thus, the country's population remains young. The median age is 25.3 years, and only 3 percent of the population is over 65 years of age. Saudi Arabia has experienced considerable demographic transition. The total fertility rate in 2010 was 2.26, or slightly above replacement level.

Migration has also been responsible for rapid population growth in Saudi Arabia. Much of this immigration is associated with the growth of the petroleum industry, which has been a mainstay of the Saudi economy since the 1930s. Saudi Arabia produces and exports more than 3 billion barrels of crude oil annually. Petroleum represents more than 90 percent of Saudi Arabia's export income, and Saudi Arabia produces about 13 percent of all petroleum produced worldwide. As a result, Saudi Arabia's per capita income is among the highest in the world. The 2010 census showed that about 31 percent of Saudi Arabia's residents were born outside Saudi Arabia. Most of these expatriates moved to oil-rich Saudi Arabia in search of employment opportunities. Some are Americans and Europeans, many of whom work in management-level jobs in the petroleum industry. Many of these Westerners live in foreign-dominated compounds in large cities. In 2009, it was estimated that about 150,000 Western expatriates were living in Saudi Arabia.

The large majority of temporary or permanent immigrants to Saudi Arabia, however, are natives of poorer and less developed countries. In 2012, it was estimated that more than 1 million work visas were granted by the Saudi government to foreign-born workers, while only 83,000 jobs went to native-born Saudis. These expatriates move to Saudi Arabia in search of employment. Some work in the petroleum industry, and many others work as shopkeepers, domestic servants, construction workers, and in other service-related activities. In 2009, an estimated 1 million expatriates had come to Saudi Arabia from Yemen. About 300,000 expatriates had come each from Egypt, India, and Pakistan. All of these countries are much poorer than Saudi Arabia and are lacking in significant oil and mineral reserves. Many send portions of their incomes to their native countries as remittances.

See Also: Census; Crude Birth Rate; Crude Death Rate; Egypt; India; Median Age; Migration; Pakistan; Rate of Natural Increase; Remittances

Further Reading

Al Arabiya. "Foreign Workers in Saudi Arabia Weaken Nationalization Effort." August 13, 2012. http://www.alarabiya.net/articles/2012/08/13/232028.html.

American Bedu. "The Expatriate Population of Saudi Arabia." June 6, 2009. http://americanbedu.com/2009/06/06/the-expatriate-population-in-saudi-arabia/.

Singapore

Singapore, whose formal name is the Republic of Singapore, is an island country located off the coast of the Malay Peninsula in Southeast Asia. Singapore is separated from Malaysia on the mainland by the Straits of Johor, which are less than a mile wide at their narrowest point and are crossed by two bridges connecting the island and the Malaysian mainland. To the south, Singapore is separated by the Straits of Singapore, which are 12 miles wide at their narrowest point, from the Riau Islands in Indonesia.

Given its location on the main maritime route between East Asia and South Asia, Singapore has been an important trading and commercial center for at least 2,000 years. Singapore was a British colony from 1826 until 1963, when it became part of the independent Federation of Malaysia. It seceded from the federation in 1965 and became an independent country. Today Singapore is among the 20 wealthiest countries in the world, with a per capita gross domestic product of nearly $50,000 as of 2012. Singapore is a multi-ethnic state, but its population is dominated by people of Chinese ancestry, who make up about 75 percent of the population. About 14 percent are ethnic Malays, with about 9 percent of Indian and 2 percent of European ancestry. Ethnic conflict was a factor that led to the separation between Singapore and Malaysia, a majority of whose population is of Malay ancestry.

Singapore's population has risen steadily, increasing from about 1.9 million at the time of independence in 1965 to about 3 million in 1990 to about 5.2 million today. However, Singapore's crude birth rate is among the lowest in the world. In 2011, Singapore's total fertility rate was estimated at 1.15 children born to each woman in the population. The total fertility rate for the majority Chinese population was estimated at 1.02. (The *CIA World Factbook* estimated an even lower figure of 0.98 in 2012.) Thus Singapore's continuing population growth is dependent entirely on immigration. This is recognized by the government of Singapore, which has emphasized that a combination of continued immigration and increasing fertility rates will be necessary to maintain Singapore's population in the future.

Currently, only about 63 percent of Singapore's residents are Singaporean citizens and only about half of Singapore's people were born in Singapore. The remaining 37 percent of Singapore's people are noncitizens. Singaporean law divides immigrant workers between "foreign workers" and "foreign talents." The former represent international labor migrants; the latter represent the brain drain. The large majority of foreign-born residents of Singapore are foreign workers. Foreign workers hold unskilled and semiskilled jobs in construction, shipyard work, and other fields. The majority of foreign workers in Singapore come from the poorer countries of Asia, including India, Bangladesh, the Philippines, Thailand, and Sri Lanka. Foreign workers are recruited under contracts between employment agencies and the Singaporean government. Most stay in Singapore only for fixed terms of employment and are required to leave the country when their contracts have ended.

Many foreign workers come to Singapore to work as domestic servants. An estimated 200,000 foreign workers hold jobs as domestic servants in Singapore. The large majority of these domestic servants are female, and most come from less developed countries in Asia, particularly from Indonesia. International human rights organizations have expressed concerns about the treatment of these domestic servants, some of whom have been physically abused by employers and/or were expected to work more than 12 hours a day, seven days a week. In March 2012, however, the government of Singapore enacted a law requiring employers of domestic workers to grant these workers one day off per week with pay.

Foreign talents are persons such as engineers and physicians who have professional skills that are regarded as especially useful to Singapore's economy. Foreign talents are encouraged to remain in Singapore and to become Singaporean citizens. Highly qualified students from overseas are granted scholarships to study at universities in Singapore in exchange for their agreement to stay and work in Singapore for at least three years after graduation. The foreign-talent system has been extended to sports in that highly qualified athletes are recruited to become Singaporean citizens and to compete for Singapore in the Olympic Games, the World Cup, and other international sporting competitions.

See Also: Bangladesh; Crude Birth Rate; India; Indonesia; Migration; Philippines; Thailand; Total Fertility Rate

Further Reading

Human Rights Watch. "Singapore: Domestic Workers to Get One Day of Rest." March 6, 2012. http://www.hrw.org/news/2012/03/05/singapore-domestic-workers-get-weekly-day-rest.

Jakarta Globe. "Singapore's Fertility Rate Dropped to a Record Low." September 28, 2011. http://www.thejakartaglobe.com/international/singapores-fertility-rate-dropped-to-a-record-low/468263.

State of Singapore Prime Minister's Office, National Population and Talent Division. "Citizen Population Scenarios." Occasional Paper, April 2012. https://www.nptd.gov.sg/content/dam/nptd/Occasional%20Paper%20-%20Citizen%20Population%20Scenarios.pdf.

United Arab Emirates

The United Arab Emirates is a state located in the southeastern portion of the Arabian Peninsula. The United Arab Emirates is a federation of seven emirates, or small kingdoms, each of which is ruled by a hereditary monarch who has absolute

The United Arab Emirates is one of the wealthiest countries in the world, and the rapidly growing city of Dubai is one of the richest places in the United Arab Emirates. Dubai's wealth has attracted immigrants from throughout Asia and North Africa, and less than half of Dubai's people are United Arab Emirates citizens. (AP Photo/Kamran Jebreili)

authority within his emirate. The seven emirates that make up the United Arab Emirates include Abu Dhabi, Ajman, Dubai, Fujairah, Ras al-Khaimah, Sharjah, and Umm al-Quwain. About 8 million people live in the United Arab Emirates, with about half living in the two largest emirates of Abu Dhabi and Dubai. Most of the people of the United Arab Emirates live in cities along the coast, with very few people living in the extremely hot, dry interior of the country.

The major cities of the United Arab Emirates are located on the Persian Gulf west of the Strait of Hormuz, which connects the Persian Gulf with the Arabian Sea and the Indian Ocean. These cities are thus located along trade routes that have been used for thousands of years. Dubai, which is the largest city in the United Arab Emirates today, is over a thousand years old. Ships from Dubai traded as far away as India and China during the Middle Ages, after which European colonial powers assumed control of much of the region's trade. In 1892, the rulers of the emirates that now comprise the United Arab Emirates signed a treaty with Britain that guaranteed them freedom of navigation in the Persian Gulf and protection against possible attacks from foreign powers. The United Arab Emirates achieved full political independence in 1971.

Pearl diving had been a mainstay of the economy of Dubai and the United Arab Emirates for hundreds of years before the invention of artificial pearls in the early

20th century, after which the pearl-diving industry collapsed. In an effort to resurrect Dubai's economy, Dubai's Sheik Rashid bin Saeed al-Maktoum made Dubai a duty-free port. The port facilities were dredged and expanded in order to handle large ocean-going ships. Dubai joined the United Arab Emirates in 1971 only under the condition that Dubai be allowed to maintain its status as a duty-free port. Dubai's trading activities along with profits from the extraction of oil deposits first found and exploited in the 1960s have made the United Arab Emirates one of the wealthiest countries in the world.

The wealth of the United Arab Emirates has contributed to its explosive population growth. The population of the United Arab Emirates at the time of independence has been estimated at about 300,000. The population more than tripled to over 1 million in 1980, tripled again to 3 million in 2000, and doubled again between 2000 and 2009. It continues to increase at a rate of several hundred thousand per year. The population of Dubai has grown from an estimated 20,000 in 1950 to over 60,000 at the time of United Arab Emirates independence in 1971. It reached 1.4 million in 2006 and is believed to be more than 2 million today.

The United Arab Emirates has experienced demographic transition over the course of the last half-century. The crude birth rate has fallen from over 45 per 1,000 between 1950 and 1965 to less than 14 per 1,000 in 2010. The crude death rate was more than 19 per 1,000 in the 1950s, but is below 2 per 1,000 in 2010—one of the lowest crude death rates in the world. The United Arab Emirates' death rate is low because the country contains a large number of young adult immigrants. Because of the low death rate, the rate of natural increase in the United Arab Emirates remains high. In 2010, it was estimated at 1.2 percent per year. The total fertility rate, which was between 6 and 7 between 1950 and 1975, dropped to slightly below 2 for the first time by 2010.

Although the United Arab Emirates has a high rate of natural increase, most of the population growth in the United Arab Emirates is the result of immigration from other countries. The United Arab Emirates has the highest net migration rate in the world. Today only about 17 percent of United Arab Emirates' people are native-born Emiratis and United Arab Emirates citizens, and about 83 percent are expatriates. The largest source of expatriates is South Asia, including India, Bangladesh, and Pakistan. Emigrants from these countries are believed to comprise more than half of the United Arab Emirates' current total population. Other large expatriate populations have come from the Philippines, Iran, and other countries throughout the Arab world. Several hundred thousand Americans and Europeans also live in the United Arab Emirates, principally in Abu Dhabi and Dubai. Many expatriates, especially those from the Arab world and Asia, have lived in the United Arab Emirates for many years. However, in most cases the United Arab Emirates does not give these long-term resident expatriate the opportunity to achieve United Arab Emirates citizenship.

The high population of expatriates has had other significant effects on the demographics of the United Arab Emirates. Many expatriates are young men, many of whom send remittances to relatives in their native countries. Because so many expatriate workers are young, the United Arab Emirates has the lowest crude death rate in the world. According to the CIA World Factbook, the crude death rate of the United Arab Emirates was estimated to be 2.11 per thousand as of 2009. Kuwait, Qatar, and Saudi Arabia, all of which are oil-rich countries with large expatriate populations, also have very low crude death rates. The very low crude death rates in the United Arab Emirates and other oil-rich countries are associated with the fact that age-specific death rates for persons under 50 years of age are much lower than are those for older adults. The majority of expatriates are men, and therefore more than 70 percent of the total population of the United Arab Emirates is male.

See Also: Bangladesh; China; Crude Birth Rate; Crude Death Rate; Demographic Transition Model; India; Iran; Pakistan; Philippines; Rate of Natural Increase; Remittances; Saudi Arabia; Total Fertility Rate

Further Reading

Dylan Bowman. "GCC Residents Demand Gulf States Grant Citizenship." *Arabianbusiness .com*, December 17, 2007. http://www.arabianbusiness.com/gcc-residents-demand-gulf -states-grant-citizenship-122557.html.

Andy Sambridge. "United Arab Emirates Population Hits 6m, Emiratis Make Up 16.5%." *Arabianbusiness.com*, October 9, 2009. http://www.arabianbusiness.com/uae-popu lation-hits-6m-emiratis-make-up-16-5--12137.html.

Part III: Cities

Tokyo

Tokyo is the capital city of Japan. It is the center of the largest metropolitan area in the world. This region, known officially as Tokyo Metropolis, has a population of more than 35 million people. Of these, about 8.5 million live in the city of Tokyo itself. In addition, the Tokyo metropolitan area includes the cities of Chiba, Kawasaki, Saitama, and Yokohama. The overall land area of metropolitan Tokyo, as designated by the government of Japan, is 5,240 square miles—a region nearly as large as the U.S. state of Connecticut. Thus, metropolitan Tokyo has a population density of about 6,800 people per square mile. Nearly 30 percent of Japan's people live in the Tokyo metropolitan area. Tokyo is Japan's primate city. Tokyo is a center for global finance as well as the political and economic center of Japan. The Tokyo Stock Exchange is the second largest in the world.

Tokyo was founded in the 15th century as a fishing village known as Edo. It grew rapidly during the 17th and 18th centuries, when Japan was isolating itself almost completely from the outside world. Edo's population is believed to have exceeded 1 million by the 1720s, and it emerged as Japan's cultural and economic center. In 1869, the Japanese government moved the capital city from Kyoto to Edo. The city was renamed Tokyo, meaning "Eastern Capital."

The Tokyo area has remained one of the largest metropolitan areas in the world for the past three centuries. An 1889 census of Tokyo counted about 1.4 million people. The population reached about 5 million in 1950 and nearly 9 million by 1965. Since that time, the population of the city of Tokyo itself has been stable. Most of the population growth in the Tokyo metropolitan area has taken place outside the city as Tokyo has undergone considerable suburbanization. Suburban relative to central-city growth in Tokyo paralleled similar developments in Europe and the United States. In 1950, the population of the Tokyo metropolitan area outside Tokyo itself was about 7 million. At that time, more than 40 percent of the metropolitan area's residents lived in the city. In 2010, the suburban population of the metropolitan area exceeded 26 million. Thus more than three-quarters of the metropolitan area's residents were living outside the city limits of Tokyo.

The immense population of Tokyo has resulted in a host of problems faced by metropolitan and national government officials. Like other Japanese cities, Tokyo suffers from a shortage of space. This is due in part to Tokyo's geography. The Kanto Plain region, in which Tokyo is located, is one of the few extensive areas of flat land in Japan. However, this region is now urbanized almost entirely and there is little room for Tokyo to expand further to the west and north. To the east and south, Tokyo Metropolis has a coast on the Sea of Japan. Lack of room for expansion contributes to Tokyo's very high population density relative to other very large cities throughout the developed world, although Tokyo's population density is comparable to the population densities of other large Asian cities including Beijing, Jakarta, Manila, Mumbai, and Seoul.

Tokyo is also subject to natural hazards and disasters. Tokyo is located near the boundaries between three tectonic plates and thus is subject to major earthquakes. In 1923, an earthquake measuring 7.9 on the Richter scale struck the Tokyo area, causing between 70,000 and 100,000 fatalities. In addition to the 1923 earthquake, Tokyo has been devastated by earthquakes in 1703, 1782, 1812, and 1855. Although Japanese law requires all buildings to be constructed in such a way as to withstand earthquakes, a major earthquake near the center of Tokyo today could result in substantial loss of life, great damage to property, and severe disruption to the Japanese economy.

The high population density of Tokyo has contributed to substantial pollution and traffic congestion. During the 1950s and 1960s, Tokyo was one of the most polluted cities in the world. Since that time, levels of air pollution in Tokyo have decreased because manufacturing has declined and because the Japanese government has enacted and enforced far more stringent environmental protection laws. Nevertheless, congestion has contributed to very long commuting times to work. Commutes of two hours or more each way are not uncommon for Japanese workers. Housing is highly expensive. The combination of high housing costs and long commuting times has driven up housing prices even more near the center of Tokyo, pushing less affluent workers further and further from the center of the city.

Although the Tokyo metropolitan area remains the largest in the world by population, many demographers predict that it will be surpassed in population by other large cities in less developed countries such as Jakarta and Manila by 2030. Japan's rate of natural increase is negative and its total fertility rate is low. One Japanese government projection suggests that Tokyo may lose more than 2 million residents by 2035. However, areas of Japan outside Tokyo are expected to lose population at a faster rate, meaning that the Tokyo metropolitan area will contain an even larger share of Japan's population than is the case today.

See Also: Beijing; Census; Demography; Jakarta; Japan; Manila; Mumbai; Population Density; Primate City; Rate of Natural Increase; Seoul; Total Fertility Rate; United States of America

Further Reading

Wendell Cox. "The Evolving Urban Form: Tokyo." *newgeography.com*, June 20, 2012. http://www.newgeography.com/content/002923-the-evolving-urban-form-tokyo.

Alexandra Harney. "Japan's Pollution Diet." *New York Times*, February 15, 2013. http://latitude.blogs.nytimes.com/2013/02/15/japans-pollution-diet/?_r=0.

Edwin Seidensticker. *Tokyo Rising: The City since the Great Earthquake*. Cambridge, MA: Harvard University Press, 1991.

Jakarta

Jakarta is the capital city and largest city in Indonesia. The city of Jakarta has a population of about 11 million, with more than 28 million people living in the Jakarta metropolitan area. In 2011, Jakarta was the 17th-largest city by population in the world, and its metropolitan population was the second largest in the world behind Tokyo. Some experts predict that the population of Jakarta's metropolitan area will exceed that of the Tokyo metropolitan area by 2030. As is the case with many large metropolitan areas throughout the world, suburban and outlying areas of Jakarta are currently growing at a considerably faster rate than is the city itself.

Jakarta is located on the northwest coast of the island of Java, on the Java Sea. Java is the most populous island in the world, with a population of over 135 million living in an area about the size of the U.S. state of Illinois. Java contains about 60 percent of Indonesia's population, and thus more than 10 percent of all Indonesians live in greater Jakarta.

Jakarta's recorded history has been traced to the fourth century CE. Beginning in the seventh century CE, present-day Jakarta was a major port city of the Sunda kingdom, which ruled western Java until the arrival of Europeans in the 16th century. In the early 17th century, the Dutch East India Company built a settlement known as Batavia on the site of present-day Jakarta near the Sunda port of Kelapa. Batavia later became the capital of Dutch Indonesia and was renamed Jakarta by

Jakarta, the capital city of Indonesia, is one of the largest and most densely populated cities in the world. Like many megacities in less developed countries, Jakarta experiences massive traffic jams. (SUPRI/Reuters/Corbis)

Indonesian nationalists in 1942. Jakarta was occupied by the Japanese during World War II. After the war ended, the Netherlands recognized Indonesia's independence in 1949. Jakarta became the capital city of independent Indonesia.

Jakarta, like other large Asian cities such as Tokyo, Seoul, and Manila, is a primate city and the major political, economic, and cultural center of Indonesia. Like many primate cities in less developed countries, Jakarta has experienced very rapid population growth since Indonesia achieved independence. Economic development and the growth of government created numerous jobs, and large numbers of people from rural areas across Java flocked to Jakarta in search of employment. The city's population began to grow very rapidly. The population of the city of Jakarta proper has been estimated at about 100,000 in 1880 to about 530,000 in 1940, before the city was taken over by Japan. The census of 1950, taken shortly after Indonesia became independent, counted about 1.7 million residents. Thus Jakarta's population has increased to nearly six times its 1950 level over the 60 years following Indonesian independence. Moreover, the census figures released by the Indonesian government include only legal residents. It is estimated that hundreds of thousands of illegal residents, transients, and people residing in squatter settlements also live in Jakarta. Thus the actual number of people who live in Jakarta is believed to be considerably higher than the number shown in official Indonesian government statistics.

THE TRAFFIC JOCKEYS OF JAKARTA

In Jakarta, traffic jams have been estimated to cost Indonesia more than 1.2 billion dollars a year while contributing greatly to air pollution. In an effort to reduce traffic congestion and pollution, Jakarta's government introduced a "three-in-one" rule in 1992. This law requires at least three occupants of each automobile on many highways during rush hours.

In order to help drivers to circumvent this policy, some Indonesians work in the informal sector of the economy as "jockeys." A jockey is someone paid by a driver to ride as a passenger, so that the driver can comply with the three-in-one rule, reducing the driver's travel time. Jockeys are paid roughly a dollar to ride to or from downtown. They then pay 20 cents to take a bus back to their original starting point and repeat the process. Men, women, and children, some as young as 10 years old, work as traffic jockeys. The Indonesian government is considering adopting a system of electronic road pricing which, if implemented, would eliminate the jockeys' jobs.

Further Reading

Norimitsu Orishi. "Finding a Detour to Earn a Living in Indonesian Traffic Jams." *New York Times*, May 12, 2009. http://www.nytimes.com/2009/05/13/world/asia/13indo.html?pagewanted=all.

Jakarta's explosive growth has resulted in a very high population density. Jakarta is one of the most densely populated cities in the world, with an estimated population density of about 40,000 per square mile in the city proper and about 12,000 per square mile in the entire metropolitan areas. High density and crowding have created a substantial number of problems currently faced by Indonesian leaders, foreign government experts, and nongovernmental organizations. Traffic is highly congested and drivers face very long commutes within the metropolitan area. Indeed, some experts on transportation have predicted that central Jakarta could face gridlock within the next two decades.

In order to reduce traffic congestion, the law requires each car traveling on major roads to have three or more occupants. This law has created a market for "traffic jockeys" who are paid by drivers to ride with them along these major roads. Traffic jockeys are paid the equivalent of two to three dollars to ride into the central city. They then take public transportation back to outlying areas and repeat the process over the course of the business day. Other problems associated with Jakarta's very large and dense population include shortages of potable water, lack of sanitation, and piles of garbage in slum areas. These problems have contributed to poor nutrition, inadequate public health, air pollution, and the spread of infectious diseases throughout the city.

See Also: Indonesia; Manila; Population Density; Primate City; Seoul; Squatter Settlements; Tokyo

Further Reading

Evi Nurvidya Arifin and Aris Ananta. "Is Jakarta's Population Growing Too Fast?" *Jakarta Post*, August 28, 2010. http://www.thejakartapost.com/news/2010/08/28/is-jakarta%E2%80%99s-population-growing-too-fast.html.

Michael Bachelard. "Jakarta Grinds to a Halt as Traffic Nears Gridlock." *Sydney Morning Herald*, February 4, 2012. http://www.smh.com.au/world/jakarta-grinds-to-a-halt-as-traffic-nears-gridlock-20120203-1qxjr.html.

Wendell Cox. "The Evolving Urban Form: Jakarta (Jabotabek)." *newgeography.com*, May 31, 2011. http://www.newgeography.com/content/002255-the-evolving-urban-form-jakarta-jabotabek.

Seoul

Seoul is the capital and largest city of South Korea. The Seoul metropolitan area has a population of nearly 26 million people, making it the second-largest metropolitan area in the world. The city of Seoul itself has a population of approximately 10 million. About 20 percent of all South Koreans live in Seoul's central city, and about half of the country's residents live in the Seoul metropolitan area.

Seoul is located in northwestern South Korea on the banks of the Han River. The city proper is approximately 25 miles east of the Yellow Sea, which separates South Korea from China. At its closest point, central Seoul is located about 25 miles southeast of the heavily guarded boundary between South Korea and North Korea. The northernmost of Seoul's suburbs are located less than eight miles from the demilitarized zone that separates the two countries.

Seoul has been an important trading and administrative center for over 2,000 years. In approximately 18 BCE, the kingdom of Baekje established its capital at the site of present-day Seoul. At that time, this site was a very important center for trade. The Baekje kingdom was one of the Three Kingdoms of Korea. It was captured by the Silla kingdom in the seventh century CE, and Seoul's capture was very important to the political unification of the Korean peninsula.

The Joseon Dynasty established full control over the peninsula in the late 14th century. The Joseons reaffirmed Seoul as Korea's capital city, and Seoul has remained the political center of Korea ever since. Between 1910 and 1945, Korea was a Japanese colony also administered from Seoul. Seoul remained the capital of an independent Korea after the end of the war, and the city became the capital of South Korea after the peninsula was partitioned after the Korean War. Today, Seoul is South Korea's primate city. It is not only the political capital of South Korea but is also an important commercial, financial, and industrial center with an international reputation for high technology. The city hosted the 1988 Olympic Games and co-hosted the World Cup (along with Tokyo) in 2002. Nearly half of South Korea's residents live in the Seoul metropolitan area.

Seoul grew rapidly in the late 19th and early 20th centuries. The population of the city was estimated at about 250,000 in 1890. Shortly before Korea's partition, Seoul's population was estimated at about 1.5 million in 1949. Over the next four decades, the city's population grew to 10 million by 1990. Much of this growth occurred because of rapid migration from rural areas of South Korea into the city. Since that time, Seoul's population has stabilized. However, the Seoul metropolitan area population continues to grow rapidly from about 5 million in 1960 to more than 17 million in 1980 to 22 million in 2000. The metropolitan area population continues to increase at about 1 percent per year. Because South Korea's birth rate is among the lowest in the world, continuing population growth in the Seoul region occurs only because of net in-migration from other parts of the country. More than 97 percent of the city proper's population consists of ethnic Koreans, with small numbers of people from China, Japan, and other countries.

The central city of Seoul is very densely populated. Its population density of about 43,000 people per square mile is considerably greater than the densities of other very large cities in developed countries, although the overall population density of the metropolitan area is decreasing as it expands outward away from the city center. Hundreds of thousands of Seoul's residents live in high-rise condominiums within the central city's boundaries.

Seoul shares many problems with densely populated megacities throughout the world, including smog, air pollution, and traffic congestion. In order to slow Seoul's metropolitan-area growth and also to move the capital further from the North Korean border, the South Korean government has considered seriously moving the capital from Seoul to another less densely populated location. In recent years, the municipal and national governments have made concerted efforts to reduce traffic congestion and pollution through a variety of incentive programs intended to reduce driving and encourage people to use public transportation.

See Also: Crude Birth Rate; Population Density; Primate City; South Korea; Tokyo

Further Reading

Cindy Bae. "Congestion Pricing Scheme in Seoul, Korea." University of British Columbia, March 22, 2013. http://blogs.ubc.ca/cindybae/2013/03/22/congestion-pricing-scheme-in-seoul-korea/.y

CNN Travel. "Don't Hold Your Breath: Seoul's Air Gets Cleaner." August 16, 2011. http://travel.cnn.com/seoul/life/dont-hold-your-breath-seouls-air-gets-cleaner-987513.

Wendell Cox. "The Evolving Urban Form: Seoul." *newgeography.com*, February 17, 2011. http://www.newgeography.com/content/002060-the-evolving-urban-form-seoul.

Delhi and New Delhi

Delhi, including the nearby capital city of New Delhi, is the center of India's second-largest metropolitan area. With an estimated population of about 20 million, the Delhi conurbation is among the 10 largest metropolitan areas in the world.

Delhi is located on the Yamuna River, which is an important tributary of the Ganges River, in northern India. The Delhi area is believed to have been inhabited for at least 4,000 years. Since the 13th century, it has served as an administrative center for various rulers of present-day India. In 1526, the Mughal conqueror Babur conquered Delhi and made it the administrative seat of the Mughal Empire, which was ruled by a Muslim dynasty that claimed descent from Genghis Khan. The Mughals controlled much of present-day northern India for the next 300 years, although control of Delhi itself was contested between the Mughals and the Hindu Marathas during the 17th and 18th centuries.

In 1857, Delhi was captured by the British East India Company, which deposed and ousted the Mughals. The British government, which took over administration of India from the company in 1858, assumed direct control over Delhi. Britain moved the administrative center of its colonies in India from Kolkata in 1911, in large part because of Delhi's more centralized location within British India (which also included present-day Pakistan and Bangladesh).

After moving the capital of British India to Delhi, the British began a program of constructing buildings to house government operations. Construction of these British administrative buildings began in 1911 and was completed in 1931. The region containing these buildings became British India's capital of New Delhi and was administered separately from the older city of Delhi. New Delhi became the capital of independent India in 1947. Today, the population of New Delhi proper is about 250,000.

Since it became the capital of British India, and especially since Indian independence, the Delhi region has been one of the most rapidly growing areas of India. Its relative prosperity, in combination with the opportunity for government employment, has brought large numbers of people into Delhi from rural areas. The Delhi area's population in 1911 was estimated at about 413,000. It reached 1.7 million in 1951, when the first census of independent India was conducted by the Indian government. It more than doubled, to 4 million, in 1971, and more than doubled again, to 9.4 million, in 1991, doubling again in the next two decades.

For many years, Delhi experienced a high rate of natural increase and population growth that was driven by both natural increase and migration. Today, declining birth rates and total fertility rates have meant that migration is the primary driver of population growth in Delhi and New Delhi. The Delhi metropolitan area continues to grow quickly. Recent estimates suggest that about 200,000 people move into Delhi each year, primarily from other parts of India. Given its ongoing rapid growth, some experts have predicted that Delhi will become the third-largest metropolitan area in the world, following Tokyo and Mumbai, by 2020. Delhi and New Delhi have found it difficult to provide adequate housing and infrastructure to meet the demands of its rapidly growing population. As many as 30 percent of the Delhi region's people are believed to live in squatter settlements, which in India are known as "unauthorized colonies."

As in other major cities in developing countries, Delhi has experienced considerable numbers of environmental problems in recent years. Many of these problems are associated with the rapid population growth that Delhi has experienced over the past several decades. Delhi has been identified as one of the most polluted cities in the entire world, with much of this pollution caused by motor vehicles and by industrial activity. The Yamuna has also been identified as a highly polluted stream, with pollution levels also heightened by Delhi's congestion and rapid population growth. Water shortages are commonplace, especially in the winter months in which very little rain falls in the area.

See Also: Bangladesh; Census; Crude Birth Rate; India; Kolkata; Mumbai; Pakistan; Rate of Natural Increase; Squatter Settlements; Tokyo; Total Fertility Rate

Further Reading

India Today. "Falling Fertility Rates, Shrinking Family Sizes Pull Down Delhi's Population Growth to 21 Percent." June 12, 2013. http://indiatoday.intoday.in/story/delhi-population-growth-rate-slumps-in-last-decade/1/279641.html.

John Upton. "Where Is the Worst Air in the World?" *Slate*, February 5, 2013. http://www.slate.com/articles/health_and_science/medical_examiner/2013/03/worst_air_pollution_in_the_world_beijing_delhi_ahwaz_and_ulaanbaatar.html.

Jim Yardley. "Illegal Districts Dot New Delhi as City Swells." *New York Times*, April 27, 2013. http://www.nytimes.com/2013/04/28/world/asia/unauthorized-colonies-dot-new-delhi-seeking-legal-status.html?nl=todaysheadlines&emc=edit_th_20130428&_r=0.

Shanghai

Shanghai is the largest city in China. With a population of nearly 18 million, Shanghai is the largest city (not including suburbs) by population in the world. Its metropolitan-area population is more than 23 million. The city is China's major commercial and financial center, and it is the largest container port in the world. Its population density is considerably higher than that of many European cities, but not as great as the densities of other very large metropolitan areas in poorer countries of Asia, including Mumbai, whose population density has been estimated at four times greater than that of Shanghai.

Shanghai is located near the mouth of the Yangtze River near the coast of the East China Sea. The city was first established as a fishing village on the Huangpu River about 10 miles from its confluence with the Yangtze about 1,500 years ago. During the 15th century, the Huangpu was dredged in order to provide Shanghai with ocean access. Thus Shanghai became a major port. Shanghai's importance as a trading center increased during the 16th, 17th, and 18th centuries.

In 1842, the Chinese government and Britain signed the Treaty of Nanjing, which forced China to open up Shanghai and other Chinese ports to the British and other Western colonial powers. By 1850, trading operations from Britain, France, Germany, and the United States had become established in Shanghai. By the early 20th century, Shanghai was the major financial center of East Asia.

Shanghai's importance declined after 1949, when the People's Republic of China was established under the leadership of Mao Zedong (1893–1976). During the 1950s and 1960s, Mao's government pursued a policy of agricultural and industrial self-sufficiency and isolated itself considerably from trade relationships with the rest of the world. Shanghai's economy, which had long been based on commerce and international finance, suffered as a result. In the 1970s, however, China reversed its course and began to open itself up once again to international trade. As China became more and more active in the global economy, Shanghai boomed once again and became a major focal point of economic development.

Shanghai's population has grown rapidly since it became established as the major port on the Yangtze. Its population has been estimated at about 200,000 around 1700. A census taken in 1881 counted about 302,000 people. The population rose quickly throughout the early 20th century, reaching 6.2 million in 1953. Despite reduced importance of trade and global finance during the Maoist era, Shanghai continued to grow quickly. The city's metropolitan area population was 11.9 million in 1980. The rate of population growth increased as China's economy burgeoned, reaching 13.3 million in 1990 and 16.4 million by 2000. It has grown by more than 40 percent since.

Shanghai's rapid population growth is due to internal migration. According to the 2010 census, about 40 percent of Shanghai's people were born in other parts of China. Shanghai's rate of natural increase has been negative. Its total fertility rate has been estimated at only 0.6, implying that the city's population would decrease quickly absent in-migration from other areas. Because of the low total fertility rate, which is due in part to the implementation and enforcement of China's one-child population policy, Shanghai has a high median age and a large elderly population. As of 2012, about 25 percent of Shanghai's residents were over 60, as compared with 8.3 percent under 14. International migration into Shanghai has been negligible, with only 1 percent of Shanghai's people born outside China.

In recent years, the Chinese government has worked to limit migration into Shanghai by requiring migrants to apply for permanent residency. A point system has been established in order to prioritize issuing permanent residency permits. However, this system is highly controversial. Some also have expressed concern that strict limits on rural to urban migration into Shanghai will result in labor shortages in a city whose elderly population is increasing rapidly relative to its overall population.

See Also: Census; China; France; Germany; Median Age; Mumbai; Population Density; Rate of Natural Increase; Rural to Urban Migration; Total Fertility Rate; United Kingdom; United States of America

Further Reading

Wendell Cox. "Shanghai: Torrid Population Growth." *newgeography.com*, April 17, 2011. http://www.newgeography.com/content/002187-shanghai-torrid-population-growth.

Katie Hunt. "Shanghai: China's Capitalist Showpiece." *BBC News*, May 21, 2008. http://news.bbc.co.uk/2/hi/business/7373394.stm.

Sherry Tao Kong. "China's Migrant Problem: The Need for *Hokuo* Reform." *East Asia Forum*, January 29, 2010. http://www.eastasiaforum.org/2010/01/29/chinas-migrant-problem-the-need-for-hokuo-reform/.

Manila

Manila is the center of the National Capital Region, also known as Metropolitan Manila or Metro Manila, in the Philippines. The population of Metro Manila has been estimated at more than twelve million. Including people living in nearby suburban areas, there are about 20 million people in the greater Manila region. About 2.5 million live in Manila proper. Nearby Quezon City, which is also part of Metro Manila, is slightly larger with about 2.8 million residents.

Metro Manila is located on the west coast of the island of Luzon, which is the largest and most populated of the islands comprising the Philippines. It is a primate city and is the economic, political, and cultural capital of the entire country. More than 20 percent of the Philippines' people live in the Metro Manila region.

In less developed countries throughout the world, millions of people live in squatter settlements in and near very large cities. Rapid population growth along with poverty and a lack of infrastructure has contributed to the growth of squatter settlements such as this one near Manila in the Philippines. (AP Photo/Bullit Marquez)

Manila's history goes back at least 1,000 years. By the 13th century, Manila had become an important seaport and administrative center. The Spanish took control of the Philippines in 1565 and took over Manila, making the city the seat of the colonial administration. In 1898, control over the Philippines was transferred from Spain to the United States and Manila remained the colonial capital. The area was the site of fierce fighting between American and Japanese forces during World War II, and much of the city's infrastructure was destroyed or heavily damaged. Despite this damage, Manila became the capital of the Philippines when the Philippines was granted independence in 1946. The capital was moved to Quezon City in 1948, but was returned to Manila proper in 1976. The area containing Manila, Quezon City, and other surrounding urbanized areas was designated as the National Capital Region in 1975.

Metro Manila has experienced rapid population growth over the course of its history. Prior to the independence of the Philippines, most people who resided in present-day Metro Manila lived in Manila itself. In 1900, the population of Manila proper was estimated at about 1.5 million. The population of the city increased to about 2.5 million in 1950, and has remained at about this level ever since. Growth in Metro Manila has taken place outside Manila itself. For example, the site of present-day Quezon City consisted of a few small towns until the city was established in the late 1930s. According to a census, about 39,000 people lived in present-day Quezon City in 1939. Quezon City's population grew to nearly 400,000 in 1960 and nearly one million in 1975. Even after the capital was transferred back to Manila in 1976, Quezon City continued its rapid growth, reaching 2 million by 1995 and more than 2.8 million today.

Soon after its creation, the population of Metro Manila was estimated at 5.9 million, of whom more than half lived in Manila itself or in Quezon City. By 2010, the population of Metro Manila had nearly doubled. In light of the fact that the Philippines has undergone considerable demographic transition, much of the ongoing increase in Metro Manila's population is the result of rural to urban migration from outlying areas of the country. As in many other large metropolitan areas, population growth rates in suburbs now exceed those in the central cities that comprise Metro Manila. Today only about a quarter of the people living in the Metro Manila urban agglomeration live in Manila or in Quezon City.

Metro Manila shares many serious problems with other rapidly growing megacities located in less developed countries. Many in-migrants to Metro Manila are impoverished, and the metropolitan region lacks the resources necessary to provide needed housing and infrastructure. It has been estimated that about a third of Metro Manila's inhabitants live in slums or squatter settlements. These slums and shantytowns have experienced numerous devastating fires, many of which have resulted in substantial numbers of fatalities and injuries. Traffic congestion and air pollution are also major problems. Given its coastal location, low-lying areas of

Metro Manila are also subject to the possibility of sea-level rise associated with continuing global warming.

See Also: Census; Demographic Transition Model; Megacities; Philippines; Primate City; Rural to Urban Migration; Squatter Settlements

Further Reading

Wendell Cox. "The Evolving Metropolitan Form: Manila." *newgeography.com*, April 24, 2011. http://www.newgeography.com/content/002198-the-evolving-urban-form-manila.

Kara Santos. "Philippines: Economic Recovery Unfelt by Urban Poor." *Global Issues*, February 3, 2010. http://www.globalissues.org/news/2010/02/03/4420.

Karachi

Karachi is the largest city in Pakistan and is Pakistan's major commercial, economic, industrial, and financial center. Karachi is believed to be the third-largest city in the world by population within its city limits, with more than 13 million residents. The greater Karachi metropolitan area includes more than 23 million people.

Karachi proper is located on the coast of the Arabian Sea in southern Pakistan, near the mouth of the Indus River. It has been an important trading center for more than 2,000 years. Historians believe that Karachi was founded as a small fishing village more than 2,500 years ago. It was used by Alexander the Great to launch military campaigns in South Asia. By 2,000 years ago, Karachi had become an important seaport used for trade between Asia, the Arab world, and the Roman Empire. The city was visited by Portuguese and Ottoman mariners and traders during the 16th century, but it retained its status as an independent city until the early 19th century.

In 1839, the British East India Company captured Karachi. Control of Karachi was transferred to the British Empire in 1858. The city was selected as the capital of newly independent Pakistan, including present-day Bangladesh, in 1947. At that time, thousands of Muslims from Hindu-majority India moved across the newly delineated international boundary and settled in Karachi, swelling its already increasing population. In 1958, the capital was transferred to the new city of Islamabad in northeastern Pakistan, but Karachi remained Pakistan's economic center and largest city.

In keeping with its political and economic importance, Karachi has experienced ongoing and rapid population growth since the late 19th century. Its population in 1901 has been estimated at about 137,000. The city grew to about 800,000 people at the time of independence in 1947. Since that time, population growth rates have increased sharply. The population quadrupled to about 3.4 million in 1972, shortly after Bangladesh split from Pakistan and became an independent country. It tripled again over the next three decades, reaching 10 million by 2000. Currently, Karachi's population is increasing by about 4 to 5 percent per year. If this growth rate continues, Karachi's population may surpass 25 million by 2025.

Karachi's population growth is the result of both natural increase and in-migration, especially from other areas of Pakistan. The city has more ethnic diversity than is the case in other areas of Pakistan, as large numbers of people from all of Pakistan's major ethnic groups have moved to the Karachi area. Karachi is home to many immigrants, including thousands of refugees from Afghanistan and Iran.

Like other megacities around the world, Karachi experiences a large number of difficult urban problems. These problems have been exacerbated by Karachi's continuing very high rate of population growth relative to most other megacities, making it very difficult for Karachi and Pakistani government officials to keep up with growth. Karachi contains some of the largest and most sprawling slums in Asia. The largest of these slums is located in the Karachi suburb of Orangi Town. It extends across nearly 50 square miles and is home to well over a million people. Efforts to improve conditions in Orangi Town and other slum areas have been stymied by lack of resources, poor planning, and activities of criminal gangs.

Environmental problems also plague Karachi. As a coastal city, Karachi is subject to major tropical storms. In 2007, Cyclone Yemyin formed in the Arabian Sea and made landfall near Karachi, resulting in 213 fatalities within the city and causing millions of dollars in property damage. Karachi is also subject to flooding, both because of runoff from the Indus River and because of tropical cyclones along with severe storms associated with the summer monsoon during which most of Karachi's rain falls. Karachi's climate is normally dry, but monsoon rains far exceed normal levels in some summers. In 2009, unusually high levels of monsoon rain caused major flooding over large areas of downtown Karachi. Flooding problems could also be exacerbated as a result of sea level rise.

See Also: Bangladesh; India; Iran; Megacities; Pakistan; Rate of Natural Increase; Refugees

Further Reading

Umar Farooq. "In Asia's Largest Slum, Development, Danger." *The Wall Street Journal India*, June 13, 2013. http://blogs.wsj.com/indiarealtime/2013/06/13/in-asias-largest-slum -development-danger/.

Salman Qureshi. "The Fast Growing Megacity Karachi as a Frontier of Environmental Challenges: Urbanization and Contemporary Urbanization Issues." *Journal of Geography and Regional Planning* 3 (2011): 306–21.

Zia Ur Rahman. "Afghan Refugees in Karachi Face a Trifecta of Woes." *Central Asia Online*, May 3, 2010. http://centralasiaonline.com/en_GB/articles/caii/features/pakistan/2010/05/03/feature-02.

New York

New York is the largest city in the United States and also the center of the largest metropolitan area in the United States. The population of New York City proper is about 8.3 million. Its metropolitan area, including parts of New York State, New Jersey, and Connecticut, contains about 19 million people. It is the major economic, financial, and commercial center of North America.

New York's location at the mouth of the Hudson River provides an excellent natural harbor along with access to the North American interior via the Hudson. The city was founded originally by the Dutch, who named the settlement New Amsterdam. The Dutch selected the site in order to control trade between the Atlantic and the interior. In 1664, New Amsterdam was taken over by the British, who renamed the city New York. In 1674, Britain and the Netherlands agreed to the Treaty of Westminster, under which the Dutch agreed to give up their claims to New York

New York City has been an important point of entry for immigrants to the United States for more than 200 years. Today, large numbers of immigrants continue to call New York home. (SuperStock/Getty Images)

in exchange for control of Surinam (the present-day independent country of Suriname) in South America.

New York became the United States' dominant city in the early 19th century. At the time of U.S. independence in the 1780s, New York was only slightly larger in population than Philadelphia and Boston. The first United States census, taken in 1790, counted 33,131 people in New York, 28,522 in Philadelphia, and 18,320 in Boston. By 1850, however, New York's population of 696,115 was about five times as large as that of either Philadelphia, with 121,376 people, or Boston, with 136,881. New York owed its rapid growth relative to its rivals to access to the interior. The valley of the Hudson River and its eastward-flowing tributary, the Mohawk River, are the only extensive areas of relatively flat land between the Atlantic coast to the east and the Great Lakes and the Mississippi River drainage basin to the west. Recognizing this geographic advantage, officials in New York State appropriated funds to build the Erie Canal, which connected the Great Lakes with the Mohawk and the Hudson. Construction began in 1817 and the canal was completed in 1825. The canal provided easy water access to the interior, enabling New York to dominate this trade and propelling its growth.

New York's population increased even more rapidly during the second half of the 19th century. The city became a major industrial center. In addition, New York became the United States' major center for immigration and was the point of entry for millions of immigrants from Europe, who arrived in New York during the late 19th and early 20th centuries. Many of these immigrants settled in New York itself, where they provided the labor force for the city's growing industries. Ever since, New York has been a magnet for immigrants from all over the world. Although relatively few immigrants to New York today come from Europe, large numbers of immigrants from Latin America, Asia, Africa, the Caribbean, and other parts of the world call New York home.

Originally, the city of New York included Manhattan Island and the Bronx. In 1898, the city of New York was consolidated with Brooklyn, Queens, and Staten Island to form the present city. In 1900, New York's population was 3.4 million, of whom about 1.5 million lived within the original city limits. The population of New York more than doubled over the next 50 years, reaching 7.9 million in 1950. Since then, the city's population has been stable, with a population of 8.15 million in 2010.

Most of the growth in the New York metropolitan area's population since World War II has taken place in its suburbs, as is the case with other American cities. However, New York's stable population over the past six decades contrasts with that of many other American central cities, most of which have lost population since the 1950s. Experts predict that the central city's population will continue to increase, in part because of New York's increasing reliance on white-collar employment. New York's population density is the highest of any American city, and the boroughs of

Manhattan and Brooklyn are the two most densely populated counties in the United States.

See Also: Census; Migration; Population Density; United States of America

Further Reading

Wendell Cox. "The Accelerating Suburbanization of New York." *newgeography.com*, March 29, 2011. http://www.newgeography.com/content/002157-the-accelerating-suburbanization-new-york.

Laura Kosisto. "City's Boom Spurs a Need for Housing." *Wall Street Journal*, June 10, 2013. http://online.wsj.com/article/SB10001424127887323495604578537714265145672.html.

São Paulo

São Paulo is the largest city in Brazil. With a population of about 11.4 million, the city of São Paulo is the eighth-largest central city in the world. The São Paulo metropolitan area has a population of about 20 million. São Paulo is the largest city in the world located in the southern hemisphere. It is the world's second-largest inland city by population, trailing only Delhi.

São Paulo is located in southeastern Brazil, about 50 miles inland from the Atlantic Ocean coast. The current location was settled in 1554 by 12 Portuguese Jesuit priests, who named the settlement São Paulo dos Campos de Piratininga. The name of the village was chosen because it was founded on January 25, which is celebrated by Roman Catholics as the feast day of the Apostle Paul. At the time, São Paulo was the only significant Portuguese settlement in the interior of Brazil.

São Paulo remained relatively isolated and impoverished until after Brazil achieved its independence from Portugal in 1822. During the 19th century, the São Paulo area became a center for the growing of coffee and other agricultural products. Railroads were constructed between São Paulo and the coastal port of Santos, providing international market access to local farmers. In the late 19th century, São Paulo became an important railroad center. It also emerged as Brazil's major manufacturing center. São Paulo also became Brazil's financial and commercial center, hosting Brazil's largest stock exchange and serving as the headquarters for many Brazilian banks and other commercial activities.

All of these economic developments have contributed to São Paulo's steady population growth over the past two centuries. São Paulo's population was estimated at 32,000 in 1872 and at about 240,000 in 1900. By 1950, its population had reached 2.2 million. The city's population nearly quadrupled between 1950 and 1980, when its population was about 8.4 million. During the 1960s, São Paulo became the largest city in Brazil by population, with its population exceeding that of Rio de Janeiro. Growth in the city has slowed down since 1980, but suburbs and outlying areas continue to grow rapidly.

Historically, population growth in São Paulo has been attributed to natural increase, internal migration, and migration from outside Brazil. However, Brazil's total fertility rate dropped below 2, or less than replacement-level fertility, for the first time in the country's history in 2001. Hence population growth in São Paulo and its suburbs is now due increasingly to in-migration. São Paulo has attracted large numbers of immigrants throughout its history. In the 19th century, Brazil attracted thousands of immigrants from Italy, Germany, Spain, Switzerland, and other European countries in addition to Portugal. During the early 20th century, these immigrants were joined by many from Asia, especially from Japan. As Brazil's major manufacturing and commercial center, São Paulo attracted more international immigrants than did any other place in Brazil. During the 1950s and 1960s, the Brazilian government actively encouraged migration of factory workers into São Paulo. Over the past several decades, São Paulo has also experienced large-scale in-migration of people from poorer and less developed parts of Brazil, notably the impoverished states of Brazil's northeast.

São Paulo shares many problems with other megacities in the developing world. Levels of traffic congestion are very high. One of São Paulo's major problems is the existence of squatter settlements, which are known in Brazil as *favelas*. Although *favelas* are often associated with Rio de Janeiro, in fact São Paulo has more *favelas* and more *favela* residents. Estimates have suggested that as many as 25 to 30 percent of São Paulo's inhabitants live in *favelas*, whose housing is substandard and whose services are inadequate despite the fact that most now have electricity and running water. Government officials, with help from international organizations, have attempted to upgrade São Paulo's *favelas* and improve their quality of life.

See Also: Brazil; Delhi and New Delhi; Germany; Italy; Megacities; Spain; Squatter Settlements; Total Fertility Rate

Further Reading

Wendell Cox. "Emerging Urban Form: São Paulo." *newgeography.com*, August 29, 2012. http://www.newgeography.com/content/003054-evolving-urban-form-s%C3%A3o-paulo.

Beth Matias. "São Paulo Revitalizes Favelas and Illegal Subdivisions." March 9, 2012. http://infosurhoy.com/cocoon/saii/xhtml/en_GB/features/saii/features/main/2012/09/03/feature-02.

Mexico City

Mexico City is the center of the largest metropolitan area by population in Mexico. With a population of more than 21 million, the Mexico City metropolitan area is the largest in the western hemisphere and the third largest in the world. Mexico City is a primate city and it is Mexico's financial and commercial center, political capital, and cultural center. The Mexico City metropolitan area contains nearly 20 percent of Mexico's population.

The Aztec Empire established its capital of Tenochtitlan on the site of present-day Mexico City in approximately 1325. Tenochtitlan was built on an island in natural Lake Texcoco. Spanish conquistadors overthrew the Aztecs in 1521. The Spanish destroyed Tenochtitlan, but began to rebuild on the site and gave the city its present name. Most of Lake Texcoco was drained and parts of the city were constructed on the lakebed. Mexico City became the capital of the Spanish colony of New Spain. Its location in the center of New Spain and convenient connections to both the Atlantic and Pacific Oceans helped to make Mexico City a trade center. After Mexico became an independent country in 1821, the new Mexican government created and placed the city within the Mexican Federal District, making Mexico City the country's capital.

Historians of the Aztec Empire believe that as many as 200,000 people lived in Tenochtitlan in the early 16th century before the arrival of the Spanish. Thus Tenochtitlan had more people at that time than any city in Europe. Mexico City grew steadily during its period of Spanish rule and after independence. In 1900, its population was estimated at about 500,000. It reached 1 million during the 1920s and exceeded 3 million by the 1950s. The population of Mexico City proper peaked at about 8.7 million around 1990. Since then, the population of Mexico City itself has been stable, but the metropolitan area has continued to grow, although the rate of population growth has slowed as Mexico's rate of natural increase began to decline.

As Mexico's rate of natural increase slowed down, more and more of Mexico City's population growth has been caused by rural to urban migration from other parts of the country. Most migrants into Mexico City have come from within Mexico, although there are substantial populations of expatriates from the United States, Central and South America, and elsewhere.

Rapid population growth associated with high rates of in-migration has caused or exacerbated many urban problems in Mexico City. Mexico City has one of the highest levels of air pollution of any megacity in the world. Much of this pollution is the result of Mexico City's very large number of motor vehicles. The problem is intensified by Mexico's high elevation. At more than 7,300 feet above sea level, Mexico City has the highest altitude of any large megacity in the world. Mexico's location in the Valley of Mexico, surrounded by high mountains, also creates temperature inversions that trap polluted air and create smog. The thin, polluted air has meant that Mexico City has a much higher rate of respiratory infections than elsewhere in Mexico. However, in recent years Mexico's government has made a concerted effort to address problems associated with air pollution. Pollution levels have declined in recent years despite considerable increases in the city's population.

Mexico City also suffers from water pollution. Untreated sewage, agricultural chemicals, and industrial waste enter the city's water system, polluting drinking water. Mexico City's location on a drained lakebed has meant that many building foundations are unstable. This instability is exacerbated by the fact that Mexico City is located in an earthquake-prone region, putting buildings constructed on the lakebed at risk of collapse. In 1985, an earthquake measuring 8.1 on the Richter scale caused more than 10,000 fatalities in Mexico City and destroyed or damaged more than 500,000 houses, although the epicenter of the earthquake was actually more than 200 miles away in the Pacific Ocean.

See Also: Megacities; Mexico; Primate City; Rate of Natural Increase; Rural to Urban Migration

Further Reading

David Agren. "A Model for Megacities? Mexico City Cleans Up Its Air." *Christian Science Monitor*, April 22, 2013. http://www.csmonitor.com/World/Americas/2013/0422/Model-for-megacities-Mexico-City-cleans-up-its-air.

Wendell Cox. "The Evolving Urban Form: The Valley of Mexico." *newgeography.com*, March 2, 2011. http://www.newgeography.com/content/002088-the-evolving-urban-form-the-valley-mexico.

Beijing

Beijing is the capital city of China and its second-largest city, following Shanghai. It is China's political capital, its dominant cultural center and the site of China's most prestigious universities, as well as the economic center for northern China.

The site of Beijing has been occupied for at least 3,000 years. The walled city of Ji was constructed at the site of present-day Beijing about 3,000 years ago. After China was unified politically under the Han Dynasty in the late third century BCE, the Great Wall of China was constructed to keep out foreign invaders. At that time the area near Beijing was on the frontier of Chinese civilization, and sections of the wall, some of which still stand, were built within 50 miles of the present-day city. Beijing achieved national importance within China during the thirteenth century, when the Mongols under Kublai Khan made Beijing the administrative seat of the Yuan Dynasty.

Beijing remained China's capital under the rule of the Ming Dynasty between 1368 and 1644. The Ming reinforced and fortified the Great Wall, especially in the area near Beijing, in order to prevent further invasions from the north. However, the Qing Dynasty coming from Manchuria overthrew the Ming in 1644. Beijing remained the capital of the Qing Dynasty between 1644 and 1912, when the Qing Dynasty was overthrown by what would become the Republic of China. The Nationalist government of the Republic of China moved the capital to Nanjing. However, the capital was returned to Beijing after the Nationalists were ousted by the Chinese Communists, who established the People's Republic of China in 1949. Beijing has remained the capital of the People's Republic ever since.

Historians have documented steady growth in Beijing's population over most of China's history. The population of Beijing and nearby areas has been estimated at about 450,000 in the early seventh century BCE and at about 580,000 in the 11th century. During the 11th and early 12th centuries, Beijing was the scene of conflict between the Jin dynasty, which ruled northern China at the time, and the invading Mongols. Beijing began to grow more rapidly after the Mongols ousted the Jin and made Beijing the capital of the Yuan Dynasty. It continued to grow after the Yuan were replaced by the Ming. A census conducted by the Ming government in 1448 counted about 960,000 people within Beijing itself, with another 2 million people living in the surrounding area. Thus Beijing was probably the largest city in the world at that time. In the late 18th century, historical estimates suggest that about 3 million people lived in what is now the Beijing metropolitan area.

Beijing began its most rapid period of growth after the establishment of the People's Republic. In 1953, Beijing's population was estimated at nearly 2.8 million. The population reached 11 million in the early 1990s and has nearly doubled in the past two decades.

Beijing's annual rate of population growth is estimated currently at nearly 4 percent a year, or nearly eight times the national population growth rate of about 0.5 percent annually. Because China has completed demographic transition and has a low crude birth rate because of its one-child population policy, Beijing's contemporary growth is the result of large-scale migration into the metropolitan area from other parts of China. It has been estimated that more than 7 million residents of Beijing and its suburbs were born outside the Beijing area. Nearly all of this population growth is taking place in Beijing's expanding suburbs. Many of Beijing's numerous in-migrants come from rural areas. As elsewhere, many rural migrants decide to move to Beijing as a result of both push factors, such as lack of opportunity, and pull factors, including job prospects and better public services. However, many of these migrants lack education and job skills, and many are victimized by poor infrastructure, discrimination, and substandard housing.

Beijing's rapid growth and increased prosperity have contributed to the city's ongoing problems with air pollution, much of which is caused by automobile emissions and by Beijing's numerous industries. Frequently, particulate levels in and near Beijing reach levels much higher than pollution levels identified as "safe" by the United States Environmental Protection Agency. Beijing's air pollution problem was brought to worldwide attention in 2008, when Beijing hosted the Olympic Games. In early 2014, the amount of fine particulates in the atmosphere of Beijing reached as much as 500 micrograms per cubic meter of air. This figure is nearly 20 times the World Health Organization's standard defining more than 25 micrograms per cubic meter of air as hazardous to human health.

Although much of Beijing's pollution problems are the result of locally generated automobile exhaust and industrial emissions, air pollution problems in Beijing are exacerbated by dust storms. Dust and fine particulates originating in the deserts of western China and Mongolia are swept into the atmosphere and carried to Beijing and nearby areas by prevailing westerly winds. The dust contributes to the very high levels of fine particulates in Beijing itself. Although the government of China has made efforts to curb air pollution in Beijing, in general air pollution levels have continued to increase.

See Also: Census; China; Crude Birth Rate; Demographic Transition Model; Great Wall of China; One-Child Policy; Push Factors and Pull Factors; Shanghai

Further Reading

Wendell Cox. "The Evolving Urban Form: Beijing." *newgeography*.com, August 29, 2011. http://www.newgeography.com/content/002406-the-evolving-urban-form-beijing.

The Economist. "Blackest Day." January 14, 2013, http://www.economist.com/blogs/analects/2013/01/beijings-air-pollution.

Hsiao-Hung Pai. "Despite China's Growth, Its Workers Endure a Fundamental Evil." *The Guardian*, September 20, 2011. http://www.theguardian.com/commentisfree/2011/sep/20/china-migrant-workers.

Guangzhou

Guangzhou, which was formerly known as Canton, is the third-largest city in China and the largest in South China. Guangzhou is located on the navigable Pearl River about 75 miles north of Hong Kong on the coast of the South China Sea. Its population has been estimated at about 13 million. The region along the Pearl River between Guangzhou and Hong Kong, including the megacity of Shenzhen, has a population estimated at 40 million, and thus might be considered the largest conurbation by population in the world.

Guangzhou was first settled more than 2,000 years ago. Then known as Panyu, Guangzhou became the capital of the Nanyue Kingdom, which included also part of northern Vietnam, around 200 BCE. In 111 BCE, the Nanyue Kingdom was absorbed into the Han Empire. Guangzhou became an important seaport, conducting trade as far away as present-day India and the Arab world throughout the Middle Ages.

Portuguese mariners visited Guangzhou in the early 16th century. Over the next three centuries, other European powers established presences in the city. Guangzhou, which at the time was known as Canton, became one of the world's largest seaports throughout the 18th, 19th, and early 20th centuries, conducting trade with Europe and the Americas, and throughout the entire world. The city was captured by Japanese forces in 1938 and remained under Japanese occupation until the end of World War II. In 1949, Guangzhou became one of Nationalist China's last strongholds until the Nationalists were expelled from mainland China by the Chinese Communists.

As with other megacities, Guangzhou grew very rapidly in the late 19th and the 20th centuries. Its population was estimated at about 400,000 in 1879. It nearly tripled, to about 1.1 million, in 1936, shortly before it was occupied by Japanese troops. Its population was about 3 million in 1964 and more than doubled to about 7.2 million in 1992. It reached 10 million around 2000.

Guangzhou continues to grow, but at a slower rate. Given China's one-child population policy and its current negative rate of natural increase, Guangzhou's current population growth is occurring because of in-migration from other parts of China. As China's economy expanded in the 1980s and 1990s Guangzhou benefited from its location on the Pearl River and became a major center for manufacturing. Hence Guangzhou grew especially rapidly in the 1990s. Today, Guangzhou is China's major center for automobile manufacturing.

In 2010, the Chinese government identified Guangzhou as one of China's five National Central Cities, along with Beijing, Shanghai, Tianjin, and Chongqing. These National Central Cities have been designated as economic and cultural centers for their regions of China, and thus Guangzhou is maintaining its status as a major growth center within South China. The Chinese government has estimated that as many as 3 million unregistered migrants live in and near Guangzhou, impeding efforts to provide housing, infrastructure, and services to Guangzhou's burgeoning population. According to some experts, Guangzhou's population has reached the maximum needed to ensure long-run stability. However, it is estimated that 200,000 to 300,000 people, most of whom come from rural areas of southern China, move to Guangzhou every year.

Guangzhou has taken major steps to address problems associated with its long history of population growth. As is the case with many other large cities in China, Guangzhou is heavily polluted. Air pollution in Guangzhou is attributed to emissions from Guangzhou's many heavy industries as well as to increasing levels of automobile traffic. In 2012, the Guangzhou government initiated policies intended to reduce air pollution levels by half by restricting automobile ownership and access.

See Also: Beijing; China; India; Megacities; One-Child Policy; Rate of Natural Increase; Shanghai; Shenzhen; Tianjin; Vietnam

Further Reading

Keith Bradsher. "A Chinese City Moves to Limit New Cars." *New York Times*, September 4, 2012. http://www.nytimes.com/2012/09/05/business/global/a-chinese-city-moves-to-limit-new-cars.html?pagewanted=all&_r=0.

Wendell Cox. "The Evolving Urban Form: Guangzhou-Foshan." *newgeography.com*, February 1, 2012. http://www.newgeography.com/content/002652-the-evolving-urban-form-guangzhou-foshan.

Xiaochu Hu. "China's Young Rural-to-Urban Migrants: In Search of Fortune, Happiness, and Independence." *Migration Policy Institute*, January 4, 2012. http://www.migrationpolicy.org/article/chinas-young-rural-urban-migrants-search-fortune-happiness-and-independence.

Mumbai

Mumbai, formerly known as Bombay, is the largest city in India, with a population of more than 12.5 million. Its metropolitan area has a population of about 21 million, and is the fourth largest in the world. It is the financial center of India and one of the wealthiest cities in Asia, although it is much poorer than New York, London, Paris, and other Western megacities.

Mumbai is located in the state of Maharashtra on the west coast of India, on the Arabian Sea. The original city was constructed on seven islands located at the mouth of the Ulhas River, which flows into the Arabian Sea from the northeast. During the 18th and 19th centuries, some of the hills on these islands were razed and were used to reclaim and fill in the shallow water that had separated the islands from one another. Today, the seven islands have become a single island known as Salsette Island. More recently, Mumbai has expanded from Salsette Island north and east onto the mainland between the Ulhas and the Arabian Sea coast.

The site of present-day Mumbai has been inhabited for at least 2,500 years. Before the arrival of European colonists, it was ruled successively by various Indian kingdoms and empires. Mumbai boasts the best deep-water harbor in western India, and the present-day city has been an important center for transoceanic trade

Mumbai is the largest city in India, which is the second-largest country by population in the world. As is the case with many megacities, Mumbai has a very high population density and it experiences great contrast between wealth and poverty. (AP Photo/Rafiq Maqbool)

for more than 2,000 years. During the Middle Ages, trade flourished between Mumbai and other ports on the Arabian Sea and the Indian Ocean on the Arabian Peninsula, East Asia, and East Africa.

In 1508, the Portuguese mariner Francisco de Almeida became the first European sailor to visit Mumbai after having circumnavigated Africa. In 1534, Sultan Bahadur Shah of Gujarat agreed to the Treaty of Bassein, which gave control over the seven islands comprising present-day Mumbai to Portugal. Control of the island of Bombay passed from Portugal to Britain in 1661. At that time the population of present-day Mumbai was estimated at about 10,000. In 1668, Britain's King Charles II gave control of Bombay to the English East India Company, which was renamed the British East India Company in 1707. The company made Bombay its headquarters for the Indian subcontinent, developed its port facilities, and promoted trade. Salsette was taken over by the British East India Company in 1774. By the 19th century, Mumbai had become the leading commercial and financial center of India. Expanding port facilities and employment opportunities brought large numbers of workers from rural Maharashtra and other nearby areas, and Mumbai's population grew quickly.

Today Mumbai remains India's major commercial center. It remains a major port, accounting for more than two-thirds of India's maritime trade. Mumbai is also the headquarters for India's major financial institutions, including the National Stock Exchange of India and the Reserve Bank of India. Mumbai is also a center for scientific research, and is India's leading entertainment center. Bollywood, which produces films in Hindi and other Indian languages that are distributed throughout India and other countries particularly in Asia and Africa, is based in Mumbai. The financial success of Bollywood has made Mumbai one of the leading film-producing cities in the world.

Mumbai's commercial activities and wealth relative to the rest of India has made the city a magnet for migrants for more than 300 years. Although early population estimates are unreliable, historians believe that Mumbai's population reached 100,000 by the 1750s. In 1901, a census of British India gave Mumbai's population as 812,912. Its population is believed to have reached more than 2 million when India became independent in 1947. Since independence, Mumbai has experienced explosive growth. Its current population of 21.5 million is more than 10 times its population in 1947, making it one of the fastest-growing cities in the world.

Having attracted immigrants from throughout India over several centuries, Mumbai has a highly diverse population. About 68 percent of Mumbai's residents are Hindus, a percentage considerably less than the national average of over 80 percent; 17 percent are Muslims; and there are substantial communities of Christians, Buddhists, Sikhs, Zoroastrians, Jains, and Jews. In light of the fact that many single men from other parts of India and other countries have continued to move to Mumbai in search of work, Mumbai's population consists of only about 81 females per 100 males.

As is the case with many cities in developing countries, Mumbai has had difficulty keeping up with its rapid population increases. In 2005, the World Bank estimated that 54 percent of Mumbai's people lived in slums. These slums made up only about 6 percent of Mumbai's land area, and some estimates suggest that the most densely populated slums of Mumbai contain as many as 120,000 people per square mile. The film *Slumdog Millionaire* depicts vividly the contrast between Mumbai's wealth and its extreme poverty in its slums.

Mumbai's rapid population growth has contributed to various environmental problems. Although Mumbai's average annual rainfall is more than 80 inches, most of the rainfall is concentrated in the summer and water shortages have become commonplace in the dry season. Especially in slum areas, water supplies are not only lacking, but what water is available is heavily polluted and of poor quality. Concerns that sea-level rise will affect and potentially flood areas along Mumbai's coastline have also been raised, given that much of the city is located on low-lying land at or near sea level.

See Also: Census; India; London; Megacities; New York; Paris

Further Reading

Wendell Cox. "The Evolving Urban Form: Mumbai." *newgeography.com*, April 5, 2011. http://www.newgeography.com/content/002172-the-evolving-urban-form-mumbai.

Infochange India. "54% of Mumbai Lives in Slums: World Bank." January 9, 2006. http://infochangeindia.org/poverty/news/54-of-mumbai-lives-in-slums-world-bank.html.

Delnaaz Irani. "Mumbai Disrupted by Water Shortages." *BBC News*, August 2, 2009. http://news.bbc.co.uk/2/hi/business/8178729.stm.

Keihanshin

The Keihanshin metropolitan area, which includes the cities of Osaka, Kyoto, and Kobe, is the second-largest metropolitan area in Japan following Tokyo. The overall population of the Keihanshin metropolitan area is estimated at about 18.6 million, or about 15 percent of Japan's population. More than 12 million people live in the Osaka Prefecture, with about 2.5 million in the city of Osaka itself. About 2.5 million live in Kyoto and about 2 million live in Kobe. Keihanshin is located about 350 miles southwest of Tokyo on the island of Honshu. Its name is derived from the Japanese names of its three major cities.

The area containing the present-day cities of Osaka, Kyoto, and Kobe has been inhabited continuously for at least 2,500 years. Osaka became an important center for land and ocean transportation and it emerged as Japan's commercial center. Nearby Kobe became a major seaport. Meanwhile, the more inland city of Kyoto became the capital of the Japanese empire in 794 CE. It remained the imperial capital of Japan until after the Meiji Restoration in 1868, after which the capital was moved to Tokyo. Kyoto was Japan's largest city by population until the seventeenth century, when its population was exceeded by both Tokyo (then known as Edo) and Osaka.

Although Tokyo became Japan's most prominent city in the 19th century, the cities comprising Keihanshin remained important economic and cultural centers as Japan modernized and developed into a global power. Osaka also emerged as an important industrial center and serves today as the headquarters for Mitsubishi and Sanyo. Both Kobe and Osaka are among the largest container ports in Asia.

All three major cities comprising Keihanshin have experienced rapid population growth, especially in the 20th century. Population growth was the result of both natural increase and in-migration during the 19th and early 20th centuries. As Japan completed the process of demographic transition by the middle of the 20th century, migration became the major source of Keihanshin's population increases. Osaka Prefecture's population has been estimated at 1.6 million in 1900 and tripled to about 4.8 million on the eve of World War II in 1940. Osaka was damaged heavily by American bombings during the war, and many people left the region. The port of Kobe was also bombed. After the war, however, the prefecture's population continued to grow rapidly in part because industrial development created large numbers of jobs for people from other less developed parts of Japan. In contrast, Kyoto was spared American bombing given its cultural and historical significance.

The Keihanshin region, like other areas of Japan, is highly susceptible to natural disasters. In 1995, an earthquake measuring 7.2 on the Richter scale struck near Kobe. The Great Hanshin Earthquake caused about 6,400 fatalities, with about 4,600 in the city of Kobe itself. More than half of the buildings located in the worst-hit areas of Kobe were destroyed or damaged heavily. The earthquake triggered government efforts to improve emergency management planning and to strengthen building codes so that buildings would be able to withstand future earthquakes better.

Japan's population has begun to decline in light of its low birth rate relative to its death rate, resulting in a negative rate of natural increase. However, the Keihanshin region, along with Japan's other very large cities, continues to increase in population as a result of continuing in-migration from smaller cities and rural areas.

See Also: Crude Birth Rate; Crude Death Rate; Demographic Transition Model; Japan; Rate of Natural Increase; Tokyo

Further Reading

Wendell Cox. "The Evolving Urban Form: Osaka-Kobe-Kyoto." *newgeography.com*, March 28, 2012. http://www.newgeography.com/content/002750-the-evolving-urban-form-os aka-kobe-kyoto.

Kanako Itamae and Pierre Leblanc. "Population of Japan Continues to Decline but Tokyo, Osaka, and Nagoya Expand." *Modern Tokyo Times*, August 9, 2012. http://moderntokyo- times.com/2012/08/09/population-of-japan-continues-to-decline-but-tokyo-osaka-and -nagoya-expand/.

Shabbar Sagarwala. "Shrinking Japan: Kyoto's Machiya Districts Signal the Demographic Decline and the Way Forward." *Architokyo*, September 15, 2010. http://architokyo .wordpress.com/2012/09/15/kyomachiya/.

Moscow

Moscow is the capital city of Russia. With a metropolitan-area population of more than 11.5 million, Moscow is the largest city in Russia and the second-largest megacity in the world, following London. The greater Moscow metropolitan area has a population of about 16 million.

Moscow is located on the banks of the Moskva (Moscow) River, after which the city was named. A settlement near present-day Moscow was established around 1100, but was destroyed by the Mongol Golden Horde during the 13th century. It was rebuilt later, and became the capital of the Grand Duchy of Moscow during the 14th century. By the late 15th century, the Grand Duchy had expanded into much of present-day western Russia and became the Russian Empire. Ivan III the Great became the first Tsar of the Russian Empire in 1462, with Moscow becoming the capital of the Russian Empire. Moscow remained the capital of the Russian Empire until 1712, when Tsar Peter the Great moved the capital to the newly constructed city of St. Petersburg.

After World War I and the Russian Revolution, Russia's new Communist government returned the capital of what had become the Soviet Union to Moscow in 1918. The Soviet Union included present-day Russia as well as 14 other Soviet republics including present-day Estonia, Latvia, Lithuania, Ukraine, Armenia, and Kazakhstan. The Soviet Union collapsed in 1991, and each of the 15 constituent republics of the Soviet Union became an independent country. Moscow became the capital of the Russian Federation, which contained about half of the former Soviet Union's population and three-quarters of its land area.

Moscow evolved from a small village into a major city as the Grand Duchy of Moscow grew in size, power, and influence. The population of Moscow in 1500 has been estimated at 100,000. Over the next 70 years, its population doubled. However, in 1571, the city was captured by the Crimean Tatars and more than 80 percent of the people perished. An epidemic of bubonic plague and a major famine in the early 17th century resulted in several thousand additional fatalities. Nevertheless, Moscow's population rebounded from these disasters and is believed to have been about 200,000 in 1712, when the capital was moved to St. Petersburg.

During the first few decades after the movement of the capital, Moscow's population declined. After 1750, however, it began to grow rapidly. The population of Moscow increased from about 150,000 around 1750 to about 1.8 million at the outset of World War I around 1915, shortly before Moscow regained its status as its country's capital city. Hundreds of thousands of Muscovites lost their lives during the war and the Russian Revolution, but the population began to grow quickly again after the Communists took control of the country. Its population was about 5 million in 1950 and 9.5 million in 2000.

Russia's population as a whole has been in decline since the Soviet Union collapsed in 1991, but the Moscow metropolitan area has been growing in population. During the first decade of the 21st century, the population of metropolitan Moscow increased by more than 10 percent. Given Russia's negative rate of natural increase, Moscow's population growth has been driven by in-migration from other parts of Russia and to a lesser extent from former Soviet satellites in Central Asia and elsewhere. The governments of Moscow and of Russia have worked to address this growth by annexing nearby land areas. Because most government offices and businesses in Moscow have been located near the center of the city, the government has been moving government offices to outlying areas and encouraging private businesses to do the same. These policies are intended also to alleviate Moscow's ongoing problems with traffic congestion.

See Also: Black Death; Famine; London; Megacities; Rate of Natural Increase; Russia

Further Reading

Wendell Cox. "The Evolving Urban Form: Moscow's Auto-Oriented Expansion." *newgeogra phy.com,*February 22, 2012. http://www.newgeography.com/content/002682-the-evolving-urban-form-moscows-auto-oriented-expansion.

Miriam Elder. "Moscow to Double in Size to Ease Overcrowding." *The Guardian*, July 14, 2011. http://www.theguardian.com/world/2011/jul/14/moscow-double-size-overcrowding.

Gregory Ioffe and Zhanna Zayonchkovskaya. "Spatial Shifts in the Population of Moscow Region." *Eurasian Geography and Economics* 52 (2011): 543–66.

Cairo

Cairo is the capital and largest city of Egypt. It is a primate city and is Egypt's major financial and cultural center as well as its political capital. The Cairo metropolitan area contains more than 17 million people, or roughly 20 percent of Egypt's population. It is the largest city by population on the continent of Africa, as well as in the Middle East. It is an important commercial hub not only for Egypt, but throughout the Middle East and North Africa.

The area around Cairo, which is located on the banks of the Nile River, has been inhabited for several thousand years. The Great Pyramid of Giza and the Sphinx, which are believed to have been constructed more than 4,500 years ago, are both located at Giza, on the outskirts of contemporary Cairo. However, the modern city of Cairo was not established until the tenth century CE, when it was founded on the eastern bank of the Nile by the Fatimid Caliphate. It became the Caliphate's capital city in 1168. Around 1250, power in Egypt was seized by the Mamluk dynasty. Given its location on the Nile just upstream from where the main channel of the river branches into the Nile Delta before flowing into the Mediterranean Sea, Cairo became an important trading center as well as the Mamluk's political capital.

In 1517, the Ottoman Empire, which was centered in Constantinople (present-day Istanbul), took control of Egypt. Cairo lost its status as a capital city at that time, and its importance as a trading center declined after European mariners began to circumnavigate Africa at around the same time. Cairo along with the rest of Egypt was occupied by the British during the 19th century, and the British continued to occupy the city until Egypt became independent in 1922. Cairo became the capital of newly independent Egypt, and has grown in population and influence ever since. In 2011, Cairo was the focal point for demonstrations associated with Arab Spring, during which dictatorships in Egypt and several other countries were toppled following large-scale public protests.

Cairo's population fluctuated between the 10th and the 19th centuries, but it has experienced steady and rapid population growth ever since. Historians have estimated that the population of Cairo was about 500,000 during the middle of the 14th century. However, by the 16th century, its population declined to less than 300,000 because of its reduced economic importance, and also because several epidemics of bubonic plague caused thousands of fatalities. Cairo grew only slowly during most of the period of Ottoman rule, with a population estimated at about 350,000 in the 1880s. Since then, its population has grown rapidly. Its population grew to more than a million people at the time of Egyptian independence in the 1920s, and to over 3 million in 1960. By this time, suburbs outside of Cairo's city limits had also begun to grow quickly, although the growth rate has slowed as Egypt has completed demographic transition. Today less than half of metropolitan Cairo's people live within the city limits of Cairo proper.

Cairo is among the most densely populated very large cities in the world. The population density of the city itself has been estimated at over 100,000 people per square mile, or almost twice that of Manhattan Island in New York. Cairo's high population density is associated with water shortages. Cairo averages only about 3.5 inches of rainfall per year, considerably less than any other megacity in the modern world. Thus the city is entirely dependent on the Nile as a source of fresh water, with the cost of pumping and supplying water increasing with distance from the river. Thus most of Cairo's development has occurred near the river, upstream and downstream from its main channel.

Cairo's high population density coupled with its rapid growth rate has contributed to various problems, notably traffic congestion and air pollution. Millions of cars choke Cairo's streets each day, and the city's lack of rainfall impedes the dispersion of pollutants. Air pollution is also caused by factories and smelters, many of which lack emission controls. According to one Egyptian government estimate, more than 25,000 people in Cairo die each year from diseases caused directly by air pollution. Water pollution in the Nile has also become a significant problem, especially given that the river is Cairo's sole source of potable water.

See Also: Black Death; Demographic Transition Model; Egypt; Istanbul; Megacities; New York; Population Density; Primate City

Further Reading

Wendell Cox. "The Evolving Urban Form—Cairo." *newgeography.com*, June 13, 2012. http://www.newgeography.com/content/002901-the-evolving-urban-form-cairo.

Andy Soos. "The Thick Haze of Cairo." *Environmental News Network*, January 3, 2013. http://www.enn.com/pollution/article/45410.

Los Angeles

Los Angeles is the second-largest city in the United States and the largest city on the American side of the Pacific Ocean. About 18 million people live in the Los Angeles metropolitan area, with about 3.7 million within the city limits of Los Angeles itself.

The area containing present-day Los Angeles was inhabited by Native Americans for thousands of years. Spain claimed present-day California, including Los Angeles, in 1542. In 1771, Father Junipero Serra established a mission on the site of Los Angeles, and settlers began moving northwestward from present-day Mexico, which took control of California after becoming independent from Spain in 1821. California was ceded from Mexico to the United States in 1848.

In 1870, Los Angeles had only about 5,000 residents. During the late 19th century, however, several factors resulted in rapid growth that continues to the present day. Los Angeles' importance as a commercial center increased with the completion of transcontinental railroads in the 1870s. Harbors were constructed, making Los Angeles and nearby Long Beach major ports. The discovery of oil in the 1890s also contributed to Los Angeles' economic boom. According to the United States census, the population of Los Angeles was about 50,000 in 1890 and doubled to about 102,000 in 1900. At that time, Los Angeles was the 36th-largest city by population in the United States.

Los Angeles grew quickly into a megacity during the 20th century. The city became the major headquarters for the motion picture industry and also became an increasingly important center for manufacturing. Water shortages associated with the movement of large numbers of people into the semi-arid Los Angeles basin were alleviated by the construction of aqueducts that transferred water from the Sierra Nevada mountain range, with its very heavy winter snows, to the area in the early 20th century. The city gained worldwide attention as the site of the Olympic Games in 1932. During World War II, the city became a manufacturing center for aircraft, ships, ammunition, and other war supplies. These industries provided thousands of jobs for incoming residents, and growth increased after the war ended in part because many military personnel as well as civilians who had worked in plants producing military supplies elected to remain in southern California.

The rapid growth of Los Angeles is reflected in population data. Its population grew to more than 575,000 in 1920 and to nearly 2 million by 1950. The city's population passed the 3 million mark during the 1980s, and by 1990 it had surpassed Chicago to become the second-largest city by population in the United States.

Los Angeles expanded its city limits frequently during the 20th century. Today, it is one of the largest central cities by land area in the United States. However, growth in Los Angeles occurred increasingly outside the city limits, and less than a third of the residents of the Los Angeles metropolitan area live in Los Angeles itself. In 1950, the population of the present-day Los Angeles metropolitan area was about 4.5 million, with about 40 percent in Los Angeles proper. Today, only about 20 percent of the metropolitan area's residents live in the city of Los Angeles.

Los Angeles' population is characterized by considerable diversity and ethnic heterogeneity. For decades, Los Angeles has attracted immigrants from throughout the world, particularly from Mexico. Today, more than half of Los Angeles' residents describe themselves as having Latino or Hispanic ancestry. Los Angeles also has substantial populations of Asian Americans and African Americans, with about 10 percent of its residents belonging to each of these ethnic groups. The Los Angeles metropolitan area contains the largest communities in the United States of immigrants from Korea, the Philippines, Armenia, and other countries of origin.

Immigration is the major cause of population increases in contemporary Los Angeles. More than half of Los Angeles' residents today are immigrants or children of immigrants. In recent years, however, many native-born Americans have left the Los Angeles region for other places. Rates of out-migration of native-born Americans now exceed rates of in-migration, reversing a trend of net in-migration that had been prevalent throughout the 20th century.

The growth of Los Angeles during the 20th century generated a variety of social and environmental problems. Los Angeles is highly dependent on the automobile, and the suburbs have sprawled into environmentally sensitive areas. Large numbers of cars created major problems with smog and air pollution, although these problems have been abated in recent years because strict pollution controls have been imposed. The city has invested heavily in public transportation and other efforts to promote improved environmental quality throughout the area. Los Angeles is located in a region prone to seismic activity, and the possibility of a large and highly destructive earthquake affecting the city and nearby areas is ongoing.

See Also: Census; Megacities; Mexico; Migration; Philippines; South Korea; United States of America

Further Reading

James P. Allen and Eugene Turner. "Ethnic Change and Enclaves in Los Angeles." *Association of American Geographers*, March 8, 2013. http://www.aag.org/cs/news_detail?pressrelease.id=2058.

Wendell Cox. "The Emerging Urban Form: Los Angeles." *newgeography.com*, August 8, 2011. http://www.newgeography.com/content/002372-the-evolving-urban-form-los-angeles.

Stephanie Pincetl. "Los Angeles: The Improbably Sustainable City." *Association of American Geographers*, March 8, 2013. http://www.aag.org/cs/news_detail?pressrelease.id=2046.

Kolkata

Kolkata, formerly known as Calcutta, is India's third-largest city. Kolkata's population has been estimated at 5.2 million, with a metropolitan area population estimated at between 15 and 17 million. Kolkata is more crowded and poorer than India's two larger metropolitan areas, Mumbai and Delhi–New Delhi.

Kolkata is located near the east coast of India, on the east bank of the Hooghly River. The city is located about 40 miles north of the river's mouth, where it empties into the Bay of Bengal. Kolkata is the capital of the Indian state of West Bengal, which has more than 90 million inhabitants. Archaeologists have demonstrated that the site of present-day Kolkata has been inhabited for at least 2,000 years. In the 17th century, the site was occupied by three small villages that belonged to the Mughal Empire. In 1690, the British East India Company began efforts to establish the area occupied by these villages as the site of its trading operations in eastern India. Control of the area was transferred from the Mughals to the company in 1696.

During the early 18th century, the British government began construction fortifications in the Kolkata area in order to protect their interests from attacks by French and local Indian troops. Newly fortified Kolkata was named the capital and administrative center of all Indian territory controlled by the company in 1772. The city became the capital of British India after the British East India Company was dissolved in 1858 and control of India was nationalized in 1874. During this period, numerous marshes in and near the city were drained and land was reclaimed for urban development.

Kolkata remained the capital of British India until 1911, when the capital was transferred to Delhi. During the late 19th and early 20th centuries, Kolkata became a center for the Indian independence movement and was recognized as a center for science, education, and culture. However, Kolkata began to lag economically behind Mumbai, Delhi, and other major Indian cities after the capital functions were transferred. Stagnation intensified after India became independent in 1947, because the separation of India from East Pakistan (present-day Bangladesh) removed much of Kolkata's economic hinterland and Dhaka became the dominant commercial center on the Pakistani side of the international boundary. Despite its relative stagnation, Kolkata remains an important commercial, financial, and economic center and India's second-largest port.

Kolkata's population has experienced steady growth since its establishment by the British East India Company. Its population in 1750 has been estimated at 150,000. In 1911, when the capital was transferred from Kolkata to Delhi, Kolkata's population was about 900,000. The population grew slowly over the next two decades, but doubled in the 1930s. The central city population doubled between 1941 and 1991 but has remained relatively stationary since then. Between 2001 and 2011, the population of the central city dropped by about 2 percent. However, the suburbs of Kolkata continue to grow rapidly. Until the 1950s, more than half of residents of the Kolkata metropolitan area lived in the city of Kolkata itself. Since then, the suburbs have grown substantially faster than the central city itself. Today about two-thirds of the metropolitan area's people live in the suburbs.

The city of Kolkata proper is one of the most densely populated cities in the world, with an estimated population density of more than 63,000 people per square mile. The suburbs are densely populated but not as crowded as the central city, with about 25,000 per square mile. According to government and international estimates, about a third of Kolkata's central-city residents, or about 1.5 million people, live in slums. Some of Kolkata's slums are more than 100 years old, dating back well before Indian independence. Others have come into existence more recently. Some are squatter settlements in which people live on vacant land, using any available building materials to construct shacks lacking electricity, running water, or sewage treatment. Efforts to alleviate problems associated with slum life in Kolkata have been ongoing for many years. Mother Teresa (1910–1997) became renowned internationally for her work with very poor slum residents of Kolkata, winning the Nobel Peace Prize in 1979.

KOLKATA'S VULNERABILITY TO NATURAL DISASTERS

The city of Kolkata in eastern India is one of the poorest megacities in the world. It is also one of the most vulnerable to natural disasters, many of which are associated with the city's coastal location on flat, low-lying land.

Not only is Kolkata at risk of floods and intense tropical cyclones, but its ability to cope with these disasters should they occur is compromised by its lack of infrastructure. For example, much of the city's drainage system is more than 140 years old and in need of repair or replacement. Sewer lines are silted and often clogged, and thus rainwater backs up into the streets. One estimate has suggested that a storm dumping less than a third of an inch of rain per hour can cause the city's sewers to back up. Given its coastal location, Kolkata is subject to sea level rise, and some fresh water supplies have become saline, making them unsafe to drink. Kolkata has been identified as the seventh most vulnerable city to natural disasters in the world, and some Indians hope that this identification will spur the government into better planning and improved infrastructure to mitigate against future disasters.

Further Reading

Prithvijit Mitra. "Kolkata on the Edge of Disaster." *The Times of India*, November 12, 2012. http://timesofindia.indiatimes.com/kolkata-on-edge-of-disaster/articleshow/17188293.cms.

Like many very large metropolitan areas in less developed countries, the Kolkata metropolitan area faces numerous problems in addition to abject poverty, including very high levels of traffic congestion, pollution, and smog. Given its location on the Hooghly River floodplain and its elevation of only 30 feet above sea level, Kolkata has also been subject to intense flooding that has often resulted in substantial loss of life, injuries, and property damage. According to one estimate, Kolkata, Shanghai, and Dhaka are the world's large metropolitan areas most vulnerable to the impacts of coastal flooding and potential sea level rise associated with continuing global warming. Nevertheless, the Kolkata area continues to grow, as large numbers of people move from impoverished areas of India into the city.

See Also: Bangladesh; Delhi and New Delhi; Dhaka; India; Mumbai; Shanghai; Squatter Settlements

Further Reading

Stefania Balica, Nigel Wright, and Frank van der Meulen. "A Flood Vulnerability Index for Coastal Cities and Its Use in Assessing Climate Change Impacts." *Natural Hazards* 52 (2012): 73–105. http://eprints.whiterose.ac.uk/74383/2/10.1007_s11069-012-0234-1.pdf.

Wendell Cox. "The Evolving Urban Form: Kolkata: 50 Mile City," *newgeography.com*, January 10, 2010. http://www.newgeography.com/content/002620-the-evolving-urban-form-kolkata-50-mile-city.

V. Ramaswamy. "Renewing the City: Efforts to Improve Life in Calcutta's Urban Slums." Asia Society, n.d. http://asiasociety.org/policy/social-issues/human-rights/renewing-city-efforts-improve-life-calcutta%E2%80%99s-urban-slums?page=0,0.

Bangkok

Bangkok is the capital city and primate city of Thailand. With a population of 8.5 million, and a metropolitan area population of about 15 million, Bangkok is nearly 40 times as large in population as the country's second-largest city of Nonthaburi. Thus it might be regarded as the most extreme primate city in the world as measured by the ratio of its population to the population of the country's second largest city. Nearly a quarter of Thailand's people live in the Bangkok metropolitan area.

Bangkok is known in Thailand as Krung Thep Maha Nakhon, or simply Krung Thep. It is located on the delta of the Chao Phraya River, which flows across Thailand before emptying into the Gulf of Thailand. The Bangkok region has been settled for at least 700 years. Given its location near the mouth of the Chao Phraya, it became important as a port and a gateway for international trade. Bangkok became Thailand's capital city in 1782. Thailand remained independent throughout the colonial era and was never colonized by Europeans, but its importance increased during the 19th century because of extensive trade with the Western colonial powers. Between 1851 and 1910, King Mongkut and his son, King Chulalongkorn, strongly encouraged

Bangkok is the primate city of Thailand and is the largest city by population in mainland Southeast Asia. The high concentration of people along with traffic jams and industrial activities cause considerable air pollution in Bangkok. (sndrk/iStockphoto.com)

modernizing the city. Kings Mongkut and Chulalongkom built roads, bridges, and railroads, initiated formal planning for residential construction, and introduced electricity and other modern innovations. The city was occupied by Japanese forces during World War II, but was once again under Thai control after the war ended.

Throughout its history, Bangkok has grown in population very rapidly. In 1822, 30 years before King Mongkut ascended the Thai throne, a British observer estimated the population of Bangkok at about 50,000. A census conducted in 1919 counted about 437,000 residents. The population rose to 2 million in 1960. It more than doubled during the 1960s and 1970s, reaching 4.7 million by 1980. Since then, Bangkok proper has grown by more than 100,000 people annually, with much faster growth taking place in the suburbs. Much of this growth is the result of rural to urban migration from Thailand's rural areas, although Bangkok today contains nearly 400,000 expatriates.

Bangkok's economy remains oriented to trade, finance, transportation, and communications, although there is also a substantial manufacturing center. Bangkok is an important tourist center, both in itself and as a gateway for tourists visiting the whole of Southeast Asia. Its gross domestic product per capita has been estimated at nearly three times that of Thailand as a whole, and is considerably higher than that of other megacities in less developed countries of Asia, including Kolkata, Dhaka, and Jakarta. Its prosperity has helped to attract large numbers of migrants from throughout Southeast Asia, including more than 400,000 migrants from poorer Southeast Asian countries, including Myanmar and Cambodia.

With rapid and continuing population growth, however, have come many problems typical of megacities, especially in developing countries. Air and water pollution are widespread. Although Thailand's government has attempted to prioritize environmental protection, Bangkok's industrial sector and its very high volume of motor vehicle traffic cause substantial amounts of air pollution and smog. Extensive quantities of industrial and household wastes have polluted the Chao Phraya delta and other waterways. Bangkok is subject to high amounts of rainfall annually, especially during its monsoon season between June and October. Thus flooding is a significant issue. Moreover, because Bangkok is located on low-lying land near the coast, it is potentially subject to inundation as a result of sea-level rise associated with climate change.

Above and beyond these environmental issues, Bangkok faces many problems associated with its very rapid growth. Thailand has often been unable to keep up with this growth by providing infrastructure, health care, housing, and other services to its quickly increasing population. Many people, especially impoverished rural to urban migrants, live in slums. Moreover, Bangkok is recognized as an international center for prostitution and sex trafficking, and as a result Thailand has one of the highest rates of incidence of HIV/AIDS outside of Africa.

See Also: Climate Change and Population; Dhaka; Expatriates; HIV/AIDS; Jakarta; Kolkata; Myanmar; Primate City; Rural to Urban Migration; Sex Trafficking; Thailand

Further Reading

Joe Maier and Jerry Hopkins. *Welcome to the Bangkok Slaughterhouse: The Battle for Human Dignity in Bangkok's Bleakest Slums.* Hong Kong: Periplus, 2005.

Maryvelma O'Neal. *Bangkok: A Cultural History.* Oxford: Oxford University Press, 2008.

Dhaka

Dhaka is the capital city and primate city of Bangladesh. Located on the delta of the Ganges and Brahmaputra Rivers, Dhaka's population has been estimated at more than 15 million. Dhaka is the most rapidly growing large city in Asia, and some demographers have predicted that its population may exceed 25 million by 2025.

Dhaka was established 1,500 years ago and became the capital of the Buddhist kingdom of Kamarupa in the seventh century CE. It became the administrative center of the Hindu Sena dynasty, which toppled the Kamarupas in the ninth century. It was the capital of various successor kingdoms until the Mughal Empire, centered in Delhi, took control of present-day Bangladesh in the 17th century. The

Mughals were succeeded by the British, who granted independence to British India in 1947. At that time, Bangladesh was part of Pakistan and was known as East Pakistan. Bangladesh became independent in 1971, and Dhaka became the capital of the newly independent country.

Dhaka has grown very rapidly since the 19th century, both because of natural increase and because of large volumes of rural to urban migration. In 1901, a census of British India counted about 2 million people in the Dhaka metropolitan region with 130,000 in the city itself. The population of the region grew to about 3.5 million in 1931 and to about 8 million by 1975. Thus, the population of Dhaka has nearly doubled in less than 40 years. The population of Dhaka is predicted to continue to grow rapidly, and it may emerge as one of the five largest cities in the world by 2030.

Bangladesh is the most densely populated large country in the world, and Dhaka's population density is far greater than that of any other megacity. Currently, Dhaka's population density is estimated at more than 115,000 people per square mile, or 50 percent higher than Mumbai and nearly twice as much as Hong Kong and Karachi. Very high population densities in Dhaka have impeded efforts to address Dhaka's major social and economic problems.

Like other megacities in less developed countries, Dhaka suffers from many serious environmental and social problems. Rapid population growth has resulted in high levels of air and water pollution, as well as monumental levels of traffic congestion. Bangladesh is a poor country, and the country has not yet been able to provide infrastructure adequate to meet the needs of Dhaka's numerous new residents, although thousands of people from rural areas migrate to Dhaka each year. It is believed that a third of Dhaka's residents live in slums and squatter settlements. Population densities in Dhaka's more crowded slums are believed to exceed 3,000 people per acre.

Dhaka has a hot, wet climate and is subject to frequent flooding. On several occasions, 10 or more inches of rain have fallen in less than 24 hours. The impacts of floods on Dhaka are exacerbated by very poor drainage and by ineffective waste disposal systems. Garbage has been spread throughout the city during flood events. These problems are especially evident in Dhaka's many slums. Population densities in some of the more crowded slums of Dhaka have been estimated at 4,000 people or more per acre. Dhaka is also subject to tropical cyclones making landfall from the offshore Bay of Bengal. In 1991, for example, nearly 140,000 people in and near Dhaka lost their lives in a deadly cyclone.

Dhaka is located on the coast of Bay of Bengal at a very low elevation, and most of its land is flat. Thus Dhaka is also highly vulnerable to sea-level rise associated with global warming. Estimates suggest that sea-level rise associated with increased global surface temperatures as little as three to four degrees Fahrenheit could inundate as much as a third of Bangladesh's land surface, including portions of the city.

Not only will people living in the lowest portions of Dhaka be forced to move, but levels of salinity, water pollution, and drainage problems are also very likely to increase as sea levels rise.

See Also: Bangladesh; Census; Demography; Hong Kong; Karachi; Megacities; Mumbai; Pakistan; Primate City; Rate of Natural Increase; Squatter Settlements

Further Reading

Nushrat Rahman Chowdhury. "Where Dhaka Stands Today." *Financial Express*, February 26, 2013. http://www.thefinancialexpress-bd.com/index.php?ref=MjBfMDJfMjZfMTNf MV85Ml8xNjEyOTE=.

Wendell Cox. "Dhaka's Dangerous Development." *newgeography.com*, June 8, 2010. http://www.newgeography.com/content/001610-dhakas-dangerous-development.

Shairul Mashreque. "Dhaka's Environment Suffers Urban Impact." *Daily Star*, October 3, 2009. http://archive.thedailystar.net/newDesign/news-details.php?nid=107999.

Research Initiative for Social Equity Society. "A Look into Dhaka, Bangladesh—The Most Densely Populated City in the World." March 9, 2013. http://risebd.com/2013/03/09/ a-look-into-dhaka-bangladesh-the-most-densely-populated-city-in-the-world/.

Buenos Aires

Buenos Aires is the capital and largest city in Argentina. It is a primate city and is Argentina's financial, economic, and cultural center as well as its political capital. With a population of about 13 million, the Buenos Aires metropolitan area is the second-largest metropolitan area by population in South America, following only São Paulo. Nearly one-third of Argentina's people live in Buenos Aires or its suburbs.

Buenos Aires is located at the mouth of the estuary of the Rio de la Plata. The Spanish began efforts to establish a settlement in the area of present-day Buenos Aires in the early 16th century. An initial settlement was founded in 1536, but the Spanish colonists were driven away by local indigenous people. In 1580, the Spanish constructed a second settlement that eventually became the present-day city of Buenos Aires.

The Rio de la Plata provided convenient access from the Atlantic Ocean into the interior of South America, and given its location Buenos Aires soon became an important port and commercial center. In 1776, the Spanish government created the Viceroyalty of Rio de la Plata, which included present-day Argentina, Paraguay, and Bolivia. However, high taxes and difficulty of access across the Andes Mountains to the Pacific Ocean ports of Lima and Santiago impeded trade and frustrated many Buenos Aires merchants, who began to agitate for independence from Spain.

After six years of war, Argentina became independent from Spain in 1816, with Buenos Aires as its capital. Buenos Aires attempted to secede from Argentina and establish itself as an independent country in the 1850s, but these efforts were abandoned after several years of conflict and controversy. During the late 19th and early 20th centuries, Buenos Aires attracted large numbers of immigrants from Germany, Italy, and other European countries. It became an important center for industrial activity while retaining its status as Argentina's capital city and financial center, and it remains one of South America's busiest seaports. In the 1980s, the Argentine government considered relocating the capital from Buenos Aires to Viedma, some 600 miles to the south, but this proposal was rejected.

The city of Buenos Aires comprises the Capital Federal District, but the urbanized area of Buenos Aires has spread far beyond the boundaries of the district. Today, a large majority of Buenos Aires' people live outside the city limits of Buenos Aires itself. In 1869, a census conducted by the government of Argentina counted about 180,000 people within the city limits. The population of Buenos Aires grew rapidly in the late 19th and early 20th centuries, in part because of large-scale migration from Europe. Its population reached 700,000 around 1900 and grew to nearly 3 million in 1947.

The population of Buenos Aires proper remained stable for the 40 years after 1947, and then began to decrease slightly. Today, about 2.6 million people live within the boundaries of the Capital Federal District. However, outlying areas surrounding the city proper have grown very quickly over the past century. In 1947, the suburban population surrounding Buenos Aires was about 2 million. In other words, at that time about 60 percent of the residents of the Buenos Aires metropolitan area lived in the city of Buenos Aires itself. Today, more than 10 million people, or more than 80 percent of the metropolitan area population, live in the suburbs. Some of Buenos Aires' suburbs are affluent, whereas others house low-skilled and unskilled workers who often live in shoddy or substandard houses. More than 1.5 million people in the greater Buenos Aires metropolitan area live in slums, both inside and outside the city limits themselves. These slums are often called *villas miseria*, or "misery slums."

Buenos Aires also faces multiple environmental problems. Water pollution is among the most significant of these problems. Large amounts of oil have been discharged into the Rio de la Plata and other waterways near the city, and heavy metals seep into the water from old, rusted, and sometimes abandoned ships in the port of Buenos Aires. Air pollution is also a major problem that has been exacerbated by large numbers of exhaust-generating motor vehicles. The city has also experienced problems with inadequate space to store its large and growing volume of garbage and trash. Lack of disposal sites has resulted in concentration of garbage in various areas, often located near the *villas miserias*. These informal disposal sites have become breeding grounds for very large populations of disease-bearing rats, mice, and other vermin.

See Also: Argentina; Census; Germany; Italy; Primate City; São Paulo

Further Reading

Wendell Cox. "The Two Worlds of Buenos Aires." *newgeography.com*, November 11, 2011. http://www.newgeography.com/content/001862-the-two-worlds-buenos-aires.

MercoPress. "Half a Million Families Live in Buenos Aires Slums and Keep Expanding Vertically and Horizontally." October 7, 2011. http://en.mercopress.com/2011/10/07/half-a-million-families-live-in-buenos-aires-slums-and-keep-expanding-vertically-and-horizontally

Tehran

Tehran, whose name is sometimes spelled Teheran, is the capital and largest city of Iran. The population of the greater Tehran area has been estimated at more than 12 million. Tehran is the political capital and major economic and financial center of Iran. It is a primate city whose metropolitan population is more than four times larger than that of Iran's second-largest city of Mashhad. Nearly 15 percent of Iran's people live in the Tehran metropolitan area.

The area around present-day Tehran was settled more than 6,000 years ago, although it did not develop into a large city until the 19th century. Tehran is located north of the ancient city of Rey, which was founded several thousand years ago and was, for most of its history, considerably larger than Tehran. Today, Rey is a suburb of Tehran. At various times, the region around present-day Rey and Tehran was contested between various kingdoms and empires. In 1795, Tehran

Air pollution is a major environmental problem in large and rapidly growing cities, especially in less developed countries. Immense traffic jams contribute to this air pollution, which can cause major health hazards. Here women in Tehran, Iran, wear masks to keep out pollutants. (AP Photo/Vahid Salemi)

became the capital of the Persian Empire, which controlled much of present-day Iran at the time. Tehran has remained the capital of Iran, whose present name was adopted in 1938, ever since.

When Tehran became the capital city of the Persian Empire in 1795, its population was estimated at about 15,000. The city began to grow rapidly. Its population grew to more than 50,000 by 1810 and about 155,000 in 1869. It had doubled by 1915, and it began to grow even more rapidly after the Pahlavi dynasty took power in 1925. Its population was estimated at more than 1.5 million in 1950, and tripled to nearly 5 million by 1980, when the Pahlavis were ousted by the current religious-oriented regime led by the Ayatollah Ruhollah Khomeini. Tehran's growth continued after the new regime took over. However, much of the growth in the Tehran metropolitan area today is taking place outside the city limits, and Tehran's suburbs are now growing at a rate considerably faster than that of Tehran itself.

Tehran's population growth can be attributed to two major factors—natural increase and rural to urban migration. International migration has had little impact on Tehran's population in recent years, although the city has become home to many refugees from nearby Afghanistan. Iran's crude birth rate and total fertility rate remain high relative to other parts of the world, contributing to its population growth. However, much of the growth in contemporary Tehran is the result of large numbers of migrants who are moving into the Tehran metropolitan area from rural areas of Iran. The fact that many of these migrants are of childbearing age has contributed to Tehran's high birth rate relative to many other megacities. As elsewhere, Tehran has experienced considerable difficulty keeping up with demands for housing, schools, health care, and other infrastructure as its population has continued to increase.

Contemporary Tehran experiences substantial levels of air and water pollution. Tehran's location at the foot of the Alborz Mountains, which surround much of the city, creates the possibility of temperature inversions. Heavy traffic, which increases each year in light of Tehran's growth, generates pollutants that are trapped under the inversion layer and cause smog, especially in winter. Tehran has been ranked by the World Health Organization as one of the most polluted cities in the world. Along with the rest of Iran, Tehran is located in a seismic zone and is subject to sometimes destructive earthquakes.

See Also: Crude Birth Rate; Iran; Megacities; Rate of Natural Increase; Refugees; Rural to Urban Migration; Total Fertility Rate

Further Reading

Thomas Erdbrink. "Annual Buildup of Air Pollution Chokes Tehran." *New York Times*, January 6, 2013. http://www.nytimes.com/2013/01/07/world/middleeast/tehran-is -choked-by-annual-buildup-of-air-pollution.html?_r=0.

Paul Koring. "A View from the Booming, Modern Streets of Tehran." *Globe and Mail*, June 18, 2012. http://m.theglobeandmail.com/news/world/a-view-from-the-booming -modern-streets-of-tehran/article4210031/?service=mobile.

Istanbul

Istanbul is the largest city in Turkey, with a metropolitan area population of about 14 million. It is Turkey's primary economic, financial, and cultural center. Located partly in Europe and partly in Asia, Istanbul is the only major city in the world that straddles two continents.

Istanbul is located on the Bosporus, which is a strait that is part of a water connection between the Black Sea and the Mediterranean Sea along with the Sea of Marmara and the Dardanelles. Istanbul's position on the Bosporus has given it an important strategic location and made it a major center for trade and commerce for more than 2,000 years. Archaeologists have discovered artifacts on the site of present-day Istanbul that are more than 7,000 years old, confirming that the Istanbul area was inhabited long before it developed into a major city.

The history of present-day Istanbul dates back to about 660 BCE, when Greek traders established the trading town of Byzantium on the European or western bank of the Bosporus. Byzantium became part of the Roman Empire in 73 CE. In 330 CE, the Roman emperor Constantine made Byzantium the capital city of the Eastern Roman Empire and renamed the city Constantinople, after himself. The Western Roman Empire collapsed in 476 CE, but Constantinople remained the capital of the Eastern Roman Empire, which was also called the Byzantine Empire, for the next several hundred years. Constantinople was contested between Christian and Muslim forces until it fell finally to the Ottomans in 1453. The first Ottoman emperor, Sultan Mehmed II, made Constantinople the capital city of the Ottoman Empire.

Constantinople remained the Ottoman capital until the Ottoman Empire collapsed before and during World War I. In 1923, the European powers recognized Turkey, with its present-day boundaries, as the successor state to the Ottoman Empire. Independent Turkey's first ruler, Mustafa Kemal Ataturk, moved the capital of the country to inland Ankara in the same year. However, Istanbul remained newly independent Turkey's major commercial and financial center. The name of Istanbul had been used colloquially for the city during the 19th and 20th centuries and was adopted officially by the Turkish government in 1930. By this time, the urbanized area of Istanbul had expanded across the Bosporus into Asia. Today, about 40 percent of Istanbul's people live on the Asiatic side of the Bosporus.

During its period of Roman and Byzantine rule, Constantinople was one of the largest cities in the world by population. Historians have estimated that as many as

500,000 people lived in Constantinople during the seventh and eighth centuries CE. After several centuries of warfare, culminating in the Ottoman conquest in 1453, the population declined to an estimated 100,000. The population of Constantinople rebounded while it was the capital of the Ottoman Empire. At the time of Turkish independence in the early 1920s, its population was estimated at between 600,000 and 650,000.

Istanbul began to grow rapidly after Turkish independence. Not only did Turkey's rate of natural increase remain high, but very large numbers of people from rural Turkey moved to Istanbul in search of urban employment. Istanbul's population surpassed 1 million in the early 1950s. It reached 2.5 million in 1970, and then nearly tripled over the next two decades, reaching 7 million by 1990 and doubling again during the next two decades. Although much of this increase was the result of continued rural to urban migration, some of these increases were due to the fact that Istanbul's boundaries were extended to encompass virtually all of the urbanized territory on both the European and the Asiatic sides of the city. Uniquely among the megacities of the world, nearly all of metropolitan Istanbul's people live within the now-expanded city limits of Istanbul itself, rather than in suburbs. Istanbul is expected to continue to grow, with some experts predicting a population between 17 and 19 million by 2030.

Istanbul has experienced many problems typical of rapidly growing large cities in developing countries including very high population densities, traffic congestion, pollution, shortages of housing, and festering slums. However, experts on urban planning have praised the governments of Turkey and Istanbul for effective management of these problems in spite of continued rapid population growth. The expansion of Istanbul's boundaries into outlying areas of both European and Asiatic Istanbul was part of a comprehensive growth management plan, motivated in part by Turkey's efforts to become part of the European Union.

Istanbul's development and prosperity have been hampered, however, by natural hazards and disasters, notably earthquakes. Istanbul is situated on a fault line known as the North Anatolian Fault, and many severe earthquakes have occurred in and near the city since its founding. Although the last major earthquake to strike Istanbul itself occurred in 1766, in 1999 a strong earthquake struck at Izmit, about 70 miles from Istanbul. The Izmit earthquake, with a magnitude of 7.6 on the Richter scale, destroyed numerous buildings and caused hundreds of fatalities in Istanbul itself.

See Also: Megacities; Rate of Natural Increase; Turkey

Further Reading

Katherine Barnes. "Clock Ticking for an Istanbul Earthquake." *Nature*, March 12, 2010. http://www.nature.com/news/2010/100312/full/news.2010.121.html.

Eugenie L. Birch. "Istanbul—A Megalopolis That's Beginning to Work." *Citiscope*, January 2011. http://citiscope.org/stories/citiwire/2011/istanbul-megalopolis-thats-beginning-to-work.

Wendell Cox. "The Evolving Urban Form: Istanbul." *newgeography.com*, August 16, 2012. http://www.newgeography.com/content/003020-the-evolving-urban-form-istanbul.

Tianjin

Tianjin is a megacity in northern China. Its metropolitan area population is about 14 million, and it is fourth in China in population size following Shanghai, Beijing, and Guangzhou. It is located on the coast at the mouth of the Hai River on the Bo-hai Gulf, which is an arm of the Yellow Sea and thus gives Tianjin direct shipping access to the Pacific Ocean. Thus Tianjin, which is located about 70 miles southeast of Beijing, is one of China's major seaports.

The area around Tianjin has been settled by Han Chinese for more than 2,000 years. During the Middle Ages, the Chinese government opened the Grand Canal connecting present-day Beijing with present-day Shanghai. The course of the canal passes through Tianjin and also connects the Hwang Ho and Yangtze Rivers. Tianjin is the only place along the route of the canal adjacent to the coast, and hence the canal facilitated and greatly expanded domestic and international trade for many centuries. Tianjin was established formally as a city by the Ming dynasty in 1404. Its name means "port for the emperor."

In 1860, British and French traders forced the Chinese government to open up Tianjin as a treaty port in order to facilitate trade between China and Europe. As the major port city of northern China and as the gateway to the Chinese capital of Beijing, Tianjin soon developed also as an industrial center. Tianjin was captured by the Japanese in 1938, but returned to China after the end of World War II in 1945. After the People's Republic of China took over the country, Tianjin's importance as a seaport declined during the 1950s and 1960s, when China isolated itself largely from the rest of the world. However, Tianjin's importance, and its population, grew after the early 1970s, when China opened itself up once more to the global economy. Today, Tianjin is the fifth-largest port in the world.

Tianjin's population has more than quadrupled since the People's Republic of China took control of the country in 1949. Its population was estimated at 2.7 million in 1953. By 1982, the population had reached 7.7 million, with much of this growth taking place in the 1970s. It grew to 9.8 million in 2000 and has now surpassed 14 million. Given the impacts of China's one-child population policy, all of this growth is the result of large-scale migration into Tianjin from other areas of China. During the first decade of the 21st century, planning officials in Tianjin advocated capping Tianjin's population at 13.5 million, but these recommendations have not been implemented and Tianjin continues to grow. More than 97 percent of Tianjin's people are Han Chinese, and the impacts of international migration on the population of Tianjin have been negligible.

As throughout China, rapid urban development and expansion in and near Tianjin have contributed to a host of environmental problems in the region. Industrial waste and heavy use of Tianjin's port facilities have contributed to extensive levels of water pollution in the area. However, Tianjin's officials, with the help of the national government, have developed and implemented plans intended to reduce water pollution and otherwise improve the physical environment of the urbanized area. One of the most ambitious projects is the construction of an entire new community called Tianjin Eco-City, to be located on the coast south of central Tianjin primarily on reclaimed land. Tianjin Eco-City is being designed to promote recycling, reduce carbon emissions, maximize green space, and use desalinated water. When completed, Tianjin Eco-City is expected to house about 350,000 residents.

See Also: Beijing; China; Guangzhou; International Labor Migration; Megacities; One-Child Policy; Shanghai

Further Reading

Li Fusheng and Li Xiang. "Eco-Appeal Makes Tianjin 'More Livable.'" *China Watch*, February 22, 2013. http://chinawatch.washingtonpost.com/2013/02/eco-appeal-makes -tianjin-more-livable.php.

Gaia Vince. "China's Eco-Cities: Sustainable Urban Living in Tianjin." *BBC Future*, May 3, 2012. http://www.bbc.com/future/story/20120503-sustainable-cities-on-the-rise.

Shenzhen

Shenzhen is located in southeastern China near the mouth of the Pearl River, adjacent to Hong Kong and less than 70 miles downstream from Guangzhou. Uniquely among the megacities of the world, Shenzhen has grown from a small fishing village into a major world city in less than 40 years. Its population is about 10 million. Along with Hong Kong, Guangzhou, and places in between, the Pearl River region is home to about 40 million people, making this region the largest conurbation in the world.

The area around present-day Shenzhen has been occupied for at least 7,000 years. At least 2,000 years ago, the area became a center for salt production and trade. The region also held strategic importance, given its location as a water gateway to Guangzhou and as a commercial center. However, Shenzhen itself did not develop as a city until it was designated as a Special Economic Zone by the government of China in 1979.

The history of Shenzhen is tied closely to that of Hong Kong, which is located in the territory between Shenzhen itself and the South China Sea. Hong Kong was occupied by British forces in 1841 and became part of the British Empire. In 1898, the government of the United Kingdom signed a 99-year lease with the Chinese government to retain control over Hong Kong. During its period of British rule, Hong Kong became the major center of trade between China and the British Empire. It later became an important industrial center, and as a result achieved a level of prosperity much greater than that of China itself.

When the British lease expired in 1997, control of Hong Kong reverted to China. The selection of Shenzhen as a Special Economic Zone was motivated by Shenzhen's proximity to Hong Kong, perhaps in anticipation of the eventual reabsorption of Hong Kong into China. Under Chinese policy, Shenzhen and other Special Economic Zones were given the opportunity to develop market-oriented economic activities, integrate industry and trade with scientific research and high technology, and adopt innovative administrative and management structures and policies.

Once it was designated by the Chinese government as a Special Economic Zone, Shenzhen developed and grew very rapidly. Hills in the area were razed in order to provide building space, and construction of houses, shopping centers, and public buildings proceeded quickly. In 1982, according to the census of China there were about 350,000 people in Shenzhen. The population grew to 1.2 million in 1990 and reached 7 million by 2000. Thus Shenzhen is by far the fastest-growing megacity in the world. Growth is extending from the core area of Shenzhen near the Hong Kong border to outlying, formerly rural areas.

Population growth in Shenzhen is the result of very large numbers of migrants moving into the city from other areas of China. Many of Shenzhen's residents are migrant workers who live in dormitories and work in factories in Shenzhen during the week, returning to their homes elsewhere on weekends. In addition to manufacturing, and again as a result of proximity to Hong Kong, Shenzhen has also developed as a center for high-tech industry and scientific research. The per capita gross domestic product of Shenzhen is the highest in China except for that of Hong Kong.

The speed of growth in Shenzhen has contributed to its environmental problems. As elsewhere in China, Shenzhen suffers from serious problems with air pollution. Deteriorating air quality in Shenzhen is the result of industrial emissions, high levels of automobile traffic, and the impact of Shenzhen's numerous building construction projects. Among the world's megacities, Shenzhen is especially vulnerable to typhoons and is also subject to strong earthquakes. All of these factors are being taken into account as Shenzhen prepares for the future.

See Also: Census; China; Guangzhou; United Kingdom

Further Reading

Wendell Cox. "The Evolving Urban Form: Shenzhen." *newgeography.com*, May 25, 2012. http://www.newgeography.com/content/002862-the-evolving-urban-form-shenzhen.

A. J. Eckstein. "The Instant City." *Encountering Urbanization*, June 22, 2011. http://encounteringurbanization.wordpress.com/2011/06/22/shenzhen-the-instant-city/.

Lagos

Lagos is the largest city in Nigeria and the largest city in sub-Saharan Africa. In 2011, the United Nations estimated Lagos' population at over 11.2 million. The metropolitan-area population of Lagos is believed to be over 20 million, and Lagos may have surpassed Cairo as the largest metropolitan area on the African continent. More than 10 percent of Nigeria's people live in Lagos and its suburbs.

Lagos is located near the southwestern corner of Nigeria on the coast of the Gulf of Guinea, an arm of the Atlantic Ocean. The central area of the city, including its port facilities, is located on islands and a narrow stretch of land between the Gulf of Guinea and the Lagos Lagoon. The islands and the mainland are now connected to one another by roads, bridges, and causeways. The Portuguese mariner Rui de Sequeira sighted this area in 1472 and named it Lago de Curamo. The Bini people founded the present-day city in the 16th century, and in 1730, the local ruler allowed Portugal access to the harbor for the purpose of capturing and transporting slaves across the Atlantic.

In 1851, the British deposed the local regime that had been cooperating with Portugal in the slave trade, which had been abolished in the British Empire in 1834. In 1862, Lagos and its surrounding territory became a formal British colony known as Lagos Colony. In 1906, Lagos Colony was merged with the Niger Coast Protectorate to form the Colony and Protectorate of Southern Nigeria. The Colony and Protectorate included roughly the southern third of present-day Nigeria.

Shortly before World War I broke out, the Colony and Protectorate was united with the Northern Nigeria Protectorate, and Nigeria became a single British colony with Lagos as its capital city. Lagos remained the capital city when Nigeria became independent in 1960.

Lagos has experienced explosive population growth throughout the late 20th and early 21st centuries. The population of Lagos Colony, which included the islands along with territory on the mainland along the Gulf of Guinea coast east and west of the city of Lagos, was estimated at 60,000 in 1872 by British officials. Its population was estimated at about 1.4 million at the time of independence in 1960. Lagos' population doubled between 1960 and 1980, and doubled again between

1980 and 2000. Rapid population growth in Lagos has resulted from a combination of high birth rates and rapid in-migration from rural areas within Nigeria. Less than 1 percent of Nigerians were born outside the country, although Lagos has an increasing population of residents who are native to other West African countries.

As is typical of very large cities in less developed countries, Lagos has a diverse population. The three largest ethnic groups in Lagos are the Hausa and Fulani, with 29 percent, the Yoruba, with 21 percent, and the Igbo, with 18 percent. Thus Lagos' population parallels the ethnic distribution of Nigeria, in which 62 percent of the people belong to one of these three major ethnic groups. Each of the three ethnic groups is indigenous to a different area of Nigeria, with the Hausa and Fulani in the north, the Yoruba in the southwest, and the Igbo in the southeast. About 50 percent of Lagos' residents are Muslims, 40 percent are Christians, and the remaining 10 percent practice other religions. This distribution of religious affiliation parallels that of Nigeria as a whole, although its major religions are separated geographically, with Muslims in the north and Christians in the south.

After independence, Lagos was Nigeria's primate city. Not only was Lagos the political capital of Nigeria, but it was also the economic, financial, and commercial heart of Nigeria and its major cultural center. After independence, Nigerian leaders considered relocating the capital to a more centrally located site in Nigeria's interior. Another goal of Nigeria's government was to choose a location that would be seen as neutral by Nigeria's many ethnic and religious groups. However, the decision to move the capital away from Lagos was motivated also by Lagos' rapid population growth. The site for Nigeria's planned capital city was selected in the late 1970s and named Abuja. Construction of government buildings was completed by the end of the 1980s, and the capital functions were transferred formally to Abuja in 1991. Despite this move, Lagos continued to grow rapidly, although Abuja is now the fourth-largest metropolitan area in Nigeria.

Although it is no longer Nigeria's capital city, Lagos experiences many of the problems experienced by large primate cities in developing countries, including traffic congestions, inadequate housing and public services, pollution, and shortages of potable water. Given Lagos' coastal location and heavy rainfall, drainage is poor and sewage treatment is inadequate. As in many primate cities throughout the world, millions of Lagos' residents live in slums. In 2012 and 2013, the Nigerian government instituted a controversial program to demolish slums and upgrade its slum areas.

See Also: Cairo; Nigeria; Primate City

Further Reading

John Campbell. "This Is Africa's New Biggest City: Lagos, Nigeria, Population 21 Million." *Atlantic*, July 10, 2012. http://www.theatlantic.com/international/archive/2012/07/this-is-africas-new-biggest-city-lagos-nigeria-population-21-million/259611/.

Ben Ezeamalu. "Failures, Tears, Complaints, Trail Lagos' Multi-Billion Naira Slums Upgrade." *Premium Times*, April 14, 2013. http://premiumtimesng.com/news/129420 -failures-tears-complaints-trail-lagos-multi-billion-naira-slums-upgrade.html.

Ndubuisi Okezie Okeh. "Time to Save Lagos from Environmental Degradation." *allafrica .com*, September 11, 2012. http://allafrica.com/stories/201209110694.html.

Rio de Janeiro

Rio de Janeiro is the second-largest city in Brazil by population, following São Paulo, and the fourth-largest city by population in Latin America after Mexico City, São Paulo, and Buenos Aires. Rio de Janeiro is located on the Atlantic coast of southeastern Brazil, about 200 miles northeast of São Paulo. Its metropolitan-area population is about 12.5 million. It has been an important cultural and political center of Brazil ever since present-day Brazil was conquered by the Portuguese in the 16th century.

The site of present-day Rio de Janeiro was visited by Portuguese mariners beginning in 1502, and the city itself was founded in 1565. Gold and diamonds were

Rio de Janeiro is the second-largest city in Brazil. The annual Carnival celebration, held before Lent, attracts tourists from throughout the world. However, the celebration of Carnival belies the fact that millions of Rio's residents reside in slums and favelas. (Meeds/Dreamstime.com)

discovered in the region surrounding Rio de Janeiro in the 17th century, and the city became the Portuguese colony of Brazil's major seaport. The city also became a major center for the import of African slaves into Brazil. In 1763, Portugal moved its seat of administration from the city of Salvador to the north to Rio de Janeiro. Rio de Janeiro remained the capital of Brazil after the country became independent from Portugal in 1822. It remained Brazil's capital until 1960, when the government relocated the capital to the new interior city of Brasilia.

Rio de Janeiro has experienced steady growth throughout its history. The population is believed to have been about 25,000 in 1750, shortly before the Portuguese made the city Brazil's colonial capital. The population rose to about 110,000 at the time of Brazilian independence in 1822. The Brazilian census of 1890 counted about 520,000 people. The population reached 1 million by 1920 and over 1.7 million by 1940. By that time, the city had begun to expand outward from its historic core along the Atlantic coast. Rio de Janeiro's population reached about 3 million in 1960, when the capital of Brazil was transferred to Brasilia. At the same time, the nearby and more industrialized city of São Paulo grew more rapidly than did Rio de Janeiro, and by this time, its population had eclipsed that of Rio de Janeiro.

Despite the loss of the capital and the increasing primacy of São Paulo, the population of the Rio de Janeiro metropolitan area continued to grow steadily. After the 1960s, most of this growth was concentrated in the suburbs. In the 1960s, about two-thirds of the population of the metropolitan area lived in Rio de Janeiro itself. By 2000, more than half of the region's people lived in suburban areas. Today nearly all of the new growth in the Rio de Janeiro metropolitan area is taking place outside the Rio de Janeiro city limits. Much of Rio de Janeiro's contemporary population growth is the result of rural to urban migration within Brazil, and immigration no longer plays a major role in increasing Brazil's population.

Although Rio de Janeiro today is a major tourist destination and an important high-technology center, it is also notorious for its slums and squatter settlements, which in Brazil are known as *favelas*. As many as one-quarter of Rio de Janeiro's residents live in *favelas* and slums. Recently, *favelas* in and around Rio de Janeiro have emerged as centers for illegal drug trafficking. Air pollution has also increased, and a recent report by the World Health Organization indicated that air pollution levels in Rio de Janeiro now exceed those in New York, London, and Paris. Because Brazil was scheduled to host soccer's World Cup in 2014, and because Rio de Janeiro will host the 2016 Olympic Games, intensive efforts to address social and environmental problems are under way by the government of Brazil before these events take place.

See Also: Brazil; Buenos Aires; Census; London; Mexico City; Migration; New York; Paris; São Paulo; Squatter Settlements

Further Reading

Wendell Cox. "The Evolving Urban Form: Rio de Janeiro." *newgeography.com*, January 30, 2013. http://www.newgeography.com/content/003438-the-evolving-urban-form-rio-de-janeiro.

English News. "Rio More Polluted Than NY, Paris, or London: Study." September 27, 2011. http://news.xinhuanet.com/english2010/health/2011-09/27/c_131162160.htm.

Paris

Paris is the capital, largest city, and primate city of France. Its metropolitan area is the second largest in the European Union following London and the second largest in continental Europe following Moscow. It has been a major global city for hundreds of years. Its metropolitan-area population has been estimated at over 12 million, with about 2.2 million in the city itself.

The modern city of Paris began as a Celtic settlement along the Seine River in about 250 BCE. This settlement was captured by the Roman Empire in 52 BCE and taken over by Germanic tribes during the fourth and fifth centuries CE as the empire collapsed. In 987, the Parisian count Hugh Capet became King of France, establishing the Capetian dynasty and making Paris the capital of the country. Paris has remained the capital of France ever since, with short interruptions during the 14th and 15th centuries.

Paris' population has fluctuated over the course of its history, but in general the city grew between Roman times and the 18th century. Since then, the Paris metropolitan area has grown rapidly. The population of Paris has been estimated at about 250,000 during the early 14th century. However, Paris was affected heavily by numerous epidemics of bubonic plague. Historians believe that as many as 40,000 Parisians succumbed to a plague epidemic in 1466 alone. Nevertheless, Paris recovered. As France became a colonial power in the 16th, 17th, and 18th centuries, Paris' economic and political importance grew, as did its population. The population of Paris has been estimated at about 650,000 during the 1820s and the 1830s and reached a million by the 1850s. In 1860, the city limits of Paris were expanded, and its population grew accordingly to nearly 2 million around 1870.

Population growth in Paris began to slow down in the 20th century. According to the French census, the population of Paris peaked at more than 2.9 million in 1921. It remained stable into the 1960s, and then began to decline until reaching its present level. Suburbanization has been responsible for this decline, and the metropolitan area of Paris continues to grow while the city of Paris itself has been losing population. The metropolitan-area population passed the 6 million mark in the 1960s and has more than doubled in the half century since that time, and less than

20 percent of the residents of the Paris metropolitan area today live in Paris itself. Despite Paris' population decline, the city of Paris proper has one of the highest population densities of any major city in Europe or North America.

Along with London, New York, and Los Angeles, population growth in Paris is driven by immigration from outside France. The greater Paris area contains more than 40 percent of France's immigrant population, and nearly 40 percent of the city of Paris' residents are immigrants or children of immigrants. Many of these immigrants into Paris come from former French colonies, especially in the Middle East and Africa. The countries of Morocco, Algeria, and Tunisia, all of which are former French colonies located across the Mediterranean Sea from France, have sent especially large numbers of immigrants to the Paris region. Many of these immigrants live in poor, isolated suburban areas, some of which are slums with inadequate transportation, schooling, and infrastructure. Political tensions involving immigration intensified following a series of riots taking place in Paris in 2005, and some French political leaders have called for reducing immigration levels and/or expelling immigrants.

Increasing populations throughout metropolitan Paris have also spurred efforts to promote a sustainable environment. Concerted efforts have been made to reduce air pollution by encouraging the use of bicycles and public transportation.

See Also: Black Death; Census; Epidemics; France; London; Los Angeles; Migration; Moscow; New York; Population Density; Primate City

Further Reading

Beryl Magilivy. "Paris Sustainable Development: Much More Than the Environment." *Sustainable Development in the Third Era*, October 12, 2010. http://third-era.net/blog/?p=48.

Amanda Sealy. "African Flavor at the Heart of Paris." *CNN*, November 8, 2012. http://www.cnn.com/2012/11/08/world/europe/paris-africa-culture.

Lahore

Lahore is the second-largest city in Pakistan and the economic and cultural center of northern Pakistan. It is located on the Ravi River, which is a major tributary of the Indus River, in the northeastern part of the country. Lahore is the historic center of the Punjab region of the northwestern portion of the Indian subcontinent, including parts of present-day India as well as present-day Pakistan. The center of Lahore is less than 20 miles from the boundary between Pakistan and India. The population of the Lahore region has been estimated at 11 million.

Lahore's recorded history goes back more than 2,000 years. It is located along the major route of invasion by land into India, which has experienced a long history of invasions from present-day Iran, Turkey, and other areas to the west of South Asia, as well as on important trade routes. Thus Lahore has been a city of considerable strategic importance throughout its history. The present-day city is believed to have been established by Hindu rulers at some time during the first three centuries CE. Over the next 1,500 years, control over Lahore was contested between Hindu, Muslim, Afghan, and Mongol kingdoms. It was absorbed eventually into the Mughal Empire in 1524, but later captured by Sikh forces.

During the 19th century, a Sikh dynasty founded by Maharaja Ranjit Singh assumed control of Lahore. The Sikhs ruled Punjab from Lahore until they were deposed by the British East India Company in 1849. Upon the partition of British India into India and Pakistan in 1947, Lahore became the capital of Punjab Province in Pakistan. Located in a region with substantial Muslim, Hindu, and Sikh populations, however, Lahore became the scene of violent clashes during and after independence. Karachi, located on the Arabian Sea coast and much further away from the Indian border, became Pakistan's capital and soon developed into Pakistan's predominant economic center. However, Lahore has retained its economic and cultural leadership of the Pakistani portion of Punjab. Lahore's status has also been enhanced by the movement of Pakistan's capital from Karachi to the new city of Islamabad, only a hundred miles north of Lahore, in 1966.

Lahore has grown very rapidly throughout the 20th and early 21st centuries as Pakistan has undergone demographic transition. Its population was about 140,000 in the 1880s, and rose to nearly 300,000 in 1921. The first census of independent Pakistan, conducted in 1951, counted about 1.1 million people in Lahore. Since then, Lahore has grown at a faster rate. Its population more than doubled to 2.6 million in 1972 and rose to about 6.3 million in 1998 before passing the 10 million mark by 2010. Thus, Lahore's population has quadrupled over the past 40 years.

Some demographers have predicted that Lahore's population will increase to more than 13 million by 2020. This growth is the result of migration from rural areas as well as from Pakistan's relatively high crude birth rate, which has kept the country well above replacement-level fertility. Most Hindus and Sikhs who had lived in and near Lahore at the time of independence have moved across the international boundary into India, and today nearly 95 percent of Lahore's residents are Muslims.

Lahore faces many issues in adjusting to its rapid population growth. Lahore's air and water are heavily polluted. In 2009, the Pakistani government reported that Lahore was the most polluted city in the country, with particulate levels as much as three times higher than what is considered safe by the World Health Organization. Sewage and waste disposal have become major problems in light of rapid growth and lack of disposal space. Given rapid population growth, the city has not been able to keep up with demand for housing. Some estimates suggest that as many as half of Lahore's people currently live in squatter settlements or slums. Lahore's location near the boundary between Pakistan and India continues to make the city vulnerable to ethnic and political violence. Although Lahore's relatively dry climate has contributed to ongoing water shortages, the region is also subject to frequent flooding and to sometimes devastating earthquakes, and these hazards have also affected planning for Lahore's future.

See Also: Census; Crude Birth Rate; Demographic Transition Model; Demography; India; Iran; Karachi; Pakistan; Replacement-Level Fertility; Squatter Settlements; Turkey

Further Reading

Jason Burke, Issam Ahmed, and Saeed Shah. "Laid-Back Lahore Faces a Frightening Future." *The Guardian*, March 7, 2009. http://www.theguardian.com/world/2009/mar/08/pakistan-lahore-terrorism.

Fareiha Rahman. "Lahore Tops List of Most Polluted Cities." *The Nation* (Pakistan), June 18, 2009. http://www.nation.com.pk/pakistan-news-newspaper-daily-english-online/islamabad/18-Jun-2009/Lahore-tops-list-of-most-polluted-cities.

London

London is the largest city by population in the United Kingdom. Its metropolitan area of 15 million people is the largest by population in the European Union. London is a primate city, and as such it is the political capital of the United Kingdom as well as the country's cultural, economic, and financial center. London has been a very important global city for hundreds of years.

London is located near the head of navigation on the Thames River, which flows into the North Sea opposite continental Europe. It was established on its present site by the Roman Empire, which founded it around 35 BCE and named the settlement Londinium. During the second century CE, the Romans made Londinium their center of administration for the Empire's possessions in Great Britain. At that time, present-day London is believed to have contained about 60,000 residents. After the collapse of the Roman Empire, however, the city experienced several hundred years of decline and stagnation. By the 10th century CE, however, London had grown considerably in economic importance, and it became the political center of Great Britain, whose rulers by this time had united most of England. Nevertheless, London's population has been estimated at only about 20,000 at the beginning of the 12th century.

Over the next 200 years, it grew rapidly at a time when England emerged as an important European power. During the 14th and 15th century, London was affected heavily by epidemics of bubonic plague. However, in the 16th century England

London is Western Europe's largest metropolitan area and a place of great diversity. In 2012, London hosted the Olympic Games. (Robert Nickelsberg/Getty Images)

initiated active efforts to promote colonization outside Europe, and London as the center of the growing British Empire grew rapidly despite a final plague epidemic in the 1630s and the Great London Fire, which destroyed more than half of the city's buildings, in 1666. In the 18th and 19th centuries, London grew quickly again as the center for the British Empire and as one of the birthplaces of the Industrial Revolution. By the late 18th century, Britain had come to dominate the global economy, and as the capital of the empire, London became one of the most important cities in the world as well as one of its largest cities. London also began to expand outside its traditional boundaries, and today a large majority of people residing in the London metropolitan area live outside the traditional city limits.

London's population growth has reflected the increasing political and economic importance of the United Kingdom over the past several hundred years. Historians have estimated that between 50,000 and 100,000 people lived in London in 1500. The population is believed to have reached more than 500,000 in 1700 and nearly 1 million by the early 19th century. At that time, London is believed to have been the only city in the world with a population greater than 1 million. Its population increased fivefold over the course of the 19th century, reaching more than 5.5 million according to the United Kingdom's census of 1891.

The population of London proper continued to increase during the early 20th century. It peaked at 8.6 million in 1931, but dropped below 7 million in the 1980s.

Since then, the city's population has rebounded to more than 8.1 million according to the census of 2011. However, during this same period London's metropolitan area population has grown considerably. In 1891, the population of metropolitan London was about 7.7 million, of whom nearly three-quarters lived in London itself. By 1961, only half of the region's nearly 16 million people resided in London. Today, the city of London contains slightly more than 40 percent of the region's population.

The United Kingdom's rate of natural increase has been negligible in recent years, and London's contemporary growth is fueled entirely by immigration from outside the United Kingdom. As is the case with Los Angeles and other megacities in developed countries, out-migration of native-born citizens of the United Kingdom exceeds in-migration. London's immigrants come from all over the world, making it one of the most diverse cities on the planet. Many immigrants have come from former British colonies including Jamaica and other Caribbean islands, India, Pakistan, and Bangladesh. In recent years, increasing numbers of migrants have moved to London from countries throughout the Middle East. As in the United States, immigration has become a major political issue in the United Kingdom. London has also been plagued in recent years by significant levels of air and water pollution as well as other environmental issues common to very large cities with significant population concentrations.

See Also: Bangladesh; Black Death; Census; India; Los Angeles; Megacities; Migration; Pakistan; Primate City; Rate of Natural Increase; United Kingdom; United States of America

Further Reading

Wendell Cox. "The Evolving Urban Form: London." *newgeography.com*, July 23, 2012. http://www.newgeography.com/content/002970-the-evolving-urban-form-london.

Nick Robinson. "How Has Immigration Changed Britain?" *BBC News*, April 29, 2013. http://www.bbc.co.uk/news/uk-politics-22339080.

John Vidal. "London Air Pollution: Worst in Europe." *The Guardian*, June 25, 2010. http://www.theguardian.com/environment/2010/jun/25/london-air-pollution-europe.

Part IV: Documents

Adam Smith's *The Wealth of Nations*, 1776

Introduction

Adam Smith's classic book The Wealth of Nations, *first published in 1776, presents the intellectual foundations of the modern discipline of economics. In* The Wealth of Nations, *Smith set forth his theory that economic growth results from the actions of rational individuals acting in their own self-interest. Smith's work includes his insights on population and demography:*

Every species of animals naturally multiplies in proportion to the means of their subsistence, and no species can ever multiply beyond it. But in civilized society, it is only among the inferior ranks of people that the scantiness of subsistence can set limits to the further multiplication of the human species; and it can do so in no other way than by destroying a great part of the children which their fruitful marriages produce.

The liberal reward of labour, by enabling them to provide better for their children, and consequently to bring up a greater number, naturally tends to widen and extend those limits. It deserves to be remarked, too, that it necessarily does this as nearly as possible in the proportion which the demand for labour requires. If this demand is continually increasing, the reward of labour must necessarily encourage in such a manner the marriage and multiplication of labourers, as may enable them to supply that continually increasing demand by a continually increasing population. If the reward should at any time be less than what was requisite for this purpose, the deficiency of hands would soon raise it; and if it should at any time be more, their excessive multiplication would soon lower it to this necessary rate. The market would be so much understocked with labour in the one case, and so much overstocked in the other, as would soon force back its price to that proper rate which the circumstances of the society required. It is in this manner that the demand for men, like that for any other commodity, necessarily regulates the production of men, quickens it when it goes on too slowly, and stops it when it advances too fast. . . . The liberal reward of labour, therefore, as it is the effect of increasing wealth, so it is the cause of increasing population. To complain of it, is to lament over the necessary cause and effect of the greatest public prosperity. . . .

In cheap years it is pretended, workmen are generally more idle, and in dear times more industrious than ordinary. A plentiful subsistence, therefore, it has been concluded, relaxes, and a scanty one quickens their industry. That a little more plenty than ordinary may render some workmen idle, cannot be well doubted; but that it should have this effect upon the greater part, or that men in general should work better when they are ill fed, than when they are well fed, when they are disheartened than when they are in good spirits, when they are frequently sick than when they are generally in good health, seems not very probable. Years of dearth, it is to be observed, are generally among the common people years of sickness and mortality, which cannot fail to diminish the produce of their industry.

The high price of [commodities] does not necessarily diminish the ability of the inferior ranks of people to bring up families. Upon the sober and industrious poor, taxes upon such commodities act as sumptuary laws, and dispose them either to moderate, or to refrain altogether from the use of superfluities which they can no longer easily afford. Their ability to bring up families, in consequence of this forced frugality, instead of being diminished, is frequently, perhaps, increased by the tax. It is the sober and industrious poor who generally bring up the most numerous families, and who principally supply the demand for useful labour. All the poor, indeed, are not sober and industrious; and the dissolute and disorderly might continue to indulge themselves in the use of such commodities, after this rise of price, in the same manner as before, without regarding the distress which this indulgence might bring upon their families. Such disorderly persons, however, seldom rear up numerous families, their children generally perishing from neglect, mismanagement, and the scantiness or unwholesomeness of their food. If by the strength of their constitution, they survive the hardships to which the bad conduct of their parents exposes them, yet the example of that bad conduct commonly corrupts their morals; so that, instead of being useful to society by their industry, they become public nuisances by their vices and disorders. Though the advanced price of the luxuries of the poor, therefore, might increase somewhat the distress of such disorderly families, and thereby diminish somewhat their ability to bring up children, it would not probably diminish much the useful population of the country.

Source: Adam Smith. *An Inquiry into the Nature and Causes of the Wealth of Nations*. Edinburgh: Arch. Constable and Company, 1776, 1806.

Thomas Malthus's *Essay on the Principle of Population*, 1798

Introduction

Thomas Malthus's Essay on the Principle of Population, *first published in 1798, has been recognized as a major contribution to the understanding of population and demography ever since. In the* Essay, *Malthus set forth his theory that populations are limited by available resources:*

I said that population, when unchecked, increased in a geometrical ratio, and subsistence for man in an arithmetical ratio. Let us examine whether this position be just. I think it will be allowed, that no state has hitherto existed (at least that we have any account of) where the manners were so pure and simple, and the means of subsistence so abundant, that no check whatever has existed to early marriages, among the lower classes, from a fear of not providing well for their families, or among the higher classes, from a fear of lowering their condition in life. Consequently in no state that we have yet known has the power of population been left to exert itself with perfect freedom. . . .

The way in which these effects are produced seems to be this. We will suppose the means of subsistence in any country just equal to the easy support of its inhabitants. The constant effort towards population, which is found to act even in the most vicious societies, increases the number of people before the means of subsistence are increased. The food therefore which before supported seven millions must now be divided among seven millions and a half or eight millions. The poor consequently must live much worse, and many of them be reduced to severe distress. The number of labourers also being above the proportion of the work in the market, the price of labour must tend toward a decrease, while the price of provisions would at the same time tend to rise. The labourer therefore must work harder to earn the same as he did before. During this season of distress, the discouragements to marriage, and the difficulty of rearing a family are so great that population is at a stand. In the mean time the cheapness of labour, the plenty of labourers, and the necessity of an increased industry amongst them, encourage cultivators to employ more labour upon their land, to turn up fresh soil, and to manure and improve more completely what is already in tillage, till ultimately the means of subsistence become in the same proportion to the population as at the period from which we set out. The situation of the labourer being then again tolerably comfortable, the restraints to population are in some degree loosened, and the same retrograde and progressive movements with respect to happiness are repeated. . . .

The passion between the sexes has appeared in every age to be so nearly the same that it may always be considered, in algebraic language, as a given quantity. The great law of necessity which prevents population from increasing in any country beyond the food which it can either produce or acquire, is a law so open to our view, so obvious and evident to our understandings, and so completely confirmed by the experience of every age, that we cannot for a moment doubt it. The different modes which nature takes to prevent or repress a redundant population do not appear, indeed, to us so certain and regular, but though we cannot always predict the mode we may with certainty predict the fact. If the proportion of births to deaths for a few years indicate an increase of numbers much beyond the proportional increased or acquired produce of the country, we may be perfectly certain that unless an emigration takes place, the deaths will shortly exceed the births; and that the increase that had taken place for a few years cannot be the real average increase of the population of the country. Were there no other depopulating causes, every country would, without doubt, be subject to periodical pestilences or famine.

The only true criterion of a real and permanent increase in the population of any country is the increase of the means of subsistence. But even this criterion is subject to some slight variations which are, however, completely open to our view and observations. In some countries population appears to have been forced, that is, the people have been habituated by degrees to live almost upon the smallest possible quantity of food. There must have been periods in such countries when population increased permanently, without an increase in the means of subsistence. China seems to answer to this description. If the accounts we have of it are to be trusted, the lower classes of people are in the habit of living almost upon the smallest possible quantity of food and are glad to get any putrid offals that European labourers would rather starve than eat. The law in China which permits parents to expose their children has tended principally thus to force the population. A nation in this state must necessarily be subject to famines. Where a country is so populous in proportion to the means of subsistence that the average produce of it is but barely sufficient to support the lives of the inhabitants, any deficiency from the badness of seasons must be fatal. It is probable that the very frugal manner in which the Gentoos are in the habit of living contributes in some degree to the famines of Indostan.

In America, where the reward of labour is at present so liberal, the lower classes might retrench very considerably in a year of scarcity without materially distressing themselves. A famine therefore seems to be almost impossible. It may be expected that in the progress of the population of America, the labourers will in time be much less liberally rewarded. The numbers will in this case permanently increase without a proportional increase in the means of subsistence.

In the different states of Europe there must be some variations in the proportion between the number of inhabitants and the quantity of food consumed, arising from the different habits of living that prevail in each state. The labourers of the South of England are so accustomed to eat fine wheaten bread that they will suffer themselves to be half starved before they will submit to live like the Scotch peasants. They might perhaps in time, by the constant operation of the hard law of necessity, be reduced to live even like the Lower Chinese, and the country would then, with the same quantity of food, support a greater population. But to effect this must always be a most difficult, and, every friend to humanity will hope, an abortive attempt. Nothing is so common as to hear of encouragements that ought to be given to population. If the tendency of mankind to increase be so great as I have represented it to be, it may appear strange that this increase does not come when it is thus repeatedly called for. The true reason is that the demand for a greater population is made without preparing the funds necessary to support it. Increase the demand for agricultural labour by promoting cultivation, and with it consequently increase the produce of the country, and ameliorate the condition of the labourer, and no apprehensions whatever need be entertained of the proportional increase of population. An attempt to effect this purpose in any other way is vicious, cruel, and tyrannical, and in any state of tolerable freedom cannot therefore succeed. It may appear to be the interest of the rulers, and the rich of a state, to force population, and thereby lower the price of labour, and consequently the expense of fleets and armies, and the cost of manufactures for foreign sale; but every attempt of the kind should be carefully watched and strenuously resisted by the friends of the poor, particularly when it comes under the deceitful garb of benevolence, and is likely, on that account, to be cheerfully and cordially received by the common people.

Famine seems to be the last, the most dreadful resource of nature. The power of population is so superior to the power in the earth to produce subsistence for man, that premature death must in some shape or other visit the human race. The vices of mankind are active and able ministers of depopulation. They are the precursors in the great army of destruction; and often finish the dreadful work themselves. But should they fail in this war of extermination, sickly seasons, epidemics, pestilence, and plague, advance in terrific array, and sweep off their thousands and ten thousands. Should success be still incomplete, gigantic inevitable famine stalks in the rear, and with one mighty blow levels the population with the food of the world. . . .

Must it not then be acknowledged by an attentive examiner of the histories of mankind, that in every age and in every state in which man has existed, or does now exist.

That the increase of population is necessarily limited by the means of subsistence.

That population does invariably increase when the means of subsistence increase. And that the superior power of population it repressed, and the actual population kept equal to the means of subsistence, by misery and vice? . . .

It is, undoubtedly, a most disheartening reflection that the great obstacle in the way to any extraordinary improvement in society is of a nature that we can never hope to overcome. The perpetual tendency in the race of man to increase beyond the means of subsistence is one of the general laws of animated nature which we can have no reason to expect will change. Yet, discouraging as the contemplation of this difficulty must be to those whose exertions are laudably directed to the improvement of the human species, it is evident that no possible good can arise from any endeavours to slur it over or keep it in the background. On the contrary, the most baleful mischiefs may be expected from the unmanly conduct of not daring to face truth because it is unpleasing. Independently of what relates to this great obstacle, sufficient yet remains to be done for mankind to animate us to the most unremitted exertion. But if we proceed without a thorough knowledge and accurate comprehension of the nature, extent, and magnitude of the difficulties we have to encounter, or if we unwisely direct our efforts towards an object in which we cannot hope for success, we shall not only exhaust our strength in fruitless exertions and remain at as great a distance as ever from the summit of our wishes, but we shall be perpetually crushed by the recoil of this rock of Sisyphus.

Source: Thomas Malthus. *An Essay on the Principle of Population.* London: Ward, Lock and Co., 1890.

Karl Marx's *Communist Manifesto*, 1848

Introduction

Karl Marx's The Communist Manifesto *was written in collaboration with Friedrich Engels and was first published in 1848. In this book, Marx and Engels examine what they called "class struggle," or evolving relationships between capitalists, who own means of production, and the working class upon whose labor capital depends but which is oppressed by capital. They predicted that the capitalist economic system prevalent at the time would come to be replaced by socialism and eventually by communism. Marx would later set forth these ideas in more detail in* Das Kapital, *the first volume of which was published in 1876.*

In The Communist Manifesto, *Marx analyzed the struggle between capital and labor as it touched upon population change. He argued that population growth forced workers into greater and greater levels of poverty, and would therefore induce workers to rebel against continued exploitation by capitalists:*

Hitherto, every form of society has been based, as we have already seen, on the antagonism of oppressing and oppressed classes. But in order to oppress a class, certain conditions must be assured to it under which it can, at least, continue its slavish existence. The serf, in the period of serfdom, raised himself to membership in the commune, just as the petty bourgeois, under the yoke of the feudal absolutism, managed to develop into a bourgeois. The modern labourer, on the contrary, instead of rising with the process of industry, sinks deeper and deeper below the conditions of existence of his own class. He becomes a pauper, and pauperism develops more rapidly than population and wealth. And here it becomes evident, that the bourgeoisie is unfit any longer to be the ruling class in society, and to impose its conditions of existence upon society as an over-riding law. It is unfit to rule because it is incompetent to assure an existence to its slave within his slavery, because it cannot help letting him sink into such a state, that it has to feed him, instead of being fed by him. Society can no longer live under this bourgeoisie, in other words, its existence is no longer compatible with society.

The essential conditions for the existence and for the sway of the bourgeois class is the formation and augmentation of capital; the condition for capital is wage-labour. Wage-labour rests exclusively on competition between the labourers. The advance of industry, whose involuntary promoter is the bourgeoisie, replaces the isolation of the labourers, due to competition, by the revolutionary combination, due to association. The development of Modern Industry, therefore, cuts from under its feet the very foundation on which the bourgeoisie produces and appropriates products. What the bourgeoisie therefore produces, above all, are its own grave-diggers. Its fall and the victory of the proletariat are equally inevitable. . . .

In proportion as the bourgeoisie, i.e., capital, is developed, in the same proportion is the proletariat, the modern working class, developed—a class of labourers, who live only so long as they find work, and who find work only so long as their labour increases capital. These labourers, who must sell themselves piecemeal, are a commodity, like every other article of commerce, and are consequently exposed to all the vicissitudes of competition, to all the fluctuations of the market.

Owing to the extensive use of machinery, and to the division of labour, the work of the proletarians has lost all individual character, and, consequently, all charm for the workman. He becomes an appendage of the machine, and it is only the most simple, most monotonous, and most easily acquired knack, that is required of him. Hence, the cost of production of a workman is restricted, almost entirely, to the means of subsistence that he requires for maintenance, and for the propagation of his race. But the price of a commodity, and therefore also of labour, is equal to its cost of production. In proportion, therefore, as the repulsiveness of the work increases, the wage decreases. Nay more, in proportion as the use of machinery and division of labour increases, in the same proportion the burden of toil also increases, whether by prolongation of the working hours, by the increase of the work exacted in a given time or by increased speed of machinery, etc.

Modern Industry has converted the little workshop of the patriarchal master into the great factory of the industrial capitalist. Masses of labourers, crowded into the factory, are organised like soldiers. As privates of the industrial army they are placed under the command of a perfect hierarchy of officers and sergeants. Not only are they slaves of the bourgeois class, and of the bourgeois State; they are daily and hourly enslaved by the machine, by the overlooker, and, above all, by the individual bourgeois manufacturer himself. The more openly this despotism proclaims gain to be its end and aim, the more petty, the more hateful and the more embittering it is.

The less the skill and exertion of strength implied in manual labour, in other words, the more modern industry becomes developed, the more is the labour of men superseded by that of women. Differences of age and sex have no longer any distinctive social validity for the working class. All are instruments of labour, more or less expensive to use, according to their age and sex. . . .

The working men have no country. We cannot take from them what they have not got. Since the proletariat must first of all acquire political supremacy, must rise to be the leading class of the nation, must constitute itself *the* nation, it is so far, itself national, though not in the bourgeois sense of the word.

National differences and antagonism between peoples are daily more and more vanishing, owing to the development of the bourgeoisie, to freedom of commerce, to the world market, to uniformity in the mode of production and in the conditions of life corresponding thereto.

The supremacy of the proletariat will cause them to vanish still faster. United action, of the leading civilised countries at least, is one of the first conditions for the emancipation of the proletariat.

In proportion as the exploitation of one individual by another will also be put an end to, the exploitation of one nation by another will also be put an end to. In proportion as the antagonism between classes within the nation vanishes, the hostility of one nation to another will come to an end.

Source: Karl Marx. *Manifesto of the Communist Party*. Translated by Frederick Engels. Chicago: Charles H. Kerr and Company, 1906.

Johnson-Reed Act: Text of Section Establishing Immigration Quotas, 1924

Introduction

Historically, the United States allowed unlimited immigration. However, restrictions on immigration were enacted beginning in the late 19th century. These restrictions culminated in the enactment of the Johnson-Reed Act, which limited immigration especially from eastern and southern Europe by establishing immigration quotas based on the total number of immigrants who had come to the United States historically from each country of origin. The text of that portion of the Immigration Act of 1924, or the Johnson-Reed Act, dealing with the establishment of immigration quotas reads as follows:

The annual quota of any nationality shall be 2 per centum of the number of foreign-born individuals of such nationality resident in continental United States as determined by the United States census of 1890, but the minimum quota of any nationality shall be 100.

(b) The annual quota of any nationality for the fiscal year beginning July 1, 1927, and for each fiscal year thereafter, shall be a number which bears the same ratio to 150,000 as the number of inhabitants in continental United States in 1920 having that national origin (ascertained as hereinafter provided in this section) bears to the number of inhabitants in continental United States in 1920, but the minimum quota of any nationality shall be 100.

(c) For the purpose of subdivision (b) national origin shall be ascertained by determining as nearly as may be, in respect of each geographical area which under section 12 is to be treated as a separate country (except the geographical areas specified in subdivision (c) of section 4) the number of inhabitants in continental United States in 1920 whose origin by birth or ancestry is attributable to such geographical area. Such determination shall not be made by tracing the ancestors or descendants of particular individuals, but shall be based upon statistics of immigration and emigration, together with rates of increase of population as shown by successive decennial United States censuses, and such other data as may be found to be reliable.

(d) For the purpose of subdivisions (b) and (c) the term "inhabitants in continental United States in 1920" does not include (1) immigrants from the geographical areas specified in subdivision (c) of section 4 or their descendants, (2) aliens ineligible to citizenship or their descendants, (3) the descendants of slave immigrants, or (4) the descendants of American aborigines.

(e) The determination provided for in subdivision (c) of this section shall be made by the Secretary of State, the Secretary of Commerce, and the Secretary of Labor, jointly. In making such determination such officials may call for information and expert assistance from the Bureau of the Census. Such officials shall, jointly, report to the President the quota of each nationality, determined as provided in subdivision (b), and the President shall proclaim and make known the quotas so reported. Such proclamation shall be made on or before April 1, 1927. If the proclamation is not made on or before such date, quotas proclaimed therein shall not be in effect for any fiscal year beginning before the expiration of 90 days after the date of the proclamation. After the making of a proclamation under this subdivision the quotas proclaimed therein shall continue with the same effect as if specifically stated herein, and shall be final and conclusive for every purpose except (1) in so far as it is made to appear to the satisfaction of such officials and proclaimed by the President, that an error of fact has occurred in such determination or in such proclamation, or (2) in the case provided for in subdivision (c) of section 12. If for any reason quotas proclaimed under this subdivision are not in effect for any fiscal year, quotas for such year shall be determined under subdivision (a) of this section.

(f) There shall be issued to quota immigrants of any nationality (1) no more immigration visas in any fiscal year than the quota for such nationality, and (2) in any calendar month of any fiscal year no more immigration visas than 10 per centum of the quota for such nationality, except that if such quota is less than 300 the number to be issued in any calendar month shall be prescribed by the Commissioner General, with the approval of the Secretary of Labor, but the total number to be issued during the fiscal year shall not be in excess of the quota for such nationality.

(g) Nothing in this Act shall prevent the issuance (without increasing the total number of immigration visas which may be issued) of an immigration visa to an immigrant as a quota immigrant even though he is a non-quota immigrant.

Source: Excerpt from the Immigration Act of 1924. Pub.L. 68–139, 43 Stat. 153. Full text available at http://tucnak.fsv.cuni.cz/~calda/Documents/1920s/ImmigAct 1924.html.

Immigration and Nationality Act Amendments of 1965: Text of Amendment Eliminating National Immigration Quotas

Introduction

The Immigration and Nationality Act Amendments of 1965 represented a fundamental, comprehensive reform of U.S. law concerning immigration into the United States. The amendments repealed the system of immigration quotas from other countries that had been in place since the Johnson-Reed Act became law in 1924. The amendments resulted in fundamental changes in geographic patterns of international migrant origins and destinations in the United States. The following is part of the text of the amendments:

Be it enacted by the Senate and House of Representatives of the United States of America in Congress assembled:

That section 201 of the Immigration and Nationality Act (66 Stat. 176; 8 U.S.C. 1151) be amended to read as follows:

SEC. 201. (a) Exclusive of special immigrants defined in section 101(a) (27), and of the immediate relatives of United States citizens specified in subsection (b) of this section, the number of aliens who may be issued immigrant visas or who may otherwise acquire the status of an alien lawfully admitted to the United States for permanent residence, or who may, pursuant to section 203(a) (7) enter conditionally, shall not in any of the first three quarters of any fiscal year exceed a total of 45,000 and (ii) shall not in any fiscal year exceed a total of 170,000.

(b) The 'immediate relatives' referred to in subsection (a) of this section shall mean the children, spouses, and parents of a citizen of the United States: Provided: That in the case of parents, such citizen must be at least twenty-one years of age. The immediate relatives specified in this subsection who are otherwise qualified for admission as immigrants shall be admitted as such, without regard to the numerical limitations in this Act.

(c) During the period from July 1, 1965, through June 30, 1968, the annual quota of any quota area shall be the same as that which existed for that area on June 30, 1965. The Secretary of State shall, not later than on the sixtieth day immediately following the date of enactment of this subsection and again on or before September 1, 1966, and September 1, 1967, determine and proclaim the amount of quota numbers which remain unused at the end of the fiscal year ending on June 30, 1965, June 30, 1966, and June 30, 1967, respectively, and are available for distribution pursuant to subsection (d) of this section.

(d) Quota numbers not issued or otherwise used during the previous fiscal year, as determined in accordance with subsection (c) thereof, shall be transferred to an immigration pool. Allocation of numbers from the pool and from national quotas shall not together exceed in any fiscal year the numerical limitations in subsection (a) of this section. The immigration pool shall be made available to immigrants otherwise admissible under the provisions of this Act who are unable to obtain prompt issuance of a preference visa due to oversubscription of their quotas, or subquotas as determined by the Secretary of State. Visas and conditional entries shall be allocated from the immigration pool within the percentage limitations and in the order of priority specified in section 203 without regard to the quota to which the alien is chargeable.

(e) The immigration pool and the quotas of quota areas shall terminate June 30, 1968. Thereafter immigrants admissible under the provisions of this Act who are subject to the numerical limitations of subsection (a) of this section shall be admitted in accordance with the percentage limitations and in the order of priority specified in section 203. . . .

No person shall receive any preference or priority or be discriminated against in the issuance of an immigrant visa because of his race, sex, nationality, place of birth, or place of residence, except as specifically provided in section 101(a) (27), section 201(b), and section 203: Provided, That the total number of immigrant visas and the number of conditional entries made available to natives of any single foreign state under paragraphs (1) through (8) of section 203(a) shall not exceed 20,000 in any fiscal year: Provided further, That the foregoing proviso shall not operate to reduce the number of immigrants who may be admitted under the quota of any quota area before June 30, 1968.

Source: H.R. 2580 (89th): An Act to Amend the Immigration and Nationality Act, and for Other Purposes. 89th Congress, 1965–1966. Text as of October 3, 1965 (Passed Congress/Enrolled Bill). Accessed April 2, 2014. https://www.govtrack.us/congress/bills/89/hr2580/text.

International Adoptions: The Hague Convention, Preamble and Articles 1–5, 1993

Introduction

The Convention on Protection of Children and Co-operation in Respect of Intercountry Adoption is an international agreement whose provisions deal with questions associated with international adoption and child trafficking. The agreement is often referred to as the Hague Convention after the Dutch capital city in which the agreement was negotiated.

As stated in the preamble, the convention is based on the premise that "intercountry adoptions are made in the best interests of the child and with respect for his or her fundamental rights, and to prevent the abduction, the sale of, or traffic in children." The convention specifies procedures and protocols involving international adoptions, including the rights of the child, his or her birth parents, his or her adoptive parents, and the governments of the child's country of birth and country of adoption.

The convention was drafted in 1993 and went into effect on May 1, 1995. As of 2014, 90 countries have ratified the convention. Most of these countries are large and/or developed countries, including the United States, China, India, and members of the European Union.

The first part of the Convention on Protection of Children and Co-operation in Respect of Intercountry Adoption, as concluded on May 29, 1993, reads as follows:

The States signatory to the present Convention, recognising that the child, for the full and harmonious development of his or her personality, should grow up in a family environment, in an atmosphere of happiness, love and understanding,

Recalling that each State should take, as a matter of priority, appropriate measures to enable the child to remain in the care of his or her family of origin,

Recognising that intercountry adoption may offer the advantage of a permanent family to a child for whom a suitable family cannot be found in his or her State of origin,

Convinced of the necessity to take measures to ensure that intercountry adoptions are made in the best interests of the child and with respect for his or her fundamental rights, and to prevent the abduction, the sale of, or traffic in children,

Desiring to establish common provisions to this effect, taking into account the principles set forth in international instruments, in particular the *United Nations Convention on the Rights of the Child*, of 20 November 1989, and the United Nations Declaration on Social and Legal Principles relating to the Protection and Welfare of Children, with Special Reference to Foster Placement and Adoption Nationally and Internationally (General Assembly Resolution 41/85, of 3 December 1986),

Have agreed upon the following provisions—

Chapter 1 – Scope of the Convention
Article 1

The objects of the present Convention are *a)* to establish safeguards to ensure that intercountry adoptions take place in the best interests of the child and with respect for his or her fundamental rights as recognised in international law; *b)* to establish a system of co-operation amongst Contracting States to ensure that those safeguards are respected and thereby prevent the abduction, the sale of, or traffic in children; *c)* to secure the recognition in Contracting States of adoptions made in accordance with the Convention.

Article 2

(1) The Convention shall apply where a child habitually resident in one Contracting State ("the State of origin") has been, is being, or is to be moved to another Contracting State ("the receiving State") either after his or her adoption in the State of origin by spouses or a person habitually resident in the receiving State, or for the purposes of such an adoption in the receiving State or in the State of origin.
(2) The Convention covers only adoptions which create a permanent parent-child relationship.

Article 3

The Convention ceases to apply if the agreements mentioned in Article 17, subparagraph *c*, have not been given before the child attains the age of eighteen years.

Chapter II – Requirements for Intercountry Adoptions
Article 4

An adoption within the scope of the Convention shall take place only if the competent authorities of the State of origin—

a) have established that the child is adoptable;
b) have determined, after possibilities for placement of the child within the State of origin have been given due consideration, that an intercountry adoption is in the child's best interests;
c) have ensured that
  (1) the persons, institutions and authorities whose consent is necessary for adoption, have been counselled as may be necessary and duly informed of the effects of their consent, in particular whether or not an adoption will result in the termination of the legal relationship between the child and his or her family of origin,
  (2) such persons, institutions and authorities have given their consent freely, in the required legal form, and expressed or evidenced in writing,
  (3) the consents have not been induced by payment or compensation of any kind and have not been withdrawn, and
  (4) the consent of the mother, where required, has been given only after the birth of the child; and
d) have ensured, having regard to the age and degree of maturity of the child, that
  (1) he or she has been counselled and duly informed of the effects of the adoption and of his or her consent to the adoption, where such consent is required,
  (2) consideration has been given to the child's wishes and opinions,
  (3) the child's consent to the adoption, where such consent is required, has been given freely, in the required legal form, and expressed or evidenced in writing, and
  (4) such consent has not been induced by payment or compensation of any kind.

Article 5

An adoption within the scope of the Convention shall take place only if the competent authorities of the receiving State—

a) have determined that the prospective adoptive parents are eligible and suited to adopt;
b) have ensured that the prospective adoptive parents have been counselled as may be necessary; and
c) have determined that the child is or will be authorised to enter and reside permanently in that State.

Source: Hague Conference on Private International Law. "33: Convention of 29 May 1993 on Protection of Children and Cooperation in Respect of Intercountry

Adoption." Accessed April 2, 2014. http://www.hcch.net/index_en.php?act= conventions.text&cid=69. (Text of entire Convention, including a total of 37 articles.)

Genocide: The Eight Stages of Genocide, 1998

Introduction

Genocide is the systematic extermination of members of particular ethnic, religious, or national communities. But how are instances of genocide identified? How can genocide be prevented? In 1998, Gregory H. Stanton, the president of Genocide Watch, prepared an analysis of these questions called "The Eight Stages of Genocide." Mr. Stanton's remarks, which are cited on Genocide Watch's Web site, are as follows:

Genocide is a process that develops in eight stages that are predictable but not inexorable. At each stage, preventive measures can stop it. The process is not linear. Logically, later stages must be preceded by earlier stages. But all stages continue to operate throughout the process.

1. CLASSIFICATION: All cultures have categories to distinguish people into "us and them" by ethnicity, race, religion, or nationality: German and Jew, Hutu and Tutsi. Bipolar societies that lack mixed categories, such as Rwanda and Burundi, are the most likely to have genocide. The main preventive measure at this early stage is to develop universalistic institutions that transcend ethnic or racial divisions, that actively promote tolerance and understanding, and that promote classifications that transcend the divisions. The Catholic church could have played this role in Rwanda, had it not been riven by the same ethnic cleavages as Rwandan society. Promotion of a common language in countries like Tanzania has also promoted transcendent national identity. This search for common ground is vital to early prevention of genocide.

2. SYMBOLIZATION: We give names or other symbols to the classifications. We name people "Jews" or "Gypsies," or distinguish them by colors or dress; and apply the symbols to members of groups. Classification and symbolization are universally human and do not necessarily result in genocide unless they lead to the next stage, dehumanization. When combined with hatred, symbols may be forced upon unwilling members of pariah groups: the yellow star for Jews under Nazi rule, the blue scarf for people from the Eastern Zone in Khmer Rouge Cambodia. To combat symbolization, hate symbols can be legally forbidden

(swastikas) as can hate speech. Group marking like gang clothing or tribal scarring can be outlawed, as well. The problem is that legal limitations will fail if unsupported by popular cultural enforcement. Though Hutu and Tutsi were forbidden words in Burundi until the 1980s, code-words replaced them. If widely supported, however, denial of symbolization can be powerful, as it was in Bulgaria, where the government refused to supply enough yellow badges and at least eighty percent of Jews did not wear them, depriving the yellow star of its significance as a Nazi symbol for Jews.

3. DEHUMANIZATION: One group denies the humanity of the other group. Members of it are equated with animals, vermin, insects or diseases. Dehumanization overcomes the normal human revulsion against murder. At this stage, hate propaganda in print and on hate radios is used to vilify the victim group. In combating this dehumanization, incitement to genocide should not be confused with protected speech. Genocidal societies lack constitutional protection for countervailing speech, and should be treated differently than democracies. Local and international leaders should condemn the use of hate speech and make it culturally unacceptable. Leaders who incite genocide should be banned from international travel and have their foreign finances frozen. Hate radio stations should be shut down, and hate propaganda banned. Hate crimes and atrocities should be promptly punished.

4. ORGANIZATION: Genocide is always organized, usually by the state, often using militias to provide deniability of state responsibility (the Janjaweed in Darfur). Sometimes organization is informal (Hindu mobs led by local RSS militants) or decentralized (terrorist groups). Special army units or militias are often trained and armed. Plans are made for genocidal killings. To combat this stage, membership in these militias should be outlawed. Their leaders should be denied visas for foreign travel. The UN should impose arms embargoes on governments and citizens of countries involved in genocidal massacres, and create commissions to investigate violations, as was done in post-genocide Rwanda.

5. POLARIZATION: Extremists drive the groups apart. Hate groups broadcast polarizing propaganda. Laws may forbid intermarriage or social interaction. Extremist terrorism targets moderates, intimidating and silencing the center. Moderates from the perpetrators' own group are most able to stop genocide, so are the first to be arrested and killed. Prevention may mean security protection for moderate leaders or assistance to human rights groups. Assets of extremists may be seized, and visas for international travel denied to them. Coups d'état by extremists should be opposed by international sanctions.

6. PREPARATION: Victims are identified and separated out because of their ethnic or religious identity. Death lists are drawn up. Members of victim groups are forced to wear identifying symbols. Their property is expropriated. They are

often segregated into ghettos, deported into concentration camps, or confined to a famine-struck region and starved. At this stage, a Genocide Emergency must be declared. If the political will of the great powers, regional alliances, or the UN Security Council can be mobilized, armed international intervention should be prepared, or heavy assistance provided to the victim group to prepare for its self-defense. Otherwise, at least humanitarian assistance should be organized by the UN and private relief groups for the inevitable tide of refugees to come.

7. EXTERMINATION begins, and quickly becomes the mass killing legally called "genocide." It is "extermination" to the killers because they do not believe their victims to be fully human. When it is sponsored by the state, the armed forces often work with militias to do the killing. Sometimes the genocide results in revenge killings by groups against each other, creating the downward whirlpool-like cycle of bilateral genocide (as in Burundi). At this stage, only rapid and overwhelming armed intervention can stop genocide. Real safe areas or refugee escape corridors should be established with heavily armed international protection. (An unsafe "safe" area is worse than none at all.) The UN Standing High Readiness Brigade, EU Rapid Response Force, or regional forces—should be authorized to act by the UN Security Council if the genocide is small. For larger interventions, a multilateral force authorized by the UN should intervene. If the UN is paralyzed, regional alliances must act. It is time to recognize that the international responsibility to protect transcends the narrow interests of individual nation states. If strong nations will not provide troops to intervene directly, they should provide the airlift, equipment, and financial means necessary for regional states to intervene.

8. DENIAL is the eighth stage that always follows a genocide. It is among the surest indicators of further genocidal massacres. The perpetrators of genocide dig up the mass graves, burn the bodies, try to cover up the evidence and intimidate the witnesses. They deny that they committed any crimes, and often blame what happened on the victims. They block investigations of the crimes, and continue to govern until driven from power by force, when they flee into exile. There they remain with impunity, like Pol Pot or Idi Amin, unless they are captured and a tribunal is established to try them. The response to denial is punishment by an international tribunal or national courts. There the evidence can be heard, and the perpetrators punished. Tribunals like the Yugoslav or Rwanda Tribunals, or an international tribunal to try the Khmer Rouge in Cambodia, or an International Criminal Court may not deter the worst genocidal killers. But with the political will to arrest and prosecute them, some may be brought to justice.

Environmental Refugees: Living Space for Environmental Refugees (LiSER)— Mission Statement, 2002

Introduction

Global climate change and other changes in the global environment associated with human activity are likely to force as many as several hundred million people through-out the world to move within the coming decades. For example, global warming and the associated melting of glaciers at high latitudes are likely to cause increases in sea levels, which in turn will result in the flooding of coastal areas. Residents of these cities would be forced to abandon their homes and livelihoods and to move inland. Such potential migrants are known as environmental refugees. Most environmental refugees are concentrated in crowded, impoverished, and less developed countries such as Bangladesh that are already experiencing major problems in coping with growing populations.

Living Space for Environmental Refugees (LiSER) is a nongovernmental organization that is dedicated to raising awareness of problems faced by environmental refugees, at present and in the future. The following is LiSER's mission statement:

More often we read about people getting in trouble because their livelihood has been damaged due to natural or human causes. We see people sitting on the roofs of their houses, or in the tops of trees trying to escape rising water; people under the remains of their houses after an earthquake; people who become disabled for the rest of their life due to a nuclear disaster.

The number of incidents that cause people to flee from environmental problems is increasing rapidly. In 1999, Mr. Serageldin, chairman of the World Water Council, already stated that more people flee due to environmental problems than due to war. At that moment he estimated the number of environmental refugees to be 25 million and he estimated the number to be quadrupled for 2005.

Despite the huge number of people involved, there is no single organisation that focuses explicitly on the problems of—nor offers help to—these refugees, who we define as environmental refugees.

Who are we? We are an organisation called LiSER, an organisation that focuses on the identification and recognition of environmental refugees. In this leaflet we will explain who are the environmental refugees and why they deserve our explicit attention.

The UNEP, the environmental program of the United Nations, defines environmental refugees: "as those people who have been forced to leave their traditional habitat, temporarily or permanently, because of a marked environmental disruption (natural and/or triggered by people) that jeopardized their existence and/or seriously affected the quality of their life." By 'environmental disruption' is meant any physical, chemical and/or biological changes in the ecosystem (or the resource base) that render it temporarily or permanently, unsuitable to support human life. (Environmental Refugees, Essam El-Hinnawi, UNEP, 1985)

There can be a number of reasons for the deterioration of a specific environment. One can think of natural causes like hurricanes, thunderstorms, volcanic eruptions, earthquakes, etc. Other causes of deterioration are purely human-induced, for instance logging of tropical rain forests, construction of (river)dams, nuclear disasters, environmental pollution, and (biological) warfare. But very often a disaster can be a combination of human and natural factors, such as floods or drought due to extreme weather events, extreme climate events or global warming.

After some disasters, such as large scale flooding, people can return to their habitat and start rehabilitation and reconstruction; very often with a future flood as a possibility. Other disasters create permanent displacement as in the case of the construction of an electric power dam in a river valley. Sometimes—for instance after a period of drought—the displaced people indeed can go back to their original livelihoods, but in fact without any prospects for the future. Environmental refugees are not only deprived of opportunities for the future but usually also from legislative recognition and support.

The international refugee legislation is fifty years old and originally was meant for the huge number of displaced people after World War II. The Treaty of Geneva, dealing with refugees, has a number of criteria to define the status of a refugee. Only persons with a well-founded fear of persecution due to their race, religion, nationality, political convictions or social class, are considered to be 'refugees' and are granted the rights that belong to this status. The main conditions are that a person finds himself in a foreign country and does not have legal protection in the country of his nationality.

In 2010, people are on the move for other reasons than just war or violence. At this moment the international law does not yet recognise such reasons. This means that in many cases environmental refugees can not count on any material or juridical support.

LiSER foundation was founded in 2002 because, despite the huge numbers of environmental refugees, there is no organisation that focuses on environmental refugees world-wide.

Environmental refugees are often not labelled as such, and are not recognised by the general public. The main reasons for the lack of attention are the different reasons for environmental degradation, the vast variety of periods for which persons stay environmental refugees, and the needs of the people involved. Furthermore, the causes and consequences of an environmental disaster might lie far away from each other, in time as well as in space. Very often, one can not pinpoint a single and clear cause for the disaster. In some cases it is impossible to pinpoint the responsible persons.

LiSER was founded by people who are involved in refugee care, environmental organisations, human rights organisations and development agencies. The main goal of LiSER is to see these various organisations join together by broadening their original working goals and mandate to environmental refugees.

LiSER wants to enforce the material and juridical position of environmental refugees. Firstly, LiSER focuses on these refugees who lack any means or possibilities to rebuild their own subsistence.

For the near future we have the following objectives:

- an analysis of the problems of environmental refugees: who is involved, how many are involved, what are their main needs, etc.
- to enforce the juridical position of the environmental refugees where ever they are.
- putting the issue of environmental refugees on the agenda of refugee care organisations, environmental organisations, human rights organisations and the development agencies.

Source: LiSER Mission Statement. Established in 2002. Available at: http://www.liser.eu/.

One-Child Policy: Testimony of U.S. Assistant Secretary of State Arthur Dewey Concerning China's One-Child Policy, 2004

Introduction

The United States has opposed the implementation of China's one-child population policy, and in particular those aspects of the one-child policy that are associated with abortion (particularly forced or sex-selective abortion) and with compulsory sterilization. With respect to these issues, Arthur Dewey, director of the U.S. State

Department's Bureau of Population, Refugees, and Migration, testified before the House International Relations Committee on December 14, 2004. What follows is the text of Secretary Dewey's remarks:

In 2002, I began a dialogue with China regarding its birth planning law. We have had six rounds of discussions on this important issue, the most recent in early November when I traveled to Beijing to meet with senior Chinese officials to press for reforms. In all of our conversations with our Chinese counterparts, we laid out our understanding, based on the Universal Declaration of Human Rights, as well as the 1994 Cairo Declaration on Population and Development, that there should be no coercion, in any form, in any nation's population policies.

We made measurable progress in these negotiations, but fell short in getting the coercive measures lifted, which would have permitted resumption of UNFPA funding. We believe China's population policies, including the so-called "one-child" policy, are undergoing an assessment and evaluation with the Chinese leadership. The Chinese Government, in our view, may be beginning to understand that its coercive birth planning regime has had extremely negative social, economic, and human rights consequences for the nation.

In our two years of negotiations, we have seen encouraging movement in China's approach to population issues, and the reduction of coercion in birth planning programs. For example, provincial legislation in 25 of China's 31 provinces, municipalities, and autonomous regions, has been amended to eliminate the requirement that married couples must obtain government permission ("birth permits") before the woman becomes pregnant.

This may prove to be an important change. Without birth permits there may be no effective overall mechanism for systematically enforcing birth targets and quotas in each county. We hope that the elimination of this repressive mechanism of control and interference in family life will be extended throughout all of China, and, as I have said, we will be monitoring this issue very closely.

The Chinese Government has also started a new government public information pilot project to highlight the status of the girl child. This could be an important step for human rights in eliminating discrimination against women and girls in China. Such an effort responds to the continuing reports of sex selective abortions in China and abandonment of girl babies, horrific behaviors that result from the devastating combination of the one-child policy and traditional son preference. Respect for the inherent worth and human dignity of the girl child, from conception through adulthood, is an essential element of a just society. This initiative is only a small step forward, but it does indicate some acknowledgement that the birth planning regime has resulted in very negative outcomes.

The one-child policy has certainly contributed to the stark gender imbalance in China, which, according to the 2000 census, was about 117 males to 100 females.

For second births, the national ratio was about 152 to 100. Moreover, China's aging population and rising ratio of dependent to wage-earning adults pose tremendous challenges for the country. The lack of effective pension and social welfare systems for senior citizens results in a growing burden on China's working age population. Many Chinese "one-child" couples, lacking siblings, are hard-pressed to support two sets of aging parents.

Also of note, under the national birth planning law, Chinese citizens—in theory—have the ability under the Administrative Procedures Law to sue officials who violate their "family planning rights." The government has established a "hotline" for citizens to report abusive family planning practices to the federal authorities. We are gathering information on use of this hotline, and its effectiveness in dealing with alleged abuses. I want to emphasize that it is the practical implementation of these measures that matters, not public pronouncements.

In addition, the Chinese authorities I met with last month emphatically declared the end of any health and education penalties for "out-of-plan" children, such as higher school tuition fees. These children are no longer to be treated as second-class citizens. We will be watching closely to see if this is implemented, and to the extent that it is, this would be a very welcome development indeed.

Yet, let me be clear. China's birth planning law and policies retain harshly coercive elements in law and practice. Forced abortion and sterilization are egregious violations of human rights, and should be of concern to the global human rights community, as well as to the Chinese themselves. Unfortunately, we have not seen willingness in other parts of the international community to stand with us on these human rights issues.

In our discussions with the Chinese government, we have urged them to implement fully the principle recognized in the Program of Action of the International Conference on Population and Development, the ICPD, that couples, not governments, should decide the number and spacing of their children. On many occasions, the Chinese authorities have professed great commitment to the ICPD. Such statements, no matter how fervent or how frequent, will ring hollow and will be little more than empty rhetoric until that day when Chinese birth planning programs become Chinese family planning programs, fully voluntary and free of all forms of coercion.

A national Law on Population and Birth Planning went into effect on September 1, 2002. The law provides that the state shall employ measures to place population growth under control, improve the quality of the population, and conduct birth planning. The law requires married couples to employ birth control measures. While provinces have some latitude in how they implement certain aspects of the law, it also requires counties to use specific measures to limit the total number of births in each county.

The law grants married couples the right to have a single child and allows eligible couples to apply for permission to have a second child if they meet conditions stipulated in local and provincial regulations. Many provincial regulations require women to wait four years or more after their first birth before making such an application. These regulations also prohibit single women who become pregnant from giving birth, but enforcement of this prohibition reportedly varies widely throughout China.

The law specifies a number of birth limitation measures by the government that amount to coercion. Party members and civil servants who parent an "out-of-plan" child are very likely to face administrative sanction, including job loss or demotion. Couples who give birth to an unapproved child are likely to be assessed a social compensation fee, which can range from one-half the local average annual household income to as much as ten times that level.

As social compensation fee policies are set at the provincial level, and implemented locally, we understand enforcement varies greatly, with some areas waiving or greatly reducing the fees, and others imposing them at a high level. The Chinese have changed the national law so that any fees collected now go to national, not local authorities. We are told that this step has been taken to reduce the extensive corruption that had been associated with the collection of these fees. Some Chinese authorities would like to see an end to the social compensation fees, recognizing their coercive nature, and witnessing that they are especially burdensome on the poor, while more affluent citizens simply pay the fee and have additional children.

Nonetheless, as we have noted in our Human Rights Report, the social compensation fees remain a harsh and effective enforcement tool. During "unauthorized pregnancies," women are sometimes visited by birth planning workers who use the threat of the social compensation fees to pressure women to terminate their pregnancies. In many cases, these penalties and the level of harassment from officials leave women little practical alternative but to undergo abortion and therefore these fees, and related punitive measures, amount to a program of coercive abortion.

And in circumstances when social compensation fees and intense psychological and social pressure are not sufficient to compel women to have an abortion, there are reports, albeit declining, of instances where the authorities have physically forced a woman to terminate a pregnancy.

Finally, I would also like to raise the problem of forced and coerced sterilization. Forced sterilizations continue to occur, most frequently when couples have more children than the allowable number. Women may be allowed to carry the "excess" child to term, but then one member of a couple is strongly pressured to be sterilized. In some cases, they may be asked to go to a hospital under other pretenses, or sterilized without consent. Additionally, if doctors find that a couple is at risk of transmitting disabling congenital defects to their children, the couple may marry only if they agree to use birth control or undergo sterilization.

I want to assure Members that we will continue to seek engagement with the Chinese authorities on these difficult and important issues. Our embassy in Beijing and our consulates throughout China track developments in this area very closely. We will continue to urge China to move to a human rights based approach to population issues.

Source: Arthur E. Dewey. "One-Child Policy in China." U.S. Department of State. Testimony before the House International Relations Committee, Washington, DC, December 14, 2004. Accessed April 2, 2014. http://2001-2009.state.gov/g/prm/rls/39823.htm.

One-Child Policy: 2008 Report of the U.S. Congressional-Executive Committee on China on Population Planning

Introduction

The United States has continued to express its concern about China's one-child policy. In order to coordinate the policy position of the U.S. government on this question, the United States Congressional-Executive Committee on China on Population Planning has been established. The committee issued a report on China's population policy in 2008, including the following section entitled "Population Planning":

The Chinese government announced that parents who lost an only child in the May 2008 Sichuan earthquake would be permitted to have another child if they applied for a government-issued certificate. The National Population and Family Planning Commission (NPFPC) issued a directive imposing higher "social compensation fees" levied according to income on couples who violate the one-child rule. Under the directive, urban families who violate the one-child rule risk having officials apply negative marks on financial credit records.

Reports of forced abortions, forced sterilizations, and police beatings related to population planning policies continued. In some areas, government campaigns to forcibly sterilize women who have more than one female child included government payments to informants.

Public debate about the continued necessity of the one-child policy reportedly prompted the NPFPC minister to issue a statement that China would "by no means waver" in its population planning policies for "at least the next decade."

RECOMMENDATIONS

Urge Chinese officials to cease all coercive measures, including forced abortion and sterilization, to enforce birth control quotas. Urge the Chinese government to dismantle its system of coercive population controls, while funding programs that inform Chinese officials of the importance of respecting citizens' diverse beliefs.

Urge Chinese officials to promptly release Chen Guangcheng, imprisoned in Linyi city, Shandong province, after exposing forced sterilizations, forced abortions, beatings, and other abuses carried out by Linyi population planning officials.

Encourage Chinese officials to permit greater public discussion and debate concerning population planning policies and to demonstrate greater responsiveness to public concerns. Impress upon China's leaders the importance of promoting legal aid and training programs that help citizens pursue compensation and other remedies against the state for injury suffered as a result of official abuse related to China's population planning policies. Provisions in China's law on state compensation provide for such remedies for citizens subject to abuse and personal injury by administrative officials, including population planning officials. Provide funding and support for the development of programs and international cooperation in this area.

Source: Congressional-Executive Committee on China, "2008 Annual Report," Section II, section entitled "Population Planning." The complete text of the annual report can be accessed at http://www.cecc.gov/publications/annual-reports/2008-annual-report.

World Refugee Day: Remarks of U.S. Secretary of State John Kerry at the World Refugee Event, June 20, 2013

Introduction

World Refugee Day is celebrated throughout the world on June 20 of each year. The United States and many other countries organize annual events commemorating World Refugee Day, and in doing so call attention to issues faced by the millions of refugees displaced from their home countries as a result of political and/or religious persecution. On June 20, 2013, U.S. Secretary of State John Kerry spoke at the World

Refugee Day Event sponsored by the Department of State. In his comments, Secretary of State Kerry discussed the history of United States policy concerning refugees, U.S. efforts to help refugees, and the continuing problems faced by refugees throughout the world. The text of Kerry's remarks reads, in part:

Today is just the 12th official World Refugee Day, but I'm proud to say that in the United States of America, our country has had a tradition of welcoming the "huddled masses yearning to breathe free," and it runs deep in our roots. I think it's safe to say it's part of our DNA as Americans, and we're proud of that.

Roughly 150 years before the American Revolution took place and 400 years before the Statue of Liberty first stood up in New York Harbor to welcome people, a fellow by the name of John Winthrop came to this land as a Puritan refugee from England with a group of refugees on a sail vessel, the *Arabella*.

And he crossed the Atlantic. Before he arrived in Boston Harbor, he delivered a very well-known sermon, envisioning the colony they were going to create there as this "City Upon a Hill," words that have been well quoted now by President Kennedy initially and President Reagan subsequently. He challenged the congregation that came over with him to serve as a model of justice and tolerance because, as he said, "the eyes of all people are upon us."

Well, I would say to you today that they still are. The eyes of all people are upon us. And opening our docks and our doors to refugees has been part of the great tradition of our country. It defines us. It really is who we are. Most people came to this country at one point or another from another place.

And I think it's safe to say that as we look at the world today and we consider where the High Commissioner is today, this challenge is as great as ever. Nearly 1.6 million people are now refugees out of Syria, a very significant portion of them in Jordan, where the High Commissioner is now. He will tell you, as I have experienced in my trips to Jordan, the profound impact that these refugees have on a community when they come there.

Many of them are not in the camps; they're just in the general population and they seek employment, or they rent an apartment, 10 of them to the apartment, all contributing to the rent, which raises rents, which produces pressure on other people within the normal Jordanian course of life. That has an impact on Jordanian citizens; it has an impact on the politics.

In addition to that, they go to work or try to go to work. And because they're desperate to go to work, they work for less money. In working for less money, they lower wages, and that has a social impact on the rest of the community.

So there are profound impacts from refugees. And obviously we live in a world today where not all refugees are refugees as a consequence of revolution or war and violence. We have refugees because they can't find water. We have refugees because of climate change. We have refugees who are driven out by drought and the lack of food, who move accordingly because they want to be able to live.

And today we see refugees in so many new parts of the world. We see refugees in Mali, in the mountains of Burma, and in many other places. It's fair to say that as we gather here for this 12th occasion, the eyes of some 46 million displaced people around the world are upon us. And we need to be able to look back at them with the knowledge that we are doing everything that is possible to try to help.

The challenge is immense. We just put an additional huge amount of money into Syria. And I think it's safe to say that everybody comes to this table committed to try to do everything in our power to live up to our values and to meet the needs. The State Department, USAID, our partners in the U.S. Government, the United Nations, nonprofits around the world, faith-based groups, humanitarian organizations—all of them try to come together in order to try to live up to our common values.

And we don't do this just because we're trying to keep faith with the past; it's because working to resolve this issue is critical to our future. And I think it's vital to our nation's strategic interest. It's also the right thing to do.

When the stakes are high, you need to up your game, and I'm proud to say that the United States is trying to do that. Today, I announced that we are nearly doubling our contributions this year to the UNHCR. We are giving to the High Commission on Refugees a $415 million commitment that brings our 2013 total to $890 million. And I'm proud to say to you that that makes the United States of America the largest single contributor in the world. We provide more aid to the UNHCR than any other country and more than the next six countries combined. Americans should be proud of that.

What does this provide? This funding provides clean water, provides shelter, provides medicine to families around the globe. It tries to provide them with the ability to be able to survive day to day, from Afghanistan, Ecuador, from Burma to the Democratic Republic of the Congo. This funding will advance our efforts on behalf of those who simply cannot defend themselves, including the elderly and the disabled. It will help to continue all of the programs to protect women and girls from abuse and exploitation and to aid the victims of gender-based violence. And we make this investment because it makes a real difference in the lives of fellow human beings.

Source: John Kerry. "Remarks at the World Refugee Day Event." Benjamin Franklin Room, Washington, DC, June 20, 2013. U.S. Department of State. Accessed April 4, 2014. http://www.state.gov/secretary/remarks/2013/06/210935.htm.

International Migrants Day: Remarks by the Director of the U.S. Bureau of Population, Refugees, and Migration on International Migrants Day, December 18, 2013

Introduction

What follows is the text of remarks made by Anne Richard, the assistant secretary of state for Population, Refugees, and Migration Affairs and director of the Bureau of Population, Refugees, and Migration on December 18, 2013. Richard's remarks were delivered on International Migrants Day. In her comments, which are entitled "Migrants Need Protecting," Richard notes how international migration has benefited the United States and other countries. Yet she points out the lack of "international frameworks or standards to assist [international migrants] when crisis hits."

They are scattered around the world, but they are valuable members of their communities. They are often absent, but their efforts mean families can build houses, put children through school, and pay for medical care. And despite the billions of dollars they send home, they are often the last people to be helped when—after all they have sacrificed—crisis hits.

These are the world's migrants, and today there are 232 million of them across the world, enough people to populate the world's fifth-largest country. Their remittances, totaling nearly $550 billion in 2013, would power an economy greater than Norway's or Sweden's. But when they go abroad to work and crisis hits, who is responsible for them?

The answer to that question is not clear, as was made tragically obvious during and after the political instability in Libya in 2011. Hundreds of thousands of migrant workers found themselves stranded with no options in that country after they were cut loose by their employers and left homeless, exposed to exploitation, and without assistance or recourse from either their employers, governments, or the Libyan authorities.

Why was this so? Because even as migrants have come to play an increasingly important role in the global economy, there are few international frameworks or standards to assist them when crisis hits.

Today is the UN's International Migrants Day, held on December 18 each year to recognize the efforts, contributions, and rights of migrants worldwide. It's a day to highlight the urgent need for countries to put protections in place for these people.

The United States recognizes the important contribution migration has played in our own economy. As President Obama said, the steady stream of hardworking and talented people who have immigrated to the United States over the years "has made the United States the engine of the global economy and a beacon of hope around the world."

Former President George W. Bush agreed: "One of the primary reasons America became a great power in the 20th century is because we welcomed the talent and the character and the patriotism of immigrant families."

While we sometimes only focus on the negative aspects of migration like brain drain and divided families, the reality is that migration drives economic development in both countries of origin and destination. Countries with aging populations and falling birth rates have come to rely on labor provided by the hardworking citizens from around the world.

But alongside these benefits, there are important risks to the individuals who travel abroad for work. In addition to the crisis in Libya, nearly every crisis—including Hurricane Sandy in the United States—has left many migrants struggling and stranded.

This is because when crisis hits, sending countries often have not put resources and systems in place to assist their citizens abroad, while receiving countries themselves are struggling to assist their own citizens.

How can migrants be better protected? This was the key question discussed at the UN High Level Dialogue on Migration and Development held in October this year in New York. One outcome was the announcement that the United States and the Philippines, in partnership with other governments, international organizations, and civil society groups, would lead an initiative to address this challenge.

The overarching goal of the initiative is to generate a set of guidelines to improve the ability of states and others to protect migrants caught in countries in acute crisis. The key will be for both the sending and receiving countries to put specific measures and resources in place to help these individuals when disaster strikes.

It will not be an easy effort, and it will likely take years to complete—for that reason countries should begin taking their own actions now, such as by requiring employers to assist in crisis, creating contingency plans with international organizations such as the International Organization for Migration, and giving their embassies specific responsibilities to help their migrant communities.

The effort will be worth it. The millions of people helping drive global development deserve no less.

Source: Anne C. Richard. "Migrants Need Protecting." Bureau of Population, Refugees, and Migration, U.S. Department of State. Op-Ed for International Migrants Day, December 18, 2013, Washington, DC. Accessed April 2, 2014. http://www .state.gov/j/prm/releases/remarks/2013/219010.htm.

Climate Change and Population: Remarks of U.S. Secretary of State John Kerry in Jakarta, Indonesia, February 16, 2014

Introduction

The international community is coming to recognize that climate change has created increasing threats to populations throughout the world. Some of these threats are direct. For example, global sea level rise is likely to displace millions of people who live in low-lying areas as environmental refugees, especially in less developed countries such as Bangladesh. Other threats are more indirect. Climate change is likely to affect agriculture and food production. Droughts, severe storms, and other natural disasters may also threaten millions of people, with potentially devastating impacts on food supplies and increasing the likelihood of famine, especially in less developed countries with their growing populations. On February 16, 2014, U.S. secretary of state John Kerry addressed these issues in a speech given in Jakarta, Indonesia. In his comments, Secretary Kerry called for awareness and global understanding of the problems associated with climate change, called attention to the possibility of technological advances that could help to alleviate these impacts, and called for international cooperation to mitigate climate change issues. The following is excerpted from Secretary Kerry's remarks:

[The] results of our human activity are clear. If you ranked all the years in recorded history by average temperature, you'd see that 8 of the 10 hottest years have all happened within the last 10 years. Think about it this way: all 10 of the hottest years on record have actually happened since Google went online in 1998. Now, that's how fast this change is happening. And because the earth is getting hotter at such an alarming speed, glaciers in places like the Arctic are melting into the sea faster than we expected. And the sea is rising—slowly, but rising—and will rise to dangerous levels. Scientists now predict that by the end of the century, the sea could rise by a full meter. Now, I know that to some people a meter may not sound like a lot, but I'll tell you this: it's enough to put half of Jakarta underwater. Just one meter would displace hundreds of millions of people worldwide and threaten billions of dollars in economic activity. It would put countries into jeopardy. It would put countless— I mean, come to the local level—it would put countless homes and schools and parks, entire cities at risk. . . .

Climate change also means water shortages. And if you have these enormous water shortages, then you have a change in the weather—because of the weather patterns, you're going to wind up with droughts, the lack of water. And the droughts can become longer and more intense. In fact, this isn't something around the corner—this is happening now.

We are seeing record droughts right now, and they're already putting a strain on water resources around the world. We've already seen in various parts of the world—in Africa, for instance—people fighting each other over water, and we've seen more conflicts shaping up now over the limits of water. Back in the United States, President [Barack] Obama just the other day visited California, where millions of people are now experiencing the 13th month of the worst drought the state has seen in 500 years. And no relief is in sight. What used to be a 100-year or a 500-year event is now repeating itself within 10 years.

Furthermore, climate change means fundamental transformations in agriculture worldwide. Scientists predict that, in some places, heat waves and water shortages will make it much more difficult for farmers to be able to grow the regular things we grow, like wheat or corn or rice. And obviously, it's not only farmers who will suffer here—it's the millions of people who depend on those crops that the farmers grow. For example, the British government research showed that climate change may have contributed to the famine that killed as many as 100,000 people in Somalia just back in 2010 and 2011. . . .

The fact is that climate change, if left unchecked, will wipe out many more communities from the face of the earth. And that is unacceptable under any circumstances—but is even more unacceptable because we know what we can do and need to do in order to deal with this challenge.

It is time for the world to approach this problem with the cooperation, the urgency, and the commitment that a challenge of this scale warrants. It's absolutely true that industrialized countries—yes, industrialized countries that produce most of the emissions—have a huge responsibility to be able to reduce emissions, but I'm telling you that doesn't mean that other nations have a free pass. They don't have a right to go out and repeat the mistakes of the past. It's not enough for one country or even a few countries to reduce their emissions when other countries continue to fill the atmosphere with carbon pollution as they see fit. At the end of the day, emissions coming from anywhere in the world threaten the future for people everywhere in the world, because those emissions go up and then they move with the wind and they drop with the rain and the weather, and they keep going around and around and they threaten all of us.

I am very well aware that these are not easy choices for any country to make—I know that. I've been in politics for a while. I know the pull and different powerful political forces. Coal and oil are currently cheap ways to power a society, at least in the near term. But I urge governments to measure the full cost to that coal and that oil, measure the impacts of what will happen as we go down the road. You cannot simply factor in the immediate costs of energy needs. You have to factor in the long-term cost of carbon pollution. And they have to factor in the cost of survival.

And if they do, then governments will find that the cost of pursuing clean energy now is far cheaper than paying for the consequences of climate change later. Make no mistake: the technology is out there. None of this is beyond our capacity.

I am absolutely confident that if we choose to, we will meet this challenge. Remember: we're the ones—we, all of us, the world—who helped to discover things like penicillin and we eradicated smallpox. We found a way to light up the night all around the world with a flip of the switch and spread that technology to more than three quarters of the world's population. We came up with a way for people to fly and move from one place to another in the air between cities and across oceans, and into outer space. . . .

[If] we come together now, we can not only meet the challenge, we can create jobs and economic growth in every corner of the globe. We can clean up the air, we can improve the health of people, we can have greater security; we can make our neighborhoods healthier places to live; we can help ensure that farmers and fishers can still make a sustainable living and feed our communities; and we can avoid disputes and even entire wars over oil, water, and other limited resources. We can make good on the moral responsibility we all have to leave future generations with a planet that is clean and healthy and sustainable for the future.

Source: John Kerry. "Remarks on Climate Change." Jakarta, Indonesia, February 16, 2014. U.S. Department of State. Full text available at http://www.state.gov/secretary/remarks/2014/02/221704.htm.

SELECTED BIBLIOGRAPHY

Ian Angus, Simon Butler, Betsy Hartmann, and Joel Kovel. *Too Many People: Population, Immigration, and the Environmental Crisis.* Chicago: Haymarket Books, 2011.

Michael Balter. "100,000 Years of Dramatic Population Changes." *Discover Magazine*, October 18, 2012. http://discovermagazine.com/2012/oct/100-000-years-of-dramatic-population-changes#.UgKhuW0piQE.

Alexander Betts. *Forced Migration and Global Politics.* London: Wiley-Blackwell, 2009.

Ester Boserup. *The Conditions of Agricultural Growth: The Economics of Agrarian Change under Population Pressure.* London: Allen and Unwin, 1965.

Lester R. Brown. *World on the Edge: How to Prevent Environmental and Economic Collapse.* New York: Norton, 2011.

Joel E. Cohen. *How Many People Can the Earth Support?* New York: W. W. Norton, 1996.

William A. Dando. *Food and Famine in the 21st Century.* Santa Barbara, CA: ABC-CLIO, 2012.

Kingsley Davis. "World Population in Transition." *Annals*, American Academy of Political and Social Science (1945): 1–11.

Paul R. Ehrlich. *The Population Bomb.* New York: Ballantine, 1968.

Garrett Hardin. "The Tragedy of the Commons." *Science* 162 (1968): 1243–48.

Russell King. *Atlas of Human Migration.* Boston, MA: Firefly Press, 2007.

Massimo Livi-Bacci. *A Concise History of World Population.* 5th ed. New York: Wiley-Blackwell, 2012.

Ray M. Merrill. *Introduction to Epidemiology.* 6th ed. Sudbury: Jones and Bartlett, 2012.

Tom Miller. *China's Urban Billion: The Story behind the Biggest Migration in Human History.* London: Zed Books, 2012.

Population Reference Bureau. *2013 World Population Data Sheet.* http://www.prb.org/pdf13/2013-population-data-sheet_eng.pdf.

Maria Pritchard. *Genocide: A History from Carthage to Darfur.* London: RW Press, 2013.

Julian L. Simon. *The Ultimate Resource.* Princeton, NJ: Princeton University Press, 1981.

John R. Weeks. *Population: An Introduction to Concepts and Issues.* Independence, KY: Cengage Learning, 2011.

Jay Weinstein and Vijayan K. Pillaj. *Demography: The Science of Population.* New York: Pearson, 2000.

Index

Page numbers in **bold** indicate main entries.

ABOUT THE AUTHOR

Fred M. Shelley is professor of geography in the Department of Geography and Environmental Sustainability at the University of Oklahoma, Norman, OK. His research interests include political geography; the global political economy; and the political, economic, and cultural geography of the United States. His published works include *Nation Shapes: The Story behind the World's Borders* (ABC-CLIO, 2013), *Atlas of the Great Plains* (coauthor), *Atlas of the 2008 Presidential Election*, *Engaging Geopolitics*, as well as numerous articles, book chapters, and other publications.